Privilege, Privacy and Confidentiality in Family Proceedings

Privilege, Privacy and Confidentiality in Family Proceedings

David Burrows
Solicitor-advocate

Bloomsbury Professional
LONDON • DUBLIN • EDINBURGH • NEW YORK • NEW DELHI • SYDNEY

Bloomsbury Professional

Bloomsbury Publishing Plc

41–43 Boltro Road, Haywards Heath, RH16 1BJ, UK

BLOOMSBURY and the Diana logo are trademarks of

Bloomsbury Publishing Plc

First published in Great Britain 2019

British Library Cataloguing-in-Publication Data

A catalogue record for this book is available from the British Library.

ISBN: PB 9781526507891
Epub 9781526507907
E-pdf 9781526507914

Typeset by Evolution Design and Digital Ltd (Kent)
Printed and bound by CPI Group (UK) Ltd, Croydon, CR0 4YY

To find out more about our authors and books visit www.bloomsburyprofessional.com. Here you will find extracts, author information, details of forthcoming events and the option to sign up for our newsletters

Preface

Litigation privilege and statement for legal aid

As this book went to press three cases involving forms of privilege and confidentiality passed across political, legal and news screens. Each were disparate examples of the subjects covered in this book. I mention them, not because any of them – at least not at this stage – moves the law along (though the ABC case included an important analysis of the American Cyanamid principle (*American Cyanamid v Ethicon* [1975] AC 396) and Human Rights Act 1998 s 12(3) in reporting restrictions litigation). I mention them because they show how pervasive are the subjects of this book in its different forms.

In early October it was reported that applicants for judicial review had failed to obtain legal aid because, it was thought, staff at the Legal Aid Agency had passed on information about their case to the government department which was to be on the receiving end of the judicial review. Judicial review, I understand, was successfully dealt with, but without legal aid. As will appear later (see 6.11) the issue of legal aid and confidentiality – specifically the lesser branch of legal professional privilege, namely litigation privilege – was raised in *R v Snaresbrook Crown Court exp Director of Public Prosecutions* [1988] 1 QB 532. As explained in Chapter 6 in *Snaresbrook*, prosecutors wanted copy documents from the legal aid authorities (then The Law Society) to prosecute a legal aid applicant (A) on a charge attempting to pervert the course of justice. On application by the DPP for judicial review the application was refused by the Divisional Court. A was the client of a professional legal adviser. The legal aid application was a communication between him and The Law Society for legal proceedings. It was covered by litigation privilege.

Legal Aid Sentencing and Punishment of Offenders Act 2012 sections 34 and 35 says what may be disclosed by legal aid authorities to third parties; and its reach, though in an earlier form, is explained by *Snaresbrook*. The case still applies to confidentiality, legal professional privilege and the legal aid application. The brief press report I have seen is not enough to tell me if section 34(2) (subject to the exceptions in section 35) has been breached; but the confidentiality and litigation privilege principles remain the law today.

Confidentiality and parliamentary privilege

ABC & Ors v Telegraph Media Group Ltd [2018] EWCA Civ 2329 represents a more dramatic use of what was called 'privilege' by those concerned. The context was the privacy of 'ABC' and two women in his firm (jointly the 'claimants'). On appeal to the Court of Appeal, the claimants' interim reporting restrictions injunction was continued. The Court very carefully considered the meaning of 'likely' in the grant of an interim injunction in the Human Rights Act 1998 section 12(3) (explained in context at 2.55). They made an interim reporting order and ordered that there should be an urgent early hearing of whether a final confidential protective order should be made.

Not content with that, and disgruntled (probably) by the continued protection of the main claimant (Philip Green), Lord Hain took advantage of his unelected position, and used parliamentary 'privilege' to tell the world the identity of 'ABC'. That is not 'privilege' in any sense which applies in this book. It is a form which derives from the seventeenth century when MPs in the Commons probably did need some protection in respect of things they said in Parliament. In this way Hain could override a court order and, for the longer term, jeopardise the confidentiality of anyone who sought protection of the common law (strictly speaking, of equity) to defend their privacy where a judge decides to protect it. Hain may have decided Philip Green was not entitled to such protection. That was for the judges to decide, surely?

Despite this, the law as to confidentiality can still protect all citizens (though it is fair to say that you may have to be rich, or knowledgeable as to the law – or both – to benefit). In *A Man for All Seasons* (1960) Robert Bolt put the following words into Sir Thomas More's mouth in an exchange with his son-in-law, Richard Roper, who wanted to cut down all laws in England to 'get after the Devil':

> *Roper: So now you'd give the Devil benefit of law!*
>
> *More: Yes. What would you do? Cut a great road through the law to get after the Devil?*
>
> *Roper: I'd cut down every law in England to do that.*
>
> *More: Oh? And when the last law was down, and the Devil turned round on you — where would you hide, Roper, the laws all being flat? This country's planted thick with laws from coast to coast — man's laws, not God's — and if you cut them down — and you're just the man to do it — d'you really think you could stand upright in the winds that would blow then? Yes, I'd give the Devil benefit of law, for my own safety's sake.*

If Lord Hain had asked me, I would have said: keep the laws in place and let the judges decide. After all (no innuendo intended) it might be you next time …

Michael Cohen and the 'iniquity exemption'

Finally, in August 2018 it was reported that 'Michael Cohen, (President Trump's long-time lawyer and "fixer") pleaded guilty to eight charges including campaign finance violations and directly implicated Trump in paying "hush money" to women with whom he allegedly had affairs'. Since then he has been ordered to serve three years in prison. Evidence seemed to have come from his client's papers. So where does that leave the long-standing rule: that what a person tells his or her lawyer is covered by secrecy (ie, legal professional privilege (LPP) and its principal branch, legal advice privilege (LAP))? I am reliably informed that that the law of privilege – based as it is on the common law (see eg, *R (Prudential plc and anor) v Special Commissioner of Income Tax* [2013] UKSC 1, [2013] 2 AC 185) – is broadly the same in US as in English law (on which the following summary is based).

As explained Chapter 10, in *R v Cox and Railton* (1884) 14 QBD 153 Court of Criminal Requests, Stephens J explained that if the reference to a solicitor – attorney in the US – is for a fraudulent purpose there can be no legal professional privilege: it 'does not exist; the fraudulent character of the communication takes away the privilege'.

Confidentiality, privacy and professional privilege protect a variety of aspects of life (as Robert Boult's Sir Thomas More showed). Its reach benefits all of us. And it benefits children, as *Gillick v West Norfolk and Wisbech AHA* [1985] UKHL 7, [1986] 1 AC 112, [1986] 1 FLR 224 (see Chapter 3) well shows. Long may the common law – for it is mostly common law – continue to provide its protection in the various forms considered in this book.

The law is as I understand it to be on 14 January 2019.

David Burrows
January 2019

Contents

Table of Statutes

[*All references are to paragraph numbers. Paragraph numbers in **bold** indicate where the Act is set out in part or in full*]

Table of Statutory Instruments and Other Guidance

[*All references are to paragraph numbers. Paragraph numbers in* ***bold*** *indicate where material is set out in part or in full*]

Table of European Legislation

[*All references are to paragraph numbers. Paragraph numbers in* **bold** *indicate where the legislation is set out in part or in full*]

Table of Cases

[*All references are to paragraph numbers*]

B

C

D

E

F

N

O

P

R

S

T

U

V

W

X

Y

1

INTRODUCTION

1 ELEMENTS OF THE LAW

Background legal principles for privacy and confidentiality

1.1 This introductory chapter provides an overview of certain legal principles which apply to the subjects being considered in this book. As will be seen, many of the subjects – confidentiality (Chapter 3) and legal professional privilege (Chapters 5 and 6) for example – are creatures of the common law. Other aspects of privilege and immunity from disclosure can be seen in self-incrimination privilege (Chapter 7) and without prejudice rule immunity (Chapter 8).

1.2 By contrast, most of the modern law on privacy has seen the common law develop alongside principles derived from the European Convention for the Protection of Human Rights and Fundamental Freedoms 1950 (especially Article 8, though that Article does not in the least define a law of privacy) (Chapter 4).

1.3 Procedures in family proceedings – with help from the common law as defined (in many cases) in the Civil Procedure Rules 1998 (CPR 1998) – are discussed in Chapter 11. This explains the regulatory framework in family proceedings in relation to confidentiality, privilege and public interest immunity (see Chapter 16). The importance of CPR 1998 as a guide to the common law for aspects of procedure – for disclosure, confidentiality and privilege in family proceedings – will be a recurring theme, though CPR 1998 does not formally apply to family proceedings.[1] The fact that, in practice, CPR 1998 frequently codifies the common law is explained in Part 5 of this chapter and related forward to other parts of the book.

1.4 An attempt to propose a procedure for any closed material declaration (on analogy with the Justice and Security Act 2013) is put forward in Chapter 15.

---

1 CPR 1998 r 2.1(2).

Structure of the law

1.5 In order to provide a summary of certain legal principles which underlie privacy and confidentiality this chapter proceeds as follows:

- Part 2 offers a few notes on aspects of the structure of the law as it applies to clients and their lawyers in family proceedings: (1) statute law; (2) the common law and how it is formed; and (3) discretion and law contrasted.
- Part 3 summarises the position with delegated legislation, practice directions and quasi-delegated legislation and at how each of these at their varying levels of authority apply in children proceedings.
- Part 4 moves on to the more general subject of precedence in case law and stare decisis; and how these contrast with the inherent jurisdiction of the High Court in family proceedings.
- Part 5 concludes with a few comments on the importance of Civil Procedure Rules 1998 and how they codify the common law to which family proceedings (supposedly exempt from CPR 1998) are subject.

2 FRAMEWORK OF THE LAW

Statute law and delegated legislation

1.6 Statute law overrides all other law, and repeals, revokes or otherwise overrides any law which conflicts with it (save, at present, in the case of EU law). Most obviously, it can change existing common law; though if that common law defines existing or fundamental rights, any statute passed by Parliament must state in terms how it is intended that those existing rights will be altered or otherwise lost. This was stated in clear terms by Lord Hoffman in *R v Secretary of State for the Home Department, ex parte Simms R v Secretary of State for the Home Department, exp O'Brien*:[2]

Fundamental rights cannot be overridden by general or ambiguous words. This is because there is too great a risk that the full implications of their unqualified meaning may have passed unnoticed in the democratic process. In the absence of express language or necessary implication to the contrary, the courts therefore presume that even the most general words were intended to be subject to the basic rights of the individual. In this way the courts of the United Kingdom, though acknowledging the sovereignty of Parliament, apply principles of constitutionality little different from those that exist in countries where the power of the legislature is expressly limited by a constitutional document.

1.7 These words were approved recently by the Supreme Court in *R (Miller & anor) v Secretary of State for Exiting the European Union*.[3] It remains to be seen to

2 [1999] UKHL 33; [2000] 2 AC 115 at 131.
3 [2017] UKSC 5, [2017] 2 WLR 583.

what extent the *ex parte Simms* principle will be honoured in any forthcoming EU withdrawal legislation.

1.8 Much statute law depends for its effectiveness on delegated legislation. This will be explained in Part 4.

Common law

1.9 The common law is judge-made law, either where a judge comes across or has come across in the past areas of dispute where there is no answer readily provided by statute or in earlier cases; or where a judge may be asked by parties to a dispute to define an aspect of statute law where parties differ as to what it may mean. This was explained by Supreme Court in *R (Miller & anor) v Secretary of State for Exiting the European Union*[4] as follows:

> [42] … The law is made in or under statutes, but there are areas where the law has long been laid down and developed by judges themselves: that is the common law. However, it is not open to judges to apply or develop the common law in a way which is inconsistent with the law as laid down in or under statutes, ie by Acts of Parliament.

1.10 In *R (Cart & Ors, on the application of) v The Upper Tribunal & Ors*[5] the Queen's Bench Division Divisional Court (Laws LJ) explained the interpretative role of the High Court. He was dealing with a claim by the government, as a defence to judicial review proceedings brought by Mr Cart and others as to the extent to which the Upper Tribunal could be challenged by judicial review. The government said that because a statute (in that case the Tribunals, Courts and Enforcement Act 2007) stated that a court (ie, the newly set up Upper Tribunal[6]) was a 'superior court of record', then that tribunal was immune from judicial review.

1.11 The Administrative Court disagreed: saying the Upper Tribunal was a 'superior court of record' was not enough to override the existing law. Laws LJ explained his view that the High Court must remain responsible for explaining statutory provisions as follows:

> [37] The principle I have suggested has its genesis in the self-evident fact that legislation consists in texts. Often – and in every case of dispute or difficulty – the texts cannot speak for themselves. Unless their meaning is mediated to the public, they are only letters on a page. They have to be interpreted. The interpreter's role cannot be filled by the legislature or the executive: for in that case they or either of them would be judge in their own cause, with the ills of arbitrary government which that would entail … The interpreter must be impartial, independent both of the legislature and of the persons affected by the texts' application,

4 [2017] UKSC 5. [2017] 2 WLR 583.

5 [2009] EWHC 3052 (Admin) [2010] 2 WLR 1012; this decision was upheld in the Court of Appeal and in the Supreme Court.

6 The Tribunals, Courts and Enforcement Act 2007.

and authoritative – accepted as the last word, subject only to any appeal. Only a court can fulfil the role.

1.12 Many of the principles laid down in the European Convention for the Protection of Human Rights and Fundamental Freedoms 1950 (the Convention) derive from the common law, since much of the drafting of the Convention was done after the Second World War by English common lawyers. In particular, a number of the principles on which Articles 6 and 10 are based derive from English common law doctrines; they still draw from English common law despite the passing of the Human Rights Act 1998 (as will be shown shortly in relation to the open court principle).

Common law and family courts

1.13 The common law applies to family courts in exactly the same way as in any other jurisdiction. One of the more controversial areas of family courts' procedure is whether a hearing should be in private or in open court. The general rule is a common law rule, now confirmed by Article 6(1) of the Convention, that all hearings should be in open court with one or two exceptions (mostly, but by no means entirely, in family cases[7]). Indeed, the main case on the subject, which is still routinely referred to, is a divorce (ie, family proceedings) case, namely *Scott & Anor v Scott*.[8] Over 100 years ago the House of Lords was astonished – that is not too strong a term – that a judge should have required that nullity proceedings be heard in private and should consequently have made an order that Mrs Scott and her solicitor be held to be in contempt of court for breach of the privacy requirement. The hearing in *Scott* should have been in open court, said the House of Lords.[9] In so holding, the Lords explained the principles of open justice which applied then and which equally apply in all courts (civil, including family, and criminal).

1.14 In *R (ota Guardian News and Media Ltd) v City of Westminster Magistrates' Court (Article 19 intervening)*[10] the Court of Appeal was considering whether or not the *Guardian* was allowed to see court documents read by the judge, where the hearing itself had been in open court. The case turned on whether the open court principle applied also to the documents. In effect, the Court of Appeal had to make new law: there was no clear answer in existing case law on the subject. The court allowed the *Guardian*'s appeal and said the newspaper could have the copies they had applied for.

1.15 In giving the lead judgment of the court, Toulson LJ included his clear assertion of the root of the open court principle in the common law; and he

7 That said, the leading case on the open justice principle is *Scott & Anor v Scott* [1913] UKHL 2, [1913] AC 417.

8 [1913] UKHL 2, [1913] AC 417.

9 Divorce and nullity – if ever contested, or even as to grant of a decree – must be in open court as must committal proceedings.

10 [2012] EWCA Civ 420, [2013] QB 618, [2012] 3 WLR 1343.

distinguished those roots from the much more recent European Convention 1950:[11]

> [88] I base my decision on the common law principle of open justice. In reaching it I am fortified by the common theme of the judgments in other common law countries to which I have referred. Collectively they are strong persuasive authority … The development of the common law did not come to an end on the passing of the Human Rights Act. It is in vigorous health and flourishing in many parts of the world which share a common legal tradition …

Discretion and decision-making

1.16 Law generally, and family law in particular, demands a close attention to whether a decision of the court depends on law, or on the discretion of the individual judge or court. Many areas of family law proceed on the basis that a discretion in decision-making has been vested by statute in the judge.

1.17 Thus, for example, the court has wide powers to make a child arrangements order (the Children Act 1989 (CA 1989) section 8), subject only to restrictions in CA 1989 section 9, where a question arises as to the welfare of and arrangements for a child.

1.18 By contrast, the basis on which a care order may be made by a family court is based at the initial stage entirely on law. CA 1989 section 31(2) which vest in the family courts the power to make a care or supervision order states the threshold which the court must find that a local authority applicant has passed if an order is to be contemplated by the court; and this depends on facts being found by the court which are sufficient in law to establish 'significant harm'. It is a matter of law. CA 1989 section 31(2) states:

(2) A court may only make a care order or supervision order if it is satisfied –

- (a) that the child concerned is suffering, or is likely to suffer, significant harm; and
- (b) that the harm, or likelihood of harm, is attributable to –
  - (i) the care given to the child, or likely to be given to him if the order were not made, not being what it would be reasonable to expect a parent to give to him; or
  - (ii) the child's being beyond parental control.

11 This passage has since been approved by Supreme Court in *A v British Broadcasting Corporation* [2014] UKSC 25, [2015] 1 AC 558.

3 SUBSIDIARY LEGISLATION AND QUASI-DELEGATED LEGISLATION

Delegated legislation and court rules

Legislation delegated by Parliament

1.19 Law is a combination of statute law, the common law and a variety of delegated (mostly court rules, such as Family Procedure Rules 2010 (FPR 2010)) and of sub-delegated – or quasi-delegated – legislation (such as practice directions, guidance, practice notes and protocols). A substantial proportion of modern legislation is delegated by Parliament to government ministers or others on Parliament's behalf. In modern life this is inevitable. Children's law save in respect of court rules (ie, FPR 2010) is relatively light on properly so-called delegated legislation (eg, rules, regulations etc), but it abounds with a variety of sub-delegated guidance and the like, as explained in Section 3 below.

1.20 The making of court rules is delegated by statute to the Family Procedure Rules Committee. They are confirmed in Parliament by the negative resolution procedure. The Courts Act 2003 section 75(1) set up that Committee. Sections 75 and 76 deal with the content and scope of the rules and include, as relevant here, the following:

> **75 Family Procedure Rules**
>
> (1) There are to be rules of court (to be called "Family Procedure Rules") governing the practice and procedure to be followed in family proceedings.
>
> (2) Family Procedure Rules are to be made by a committee known as the Family Procedure Rule Committee.
>
> (3) "Family proceedings" means—
>
> (a) proceedings in the family court, and
>
> (a) proceedings in the Family Division of the High Court which are business assigned, by or under section 61 of (and Schedule 1 to) the Senior Courts Act 1981, to that Division of the High Court and no other ...
>
> (5) Any power to make Family Procedure Rules is to be exercised with a view to securing that—
>
> (a) the family justice system is accessible, fair and efficient, and
>
> (b) the rules are both simple and simply expressed.
>
> **76 Further provision about scope of Family Procedure Rules**
>
> (3) Family Procedure Rules may modify the rules of evidence as they apply to family proceedings in any court within the scope of the rules.

1.21 A definition of 'family proceedings' can be found in the Matrimonial and Family Proceedings Act 1984 Sch 1, para 3, which defines the 'business' which is assigned to the Family Division as family work.

Rules of procedure

1.22 The function of rules is to say how cases should proceed, not to create law or to extend or re-define the jurisdiction of the courts. In response to counsel's argument that a new rule (in that case CPR 1998 r 52.17[12]) Buxton LJ said in *Jaffray v The Society of Lloyds*:[13]

> [8] That approach is quite misconceived. The CPR, being rules of court, cannot extend the jurisdiction of the court from that which the law provides, but can only give directions as to how the existing jurisdiction should be exercised. That is very trite law, but if authority is needed for the proposition it can be found in the speech of Lord Herschell LC in *British South Africa Co v Companhia de Mocambique* [1893] AC 602 at 628.[14]

1.23 The purposes of procedure and the rules which define it, is to define how a case proceeds from issue to trial (or final hearing). In particular, it regulates evidence and, for example, how costs and enforcement of orders (where applicable) are to be dealt with.

Delegated powers and Henry VIII clauses

1.24 The powers delegated to government ministers by the EU Withdrawal Act 2018 section 8 constitute extensive Henry VIII powers (as explained below in 1.26). These may have limited direct application on family law and especially for the subject matter of this book. A short comment only is offered here.

1.25 Oppressive use of such Henry VIII powers can render a minister open to judicial review as happened recently in *R (The Public Law Project) v Lord Chancellor*.[15] This case suggests that if powers are exceeded by ministers the courts may review such ministerial action. In the *Public Law Project* case Lord Neuberger, who delivered the only judgment, referred to the tension between Henry VIII powers and parliamentary sovereignty:

---

12 Power of the Court of Appeal to set aside its own decision.

13 [2007] EWCA Civ 586.

14 *British South Africa Co v Companhia de Mocambique* dealt with a rule which, the plaintiffs claimed, gave English courts the power to deal with a claim in a foreign jurisdiction. The Court of Appeal explained that a rule could not do this. *British South Africa Co v Companhia de Mocambique* [1893] AC 602 per Lord Herschell LC at 628: 'The rule [under the then "Rules of the Supreme Court Order"] is, in my opinion, a mere rule of procedure, and applies only to those cases in which the Courts at that time exercised jurisdiction. It has been more than once held that the rules under the Judicature Acts are rules of procedure only, and were not intended to affect, and did not affect, the rights of parties.'

15 [2016] UKSC 39, [2016] 1 AC 1531, [2016] 3 WLR 387.

> [23] Subordinate legislation will be held by a court to be invalid if it has an effect, or is made for a purpose, which is *ultra vires*, that is, outside the scope of the statutory power pursuant to which it was purportedly made. In declaring subordinate legislation to be invalid in such a case, the court is upholding the supremacy of Parliament over the Executive. That is because the court is preventing a member of the Executive from making an order which is outside the scope of the power which Parliament has given him or her by means of the statute concerned. Accordingly, when, as in this case, it is contended that actual or intended subordinate legislation is *ultra vires*, it is necessary for a court to determine the scope of the statutorily conferred power to make that legislation.

1.26 Lord Neuberger cited *Craies on Legislation*[16] at §1.3.9: 'The term Henry VIII power is commonly used to describe a delegated power under which subordinate legislation is enabled to amend primary legislation.' He then continued:

> [25] ... When a court is considering the validity of a statutory instrument made under a Henry VIII power, its role in upholding Parliamentary supremacy is particularly striking, as the statutory instrument will be purporting to vary primary legislation passed into law by Parliament.
>
> [26] The interpretation of the statutory provision conferring a power to make secondary legislation is, of course, to be effected in accordance with normal principles of statutory construction. However, in the case of an "amendment that is permitted under a Henry VIII power", to quote again from *Craies* (*op cit*) §1.3.11: 'as with all delegated powers the only rule for construction is to test each proposed exercise by reference to whether or not it is within the class of action that Parliament must have contemplated when delegating. Although Henry VIII powers are often cast in very wide terms, the more general the words by Parliament to delegate a power, the more likely it is that an exercise within the literal meaning of the words will nevertheless be outside the legislature's contemplation.

1.27 Administrative Court litigation is likely if EU withdrawal continues. All lawyers may find themselves called upon to check the powers exercised by ministers under the EU withdrawal legislation; and to check 'Henry VIII' delegated legislation along the lines explained by Lord Neuberger in the *Public Law Project* case.

Practice directions

Practice directions and rules contrasted

1.28 Rules are made formally by the FPRC under powers delegated to them under the Courts Act 2003 (as explained above). Practice directions are issued separately by the President of the Family Division with the approval only of the Lord Chancellor. Most practice directions are incorporated into the rules.

16 *Craies on Legislation* ed. Daniel Greenberg, 10th edn (London: Sweet & Maxwell, 2015).

1.29 Rules are approved – nominally at least – by Parliament. There is no such democratic control in the case of practice directions (still less of the remainder of the forms of 'guidance', 'practice notes', 'protocols' and so on considered later).

1.30 Thus, practice directions have a formal statutory basis. Some are part of the rules (eg, *PD12G* which supports FPR 2010 r 12.73 (communication of information) or *PD16B* (representation of children)). They have the approval of the FPRC. Other practice directions are freestanding and are issued by the President with the Lord Chancellor's approval;[17] though these are rare in family proceedings.

1.31 The practice direction has no power to change procedural rules, still less to change the law. For example, in *U (A Child) v Liverpool CC*,[18] the Court of Appeal, per Brooke LJ, said:

> [48] The status of a practice direction has been authoritatively delineated by Hale LJ in *Re C (Legal Aid: Preparation of Bill of Costs)* [2001] 1 FLR 602 at 21, May LJ in *Godwin v Swindon Borough Council* [2001] EWCA Civ 1478 at [11], and Dyson LJ in *Leigh v Michelin Tyre plc* [2003] EWCA Civ 1766 at [19]–[21]. It is sufficient for present purposes to say that a practice direction has no legislative force. Practice directions provide invaluable guidance to matters of practice in the civil courts, but in so far as they contain statements of the law which are wrong, they carry no authority at all.

1.32 In *Secretary of State for Communities and Local Government v Bovale Ltd and anor*,[19] Waller and Dyson LJJ gave a joint judgment. Where a judge had put forward his own practice guidance which also differed from what the court guide on the subject (judicial review and planning cases) said, the two Lords Justice, set themselves the following questions for their judgment to deal with:

> [9] In considering any of the arguments in this case the starting point is an understanding of the legal force of the rules, the legal force of practice directions and to understand what are, and what are not, practice directions to which the [Constitutional Reform Act 2005] was intended to apply. To what extent can a judge or indeed any court vary the rules? To what extent are practice directions binding on a court? Who has the power to issue or vary practice directions? What are practice directions?

1.33 Here, we are mostly concerned with the extent to which practice directions are binding. The judges set out the statutory background (mostly from the Civil Procedure Act 1997 and the Constitutional Reform Act 2005) and to the history of practice directions in the context of CPR 1998 set out in Hale LJ's judgment in *Re C (Legal Aid: Preparation of Bill of Costs)*.[20] The court's conclusion (all three judges were agreed on the points considered here) was that where the practice direction

17 There are very few recent examples of this form of quasi-legislation, as Sir James Munby P did not trouble with formal Lord Chancellor approval but issued what are often treated as practice direction as 'President's Guidance' (see below).

18 Sub nom *KU (A Child) v Liverpool* CC [2005] EWCA Civ 475, [2005] 1 WLR 2657.

19 [2009] EWCA Civ 171, [2009] 1 WLR 2274.

20 [2001] 1 FLR 602.

has been made within the terms of the Constitutional Reform Act 2005 section 5(1) (as explained in the case) the judge has no power to go outside the practice direction.

1.34 The judges concluded with thoughts on the difference between formal practice directions and 'guidance':

> [36] There is, in our view, a distinction between directions, and guidance as to the way in which rules and practice directions will be interpreted. We accept that one object of the practice directions which supplement the rules is to provide guidance to litigants but they also contain directions as to the procedure that should be followed.

1.35 The court explained the difference between the statutory practice directions – that is, made according to the appropriate statutory formula (per the Constitutional Reform Act 2005 5) – and the non-statutory guidance:

> [36] ... The nature of the Guides is, or should be, different. They do not, or should not, contain directions; they do, or should, explain, inter alia, how practice directions apply and are interpreted. Guidance as to how a court interprets and applies practice directions and rules are not in our view themselves practice directions and have rightly not been treated as such. Furthermore, Guides as to how the rules and practice directions are operated by the court seem to us something with which the Lord Chancellor should not be concerned ... It follows that since Guides are not practice directions, judgments, in so far as they are providing guidance on how the rules and practice directions work, could not be said to be practice directions.

1.36 It follows from the above that if a practice direction conflicts with the law, the law – common law, statute law and any delegated legislation – takes precedence.

Practice guidance, guidelines, notes and protocols

Guidance and other 'quasi-legislation'

1.37 The forms of practice guidance touched on here are not law; though they may be authoritative depending on who issues them. They may provide guidance as to how the President of the Family Division or another senior judge wants practice to be conducted. They are what has been called by Wade & Forsythe part of the 'jungle of quasi-legislation'[21] in which many areas of law abound. Where they conflict with the law they should not be followed.

1.38 This will prove a testing area for judges and the rule of law if a child has to assert or even to understand that guidance is not law. The 'jungle' of which Wade & Forsythe speak must be daunting indeed for the mature self-represented child.

21 HWR Wade and CR Forsyth *Administrative Law* 11th edn (Oxford: Oxford University Press, 2014) at 732.

Statutory guidance

1.39 *Working Together 2018* is statutory guidance issued under the Children Act 2004 section 11(4). But what is the role of that 'guidance'? Guidance is not a formal type of delegated legislation (ie, codes of practice, guidance and so forth) which have proliferated alongside more conventional and formal legislation (eg, such as statutes, delegated legislation and practice directions). It is, as the name makes clear, 'guidance' – albeit of high authority. It cannot be any more.

4 PRECEDENT, *STARE DECISIS* AND RATIO

Rules of precedent

Doctrine of precedent: hierarchy of judges

1.40 The rules of precedent developed by the English common law are based on the principle that, to be fair, the law must, as far as possible, be predictable. Common law rule defines when a judge may deviate from previously decided cases; this includes judges in the Supreme Court. To form a precedent, however, it is not just a question of what the judge has said. It is also a question of whether what is said is part of the reasoning (ratio decidendi) behind the judge's decision.

1.41 The hierarchy of judges was explained by Lord Neuberger in *Willers v Joyce & Anor (as executors of Albert Gubay deceased)*:[22]

> [4] In a common law system, where the law is in some areas made, and the law is in virtually all areas developed, by judges, the doctrine of precedent, or as it is sometimes known *stare decisis*, is fundamental. Decisions on points of law by more senior courts have to be accepted by more junior courts. Otherwise, the law becomes anarchic, and it loses coherence clarity and predictability …
>
> [5] The doctrine is, of course, seen in its simplest and most familiar form when applied to the hierarchy of courts. On issues of law, (i) Circuit Judges are bound by decisions of High Court Judges, the Court of Appeal and the Supreme Court, (ii) High Court Judges are bound by decisions of the Court of Appeal and the Supreme Court, and (iii) the Court of Appeal is bound by decisions of the Supreme Court …

Stare decisis*: keep to earlier court decisions*

1.42 The doctrine of precedent leads to the doctrine of *stare decisis*, that is to say the rule that courts of equivalent level should keep to earlier decisions of the same court. This was explained by the Court of Appeal in *Young v Bristol Aeroplane*

22 [2016] UKSC 44, [2016] 3 WLR 534.

Co Ltd.[23] The court's conclusion on the subject remains the law. Lord Greene MR said the following of '*stare decisis*':[24]

> On a careful examination of the whole matter we have come to the clear conclusion that this court is bound to follow previous decisions of its own as well as those of courts of co-ordinate jurisdiction. The only exceptions to this rule [are]:
>
> (1) The court is entitled and bound to decide which of two conflicting decisions of its own it will follow.
>
> (2) The court is bound to refuse to follow a decision of its own which, though not expressly overruled, cannot, in its opinion, stand with a decision of the House of Lords.
>
> (3) The court is not bound to follow a decision of its own if it is satisfied that the decision was given 'per incuriam'.

Inherent jurisdiction of the High Court

Function of the jurisdiction

1.43 The inherent jurisdiction of the High Court has been described, in a text which is still treated as authoritative,[25] as being capable of being invoked:

> … In an apparently inexhaustible variety of circumstances and may be exercised in different ways. This peculiar concept is indeed so amorphous and ubiquitous and so pervasive in its operation that it seems to defy challenge to determine its quality and establish its limits.[26]

1.44 However, the jurisdiction cannot be used to supplement the powers of the court where its powers are already defined by statute. In *Wicks v Wicks*,[27] the Court of Appeal refused to permit an interim capital order as between spouses – much as it might have liked to do so – in an area of law which already gave the family courts a substantial quiver of powers.[28] Interim capital provision had not been provided for by Parliament, so the High Court could not add a power because it felt it might be a good idea.

1.45 The Family Court, like the County Court and the Crown Court[29] has no inherent jurisdiction. However, if the High Court has power to make an order under its inherent jurisdiction (eg, to grant an injunction), then the Matrimonial

---

23 [1944] KB 718.
24 Ibid at 730.
25 See eg, *Birmingham City Council v Riaz & Ors* [2014] EWHC 4247 (Fam) Keehan J at [42].
26 IH Jacob *The Inherent Jurisdiction of the Court* (1970) *Current Legal Problems* 23.
27 [1998] 1 FLR 470, [1998] 3 WLR 277.
28 See eg, the Matrimonial Causes Act 1973 s 23, discussed fully in Chapter 1.
29 See *R (Trinity Mirror) v Croydon Crown Court* [2008] EWCA Crim 50, [2008] QB 770.

and Family Proceedings Act 1984 section 31E(1)[30] gives the same power to the Family Court.[31]

5 FAMILY PROCEEDINGS, CIVIL PROCEDURE RULES 1998 AND THE COMMON LAW

Family Procedure Rules 2010 and common law gaps

1.46 Until April 1999, family proceedings were regulated by the then civil proceedings rules, namely the Rules of the Supreme Court 1965 and the County Court Rules 1981; save to the extent that any rule in the Family Proceedings Rules 1991 was inconsistent with those rules. For example, all procedures in relation to evidence were regulated by the Rules of the Supreme Court 1965 and the County Court Rules 1981 (eg, disclosure, then called 'discovery', opinion (expert) evidence, and so on). From April 1999, civil proceedings were regulated mostly by CPR 1998 and by an ever-diminishing number of pre-CPR 1998 rules.

1.47 Family proceedings were specifically excluded from the ambit of CPR 1998: 'These rules do not apply to [family] proceedings except to the extent that they are specifically applied by another enactment.'[32] Family proceedings, therefore, continued to be subject to the Rules of the Supreme Court 1965 and the County Court Rules 1981. This continued until April 2011, when the Family Procedure Rules 2010 came into effect. These new rules governed all family proceedings. The Civil Procedure Rules 1998 save as specifically applied to family proceedings (eg, costs rules and, later, rules on appeal to the Court of Appeal[33]) remained outlawed from the family courts.

1.48 In autumn 2013 this author realised that provision for disclosure in the new rules was thin on the ground. Three rules, where in CPR 1998 Pt 31 there were 23 rules. He suggested additional draft rules to the Family Procedure Rules Committee who replied in December 2013:

> After careful consideration the Committee concluded that the Family Procedure Rules in relation to disclosure provide as much as is needed. The Committee had not wanted to provide for open-ended disclosure by list, so had included only those provisions that were necessary. The rules in Part 9 (Applications for a Financial Remedy) and 21 (Miscellaneous Rules about Disclosure and Inspection of Documents) were not restrictive and did not undermine the common law duty of disclosure. It was considered that this was a training issue rather than one that required rule amendment.

30 In that part of the Matrimonial and Family Proceedings Act 1984, which introduced the Family Court.

31 Derived from the same provision in the County Courts Act 1981 s 38.

32 CPR 1998 r 2.1(2).

33 CPR 1998 Pts 44–47 and Pt 52.

Civil Procedure Rules 1998 as a codification of the common law

1.49 And so, the matter stands. However, as this book will show – especially Chapters 4, 11 and 16 – there are several areas where in fact and in law also – the common law is best found as codified in CPR 1998. Further, especially in the field of regulation of evidence, FPR 2010 (Pts 21, 22, 23, 24 and 25) merely rewrite, in a family proceedings context, CPR 1998 (Pts 31, 32, 33, 34 and 35); so case law under CPR 1998 Pts 31–35 help to explain the meaning of the same rules in FPR 2010 Pts 21–25.

1.50 To that extent it cannot be said that CPR 1998 'do not apply to [family] proceedings'. They plainly do to the extent that CPR 1998 and case law under those rules help to explain the same provision in FPR 2010. More significantly, many of the provisions, especially of the rules in CPR 1998 Part 31, help to explain the common law. This is demonstrated especially in relation to disclosure (see Chapter 4).

2

PRIVACY

1 INTRODUCTION

Privacy, and an 'expectation of privacy'

2.1 This chapter explains privacy in the context of family proceedings: individual confidentiality as developed by law (partly developed following the introduction of the European Convention 1950 Article 8 formally into United Kingdom law). By contrast, Chapter 3 deals with aspects of confidentiality on its own; especially in relation to children and their professional relationships (starting from doctors and *Gillick v West Norfolk and Wisbech AHA*[1]).

2.2 Since the coming into operation of the Human Rights Act 1998 and the European Convention for the Protection of Human Rights and Fundamental Freedoms 1950 anyone living in the United Kingdom has been able to expect a much greater range of privacy derived from law developed and explained by the House of Lords and the Supreme Court; but of course applied – see most recently such cases as *PJS*[2] and *Richard v BBC*[3] (both considered later in this chapter).

2.3 This chapter proceeds as follows:

- Part 2 explains the role of privacy in the common law, and how this related to the European Convention 1950 and its Article 8 (right to respect for private life).
- Part 3 considers the role of the European Convention 1950 and Article 8 balanced against Article 10 (right to freedom of expression): what are the main rights of relevance to family law and how are they balanced one against the other.

1 [1985] UKHL 7, [1986] 1 AC 112, [1986] 1 FLR 224.

2 *PJS v News Group Newspapers Ltd* [2016] UKSC 26, [2016] AC 1081, [2016] 2 FLR 251, [2016] 2 WLR 1253; considered further at 2.53.

3 *Richard v The British Broadcasting Corporation (BBC) & South Yorks Police* [2018] EWHC 1837 (Ch), Mann J; considered further at 2.31.

- Part 4 looks at the 'reasonable expectation of privacy' criterion in relation to a number of situations since the term was first developed by the House of Lords in *Campbell v MGN Ltd*.[4]
- Part 5 reviews the role of the balancing test in relation to Convention rights and their application in individual cases.
- Part 6 provides a brief introduction to the tort of privacy.
- Part 7 moves away from Convention principles and looks at privacy in the context of Family Courts proceedings.
- Part 8 provides a brief procedural introduction to reporting restrictions (interim non-disclosure) orders and to Lord Neuberger's practice guidance.[5]

2 PERSONAL PRIVACY: THE COMMON LAW

Privacy and private lives

2.4 As will be seen, much of the modern case law on privacy and its related protection of confidential information turns on the concerns of well-known individuals who attract the attention of the press and other media (individuals such as a daughter of Prince Rainier of Monaco,[6] in *Von Hannover v Germany* (below): described by the European Court of Human Rights as 'a figure of contemporary society *par excellence*') Naomi Campbell,[7] Sir Cliff Richard,[8] actors and football players;[9] and, in the nature of the cases, many remain anonymised.[10] It is the nature of that aspect of privacy and of development of law in relation to it which provides the main subject matter for this chapter.

2.5 In practice, the family lawyer will be concerned as much with the privacy and confidentiality of ordinary adults, of children and of others in the miscellany of family proceedings. Privacy is part of the question of anonymity in family courts and of the privacy of their proceedings. Especially in relation to legal professional privilege and to confidentiality of dealings with social workers and other professionals, the rights of children[11] – especially of mature children – will be as important as the rights of any adults.

4 [2004] UKHL 22, [2004] 2 AC 457.
5 *Practice Guidance (Interim Non-Disclosure Orders)* [2012] 1 WLR 1003.
6 *Von Hannover v Germany – 59320/00* [2004] ECHR 294, (2005) 40 EHRR 1.
7 *Campbell v MGN Ltd* [2004] UKHL 22, [2004] 2 AC 457.
8 *Richard v The British Broadcasting Corporation (BBC) & South Yorks Police* [2018] EWHC 1837 (Ch), Mann J.
9 *A v B plc and anor* [2002] EWCA Civ 337, [2003] QB 195.
10 See eg, *PJS v News Group Newspapers Ltd* [2016] UKSC 26, [2016] AC 1081, [2016] 2 FLR 251, [2016] 2 WLR 1253.
11 See especially Ch 14.

Privacy: formerly no right of action

2.6 The classic position of the common law has been that in English law there no right of action for breach of privacy. As Glidewell LJ said as recently as March 1990 in *Kaye v Robertson*:[12]

> It is well-known that in English law there is no right to privacy, and accordingly there is no right of action for breach of a person's privacy. The facts of the present case are a graphic illustration of the desirability of Parliament considering whether and in what circumstances statutory provision can be made to protect the privacy of individuals.

2.7 Bingham LJ commented:

> This case ... highlights, yet again, the failure of both the common law of England and statute to protect in an effective way the personal privacy of individual citizens ... If ever a person has a right to be let alone by strangers with no public interest to pursue, it must surely be when he lies in hospital recovering from brain surgery and in no more than partial command of his faculties. It is this invasion of his privacy which underlies the plaintiff's complaint. Yet it alone, however gross, does not entitle him to relief in English law.

Confidentiality

2.8 By contrast private affairs have been protected by a right of action where a duty of confidentiality is acknowledged or can be implied. For example, a marriage implies a duty of confidence. *Argyll v Argyll*[13] concerned a breach of confidentiality injunction (a form of reporting restrictions order or 'super injunction'). Following an eight-year marriage, the Duke presented an adultery divorce petition in Scotland. The Scottish judge, Lord Wheatley, commented on the Duchess that her attitude to the sanctity of marriage was 'what the moderns might call sophisticated but what in plain language can only be described as wholly immoral'.[14]

2.9 The Duke was granted a decree of divorce. In the same year, newspaper articles by the Duchess appeared, concerning the Duke's drug habit, and that he had borrowed money to do up property from the Duchess's family. Meanwhile, the Duchess sought interlocutory injunctions to restrain the Duke from communicating to the press information about her private life, personal affairs or private conduct all of which related to the period during the subsistence of their marriage and which had not, until then, been made public.

---

12 [1990] EWCA Civ 21: a well-known actor was severely injured when a tree fell on his car. A journalist ignored signs in the hospital where he had been in intensive care for three days, took photographs and secured a form of interview with him.

13 [1967] Ch 302, [1965] 2 WLR 790 Ungoed-Thomas J; approved by the Court of Appeal in *Imerman v Tchenguiz and ors* [2010] EWCA Civ 908, [2011] Fam 116, [2010] 2 FLR 814 at [33].

14 A view from the Scottish bench in 1963, the year in which *Lady Chatterley's Lover* was prosecuted – unsuccessfully – as allegedly obscene.

2.10 The Duchess of Argyll claimed that publication by the Duke of statements about her were in breach of marital confidence. Ungoed-Thomas J implied into the marital relationship a duty of confidence and that, as a matter of fact, when the confidences in question were imparted 'the relationship of the [Duchess] and the Duke was apparently … the normal confidence and trust between husband and wife'.[15] He therefore granted the Duchess her injunction to restrain publication by the Duke:[16]

> And if, as I have concluded, it is the policy of the law (which is the basis of the courts' jurisdiction) to preserve the close confidence and mutual trust between husband and wife, then that policy and the purpose of the jurisdiction would indeed be impaired if subsequent adultery by one spouse, resulting in divorce, were to release the other spouse from obligation to preserve their earlier confidences.

Causes of action: privacy and protection of confidential information

2.11 The Human Rights Act 1998 came into force on October 2000. It incorporated the European Convention 1950 into UK law. The Naomi Campbell case[17] explained the law as it was held to have developed from that. There developed into the common law two separate causes of action: the original protection of confidential information (as in the *Argyll* case) and the separate and developing action which protects privacy.

2.12 The distinction between these two was explained by Lord Nicholls in *Douglas v Hello Ltd (No 3)*.[18] Under the heading 'confidential information' he said:

> [255] As the law has developed breach of confidence, or misuse of confidential information, now covers two distinct causes of action, protecting two different interests: privacy, and secret ("confidential") information. It is important to keep these two distinct. In some instances, information may qualify for protection both on grounds of privacy and confidentiality. In other instances, information may be in the public domain, and not qualify for protection as confidential, and yet qualify for protection on the grounds of privacy. Privacy can be invaded by further publication of information or photographs already disclosed to the public. Conversely, and obviously, a trade secret may be protected as confidential information even though no question of personal privacy is involved …

2.13 By 2018 the position is clear: there is a recognised tort relating to privacy for which Sir Cliff Richard was entitled to claim damages (and successfully did so[19])

15 *Argyll v Argyll* at 331.
16 Ibid at 332.
17 *Campbell v MGN Ltd* [2004] UKHL 22, [2004] 2 AC 457.
18 [2007] UKHL 21, [2008] 1 AC 1.
19 *Richard v The British Broadcasting Corporation (BBC) & South Yorks Police* [2018] EWHC 1837 (Ch), Mann J.

and a recognised cause of action which could lead, for example, to an injunction to 'preserve privacy interests' of a person 'in the entertainment business'.[20] The progress of privacy claims and their relationship with a breach of confidence action is not essential to family law save for the extent to which privacy and confidentiality laws explain court and individual family proceedings parties' relationships with the media.

3 EUROPEAN CONVENTION 1950

The Convention rights

Convention for the Protection of Human Rights and Fundamental Freedoms 1950

2.14 The European Convention for the Protection of Human Rights and Fundamental Freedoms 1950 formally became part of English law on 2 October 2000; though its provisions and the jurisprudence under them had been influential in English law for a long time beforehand. The concept of open court trials had been part of English common law for centuries before 1950. In *W v Egdell*:[21] a psychiatrist considered it was necessary for him to release a report on a prisoner patient to the Home Office (ie, to override his confidentiality). Bingham LJ concluded his judgment by putting the decision of the Court of Appeal in a human rights and European Convention 1950 context (at the end of 1988):

> No reference was made in argument before us (nor, so far as I know, before the judge) to the European Convention for the Protection of Human Rights and Fundamental Freedoms, but I believe this decision to be in accordance with it. I would accept that article 8(1) of the Convention may protect an individual against the disclosure of information protected by the duty of professional secrecy. But article 8(2) envisages that circumstances may arise in which a public authority may legitimately interfere with exercise of that right in accordance with the law and where necessary in a democratic society in the interests of public safety or the prevention of crime. Here there was no interference by a public authority. Dr. Egdell did, as I conclude, act in accordance with the law. And his conduct was in my judgment necessary in the interests of public safety and the prevention of crime.

2.15 The Articles with which this chapter will be most concerned are Articles 6.1, 8 and 10:

> Article 6
>
> **Right to a fair trial**
>
> 1 In the determination of his civil rights and obligations or of any criminal charge against him, everyone is entitled to a fair and public hearing

20 *PJS v News Group Newspapers Ltd* [2016] UKSC 26, [2016] AC 1081, [2016] 2 FLR 251, [2016] 2 WLR 1253.

21 [1989] EWCA Civ 13, [1990] Ch 359, [1990] 2 WLR 471 at [1990] Ch 359, 425.

within a reasonable time by an independent and impartial tribunal established by law. Judgment shall be pronounced publicly but the press and public may be excluded from all or part of the trial in the interest of morals, public order or national security in a democratic society, where the interests of juveniles or the protection of the private life of the parties so require, or to the extent strictly necessary in the opinion of the court in special circumstances where publicity would prejudice the interests of justice …

Article 8

Right to respect for private and family life

1 Everyone has the right to respect for his private and family life, his home and his correspondence.

2 There shall be no interference by a public authority with the exercise of this right except such as is in accordance with the law and is necessary in a democratic society in the interests of national security, public safety or the economic well-being of the country, for the prevention of disorder or crime, for the protection of health or morals, or for the protection of the rights and freedoms of others.

Article 10

Freedom of expression

1 Everyone has the right to freedom of expression. This right shall include freedom to hold opinions and to receive and impart information and ideas without interference by public authority and regardless of frontiers. This Article shall not prevent States from requiring the licensing of broadcasting, television or cinema enterprises.

2 The exercise of these freedoms, since it carries with it duties and responsibilities, may be subject to such formalities, conditions, restrictions or penalties as are prescribed by law and are necessary in a democratic society, in the interests of national security, territorial integrity or public safety, for the prevention of disorder or crime, for the protection of health or morals, for the protection of the reputation or rights of others, for preventing the disclosure of information received in confidence, or for maintaining the authority and impartiality of the judiciary.

2.16 The Human Rights Act 1998 section 12 concerns freedom of expression specifically and will be particularly relevant in relation to the media and their reporting of court proceedings. It provides:

12 Freedom of expression

(1) This section applies if a court is considering whether to grant any relief which, if granted, might affect the exercise of the Convention right to freedom of expression.

(2) If the person against whom the application for relief is made ("the respondent") is neither present nor represented, no such relief is to be granted unless the court is satisfied—

(a) that the applicant has taken all practicable steps to notify the respondent; or

(b) that there are compelling reasons why the respondent should not be notified.

(3) No such relief is to be granted so as to restrain publication before trial unless the court is satisfied that the applicant is likely to establish that publication should not be allowed.

(4) The court must have particular regard to the importance of the Convention right to freedom of expression and, where the proceedings relate to material which the respondent claims, or which appears to the court, to be journalistic, literary or artistic material (or to conduct connected with such material), to—

(a) the extent to which—

(i) the material has, or is about to, become available to the public; or

(ii) it is, or would be, in the public interest for the material to be published;

(b) any relevant privacy code …

2.17 As can be seen, section 12 provides the media with procedural protection (s 12(2): against interim applications of which they have not been given notice); and that publication should only be restrained if the applicant satisfies the court that at a final hearing the publication will not be allowed (s 12(3)). Section 12(4) includes the 'public interest' provision to which this chapter will return.

Balancing the rights

Objectives of the Convention

2.18 In this section it will be necessary to see how the rights referred to above balance one with the other in relation to privacy and to confidentiality, and in connection with family proceedings.

2.19 Under the heading 'The objectives of the Convention' in *Brown v Stott (Procurator Fiscal, Dunfermline) and another*[22] and in what he described as 'the first real test of the Human Rights Act 1998' Lord Steyn said:

> … It is opportune to stand back and consider what the basic aims of the Convention are. One finds the explanation in the very words of the

22 [2000] UKPC D3, [2003] 1 AC 681 at 770–71.

> preambles of the Convention. There were two principal objectives. The first was to maintain and further realise human rights and fundamental freedoms. The framers of the Convention recognised that it was not only morally right to promote the observance of human rights but that it was also the best way of achieving pluralistic and just societies in which all can peaceably go about their lives. The second aim was to foster effective political democracy …

2.20 From the outset those who inspired the Convention understood that one individual right may conflict with another. The obvious example of this, considered below, is the right to respect for privacy and family life balanced against the right to freedom of expression, mostly (though not only) by the media; and especially in the reporting of legal proceedings). Then a balance must be struck between the rights of each party involved. Under the Convention system, it is an independent judiciary which is required to resolve this balance and to secure and enforce the rights under it.

2.21 In the present context, the way in which Articles 6, 8 and 10 are balanced when the rights they protect come into conflict was explained by Lord Steyn in *Re S (Identification: Restrictions on Publication)*.[23] In that case, the mother of S (aged 8) was accused of murdering his brother by salt poisoning. S's guardian (supported by a psychiatric report) argued that publicity would have a detrimental effect on him. There was a risk that he would become an object of curiosity and be subject to bullying. His brother's death had seriously increased a risk of his developing depressive illness. The stress of publicity would significantly increase the possibility of him developing a psychiatric illness.

Lord Steyn: *Re S (Identification: restrictions on publication)*

2.22 Hedley J permitted identification of the mother and the deceased brother and the publication of photographs of them. Lord Steyn considered that Hedley J had made the right order[24] (despite the reservations of the Court of Appeal[25]) and that the balance of the Article 8 and Article 10[26] rights had been correctly struck by the judge: [27]

> [19] … I am simply not convinced that, when everything is drawn together and weighed, it can be said that grounds under Art 10(2) of the [European Convention] have been made out in terms of the balance of the effective preservation of CS's Art 8 rights against the right to publish under Art 10.

23 [2004] UKHL 47, [2005] 1 AC 593, [2005] 1 FLR 591.

24 See para [37] of Lord Steyn's opinion.

25 *Re S (A Child) (Identification: Restrictions on Publication)* [2003] EWCA Civ 963, [2004] Fam 43 (Lord Phillips of Worth Matravers MR, Hale and Latham LJJ).

26 Article 10 is set out in full at 2.15. Article 10(2) includes that the freedoms in Art 10(1) 'may be subject to such formalities, conditions, restrictions or penalties as are prescribed by law and are necessary in a democratic society … for the protection of the reputation or rights of others …'

27 At para [11] of Hedley J's judgment in *Re S (Publicity)* [2003] EWHC 254 (Fam).

2.23 S's guardian's appeal to the Court of Appeal was dismissed, over the dissent of Hale LJ. The House of Lords dismissed the guardian's further appeal on his behalf and upheld Hedley J's order. Lord Steyn gave the only reasoned opinion, with which Lords Bingham, Nicholls, Hoffman and Carswell agreed. Article 6 was relevant, he said, only to the extent that it might enable the press to be restricted in reporting, 'where the interests of juveniles' so require;[28] but that Article 6 also recognises the 'prima facie rule in favour of open justice in criminal trials'.

2.24 It was 'the interaction of between Articles 8 and 10 which lies at the heart of this appeal'.[29] This 'has been illuminated by the opinions in the House of Lords in *Campbell v MGN Ltd*'.[30] From that case, he said, four propositions emerge clearly from the opinions; and it was in accordance with those propositions that he should approach the case:

> [17] … First, neither Article has as such precedence over the other. Secondly, where the values under the two Articles are in conflict, an intense focus on the comparative importance of the specific rights being claimed in the individual case is necessary. Thirdly, the justifications for interfering with or restricting each right must be taken into account. Finally, the proportionality test must be applied to each. For convenience I will call this the ultimate balancing test …

2.25 As will be seen these propositions are treated by judges, since the decision in *Re S*, as the basis on which they should weigh the balance in any conflict between Convention rights.[31]

Press: 'watchdog of the public'

2.26 In the case of open court hearings, such as criminal trials, the press 'is the watchdog of the public', said Lord Steyn, and the ordinary rule of open court trial can only be displaced in 'exceptional circumstances':

> [18] … It was accepted by both sides that the ordinary rule is that the press, as the watchdog of the public, may report everything that takes place in a criminal court. I would add that in European jurisprudence and in domestic practice this is a strong rule. It can only be displaced by unusual or exceptional circumstances. It is, however, not a mechanical rule. The duty of the court is to examine with care each application for a departure from the rule by reason of rights under Art 8.

---

28 Ibid at [15].

29 Ibid at [16].

30 [2004] UKHL 22, [2004] 2 WLR 1232, [2004] UKHRR 648.

31 See eg, Re *J (A Child)* [2013] EWHC 2694 (Fam) sub nom *Re J (Reporting Restriction: Internet: Video)* [2014] 1 FLR 523, Sir James Munby P; *City and County of Swansea v XZ and YZ* [2014] EWHC 212 (Fam), [2014] 2 FLR 1091, Moor J.

2.27 In the case of the child S, Lord Steyn concluded that while Article 8 was engaged, none of the factors in Article 8(2) justified interference.[32] It was therefore necessary 'to assess realistically the nature of the relief sought' on his behalf;[33] but that in doing so, the danger of 'piling exception upon exception to the principle of open justice' must be avoided.[34] The need for public information as to the conduct of criminal trials was important:

> [30] ... A criminal trial is a public event. The principle of open justice puts, as has often been said, the judge and all who participate in the trial under intense scrutiny. The glare of contemporaneous publicity ensures that trials are properly conducted. It is a valuable check on the criminal process. Moreover, the public interest may be as much involved in the circumstances of a remarkable acquittal as in a surprising conviction. Informed public debate is necessary about all such matters. Full contemporaneous reporting of criminal trials in progress promotes public confidence in the administration of justice. It promotes the values of the rule of law.
>
> [31] For these reasons I would, therefore, attribute greater importance to the freedom of the press to report the progress of a criminal trial without any restraint than Hale LJ did.

Transparency and private interests

2.28 In Re *J (A Child)*[35] Sir James Munby P applied the principles in *Re S*[36] especially and explained how the court may, by order, extend or reduce the automatic constraints on publicity; but to do so it must conduct a balancing exercise within the European Convention 1950 as described in *Re S (Identification: Restrictions on Publication)*.[37] It is 'necessary to measure the nature of the impact ... on the child' of what is in prospect, said Lord Steyn. Since *ZH (Tanzania) v Secretary of State for the Home Department*,[38] said Sir James, the interests of the child must be a primary consideration. The balance must be drawn between respect for the child's private life (Art 8) and the right of the press and a parent or others who might want (as was the case in *Re J*) to publicise information (Art 10).

2.29 It will now be necessary to balance the two Articles most engaged in this context – Articles 8 and 10 – and apply them in the context of family proceedings.

---

32 Art 8(2) is set out in full at 2.15.

33 At [26].

34 Ibid at [33].

35 [2013] EWHC 2694 (Fam) sub nom *Re J (Reporting Restriction: Internet: Video)* [2014] 1 FLR 523.

36 *Re S (Identification: Restrictions on Publication)* [2004] UKHL 47, [2005] 1 FLR 591.

37 [2004] UKHL 47, [2005] 1 FLR 591 per Lord Steyn at [17].

38 [2011] UKSC 4 at [33].

4 'A REASONABLE EXPECTATION OF PRIVACY'

A 'private life'

2.30 The best way to judge privacy at common law is to say that it imports a 'reasonable expectation of privacy'. This term was first defined by the House of Lords in *Campbell v MGN Ltd*,[39] a case which was decided almost in parallel with – but just before, in terms of the date publication of judgment – *Von Hannover v Germany – 59320/00*:[40] *Campbell* is dated 6 May 2006, *Von Hannover* 24 June 2004. And, as it happens, the third great human rights case of that year – *Re S*[41] – was also then on its way up to the House of Lords from the Court of Appeal (Hale LJ sat in the minority in *Re S* in the Court of Appeal and was one of the three majority in the House of Lords in *Campbell*).

2.31 In *Richard v The British Broadcasting Corporation (BBC) & South Yorks Police*,[42] Mann J (especially at paras [231]–[237]) provides an overview of the recent jurisprudence on this subject. The term 'expectation of privacy' was coined by Lord Nicholls and in effect adopted by Lord Hope and Lady Hale in *Campbell*. But first it is necessary to establish what 'private life' means for the European Court of Human Rights. In *Von Hannover* the judges found a form of words which, though as they put it, applied to a 'figure of contemporary society *par excellence*', defined privacy for anyone whose private life might be invaded:

> [78] … In the Court's opinion the criteria established by the domestic courts were not sufficient to ensure the effective protection of the applicant's private life and she should, in the circumstances of the case, have had a "legitimate expectation" of protection of her private life.

Campbell and an expectation of privacy

2.32 In *Campbell*, the model Naomi Campbell had always denied that she was a drug taker, though drugs were said to be rife in the fashion industry. She was photographed coming out of a Narcotics Anonymous meeting by a *Daily Mirror* cameraman. She refused to co-operate with the newspaper in publishing what was now known to be the truth about her drug -taking. There was a public interest in putting the facts right; but should her privacy have been interfered with as much as the taking of photos of Ms Campbell did'?

2.33 Lord Nicholls (who with Lord Hoffman would have allowed the publication and refused Campbell's appeal) defined what he saw was the then-emerging concept in English law of a 'private life':

> [21] Accordingly, in deciding what was the ambit of an individual's 'private life' in particular circumstances courts need to be on guard against

39 [2004] UKHL 22, [2004] 2 AC 457.
40 [2004] ECHR 294, (2005) 40 EHRR 1.
41 *Re S (Identification: Restrictions on Publication)* [2004] UKHL 47, [2005] 1 AC 593, [2005] 1 FLR 591.
42 [2018] EWHC 1837 (Ch) .

> using as a touchstone a test which brings into account considerations which should more properly be considered at the later stage of proportionality. Essentially the touchstone of private life is whether in respect of the disclosed facts the person in question had a reasonable expectation of privacy.

2.34 Lord Hope (with Lady Hale and Lord Carswell) allowed Naomi Campbell's appeal, and restored her relatively nominal damages (£3,500) claim. He uses similar words on privacy to those of Lord Nicholls in the previous paragraph in the passage italicised below:

> [95] ... it is well known that persons who are addicted to the taking of illegal drugs or to alcohol can benefit from meetings at which they discuss and face up to their addiction. The private nature of these meetings encourages addicts to attend them in the belief that they can do so anonymously. The assurance of privacy is an essential part of the exercise. The therapy is at risk of being damaged if the duty of confidence which the participants owe to each other is breached by making details of the therapy, such as where, when and how often it is being undertaken, public. I would hold that these details are obviously private.
>
> [96] If the information is obviously private, the situation will be one where the person to whom it relates *can reasonably expect his privacy to be respected.*

2.35 In *JR38*,[43] Lord Toulson explained Lord Nicholls's 'expectation of privacy':

> [88] In *Campbell's* case Lord Nicholls of Birkenhead said at para 21 that: "Essentially the touchstone of private life is whether in respect of the disclosed facts the person in question had a reasonable expectation of privacy." He also warned that courts need to be on guard against using as a touchstone a test which brings into account considerations which should more properly be considered at the later stage of proportionality. Applying *Campbell's* case, Sir Anthony Clarke MR said in [*Murray v Big Pictures (UK) Ltd* [2008] EWCA Civ 446, [2008] 2 FLR 599, [2009] Ch 481] at [35] that "The first question is whether there is a reasonable expectation of privacy". He said at [36] that the question is a broad one which takes account of all the circumstances of the case, including the attributes of the claimant, the nature of the activity in which the claimant was involved, the place at which it was happening, and the nature and purpose of the intrusion ...

A tort of invasion of privacy

2.36 The extent to which a tort has developed out of any right to privacy, or expectation thereof, is considered further in Part 6 of this chapter; alongside the modern use of the term in law as explained by Mann J in *Richard v BBC*.

43 *Re JR38* [2015] UKSC 42, [2016] AC 1131; see also 2.48.

5 THE BALANCE: PRIVACY AND FREEDOM OF EXPRESSION

The ultimate balancing test

'The balancing test'[44]

2.37 The *Re S* ultimate balance is appropriate to any circumstance where a balancing of human rights is called for. Thus, for example, a balancing exercise was said by MacDonald J in *Luxembourg v Luxembourg*[45] to apply in financial relief cases (as MacDonald J was considering in *Luxembourg*) as to any other family litigation. He explained this as follows:

> [56] In *Re S (A Child)(Identification: Restrictions on Publication)* [2005] 1 AC 593 at [23], and having regard to its decision in *Campbell v MGN Ltd* [2004] 2 AC 457, the House of Lords observed that, with respect to the foundation of the jurisdiction to restrain publicity to protect private and family life, or to permit publication to protect freedom of expression, the foundation is now derived from Convention rights under the ECHR. In *Re S (A Child) (Identification: Restrictions on Publication)* at [17] it was made clear that the court exercises this jurisdiction by balancing the competing rights engaged in accordance with the [principles set out above] …
>
> [56] It is clear on the authorities, that the jurisdiction to restrain publicity to protect private and family life, or to permit publication to protect freedom of expression, articulated in *Re S (A Child) (Identification: Restrictions on Publication)* at [23] applies to financial remedy proceedings. In *Spencer v Spencer*[46]at [25] and [26], in holding that the jurisdiction applied in financial remedy proceedings, Munby J (as he then was) noted that in *Re S (A Child)(Identification: Restrictions on Publication)* at [32] Lord Steyn had specifically rejected the assertion that the jurisdiction is confined to the protection of children and could equally be invoked by an adult.

2.38 Indeed, in *Spencer v Spencer*[47] Munby J asserted that the *Re S* 'analysis is entirely general'. The paragraph cited by McDonald J in *Luxembourg* (above) is as follows:

> [32] … Lord Steyn's analysis is entirely general. And if it be the case, as the House of Lords has now taught us, that the foundation of the jurisdiction

44 Per Lord Steyn in *Re S (Identification: Restrictions on Publication)* [2004] UKHL 47, [2005] 1 AC 593, [2005] 1 FLR 591 at [17].

45 *HRH Louis Xavier Marie Guillaume Prince of Luxembourg, Prince of Nassau and Prince of Bourbon-Parma v HRH Tessy Princess of Luxembourg, Princess of Nassau and Princess of Bourbon-Parma & Anor* [2017] EWHC 3095 (Fam), Macdonald J. The final financial relief hearing in this case has taken place: *HRH Louis Prince of Luxembourg v HRH Tessy Princess of Luxembourg & Anor (Application for Financial Remedy)* [2018] EWFC 77 (4 December 2018), McDonald J.

46 *Spencer v Spencer* [2009] EWHC 1529 (Fam), [2009] 2 FLR 1416, Munby J.

47 Ibid.

> to restrain publicity in such cases derives from the Convention, it does not seem to me that any previous distinction between a power in the court to grant such injunctions where children are involved, and the perceived lack of power to grant such injunctions in cases where adults are involved, can have survived the explanation in *In re S* of the effect of the Human Rights Act. After all, neither Article 6, nor Article 8, nor Article 10 of the Convention, being, of course, the Articles which are engaged in such cases, draws any distinction between adults and children. Adults and children are equally entitled to the protection of the Convention ...

2.39 Whenever a court encounters a conflict between two or more European Convention 1950 rights it is the *Re S* ultimate balancing exercise which is the starting point for evaluating operation of the rights, whatever may be the context. In the case of Article 10 the additional HRA 1989 section 12 weighting element comes into the balance and weight freedom of expression (Art 10) accordingly.[48]

Confidentiality balanced against a fair trial: 'to reconcile the irreconcilable'

2.40 In *Re A (Sexual Abuse: Disclosure)*[49] Lady Hale (with whose judgment Lords Neuberger, Clarke, Wilson and Reed SCJJ agreed), described the Supreme Court being asked 'to reconcile the irreconcilable'. She said this was because:

> [1] ... On the one hand, there is the interest of a vulnerable young woman (X) who made an allegation in confidence to the authorities that while she was a child she had been seriously sexually abused by the father of a little girl (A) who is now aged 10. On the other hand, we have the interests of that little girl, her mother (M) and her father (F), in having that allegation properly investigated and tested. These interests are not only private to the people involved. There are also public interests, on the one hand, in maintaining the confidentiality of this kind of communication, and, on the other, in the fair and open conduct of legal disputes. On both sides there is a public interest in protecting both children and vulnerable young adults from the risk of harm.

2.41 Should X, as a witness, be required to disclose information which she understood that she had passed on in confidence concerning the way she had been treated by F or should it remain confidential as between her and her confidant? Lady Hale explained what Convention rights were in issue in the case:

> [25] It is common ground that several European Convention rights are, or may be, in play in this case. There are the Art 6 rights of all three parties to the proceedings, A, M and F [ie the child and her mother and her father], to have a fair trial in the determination of their civil rights. The right to a fair trial is absolute but the question of what is fair may

48 See 2.37.

49 *Re A (Sexual Abuse: Disclosure)* [2012] UKSC 60, [2013] 1 FLR 948, [2013] 1 FCR 69 sub nom *Re A (Family Proceedings: Disclosure of Information)* [2013] 2 AC 66.

depend upon the circumstances of the case. There are the Art 8 rights of A, M and F to respect for their private and family lives. There is also the Art 8 right of X to respect for her private life. Article 8 rights are qualified and can be interfered with if it is necessary in a democratic society in order to protect the rights of others.

2.42 The court rejected X's arguments that Article 3 was engaged;[50] and – in a passage cited in Chapter 20 – rejected any form of closed material procedure.[51] The confidential information should be passed on by X's confidant's and the fair trial rights of the child and her respective parents preserved:

> [35] The only possible conclusion is that the family life and fair trial rights of all three parties to these proceedings are a sufficient justification for the interference with the privacy rights of X. Put the other way round, X's privacy rights are not a sufficient justification for the grave compromise of the fair trial and family life rights of the parties which non-disclosure would entail.

2.43 All that said, it still might not be that X would have to give evidence in person in the proceedings.[52]

Rights: recent developments in the law

Child and father's freedom of expression

2.44 *Rhodes v OPO*[53] was a claim in tort in the name of the 12-year-old son (O) of concert pianist James Rhodes against Rhodes and his publisher. They wanted to publish a book (dedicated to the son) in which Rhodes described in detail his experience of sexual abuse at school. O's mother wanted to protect the son from the material in the book and sued in tort (later taken over by O's godfather). An injunction was refused at first instance. This was reinstated by the Court of Appeal so that publication of a bowdlerised version of the book was permitted. In this case it was the son (or his representative) who alleged a possible breach of privacy; or, more correctly, of the tort of intentionally causing harm, which might impact on his privacy. In the Supreme Court it was the freedom of expression of James Rhodes which was in question.

2.45 The Supreme Court allowed publication of his book by James Rhodes. All five Supreme Court justices agreed (though with Lord Wilson, Lord Neuberger added a few words of his own): if what was said was true, if it was not defamatory and if it was not intended deliberately to injure, it could not be objectionable. Lady Hale (with Lords Toulson and Clarke) commented:

50 Prohibition of torture at [26]–[28] and [32].

51 Ibid at [34].

52 Ibid at [36].

53 [2015] UKSC 32, sub nom *O (A Child) v Rhodes* [2016] AC 219.

> [77] Freedom to report the truth is a basic right to which the law gives a very high level of protection (see, for example, *Napier v Pressdram Ltd* [2010] 1 WLR 934, at [42]). It is difficult to envisage any circumstances in which speech which is not deceptive, threatening or possibly abusive, could give rise to liability in tort for wilful infringement of another's right to personal safety. The right to report the truth is justification in itself. That is not to say that the right of disclosure is absolute, for a person may owe a duty to treat information as private or confidential. But there is no general law prohibiting the publication of facts which will cause distress to another, even if that is the person's intention ...
>
> [78] ... The book's revelation of what it meant to the father to undergo his experience of abuse as a child and how it has continued to affect him throughout his life, is communicated through the brutal language which he uses. His writing contains dark descriptions of emotional hell, self-hatred and rage, as can be seen in the extracts which we have set out. The reader gains an insight into his pain but also his resilience and achievements. To lighten the darkness would reduce its effect. The [Court of Appeal] has taken editorial control over the manner in which the father's story is expressed. A right to convey information to the public carries with it a right to choose the language in which it is expressed in order to convey the information most effectively: see *Campbell v MGN Ltd* [2004] 2 AC 457 at [59] and *Re Guardian News and Media Ltd* [2010] 2 AC 697 at [63].

2.46 Lord Neuberger added of comments of Sedley LJ in the case cited by him below:

> [96] It is true that the book contained material which some people might find offensive, in terms of what was described and how it was expressed, but "free speech includes not only the inoffensive but the irritating, the contentious, the eccentric, the heretical, the unwelcome and the provocative provided it does not tend to provoke violence": see *Redmond-Bate v Director of Public Prosecutions* (1999) 7 BHRC 375 at [20] per Sedley LJ. As he memorably added, "freedom only to speak inoffensively is not worth having".

A child's Article 8 rights

2.47 In *Re JR38*,[54] the applicant for judicial review was a 14-year-old ('John') who had been involved in 'interface violence' in Northern Ireland. The police wanted to expose his name. The Supreme Court considered the extent to which a child is entitled to a reasonable expectation of privacy; and as to whether – in assessment of that expectation by a court – the child is entitled to special treatment.

2.48 Lord Toulson and Lord Clarke (with both of whom Lord Hodge agreed) held that Article 8 rights were not engaged; but that anyway assessment of the

54 [2015] UKSC 42, [2016] AC 1131.

child's rights will depend on the circumstances of the case. Lord Kerr, who gave the lead judgment (with whom Lord Wilson agreed) was in a minority: they concluded that though Article 8 rights were engaged the police were justified, in the circumstances, in interfering with the child's rights.[55]

2.49 The questions for the Supreme Court were: (1) were John's Article 8 rights engaged at all; and if so (2) whether the circumstances justified the police (a 'public authority': Human Rights Act 1998 section 6(1)) in overriding those rights? Was what John was doing – rioting in the area between Protestant and Catholic communities – 'an aspect of his life he was entitled to keep private' at all? The Divisional Court in Northern Ireland had split: one of the three judges there had held that Article 8 was not engaged.

2.50 The case turned whether John was entitled to a 'reasonable expectation of privacy' (as already mentioned). Lord Kerr (in the minority) explained his view, 'particularly in the case of children', as follows:

> [36] ...The *engagement* of the right, as opposed to justification of interference with it, must, of necessity, cover a wide field of an individual's activity ... The concept of a reasonable expectation of a right to privacy ought to have been protected, and that that expectation was reasonable, is one to be approached with some caution ...

2.51 Anyone may be entitled to a 'reasonable expectation of privacy'.[56] In the case of a child, prominence must be given to the child's 'best interests'. However, the reasonable expectation is not determinative of a person's rights, but it is an important factor in its definition.[57] If the applicant is a child: 'publication of his photograph plays an important part in the decision whether that publication fell within the scope of his Art 8 rights ...'[58]

2.52 By contrast, Lord Toulson (with Lord Hodge and Lord Clarke) made the point that if a person has no reasonable expectation of privacy then Article 8 cannot get off the ground.[59] But does the fact that the applicant is a child make any difference to that child's expectation of privacy? The majority held that whether a person's expectation arises is an objective test. It does not matter that the applicant is a child. In John's case, seen objectively, he had no reasonable expectation of privacy, said the majority. His Article 8 rights were not engaged. For children in general, their expectations will be part of the assessment of what is reasonable in each individual case.

---

55 Ibid at [80].

56 And now see eg, *Richard v The British Broadcasting Corporation (BBC) & South Yorks Police* [2018] EWHC 1837 (Ch) (18 July 2018), Mann J.

57 At [37]–[39], [55]–[57], [62]; see *PG v United Kingdom* (2008) 46 EHRR 51.

58 At [47].

59 At [87] and [88].

Right to privacy of a claimant's children

Children who might be affected by publicity

2.53 In *PJS v News Group Newspapers Ltd,*[60] PJS (a married man with children) as already mentioned was in the 'entertainment business'. He received a proposal from a woman (AB) with whom he had had sex on occasion, that with her and her partner (CD) they should have a 'three-way'. Later AB and CD contacted the *Sun on Sunday* and proposed to sell their story. The editor contacted PJS who applied for an injunction to prevent publication. The judge at first instance refused the application. The Court of Appeal overturned that decision. The newspaper appealed to the Supreme Court who maintained the injunction: four Supreme Court justices over the dissent of Lord Toulson.

2.54 The main judgment was given by Lord Mance (with whom all but Lord Toulson agreed). Two features require comment here: the explanation of success at trial under HRA section 12(3) and 'public interest' at section 12(4) (especially in relation to children).

Human Rights Act 1998 section 12; 'public interest'

2.55 Though they followed the Court of Appeal decision on the issue before them, Lord Mance, with the support of all members of the court, held that there was a clear error of reasoning in relation to the reasoning of the Court of Appeal in relation to HRA 1998 section 12(4). This raised two points: the relative importance of Article 10 and the likelihood of a final order preventing publication on the application. Lord Mance explained this as follows, by reference in particular to his own reasoning:

> [19] ... The Court of Appeal's further self-direction, that [HRA 1998 s 12] "raises the hurdle which the claimant must overcome in order to obtain an interim injunction" is unexceptionable, in so far as section 12 replaces the general American Cyanamid test, focused on the balance of convenience, with a test of whether the claimant is "likely to establish that publication should not be allowed" at trial. The position was stated more particularly by Lord Nicholls of Birkenhead said in *Cream Holdings Ltd v Banerjee* [2005] 1 AC 253 at [22]: "... Section 12(3) makes the likelihood of success at trial an essential element in the court's consideration of whether to make an interim order ... There can be no single, rigid standard governing all applications for interim restraint orders. Rather, on its proper construction the effect of section 12(3) is that the court is not to make an interim restraint order unless satisfied the applicant's prospects of success at the trial are sufficiently favourable to justify such an order being made in the particular circumstances of the case ..."

60 [2016] UKSC 26, [2016] AC 1081, [2016] 2 FLR 251, [2016] 2 WLR 1253.

2.56 Lord Mance went on to recall the well-trodden path explained in *Re S* and the fact, confirmed by *Re S*, that there is no hierarchy of European Convention 1950 Articles; and to stress the point in relation to injunctions to restrain publicity:

> [20] The Court of Appeal's initial self-direction is however contrary to … authority at the highest level, which establishes that, even at the interlocutory stage, (i) neither article has preference over the other, (ii) where their values are in conflict, what is necessary is an intense focus on the comparative importance of the rights being claimed in the individual case, (iii) the justifications for interfering with or restricting each right must be taken into account and (iv) the proportionality test must be applied: see eg, *Re S (A Child) (Identification: Restrictions on Publication)* [(above)] at [17] per Lord Steyn …

Publicity and its effects on children: a 'trump card'

2.57 In the course of his judgment Lord Mance summarised the decision of Cranston J who had refused the injunction at first instance. He said of that decision:

> [13] When refusing an injunction on 15 January 2016, Cranston J:
>
> (i) accepted that the appellant had a reasonable expectation that his sexual activities would remain private,
>
> (ii) added that he was "especially troubled" by the children's privacy interests under ECHR article 8, though these could not operate as a "trump card",
>
> (iii) rejected the respondent's suggestion that the proposed publication went to any relevant matter of "public debate",
>
> (iv) identified the appellant and his partner as portraying an image to the world of a committed relationship …

2.58 Lady Hale (with whom the majority also agreed) gave a short judgment. She commented in particular on Cranston J's 'trump card' comment on PJS's children and on the importance of their interests:[61]

> [72] … I wish only to add a few words about the interests of the two children whom PJS has with YMA. It is simply not good enough to dismiss the interests of any children who are likely to be affected by the publication

61 A similar point to that made by Lady Hale is picked up by Eady J in *CDE v MGN Ltd* [2010] EWHC 3308 (QB), [2011] 1 FLR 1524 where he said of the children of a man who sought an interim injunction to prevent publication: '[7] As I understand the attitude of the newspaper, it is simply that a married man cannot be accorded greater rights or consideration by the court than a single man and, insofar as there may be any impact on his family, that is too bad. Yet it is now well established that the first question a court has to address on applications of this kind is whether Art 8 rights are engaged. As to that, the threatened publication would undoubtedly engage the Art 8 rights of all the persons I have identified. The fact that the first claimant has a wife and children simply means that there are more persons whose rights have to be taken into account. They cannot simply be ignored on the basis of traditional arguments along the lines of who has a cause of action and who does not. Since they would at least potentially be affected by the exercise of the defendants' Art 10 rights, their Art 8 rights have to be weighed in the balance.'

> of private information about their parents with the bland statement that "these cannot be a trump card". Of course they cannot always rule the day. But they deserve closer attention than they have so far received in this case, for two main reasons …

2.59 Lady Hale then went on two explain the two aspects of the rights of PJS's children which affected the case: their own privacy interests and the extent to which harm to their interests might result from any publication:

> [72] … First, not only are the children's interests likely to be affected by a breach of the privacy interests of their parents, but the children have independent privacy interests of their own. They also have a right to respect for their family life with their parents. Secondly, by section 12(4)(b), any court considering whether to grant either an interim or a permanent injunction has to have "particular regard" to "any relevant privacy code". It is not disputed that the Independent Press Standards Organisation Editors' Code of Practice, which came into force in January, is a relevant Code for this purpose. This, as Lord Mance JSC has explained, at para 36, provides that "editors must demonstrate an exceptional public interest to over-ride the normally paramount interests of children under 16".

2.60 At any final hearing of a reporting restriction injunction, the harm to children's interests must be borne in mind: they have 'privacy interests of their own' as she had said in [72] (above):

> [73] This means that, at trial, the court will have to consider carefully the nature and extent of the likely harm to the children's interests which will result in the short, medium and longer terms from the publication of this information about one of their parents …

2.61 The full version of the judgment has three paragraphs which are redacted in the published version. Lady Hale explains that these paragraphs – which could easily enable PJS to be recognised – are relevant, for her, to the balancing exercise under the European Convention 1950 and to how the three children should learn about what had happened.

Respect for private life and proportionality

2.62 The extent of any interference with any Article 8 right must be proportionate to the objective sought to be achieved by the state. That is to say, the measure of interference must be tested against the justification for it. In *Re A (Sexual Abuse: Disclosure)*[62] Lady Hale explained her approach to the proposed interference with the Article 8 rights of X (the witness in the proceedings concerning A), justification for the interference and proportionality of the means proposed, as follows:

> [33] However, that may not be the end of the matter, for to order disclosure in this case would undoubtedly be an interference with X's right to respect

62 [2012] UKSC 60, [2013] 1 FLR 948; and see fuller consideration of this case in Chapter 4.

for her private life. She revealed what, if true, would be some very private and sensitive information to the authorities in the expectation that it would not be revealed to others. She has acquiesced in its disclosure to her legal advisers and to the court in these proceedings, but that can scarcely amount to a waiver of her rights. She had no choice. Clearly, her rights are in conflict with the rights of every other party to these proceedings. Protecting their rights is a legitimate aim. But the means chosen have to be proportionate. Is there, therefore, some means, short of full disclosure, of protecting their rights?

6 A TORT OF PRIVACY

Sir Cliff Richard and a tort of privacy

2.63 By 2018 the tort of privacy is securely established as part of the English common law. Thus, in *Richard v The British Broadcasting Corporation (BBC) & South Yorks Police*,[63] Mann J was concerned with the balance of the privacy of an individual – Sir Cliff Richard (CR) – as against the extent of the freedom of the BBC publicise information about CR.

2.64 Unknown to himself, CR had become subject to police investigation by South Yorkshire Police (SYP) for alleged child abuse. Daniel Johnson (J), a BBC reporter, found out about it. He met with SYP and was told about an intended search. J was to be given advanced notice. The search took place on 14 August 2014 and the BBC immediately gave extensive television coverage to it, as it was happening and thereafter. CR remained under investigation until June 2016 when it was announced there would be no charges.

2.65 CR claimed that both BBC and SYP violated his rights both in privacy and under the Data Protection Act 1998 (DPA 1998). He claimed substantial damages because his life and finances have been radically affected by what happened. In May 2017 CR reached a settlement with SYP who accepted liability, apologised, made a statement in open court accepting liability, paid Sir Cliff damages of £400,000, agreed to pay his costs and paid £300,000 on account of costs. The BBC continued to resist the claim which came before Mann J in April 2018. The BBC was found liable to CR in damages. It did not appeal. Mann J's findings, though controversial in the view of some, especially in the press and other media, represent the law. This chapter looks only at the privacy aspect (ie, not at the subject of damages or other tort issues). Mann J specifically held[64] that the DPA 1998 claim added nothing to the privacy claim. The former could be ignored.

2.66 Mann J defined the privacy issues he must resolve in the case[65] as follows:

(1) Did CR have a legitimate expectation of privacy in relation to the investigation and the search of his property?

63 [2018] EWHC 1837 (Ch).
64 Ibid at [226].
65 Ibid at [225].

(2) If yes, was the BBC justified in publishing information to the investigation by virtue of its rights of freedom of expression?

(3) If he had rights of privacy, was there an infringement of them by either or both defendants and (if so) what damages follow?

Reasonable expectation of privacy

2.67 The first issue for the court was CR's 'legitimate expectation of privacy'. This starts from European Convention 1950 Article 8 (right to respect for private life) balanced against Article 10 (freedom of expression): respectively of CR and of BBC. Balancing the rights, where a conflict arises, he said[66] involves the following:

(1) Were CR's Article 8 rights engaged?

(2) How were such rights, if engaged, to be balanced against the Article 10 rights of the BBC?

(3) Was there a public interest in publishing the information that was published?

2.68 There is a no 'invariable right to privacy' said Mann J[67] ([251]); but, that said, the starting point 'as a matter of general principle [is that] a suspect has a reasonable expectation of privacy in relation to a police investigation, and I so rule'.[68] The question turns on the extent to which, first, people generally understand and give effect to the presumption of innocence; and, secondly, that everyone is capable of adopting a completely open- and broad-minded view of the fact of an investigation so that there was no risk of taint either during the investigation or afterwards.

2.69 Mann J referred to *Khuja v Times Newspapers Ltd*.[69] He accepted the minority view (Lords Kerr and Wilson) where, at their paragraph [52] they quoted Cobb J in *Rotherham MBC v M*:[70] that despite the presumption of innocence, where there are false allegations of serious crime investigation 'mud sticks'. The fact of a person being a public figure, like CR, made no difference to their entitlement to an expectation of privacy.[71] Nor was the position altered by the identity of the person or body who received the information: in *Richard* it was the highly respectable BBC. If information starts out as private, said Mann J, it remains so, 'full stop':

> [258] ... Sir Cliff's rights in respect of the information in the hands of the police are not based on a reasonable expectation of privacy as long as the information does not fall into the hands of the media; he has a reasonable expectation of privacy full stop ...

66 Ibid at [230].

67 Ibid at [251].

68 Ibid at [248].

69 [2017] UKSC 49, [2017] 3 WLR 351. Suspect in case concerning serious child abuse. Supreme Court permitted publicity (3:2).

70 [2016] EWHC 2660 (Fam), [2016] 4 WLR 177 at [39].

71 At [256]; and see eg, *K v News Group Newspapers Ltd* [2011] EWCA Civ 439, [2011] 1 WLR 1827 per Ward LJ at [10]; *Murray v Big Pictures (UK) Ltd* [2008] EWCA Civ 446, [2008] 2 FLR 599, [2009] Ch 481 per Brooke LJ at [36].

Freedom of expression

2.70 It follows from all this that Article 8 was engaged. This was the first hurdle for CR to overcome. It was the first step in decision making, as Lady Hale explained in *Campbell v MGN Ltd*:[72]

> [137] It should be emphasised that the "reasonable expectation of privacy" is a threshold test which brings the balancing exercise into play. It is not the end of the story. Once the information is identified as "private" in this way, the court must balance the claimant's interest in keeping the information private against the countervailing interest of the recipient in publishing it. Very often, it can be expected that the countervailing rights of the recipient will prevail.

2.71 What of the BBC's balancing rights under Article 10 and the Human Rights Act 1998 section 12(4); and how did each set of rights weigh one against the other? Mann J considered that CR's home rights had been invaded; but the disclosure of the police investigation overwhelmed the significance of this invasion. Of the balance between Articles 8 and 10 Mann J drew attention to Lord Steyn's 'ultimate balancing test' in *Re S (Identification: Restrictions on Publication)* (see above). The Human Rights Act 1998 section 12(4) requires the court to take into account the public interest in the publication of material. The judge considered this in the light of factors set out in *Axel Springer AG v Germany*.[73] Assessment of the public interest and its part in drawing the balance depends on the 'good faith' of the journalist and on the media providing 'reliable and precise information'.[74] The way the BBC came by information about, and then reported, the investigation weighed against them.

2.72 In defining how the balance fell in *Richard*, Mann J concluded that CR's privacy rights outweighed the BBC's right to freedom of expression ([315]). The first point he identified was the 'mud sticks' point:[75]

> [316] ... The consequences of a disclosure for a person such as [CR] are capable of being, and were, very serious. The failure of the public to keep the presumption of innocence in mind at all times means that there is inevitably going to be stigma attached to the revelation, which is magnified in this case by the nature of the allegations against him, which were allegations (especially in the then climate) of extreme seriousness. Reporting on the investigation and the search was a serious invasion which required an equally serious justification ...

Privacy, publicity and breach of privacy

2.73 A child and most private lay parties (though not most witnesses) in children proceedings are entitled to privacy; that is, they have an expectation of

72 [2004] UKHL 22, [2004] 2 AC 457.
73 (2012) 55 EHRR 6, [2012] EMLR 15 especially at [276].
74 Ibid at [288].
75 See 2.63.

privacy. If privacy is breached, in relation to court proceedings, there may be a question of contempt proceedings (Administration of Justice Act 1960 s 12(1)). Separately, whether there are court proceedings or not, the person who breaches their privacy may be sued in tort. As Mann J commented:

> [259] ... As against SYP as a public authority there is a direct complaint [by CR] against them under [HRA 1998]. As against the BBC there is the tort which has been fashioned out of the Act so as to give a remedy against non-public authorities ...

2.74 The claim is against anyone who publishes and thereby breaches a protected person's privacy. The press has the public interest card to play (HRA 1998 s 12(4)). Others who may publish or otherwise release information from children proceedings do not. 'Jigsaw identification' in children proceedings, of a child or the child's parents or other carers, surely makes the possibility of breach relatively high. The President of the Family Division published *Practice Guidance: anonymisation and avoidance of the identification of children and the treatment of explicit descriptions of the sexual abuse of children in judgments intended for the public arena* in December 2018.[76] This guidance deals with two aspects of anonymisation and the avoidance of identification of children: first, personal and geographical details which might identify in judgments and, secondly, the treatment of sexually explicit descriptions of the sexual abuse of children. Thus, avoidance of personal and geographical indicators in judgments is not confined to concealing names but extends to the avoidance of anything which might lead to the identification of a child – 'jigsaw identification'. The guidance aims to enable judges to strike a balance between the policy that more judgments should be published, and concerns expressed by and for young people at the placing of personal details and information in the public. The guidance also asks judges to consider what level of detail of sexual abuse of children it is necessary to include in published judgments; and, where possible, to consider whether it would be appropriate to summarise such incidents.

7 COURT IN PRIVATE

Private hearings

Open court, private court

2.75 This final Part of this chapter considers the privacy which is directed by FPR 2010 for family proceedings.

> **27.10 Hearings in private**
>
> (1) Proceedings to which these rules apply will be held in private, except–
>
> (a) where these rules or any other enactment provide otherwise;
>
> (b) subject to any enactment, where the court directs otherwise.

76 Available at: www.judiciary.uk/publications/practice-guidance-family-court-anonymisation-guidance.

2.76 The common law source of this rule is generally regarded as *Scott & Anor v Scott*,[77] in which the House of Lords set out a re-affirmation of open court hearing. The case is still the foundation of the modern law. Toulson LJ explained the open justice principle:

> [1] Open justice. The words express a principle at the heart of our system of justice and vital to the rule of law. The rule of law is a fine concept but fine words butter no parsnips. How is the rule of law itself to be policed? It is an age-old question. *Quis custodiet ipsos custodes*: who will guard the guards themselves? In a democracy, where power depends on the consent of the people governed, the answer must lie in the transparency of the legal process. Open justice lets in the light and allows the public to scrutinise the workings of the law, for better or for worse. Jeremy Bentham said in a well-known passage quoted by Lord Shaw of Dunfermline in *Scott v Scott* [1913] AC 417 at 477: "Publicity is the very soul of justice. It is the keenest spur to exertion and the surest of all guards against improbity. It keeps the judge himself while trying under trial."

2.77 *Scott v Scott* explained the common law recognition of the need for exceptions to the open justice principle – cases being heard in private, but only if for compelling reason. Lord Reed summarised the *Scott* exceptions in *A v British Broadcasting Corporation*[78] as follows:

> [29] Exceptions to the principle of open justice were considered in the well-known case of Scott v Scott [(above)], in which the House of Lords emphasised in the strongest terms the importance of the general principle, but also recognised that there were circumstances in which it was necessary to depart from it. Viscount Haldane LC gave the example at p 437 of a court exercising a wardship jurisdiction: such a court was sitting primarily to guard the interests of the ward, and the attainment of that object might require that the public should be excluded. Lunacy proceedings were in a similar position. Another example given by the Lord Chancellor, of greater relevance to the present case, was litigation concerning a secret process, "where the effect of publicity would be to destroy the subject-matter". All of their Lordships stressed the need for a compelling justification for any departure from the principle of open justice.

Legislation and privacy

2.78 As will be explained *Scott* was a case about contempt of court. It was a successful appeal to the House of Lords to excuse Mrs Scott and her solicitor from findings of contempt against them. The exceptions to open justice mentioned in the speeches (referred to by Lord Reed in the previous paragraph) have been repeated and elaborated upon by statute.

77 [1913] UKHL 2, [1913] AC 417.

78 *A v British Broadcasting Corporation* [2014] UKSC 25, [2015] 1 AC 558.

2.79 The Administration of Justice Act 1960 section 12(1) deals with publication of information from hearings 'in private' and says that, though publication of a hearing in public will not necessarily be a contempt, in certain instances the nature of the case will make publication concerning them a contempt. As amended, section 12(1) is as follows:

12 Publication of information relating to proceedings in private

(1) The publication of information relating to proceedings before any court sitting in private shall not of itself be contempt of court except in the following cases, that is to say—

(a) where the proceedings—

(i) relate to the exercise of the inherent jurisdiction of the High Court with respect to minors;

(ii) are brought under the Children Act 1989 or the Adoption and Children Act 2002; or

(iii) otherwise relate wholly or mainly to the maintenance or upbringing of a minor;

(b) where the proceedings are brought under the Mental Capacity Act 2005, or under any provision of the Mental Health Act 1983 authorising an application or reference to be made to the First-tier Tribunal, the Mental Health Review Tribunal for Wales or the county court;

(c) where the court sits in private for reasons of national security during that part of the proceedings about which the information in question is published;

(d) where the information relates to a secret process, discovery or invention which is in issue in the proceedings;

(e) where the court (having power to do so) expressly prohibits the publication of all information relating to the proceedings or of information of the description which is published …

(4) Nothing in this section shall be construed as implying that any publication is punishable as contempt of court which would not be so punishable apart from this section (and in particular where the publication is not so punishable by reason of being authorised by rules of court).

2.80 Broadly the same list of exceptions to the open justice principle set out in the Administration of Justice Act 1960 can be found in CPR 1998 r 39.2(3) which is as follows:

(3) A hearing, or any part of it, may be in private if –

(a) publicity would defeat the object of the hearing;

(b) it involves matters relating to national security;

(c) it involves confidential information (including information relating to personal financial matters) and publicity would damage that confidentiality;

(d) a private hearing is necessary to protect the interests of any child or protected party;[79]

(e) it is a hearing of an application made without notice and it would be unjust to any respondent for there to be a public hearing;

(f) it involves uncontentious matters arising in the administration of trusts or in the administration of a deceased person's estate; or

(g) the court considers this to be necessary, in the interests of justice.

Open justice principle

Open court: the 'servant of justice'

2.81 In *Re K*,[80] Lord Devlin found the open justice principle to be explained in *Scott*. Whilst justice must be open, the procedure by which justice was to be obtained was but a means to an end.[81] Justice was the end each proceeding must seek to achieve. Thus, said Lord Devlin, in *Re K*:

> But a principle of judicial inquiry, whether fundamental or not, is only a means to an end. If it can be shown in any particular class of case that the observance of a principle of this sort does not serve the ends of justice, it must be dismissed; otherwise it would become the master instead of the servant of justice. Obviously, the ordinary principles of judicial inquiry are requirements for all ordinary cases and it can only be in an extraordinary class of case that any one of them can be discarded. This is what was so clearly decided in *Scott v Scott*.

2.82 Lord Toulson (as Toulson LJ had by then become) cites *Scott* as a starting point for his approach to the open justice principle in *Kennedy v The Charity Commission*:[82]

> [110] It has long been recognised that judicial processes should be open to public scrutiny unless and to the extent that there are valid countervailing reasons. This is the open justice principle. The reasons for it have been stated on many occasions. Letting in the light is the best way of keeping those responsible for exercising the judicial power of the state up to the mark and for maintaining public confidence: *Scott*

79 A 'protected party' can be defined eg by FPR 2010 r 2.3(1) as: '... a party, or an intended party, who lacks capacity (within the meaning of the [Mental Capacity Act 2005]) to conduct proceedings'. .

80 Ibid at [238].

81 *Re K (Infants)* [1965] AC 201; and see per Lord Diplock in *Attorney General v Leveller Magazine Ltd* [1979] AC 440 at 451.

82 [2014] UKSC 20, [2015] 1 AC 455.

> *v Scott* [(above)]; *R (Guardian News and Media Ltd) v City of Westminster Magistrates' Court (Article 19 intervening)* [(above)].

Scott v Scott*: the case*

2.83 The head-note in *Scott* records that the Family Court (then the Probate, Divorce and Admiralty Division) has no power, either with or without the consent of the parties, to hear a nullity suit or other matrimonial suit in camera in the interest of public decency. The courts could not therefore restrict publication of details of any nullity hearing. The facts of *Scott* were not in issue. Mrs Scott filed a nullity petition based on Mr Scott's impotence. She then took out a summons asking for the appointment of medical inspectors and that the petition should be heard in camera. On her summons an order was made for such a hearing. She obtained a decree of nullity. There was nothing to differentiate the case, said Viscount Haldane LC, from many others which are heard in open Court, and, as far as the public were concerned, it might quite well have been so heard he said.

2.84 The decree was made absolute in January 1912. In August 1911 Mrs Scott and Mr Braby, her solicitor (second appellant), sent copies of the shorthand notes of the proceedings at the hearing to the husband's father and sister. Mrs Scott felt an inaccurate account of the case had been given by her ex-husband. In December 1911 Mr Scott applied to commit her and her solicitor for contempt. The High Court considered her and her solicitor to be in contempt and ordered them both to pay costs. The Court of Appeal refused to hear an appeal since – at the time – there was no appeal against a criminal case and they held that this was such a case.

2.85 Viscount Haldane summarised the issues before the House of Lords as follows:

> My Lords, the question which we have now to decide necessitates consideration of the jurisdiction to hear in camera in nullity proceedings, and of the power of the judge to make an order which not only excludes the public from the hearing, but restrains the parties from afterwards making public the details of what took place.

2.86 Unanimously the House held that the judge had no such powers in this case; and they went on to discuss the exceptions to the open justice principle. For the judge to have lawfully ordered a hearing in camera he must bring himself within an exception to the open justice principle. It is these exceptions and the principles on which they are based which makes *Scott v Scott* and the principles it laid down so important.

Scott*: exceptions to the open justice principle*

2.87 The exceptions to the open justice principle recognised by *Scott* have expanded over the last 100 years. In *A v BBC*,[83] Lord Reed stressed the ability of

83 Ibid at [39] and [40].

the common law to develop (see italicised passage below), and gave a number of examples which went beyond the exceptions envisaged in *Scott*:

> [40] Some of these examples may arguably go beyond the categories envisaged in some of the older authorities. As Lord Loreburn observed however in *Scott v Scott* at 446, it would be impossible to enumerate or anticipate all possible contingencies. Furthermore, in this area as in others *the common law is capable of development. The application of the principle of open justice may change in response to changes in society and in the administration of justice.* It can also develop having regard to the approach adopted in other common law countries, some of which have constitutional texts containing guarantees comparable to the Convention rights, while in others the approach adopted reflects the courts' view of the requirements of justice (italics supplied) …

2.88 Of this passage and its wider context, in *JX MX v Dartford & Gravesham NHS Trust & Ors* [2015] EWCA Civ 96, the Court of Appeal said:

> [9] … Lord Reed recognised that there may be many different cases in which the court must have regard to the need to do justice in a wider sense than merely reaching a just determination of the issue between the immediate parties.

2.89 In *A v BBC*, [84] as already mentioned, Lord Reed refers to the main well-known three elements in the list of exceptions to the open justice principle:

(1) Wardship and children proceedings.

(2) 'Lunacy', now Mental Capacity Act 2005.

(3) That publicity might destroy the subject matter of the case (eg, a commercial secret).

Open justice principle and family proceedings

2.90 For the family lawyer and for the proponent of open court justice (called 'transparency' by some, which slightly misses the fact of the rights of the public and the press), the use of these exceptions, with full subtlety, permits open justice in all courts (including family courts). Rightly – and lawfully – it turns family law's 'private' court impulse[85] on its head. It accords with the common law which is at present overridden in a cavalier fashion by the Family Procedure Rules Committee rule makers . The Committee's declaration in r 27.10 that all family proceedings under the rules are to be in 'private' is palpably outside any powers (ultra vires) which the Committee has under the Courts Act 2003.[86]

---

84 Ibid at [29].

85 FPR 2010 r 27.10.

86 Courts Act 2003 ss 75–76 provides the Family Procedure Rules Committee with its statutory powers.

2.91 Mr Allan found that Ms Clibbery was able, lawfully, to pass on his papers to the press (*Allan v Clibbery*[87]). If the same case were tried today and if FPR 2010 r 27.10 were indeed lawful, the case would go the other way: Ms Clibbery would have been considered to be in contempt of court. A rule cannot change the common law (*Jaffray v The Society of Lloyds*[88]). FPR 2010 cannot alter what the Court of Appeal found in *Allan v Clibbery*. Despite what FPR 2010 r 10.5 (hearings in private: the *Allan* case would now be dealt with under FPR 2010 Pt 10) and r 27.10 say, save in the cases referred to in AJA 1960 section 12(1) or where the court otherwise orders, all civil proceedings must be in open court (*Scott v Scott*) unless the court otherwise orders.

Private hearings, open court appeals

2.92 Because a first instance hearing had been in private, does not mean an appeal should be in private. If it is to the Court of Appeal (under CPR 1998 Pt 52), the appeal is governed by CPR 1998 r 39.2(3). This was explained by Gloster LJ in *Norman v Norman*.[89] With effect from 10 December 2018, FPR 2010 Part 30 (appeals to the Family Court in family proceedings) has been amended[90] to enable appellate judges to direct that family proceedings appeals be heard in open court.[91]

2.93 In *Norman*, three years after a couple's divorce a wife (W) applied in 2008 to extend the periodical payments aspect of an earlier consent order. In 2014 the wife made a second attempt to set aside the consent order on the basis of H's non-disclosure. The application was dismissed and the wife now sought to appeal that decision in the Court of Appeal. In 2016 an *ex tempore* judgment included a quote from a previous judgment in which the parties were named and the wife complained that this had been in breach of an earlier anonymity order. In advance of the appeal she sought to continue the anonymity order made in 2011; or she wanted imposition of a fresh anonymity order.

8 RESTRICTIONS ON PUBLICITY

Reporting restrictions orders

2.94 This Part serves as an introduction to Lord Neuberger's practice guidance on the making of 'interim non-disclosure orders' which he introduces as a 'recommended practice' for restraint of publication; but in practice it will also serve

87 [2002] EWCA Civ 45, [2002] Fam 261, [2002] 1 FLR 565.
88 [2007] EWCA Civ 586.
89 [2017] EWCA Civ 49, [2017] 1 WLR 2523, [2018] 1 FLR 426.
90 FPR 2010 r 30.12A (introduced by Family Procedure (Amendment No 2) Rules 2018.
91 See eg 'Open Court for Appeals to Family Judges' by David Burrows at Transparency Project. Available at: www.transparencyproject.org.uk/open-court-for-appeals-to-family-judges/ and 'Public Hearings of Family Proceedings Appeals'. Available at: https://dbfamilylaw.wordpress.com/2018/12/03/public-hearings-of-family-proceedings-appeals.

where anonymity is in issue; where confidentiality or privacy are in issue; or where there is threatened contempt of court.[92] The guidance is set out in full at the end of this chapter.

2.95 Lord Neuberger uses a variety of terms for the orders in question. In family proceedings they are generally referred to as reporting restrictions order. They are a common law remedy which restricts access to court material which would otherwise be at large. Most family proceedings are in private; and most the parties themselves (other than adults on appeal) are anonymous. The use of the orders will therefore be rare.

2.96 This chapter – indeed this book, as a whole – does not discuss the procedure whereby civil proceedings may be issued and pursued based on any tort related to privacy and confidentiality.

2.97 The guidance emphasises that any non-disclosure order – or as they are often termed in family proceedings, reporting restrictions order – restricts European Convention 1950 Article 10 (freedom of expression) rights as it restricts disclosure of information and is in breach of the open justice principle.

Procedure: Family Procedure Rules 2010 r 20.2

2.98 Application is made under Family Procedure Rules 2010 (FPR 2010) Part 20, which is derived from, and almost exactly the same as, CPR 1998 r 25. Lord Neuberger's references are to CPR 1998 Part 25. Examples of orders under discussion here include:

- To prevent publicity in respect of a party to proceedings.
- To provide anonymity of a witness (including experts) during the course of proceedings.
- Orders made following the conclusion of proceedings for anonymity for a party or a witness for a period.[93]

2.99 An application for a restriction order must be in the High Court.[94] Application is by the Part 18 procedure supplemented by Lord Neuberger's guidance: see for example, paragraph 17: that the applicant should prepare (a) the application/claim form; (b) a witness statement or statements justifying the need for an order; (c) legal submissions; (d) a draft order; and (e) an explanatory note (explained further in PG of 11 August 2011).

92 *Practice Guidance (Interim Non-Disclosure Orders)* [2012] 1 WLR 1003, para 1.

93 See eg, the abused girl (until 18) in *Birmingham City Council v Riaz & Ors* [2014] EWHC 4247 (Fam), [2015] 2 FLR 763 Keehan J; but no anonymity for the men concerned); or, exceptionally, for life *X v Dartford and Gravesham NHS Trust* [2015] EWCA Civ 96, [2015] 1 WLR 3647).

94 See eg, *Re J (Reporting Restriction: Internet: Video)* [2013] EWHC 2694 (Fam), sub nom *Re J (A Child) (contra mundum injunction)* [2014] 1 FLR 523, [2014] 2 FCR 284 Sir James Munby P.

2.100 In proceedings under FPR 2010 (save where otherwise provided for) proceedings are in private. Where proceedings are not in private[95] it is for the person seeking to depart from the general rule to establish why on 'clear and cogent evidence' (*Guidance* paragraph 13 and the authorities there referred to).

2.101 Applicants must comply with HRA 1998 section 12(2) (no order if a respondent is not represented: as the husband found in *Luxembourg*[96]at [16]); FPR 2010 r 20.3(2) and (3); *PD20A* paragraph 4.3(c) (informal notification to respondent) (*Guidance* paragraph 18).

2.102 Service on press legal representatives can be made in a way that those representatives will know what is part of proceedings (ie no further disclosure) and what is for 'editorial use'.[97] This press concern arose in *Luxembourg* in relation to *PD12I* paragraph 3.3, which says:

> 3.3 The court will bear in mind that legal advisers to the media –
>
> (i) are used to participating in hearings at very short notice where necessary; and
>
> (ii) are able to differentiate between information provided for legal purposes and information for editorial use.
>
> Service of applications via the CopyDirect service should henceforth be the norm

Practice Guidance (Interim Non-disclosure Orders)

1 This guidance sets out recommended practice regarding any application for interim injunctive relief in civil proceedings to restrain the publication of information: an interim non-disclosure order. It is issued as guidance (not as a practice direction) by Lord Neuberger of Abbotsbury MR, as Head of Civil Justice. Such applications may be founded on rights guaranteed by the European Convention for the Protection of Human Rights and Fundamental Freedoms ("the Convention"), or on grounds of privacy or confidentiality. They may also be made in respect of a threatened contempt of court, a threatened libel or malicious falsehood, harassment, or a *Norwich Pharmacal* application (see *Norwich Pharmacal Co v Customs and Excise Comrs* [1974] AC 133) in support of such actions. All such orders will seek to restrict the exercise of the Article 10 Convention right of freedom of expression through prohibiting the disclosure of information.

95 See eg, divorce of FLA 1996 Pt 4 proceedings per *Clibbery v Allan* [2002] EWCA Civ 45, [2002] 1 FLR 565.

96 [2017] EWHC 3095 (Fam), [2018] 1 FLR 480, Macdonald J. The final financial relief hearing in this case has now taken place: *HRH Louis Prince of Luxembourg v HRH Tessy Princess of Luxembourg & Anor (Application for Financial Remedy)* [2018] EWFC 77 (04 December 2018), McDonald J.

97 FPR 2010 *PD12I* para 3.3 *Luxembourg v Luxembourg & Anor* [2017] EWHC 3095 (Fam), [2018] 1 FLR 480, Macdonald J (at [16]).

2 It also provides guidance concerning the proper approach to the general principle of open justice in respect of such applications and explains the proper approach to the model interim non-disclosure order a copy of which is attached to this guidance.

3 The law set out in this guidance is correct as at 1 August 2011.

Statutory provisions

4 Applications which seek to restrain publication of information engage Article 10 of the Convention and section 12 of the Human Rights Act 1998 ('HRA'). In some, but not all, cases they will also engage Article 8 of the Convention. Articles 8 and 10 of the Convention have equal status and, when both have to be considered, neither has automatic precedence over the other. The court's approach is set out in *In re S (A Child) (Identification: Restrictions on Publication)* [2005] 1 AC 593, paragraph 17.

5 Section 12 of the HRA applies whenever the court is considering whether to grant relief which might affect the exercise of the article 10 Convention right. Section 12(2) of the HRA requires advance notice to be given to persons against whom the application is made, except in the exceptional circumstances set out in section 12(2)(a)(b).

6 Section 12(3) of the HRA requires the applicant to satisfy the court that they are likely to establish, at trial, that publication should not be 1004allowed. Guidance on the application of section 12(3) is set out in *Cream Holdings Ltd v Banerjee* [2005] 1 AC 253, paras 22–23.

7 Section 12(4) of the HRA requires that court to have particular regard to the fundamental importance of the Article 10 Convention right of freedom of expression, where proceedings relate to material which a respondent claims, or which appears to the court, to be journalistic, literary or artistic material, or conduct connected with such material, the extent to which the material has or is about to become available to the public, or it is or would be in the public interest for it to be published. It also requires the court to have regard to any relevant privacy code. The code of the Press Complaints Commission is one such code.

Civil Procedure Rules

8 CPR r 25.3 and paragraph 5.1(1)–(5) of Practice Direction 25A—Interim Injunctions supplementing CPR Pt 25 apply to all interim injunction applications, including those for interim non-disclosure orders.

Open justice

9 Open justice is a fundamental principle. The general rule is that hearings are carried out in, and judgments and orders are, public: see Article 6.1 of the Convention, CPR r 39.2 and *Scott v Scott* [1913] AC 417. This

applies to applications for interim non-disclosure orders: *Micallef v Malta* (2009) 50 EHRR 920, para 75ff; *Donald v Ntuli (Guardian News & Media Ltd intervening)* [2011] 1 WLR 294, para 50.

10 Derogations from the general principle can only be justified in exceptional circumstances, when they are strictly necessary as measures to secure the proper administration of justice. They are wholly exceptional: *R v Chief Registrar of Friendly Societies, Ex p New Cross Building Society* [1984] QB 227, 235; *Donald v Ntuli* [2011] 1 WLR 294, paras 52–53. Derogations should, where justified, be no more than strictly necessary to achieve their purpose.

11 The grant of derogations is not a question of discretion. It is a matter of obligation and the court is under a duty to either grant the derogation or refuse it when it has applied the relevant test: *M v W* [2010] EWHC 2457 (QB) at [34].

12 There is no general exception to open justice where privacy or confidentiality is in issue. Applications will only be heard in private if and to the extent that the court is satisfied that by nothing short of the exclusion of the public can justice be done. Exclusions must be no more than the minimum strictly necessary to ensure justice is done and parties are expected to consider before applying for such an exclusion whether something short of exclusion can meet their concerns, as will normally be the case: *Ambrosiadou v Coward* [2011] EMLR 419, paras 50–54. Anonymity will only be granted where it is strictly necessary, and then only to that extent.

13 The burden of establishing any derogation from the general principle lies on the person seeking it. It must be established by clear and cogent evidence: *Scott v Scott* [1913] AC 417, 438–439, 463, 477; *Lord Browne of Madingley v Associated Newspapers Ltd* [2008] QB 103, paras 2–3; *Secretary of State for the Home Department v AP (No 2)* [2010] 1 WLR 1652, para 7; *Gray v W* [2010] EWHC 2367 (QB) at [6]–[8]; and *H v News Group Newspapers Ltd (Practice Note)* [2011] 1 WLR 1645, para 21.

14 When considering the imposition of any derogation from open justice, the court will have regard to the respective and sometimes competing Convention rights of the parties as well as the general public interest in open justice and in the public reporting of court proceedings. It will also adopt procedures which seek to ensure that any ultimate vindication of Article 8 of the Convention, where that is engaged, is not undermined by the way in which the court has processed an interim application. On the other hand, the principle of open justice requires that any restrictions are the least that can be imposed consistent with the protection to which the party relying on their Article 8 Convention right is entitled. The proper approach is set out in *H's* case [2011] 1 WLR 1645.

15 It will only be in the rarest cases that an interim non-disclosure order containing a prohibition on reporting the fact of proceedings (a super-injunction) will be justified on grounds of strict necessity, ie, anti-tipping-off situations, where short-term secrecy is required to ensure the applicant can notify the respondent that the order is made: *T v D* [2010] EWHC 2335 (QB). It is then only in truly exceptional circumstances that such an order should be granted for a longer period: *Terry v Persons Unknown* [2010] EMLR 400, para 41.

Consent orders

16 Interim non-disclosure orders which contain derogations from the principle of open justice cannot be granted by consent of the parties. Such orders affect the Article 10 Convention rights of the public at large. Parties cannot waive or give up the rights of the public. The court's approach is set out in *H's* case [2011] 1 WLR 1645, para 21.

Application

17 The applicant should prepare (a) the application/claim form; (b) a witness statement or statements justifying the need for an order; (c) legal submissions; (d) a draft order; and (e) an explanatory note: see para 33 below. In the rare or urgent case where it is not possible to prepare such documentation prior to the hearing, the applicant should file a statement at the earliest practicable opportunity, setting out the information placed orally before the court.

Notice of application

18 Applicants must comply with the requirements set out in section 12(2) of the HRA, CPR r 25.3(2)(3), and paragraph 4.3(3) of Practice Direction 25A.

19 Section 12(2) of the HRA applies in respect of both (a) respondents to the proceedings and (b) any non-parties who are to be served with or otherwise notified of the order, because they have an existing interest in the information which is to be protected by an injunction: *X v Persons Unknown* [2007] EMLR 290, paras 10–12. Both respondents and any non-parties to be served with the order are therefore entitled to advance notice of the application hearing and should be served with a 1006 copy of the application notice and any supporting documentation before that hearing.

20 Applicants will need to satisfy the court that all reasonable and practical steps have been taken to provide advance notice of the application. At the hearing they should inform the court of any non-party which they intend to notify of the order as the court is required to ensure that the requirements of section 12(2) of the HRA are fulfilled in respect of each of them. A schedule to any interim non-disclosure order granted should provide details of all such non-parties.

21 Failure to provide advance notice can only be justified, on clear and cogent evidence, by compelling reasons. Examples which may amount to compelling reasons, depending on the facts of the case, are: that there is a real prospect that were a respondent or non-party to be notified they would take steps to defeat the order's purpose (*RST v UVW* [2010] EMLR 355, paras 7, 13), for instance, where there is convincing evidence that the respondent is seeking to blackmail the applicant: *G v A* [2009] EWCA Civ 1574 at [3]; *T v D* [2010] EWHC 2335 at [7].

22 Where a respondent, or non-party, is a media organisation only rarely will there be compelling reasons why advance notification is or was not possible on grounds of either urgency or secrecy. It will only be in truly exceptional

circumstances that failure to give a media organisation advance notice will be justifiable on the ground that it would defeat the purpose of an interim non-disclosure order. Different considerations may however arise where a respondent or non-party is an Internet-based organisation, tweeter or blogger, or where, for instance, there are allegations of blackmail.

23 Where notice of the application is to be given to a media organisation it should be effected on the organisation's legal adviser, where it has one. The court will bear in mind that such legal advisers are: (i) used to participating in hearings at short notice where necessary; and (ii) able to differentiate between information provided for legal purposes and information for editorial use.

Notice and undertakings to the court–non-parties

24 In order to provide effective protection of private and/or confidential information and information contained in private and/or confidential documents provided by applicants to non-parties: (i) where an applicant is to provide advance notice of an application to a non-party; or (ii) where an applicant notifies a non-party of an order, material supplied to the non-party by the applicant shall be supplied upon the applicant receiving an irrevocable written undertaking to the court that the material and the information contained within it, or derived from such material or information, will only be used for the purpose of the proceedings. A standard form of wording for the undertaking is set out in the notes to clause 13 of the model order, contained in the model order guidelines.

25 Where an applicant is to provide advance notice of an application to a non-party they should first provide the non-party with a copy of the explanatory note, which may where strictly necessary refer to the applicant and/or respondent by three anonymised initials. If the non-party is willing to provide the irrevocable written undertaking, the applicant should then supply the materials, including the applicant's and respondent's names, to the non-party upon receipt of the undertaking. Where the non-party is unwilling to provide the undertaking, no further information need be supplied by the applicant. (Information concerning when and where the application is to be heard should be set out in the explanatory note.)

26 Where an applicant notifies a non-party of an order, which should contain the provision set out in clause 13 of the model order, provision of material to a non-party shall be effected promptly by the applicant upon request, and upon receipt of the irrevocable written undertaking. Prior to notifying the non-party of the order and where urgency does not preclude it, the applicant should ascertain whether the non-party will require a copy of any materials referred to in clause 13 of the model order. Where the non-party indicates it will do so, it should at that stage provide the applicant with the written irrevocable undertaking. The applicant will then be in a position to, and should, serve a copy of the order and the relevant materials together. Where the non-party is unwilling to give the undertaking in advance of service of the order, the applicant will not be required to supply any relevant materials to the non-party until such time as the undertaking is given or further order of the court.

27 The undertaking should be provided on behalf of the non-party by its legal adviser where it has one. It should be provided by the non-party itself where it has no legal adviser. Breach of the undertaking may be held to be a contempt of court, which would render the non-party liable to imprisonment, a fine or having their assets seized.

28 For the purpose of para 24, material includes: the application and any supporting documentation; and a copy of any materials specified under paragraph 9.2 of Practice Direction 25A.

Hearing – scrutiny of application

29 The onus is on the applicant to satisfy the court that an interim non-disclosure order is justified. Where the applicant seeks derogations from open justice reference should be made to paras 8–13 of this guidance.

30 Particular care should be taken in every application for an interim non-disclosure order, and especially where an application is made without notice, by applicants to comply with the high duty to make full, fair and accurate disclosure of all material information to the court and to draw the court's attention to significant factual, legal and procedural aspects of the case. The applicant's advocate, so far as it is consistent with the urgency of the application, has a particular duty to see that the correct legal procedures and forms are used; that a written skeleton argument and a properly drafted order are prepared personally by her or him and lodged with the court before the oral hearing; and that, at the hearing, the court's attention is drawn to unusual features of the evidence adduced, to the applicable law and to the formalities and procedure to be observed including how, if at all, the order submitted departs from the model order.

31 Applications, especially those which seek derogations from open justice, must be supported with clear and cogent evidence which demonstrates that without the specific exception, justice could not be done.

32 Each application shall be subject to intense scrutiny. The need for intense scrutiny is particularly acute on without notice applications, or where non-parties are or have been served with orders containing restrictions on access to documents, because, for instance, the order contains derogations from paragraph 9.2 of Practice Direction 25A.

Explanatory notes

33 It is helpful if applications and orders are accompanied by an explanatory note, from which persons served can (a) readily understand the nature of the case, (b) ascertain whether they wish to attend the application hearing, and/or be legally represented at it, or, (c) where the application was heard without notice, whether they wish to challenge the order.

34 Where an interim non-disclosure order contains restrictions on access to documents it must be accompanied by an explanatory note when served on any non-party who was not present at the hearing of the application.

35 An example of an explanatory note is attached to this guidance.

Applicant's continuing duty

36 Where an interim non-disclosure order is granted applicants are required to keep any respondent or non-party subject to the order, informed of any developments in the progress of proceedings which affect the status of the order. They are required to do so in order to satisfy the court that that there has been compliance with the obligation imposed by CPR r 1.3 and any requirements specified in any order or directions given by the court. Applicants are particularly required to inform any non-parties whom they have served with the order when it ceases to have effect.

Active case management

37 Interim non-disclosure orders, as they restrict the exercise of the Article 10 Convention right and, whether or not they contain any derogation from the principle of open justice, require the court to take particular care to provide active case management.

38 Active case management requires the court to ensure that a return date is specified in such orders and that, as a general rule, the return date is kept. The applicant is required to inform the court at the return date which, if any, non-parties have been served with any interim non-disclosure order granted at an earlier, without notice, hearing.

39 It will not always be necessary for any parties to attend court on the return date: the hearing could be dealt with by the court on the papers, provided that sufficient material is before the court to enable scrutiny and effective case management to take place: see *Goldsmith v D* [2011] EWHC 674 (QB) at [60]–[62]. Any order should however be given in public and be publicly available.

40 A return date is particularly important where an order contains derogations from the principle of open justice. It is the means by which the court ensures that those derogations are in place for no longer than strictly necessary. It is also the means by which the court ensures that the interim non-disclosure order does not become a substitute for a full and fair adjudication: *X v Persons Unknown* [2007] EMLR 290, para 78.

41 Where an interim non-disclosure order, whether or not it contains derogations from open justice, is made, and return dates are adjourned for valid reasons on one or more occasions, or it is apparent, for whatever reason, that a trial is unlikely to take place between the parties to proceedings, the court should either dismiss the substantive action, proceed to summary judgment, enter judgment by consent, substitute or add an alternative defendant, or direct that the claim and trial proceed in the absence of a third party: *A v News Group Newspapers Ltd* [2010] EWHC 3174 (QB) at [13]; *Gray v W* [2010] EWHC 2367 at [37]; *Terry v Persons Unknown* [2010] EMLR 400, paras 134–136.

Hearing notes and judgments

42 The court's approach to judgments and hearing notes is set out in *Terry's* case [2010] EMLR 400, para 4; *H v News Group Newspapers Ltd (Practice Note)* [2011] 1 WLR 1645, paras 21(9), 35.

43 It is of particular importance that a full and accurate note of the hearing is taken of a without notice hearing: *G v Wikimedia Foundation Inc* [2010] EMLR 364, paras 28–32. It is the duty of counsel and solicitors to ensure that such a note is taken during the hearing, or, if that is not possible, to prepare such a note after the hearing is over. The note should be drafted so that anyone supplied with a copy of it is properly informed of: what documents were put before the court at the hearing; which legal authorities were relied on by the applicant; and what the court was told in the course of the hearing.

44 Where, and to the extent, strictly necessary hearing notes may be redacted, if they are to be supplied under paragraph 9.2 of Practice Direction 25A to a non-party who is served with an order but who is unwilling or unable to provide a written irrevocable undertaking.

45 The court should wherever possible give a reasoned, necessarily redacted, judgment. Where a judgment of the type given in *Terry's* case [2010] EMLR 400 or *H's* case [2011] 1 WLR 1645 would be disproportionate in terms of time or cost a short note or judgment should be given setting out any points of general interest, the reason why those points were raised and brief reasons for the decision: see *I v The Person Known as 'Lina'* [2011] EWHC 25 (QB).

Appeals

46 Any appeal from an interim non-disclosure order may be expedited: *Unilever plc v Chefaro Proprietaries Ltd (Practice Note)* [1995] 1 WLR 243, 246–247. It will depend on the circumstances of each case whether, and to what extent, expedition is necessary.

3

CONFIDENTIALITY

1 INTRODUCTION

Confidentiality

3.1 Confidentiality is essential to many professional relationships, including lawyers, doctors, accountants, social workers and bankers. It protects the information the client or other confidor has given to the professional (confidant). Where legal advice from a lawyer is the basis of the professional relationship, the confidence will be protected by the additional layer of legal professional privilege. This will be explained in Chapter 4.

3.2 In *Gillick v West Norfolk and Wisbech AHA*[1] the House of Lords explained why the confidentiality of a mature child should be protected by her doctor. This principle is undercut by *Working Together 2018* in a way which, it will be suggested in Part 4 of this chapter, is unlawful. Professionals who are dealing with children are encouraged to share what they are told by a child, regardless – it seems – of respect for the confidentiality of the mature (*Gillick*-competent) child. As the Court of Appeal has explained,[2] a child of age and understanding is as entitled to have the child's confidentiality respected as is any adult, just as, on the subject of confidentiality, a mature child is entitled to make the child's own decision.

Confidences: protection and overriding

3.3 In the short passage from Lord Goff's speech quoted at the beginning of Part 2 of this chapter he says 'there is such a public interest in the maintenance of confidences, [and] that the law will provide remedies for their protection'. Confidences will be protected by law, including those of a mature child. The means of protection will be explained in this chapter.

1 [1985] UKHL 7, [1986] 1 AC 112, [1986] 1 FLR 224.

2 See eg, *Re E (A Child)(Family Proceedings: Evidence)* [2016] EWCA Civ 473, [2017] 1 FLR 1675, [2016] 4 WLR 105.

3.4 By the same token, if a person entitled to the confidence wishes to, they may waive the confidence. If it is their choice because the confidence is theirs, they can publish otherwise confidential information. By contrast, in very rare, but appropriate, circumstances an individual's confidence may be overridden.

3.5 This chapter proceeds as follows

- Part 2 provides a definition of confidentiality.
- Part 3 looks at confidentiality in matrimonial and other family proceedings: especially in relation to formerly married couples and their documents.
- Part 4 considers a variety of aspects of the law on confidentiality, specifically in relation to a mature (*Gillick*-competent) child:
  - By contrasting confidentiality and the 'sharing' ethic in *Working Together 2018*.
  - By reviewing the confidentiality of the *Gillick*-competent child (*Gillick* was a case specifically about the confidentiality of a hypothetical mature child).
  - The mature child is considered as patient alongside doctor's duties and *GMC Guidance*.
  - 'Sharing' and the guidance of *Working Together 2018* contrasted with the common law in eg, *Gillick*.
  - How does confidentiality in law compare with 'sharing'?
  - Children Act 2004 section 11; *Working Together 2018* and the duty to safeguard: how do these fit with the confidentiality and older children?
  - Overriding the confidentiality of a mature child.
- Part 5 looks at the importance of confidentiality in the relationship between solicitors and their clients and in particular:
  - Confidentiality as to client's affairs and the *Solicitors' Regulation Authority Code*.
  - Lawyers (especially solicitors) and confidentiality and litigation: acting for a client with a contrary interest and the *Bolkiah* case.

3.6 Confidentiality in the context of dealings with a lawyer – legal professional privilege: legal advice privilege and litigation privilege – will be dealt with in Chapter 4.

2 A DEFINITION OF CONFIDENTIALITY

'A broad general principle'

3.7 In *Attorney General v Guardian Newspapers Ltd (No 2)*,[3] Lord Goff offered, modestly – not intended in any way to 'be definitive', he said – a definition of 'confidentiality' which is still used by many lawyers as a starting point:[4]

> I start with the broad general principle (which I do not intend in any way to be definitive) that a duty of confidence arises when confidential information comes to the knowledge of a person (the confidant) in circumstances where he has notice, or is held to have agreed, that the information is confidential, with the effect that it would be just in all the circumstances that he should be precluded from disclosing the information to others. I have used the word "notice" advisedly, in order to avoid the (here unnecessary) question of the extent to which actual knowledge is necessary; though I of course understand knowledge to include circumstances where the confidant has deliberately closed his eyes to the obvious. The existence of this broad general principle reflects the fact that there is such a public interest in the maintenance of confidences, that the law will provide remedies for their protection.

3.8 Lord Goff continued that, in his opinion there were three important 'limiting principles' on the scope of confidentiality. The first two are of restricted importance: that the information should not have already entered the public domain; and that the duty of confidence attaches 'neither to useless information, nor to trivia'.

3.9 The third principle Lord Goff defined as follows:

> The third limiting principle is of far greater importance. It is that, although the basis of the law's protection of confidence is that there is a public interest that confidences should be preserved and protected by the law, nevertheless that public interest may be outweighed by some other countervailing public interest which favours disclosure. This limitation may apply, as the learned judge pointed out, to all types of confidential information. It is this limiting principle which may require a court to carry out a balancing operation, weighing the public interest in maintaining confidence against a countervailing public interest favouring disclosure. Embraced within this limiting principle is, of course, the so-called defence of iniquity. In origin, this principle was narrowly stated, on the basis that a man cannot be made

3 [1988] UKHL 6, [1990] 1 AC 109, [1987] 1 WLR 776, (the *Spycatcher case*) at 281.

4 Lord Goff's definition was referred to in economic terms by the Court of Appeal in *Tchenguiz v Imerman* (see later) as follows: '[64] It was only some twenty years ago that the law of confidence was authoritatively extended to apply to cases where the defendant had come by the information without the consent of the claimant. That extension, which had been discussed in academic articles, was established in the speech of Lord Goff in *Attorney General v Guardian Newspapers Ltd (No 2)* [1990] 1 AC 109. He said (p 281) that confidence could be invoked "where an obviously confidential document is wafted by an electric fan out of a window ... or ... is dropped in a public place, and is picked up by a passer-by".'

> "the confidant of a crime or a fraud": see *Gartside v Outram* (1857) 26 LJCh 113, 114, per Sir William Page Wood VC. But it is now clear that the principle extends to matters of which disclosure is required in the public interest ...

3.10 The importance of not breaching confidentiality, but of recognising its place in the context of human rights principles, was explained by the Court of Appeal in *HRH Prince of Wales v Associated Newspapers Ltd*[5] by Lord Phillips (giving the judgment of the court, with Sir Anthony Clarke MR and May LJ):

> [32] Before the Human Rights Act 1998 came into force, the English law of confidence had recognised that there were circumstances where the public interest in disclosure overrode the duty of confidence, and that these circumstances could differ depending upon whether the duty was owed to a private individual or to a public authority ...

3.11 In the *Prince of Wales* case, private diaries kept by the Prince – in this case on a trip to Hong Kong – were taken by a temporary member of his staff (who had signed a contract with a confidentiality clause) and were passed to the press. The judge at first instance made an order intended to prevent publication beyond what had already occurred. Lord Phillips CJ (giving the judgment of the Court of Appeal with Sir Anthony Clarke MR and May LJ) explained the court's view of confidentiality:

> [26] The English court has been concerned to develop a law of privacy that provides protection of the rights to "private and family life, his home and his correspondence" recognised by article 8 of the Convention. To this end the courts have extended the law of confidentiality so as to protect article 8 rights in circumstances which do not involve a breach of a confidential relationship. Although their Lordships differed as to the result in Campbell v MGN Ltd [2004] 2 AC 457, there was little between them as to the applicable legal principles. Lord Nicholls of Birkenhead described the position as follows, at [14]:
>
> Now the law imposes a "duty of confidence" whenever a person receives information he knows or ought to know is fairly and reasonably to be regarded as confidential. Even this formulation is awkward. The continuing use of the phrase "duty of confidence" and the description of the information as "confidential" is not altogether comfortable. Information about an individual's private life would not, in ordinary usage, be called "confidential". The more natural description today is that such information is private. The essence of the tort is better encapsulated now as misuse of private information.

3.12 The relationship of the Prince of Wales with his member of staff was amongst those which the law recognised as importing a 'relationship of confidence': the defendant was employed by him. That duty of confidence may trump the freedom of expression claimed by her:

5 [2006] EWCA Civ 1776, [2008] Ch 57.

> [28] ... The information was disclosed in breach of a well-recognised relationship of confidence, that which exists between master and servant. Furthermore, the disclosure was in breach of an express contractual duty of confidentiality. The newspaper was aware that the journals were disclosed in breach of confidence.
>
> [29] Article 10(2) provides that the freedom to receive and impart information and ideas "may be subject to such formalities, conditions, restrictions or penalties as are prescribed by law and are necessary in a democratic society ... for preventing the disclosure of information received in confidence" ... The Convention recognises that it may be necessary in a democratic society to give effect to a duty of confidence in the old sense at the expense of freedom of expression.

3.13 There is a public interest in confidences being protected or as Lord Goff explained it in *Spycatcher* (above): 'there is such a public interest in the maintenance of confidences, that the law will provide remedies for their protection.' But exceptional circumstances might override a duty of confidence in the public interest.[6] The Court of Appeal in the *Prince of Wales* case continued:

> [67] There is an important public interest in the observance of duties of confidence. Those who engage employees, or who enter into other relationships that carry with them a duty of confidence, ought to be able to be confident that they can disclose, without risk of wider publication, information that it is legitimate for them to wish to keep confidential. Before the Human Rights Act 1998 came into force the circumstances in which the public interest in publication overrode a duty of confidence were very limited. The issue was whether exceptional circumstances justified disregarding the confidentiality that would otherwise prevail. Today the test is different. It is whether a fetter of the right of freedom of expression is, in the particular circumstances, "necessary in a democratic society". It is a test of proportionality.

3 CONFIDENTIALITY AND PARTIES TO PROCEEDINGS

Financial relief proceedings

3.14 A view of confidentiality in relation to separating or divorcing couples and their finances is provided by the Court of Appeal in *Tchenguiz & Ors v Imerman*[7] (the judgment of the court: Lord Neuberger MR, Moses and Munby LJ). In particular, the case explains the ambit of confidentiality in relation to the documents and other private information as between one member of the couple and another. It seeks to make impossible the taking of undisclosed documents by one party from

6 See eg *W v Egdell* [1989] EWCA Civ 13, [1990] Ch 359, [1990] 2 WLR 471 considered fully in Chpater 10 Part 5.

7 [2010] EWCA Civ 908, [2010] 2 FLR 814 sub nom *Imerman v Tchenguiz and others* [2011] Fam 116.

the other. This case must be contrasted to the earlier Court of Appeal case of *Lifely v Lifely* which clarified the circumstances in which confidential information (eg, a diary) can be taken.[8]

3.15 In *Tchenguiz v Imerman*, Mr Imerman (I) shared a computer server with the brothers of Mrs Tchenguiz (T). Following T filing a divorce petition, one of her brothers downloaded a large number of I's documents. He was looking for documents concerning I's finances. There was a concern that I would try to disguise assets. A barrister considered the documents for legal professional privilege. The remaining seven files of material were given to T's solicitors, who eventually, in response to a specific request from I's solicitors, passed on a copy of the files.

3.16 In the Queen's Bench Division, I had obtained summary relief, namely injunctions which were intended (a) to prevent further communication or disclosure of the information obtained to any third party, including T and her solicitors; and (b) the copying or use in any other way of the information obtained, except in the ancillary relief proceedings. The brothers appealed against those orders.

3.17 In T's ancillary relief proceedings I sought the return of the seven files and any copies made of them and an order enjoining the wife and her solicitors from using any of the information obtained from the files. The parties had not yet exchanged Form E (financial statements), which the court held was the time at which the duty to disclose arose.[9] Moylan J, in the Family Division, said that the seven files must be returned to the husband for the purpose of enabling him to remove any material for which he claimed privilege, but that the remainder of the files should then be returned to the wife for use by her in connection with the proceedings. I appealed, saying he had a right to protect the confidentiality of documents stored on his computer. T cross-appealed, saying she needed the documents in order to identify I's assets for ancillary relief purposes.

3.18 The court allowed the husband's appeal.[10] They reviewed the law on confidentiality, and its history, extensively. They looked at it in particular in the context of a couple living together. The court defined their view of confidentiality in these circumstances, first by defining the extent of the right to confidence and then by explaining the remedy in the case of a threat of breach:

> [69] In our view, it would be a breach of confidence for a defendant, without the authority of the claimant, to examine, or to make, retain, or supply copies to a third party of, a document whose contents are, and were (or ought to have been) appreciated by the defendant to be, confidential to the claimant. It is of the essence of the claimant's right to confidentiality that he can choose whether, and, if so, to whom and in what circumstances and on what terms, to reveal the information which has the protection of the confidence.

8 For a discussion of *Lifely* see 3.24.

9 Explained further at 4.10.

10 A controversial aspect of the case and the date from which a duty to disclose runes, is considered at 4.44.

3.19 And then the remedy for the threat to breach of confidence:

> [69] ... It seems to us, as a matter of principle, that, again in the absence of any defence on the particular facts, a claimant who establishes a right of confidence in certain information contained in a document should be able to restrain any threat by an unauthorised defendant to look at, copy, distribute any copies of, or to communicate, or utilise the contents of the document (or any copy), and also be able to enforce the return (or destruction) of any such document or copy ... The claimant should not be at risk, through the unauthorised act of the defendant, of having the confidentiality of the information lost, or even potentially lost.

3.20 It had been said on behalf of T (the wife) that there was no confidence as between a husband and a wife. The Court of Appeal replied:

> [86] The submission that there is no confidence as between husband and wife is particularly unacceptable, indeed, deeply unattractive, in circumstances such as arise in this case. The submission invokes the special relationship between husband and wife in order to defeat Mr Imerman's claim for confidentiality against her. But it is invoked at a time when that relationship had broken down, for the material was copied after Mrs Imerman had petitioned for divorce and Mr Imerman had left the matrimonial home. And it is invoked for the purpose of justifying an action which was and is solely concerned with the financial terms on which the parties are to be divorced.

3.21 They went on to explain how, in practice, confidentiality between husband and wife might be overridden. The issue was fact-dependant:

> [88] ... Thus, if a husband leaves his bank statement lying around open in the matrimonial home ... it may well lose its confidential character as against his wife. The court may have to consider the nature of the relationship and the way the parties lived, and conducted their personal and business affairs. Thus, if the parties each had their own study, it would be less likely that the wife could copy the statement without infringing the husband's confidence if it had been left by him in his study rather than in the marital bedroom, and the wife's case would be weaker if the statement was kept in a drawer in his desk and weaker still if kept locked in his desk. But, as we have already said, confidentiality is not dependent upon locks and keys. Thus, the wife might well be able to maintain, as against her husband, the confidentiality of her personal diary or journal, even though it was kept visible and unlocked on her dressing table.

3.22 If a document is in fact to be treated as confidential, that is an end of the matter. The relationship between the parties is irrelevant:

> [89] But it is important to emphasise that the relationship between the parties and the circumstances in which the information or document is obtained is relevant only to the question as to whether the information

or document is to be cloaked with confidentiality. Once it is determined that the document is properly to be regarded as confidential to one spouse but not to the other, the relationship has no further relevance in relation to the remedy for breach of that confidentiality.

Overriding the confidentiality if evidence of injustice: Lifely

3.23 There is an irony in all this, in relation to when confidentiality may be overridden. Rhetorically the court asked in *Tchenguiz* whether a spouse was entitled to 'borrow and read' the other spouse's diary or that other spouse's confidential papers (whether relating to his work or to the affairs of his parents or siblings)? 'Surely not'[11] said the court. And yet, almost in passing, the court mentioned *Lifely v Lifely*:[12]

> [176] It would be surprising if the court in ancillary relief proceedings had no power to exclude evidence which was confidential to the husband and had been wrongly obtained from his records, however outrageous the circumstances of the obtaining of the evidence and however unfair on the husband it would be to admit the evidence. It would be all the more surprising in the light of the Human Rights Act 1998. As was explained by Ward LJ in *Lifely v Lifely* [(above)], in a case of this type, the decision whether to admit or exclude evidence involves weighing one party's (in this case, the wife's) Art 6 right to a fair trial with all the available evidence, against the other party's (the husband's) Art 8 right to respect for privacy …

3.24 In *Lifely*, it was precisely that one brother's diary was taken by the other brother. It was read by that brother and by his solicitors. The diary was then made the basis for a successful application out of time to appeal and to adduce fresh evidence. Ward LJ explained this by asking what use might be made of evidence obtained unlawfully or in breach of another party's confidence:

> [37] … What forensic use, if any, should be permitted of an opponent's private information when it has been obtained criminally, or unlawfully, or opportunistically, or even adventitiously gives rise to current problems – see, for example *L v L* [2007] EWHC QB 140 [[2008] 2 FLR 171, Tugendhat J]. My judgment will not be and should not be the last word on this expanding jurisprudence as it is deliberately fact centred and fact sensitive.

Balance of European Convention 1950 rights

3.25 As Lord Neuberger MR explained in *Tchenguiz*, the court is required to direct itself as to the balance to be struck as between competing European Convention 1950 rights: '… something which, we are well aware, is easy to say in

11 At [85].
12 [2008] EWCA Civ 904.

general terms but is often very difficult to effect in individual cases in practice'. The facts of *Lifely* will be considered before Ward LJ's approach to European Convention 1950 rights is looked at.

3.26 In *Lifely*, the Court of Appeal considered an appeal by one brother (A) in a farming dispute over milk quotas.[13] The quotas had been divided by agreement of the brothers (A and B) and their father, before the father died. After his death, the two brothers could not agree what had been agreed and applied in the Chancery Division for a declaration. After the order had been made, A found a diary belonging to B. The diary, said A, showed that B originally accepted what he (A) had said all along. A applied to the Court of Appeal to adduce the diary as fresh evidence on appeal; and, subject to that, for the order of the first instance judge to be set aside and the case remitted for rehearing. The respondent brother asserted that the diary was obtained tortiously and that, in any event, it was private information and therefore protected from disclosure.[14]

3.27 The matter was not as simple as B asserted, said Ward LJ: the court has always 'had a discretion whether or not to admit evidence which was wrongfully obtained'. He continued, citing Lord Woolf CJ in *Jones v Warwick University*[15] (where an enquiry agent trespassed in the home of a claimant for damages for personal injuries and took a secret video of the claimant showing that she was far from as badly injured as she was asserting). When the claimant in that case sought to exclude the evidence Lord Woolf MR explained his view, based on the defendant's breach of European Convention 1950 Article 8 (here turning on the 'outrageousness' of the action of a party). Lord Woolf MR said:

> [28] That leaves the issue as to how the court should exercise its discretion in the difficult situation confronting the district judge and Judge Harris. The court must try to give effect to what are here the two conflicting public interests. The weight to be attached to each will vary according to the circumstances. The significance of the evidence will differ as will the gravity of the breach of article 8, according to the facts of the particular case. The decision will depend on all the circumstances. Here, the court cannot ignore the reality of the situation. This is not a case where the conduct of the defendant's insurers is so outrageous that the defence should be struck out. The case, therefore, has to be tried. It would be artificial and undesirable for the actual evidence, which is relevant and admissible, not to be placed before the judge who has the task of trying the case. We accept Mr Owen's submission that to exclude the use of the evidence would create a wholly undesirable situation.

13 Ward LJ started his judgment: '[1] No dispute can be bloodier than when the blood, thicker than water, is spilled copiously in uncompromising and uncompromised litigation between brothers in a fight over their inheritance and their farming business. When it happens, one hopes that the judgment of the court will at least bring an end to the wrangling, if not to the continuing reverberations of the fractured relationships and the wounded feelings.'

14 *Campbell v MGN Ltd* [2004] UKHL 22, [2004] 2 AC 457.

15 [2003] EWCA Civ 151.

3.28 In *Lifely*, the Court of Appeal admitted the evidence.[16] The diary should have been disclosed by B (ie, its existence should have been stated by him[17]). That would have promoted the likelihood of a fair trial. This overrode the fact that as a private document it was entitled to be protected on the basis of the public interest in confidentiality and privacy. The evidence was admitted and the case must be remitted to the court below for retrial with the fresh evidence. The interest in the privacy of one party must be balanced against the right of both or all parties to a fair trial and with all relevant documents before the court. As with *Jones v Warwick* (above), the reality of the parties' positions cannot be overlooked.

3.29 As to the European Convention 1950 position: Ward LJ cited the opinion of Lord Steyn *Re S (Identification: Restrictions on Publication)*[18] and then of the 'ultimate balancing exercise' he said:

> [37] In my judgment the result of undertaking this balancing exercise is plain. Here there was no trespass or burglary. The diary was left on [A's] property and had been there for many years. Though he can, perhaps, be criticised for reading a private diary, his conduct, like the enquiry agent in Jones was not so outrageous. If [B] had disclosed the existence of his diary, as strictly he ought to have done, then this information would have emerged at the trial. It was not privileged and no claim to confidentiality could then have prevailed. Now to allow him to assert it and to exclude this evidence could, I say no more than that, lead to a finding which is far removed from the truth of what happened at that family meeting three weeks before [the father's] death. It would be wholly disproportionate to exclude this evidence and I have no hesitation whatsoever in rejecting [B's submission in the point] …

3.30 To an extent this position is affirmed by the *Tchenguiz* case where the Court of Appeal said:

> [142] … Of course, a claim for breach of confidentiality may be defeated by showing that the documents or information revealed unlawful conduct or intended unlawful conduct by the claimant: see *Istil.*[19] But in the instant appeal it is not suggested that the documents themselves disclose measures taken to defeat the wife's claim …

Guidance on Tchenguiz

3.31 In *L v K (Freezing Orders: Principles and Safeguards),*[20] Mostyn J considered the position of a wife who had taken her husband's private documents. 'Illegality' (as Mostyn J calls it) must be judged against the date or time at which the common law says disclosure takes place, a date which is not clear in civil proceedings. Thus,

---

16 *Ladd v Marshall* [1954] 1 WLR 1489, (1954) FLR Rep 422.

17 CPR 1998 r 31.2.

18 [2004] UKHL 47, [2005] 1 AC 593, [2005] 1 FLR 591 at [17]; considered fully in Chapter 2.

19 *Istil Group Inc & Anor v Zahoor & Ors* [2003] EWHC 165 (Ch), Collins J.

20 [2013] UKHC 1735 (Fam), [2014] Fam 35 (also called *UL v BK*), Mostyn J.

if a party such as Mrs Livesey ((*Livesey (formerly Jenkins) v Jenkins*)[21] or Mr Sharland (*Sharland v Sharland*[22])) has not disclosed material information where their case is settled or a consent order is made, their non-disclosure may lead to a financial relief court order being set aside by later order of the court.

3.32 In *Vernon v Bosley (No 2)*,[23] it will be recalled, the defendant's leading counsel (A) received from an undisclosed source, and read, confidential documents (medical reports: highly private) about Mr Vernon (B). These provided information which, said the Court of Appeal, should have been disclosed. It was relevant evidence which had become available between the High Court hearing and the appeal hearing. This is the common law, said Stuart Smith LJ. The principle is now confirmed by Civil Procedure Rules 1998 r 31.11.

3.33 In each of these cases the documents were confidential: what could be more confidential than a diary or a medical report? They belonged to someone who had not authorised their being read. They were obtained and read unlawfully (in this sense) and in breach of B's or Mr Vernon's rights under the European Convention 1950 Article 8. At [32] Ward LJ said in *Lifely*: 'I am prepared to accept ... that there is at least a good arguable claim for misuse of private information which is protected by Article 8 of the ECHR [ie all A's in the above examples were in the wrong]. However, the matter does not end there...'

'Imerman principles': date of duty of disclosure

3.34 In *L v K* Mostyn J set out what he called '*Imerman* principles'. These are his deductions from the case. They are not what was said by the Court of Appeal in the *Tchenguiz* case itself. What Mostyn J says about the *Tchenguiz* case has nothing to do with the decision he was being asked to make. They are *obiter* and are made without reference to such Court of Appeal cases as *Jones v Warwick*, *Lifely* and *Vernon*.

3.35 As each of these cases confirm, as does the common law,[24] a fair trial requires that the court has access to all relevant material, which mostly means documents (such as diaries and further relevant information about a party). Therefore, parties to a case must tell each other what documents or other information they have (such as Mrs Livesey's plans to remarry).

3.36 It seems Mostyn J was not referred to *Lifely v Lifely* (above) or *Jones v Warwick* (above).[25] *In L v K* he concluded:

> (1) ... It is simply and categorically unlawful for [A] to breach her husband's privacy by furtively copying his documents whether they exist in hard copy or electronically ...

---

21 [1985] AC 424, [1985] FLR 813.
22 [2015] UKSC 60, [2015] 2 FLR 1367.
23 [1999] QB 18, CA.
24 As explained in Chapter 4.
25 In fairness to counsel for the parties, it appears that Mostyn J issued his 'guidance' without hearing submissions from them and without inviting them to refer him to relevant authorities.

(2) If [A] supplies such documents to her solicitor then the solicitor must not read them but must immediately seek to obtain all of them from the wife and must return them, and all copies (both hard and soft), to [B's] (if he has one). [B's] solicitor, who owes a high duty to the court, will read them and disclose those of them that are both admissible and relevant to the wife's claim, pursuant to [B's] duty of full and frank disclosure.

(3) If [B] does not have a solicitor [A's] solicitor must retain the documents, unread, and in sealed files, and must approach the court for directions.

3.37 The question of disclosure and the decision about the evidence obtained was part of the *ratio decidendi* of the Court of Appeal's determinations in *Jones v Warwick* and *Lifely*. By contrast, Mostyn J's comments are *obiter* (he was asked to make a decision as to whether a freezing order should be continued); in any event, his is the decision of a judge of lesser level in the judicial hierarchy than the Court of Appeal.

3.38 Once the duty of disclosure has arisen then a party – like brother A in *Lifely* – who finds a private document or other material which should have been disclosed is entitled to consider it. Their lawyer must consider what is in the document or documents. To hand it back unread might leave Mr Sharland[26] with his, now set aside, order intact or Mr Vernon with the entirety of his damages.[27]

3.39 The above analysis assumes the duty of disclosure has already arisen. In view of what the Court of Appeal says in *Tchenguiz*, the position is unclear.[28] That said, most lawyers can be trusted to read papers brought in by a spouse, and to recognise that they are covered by legal professional privilege. If so, they must be returned and taken no account of. It is submitted that they must be read, like the *Lifely* diary, despite Mostyn J's guidance.

4 CONFIDENTIALITY OF A MATURE CHILD

Confidentiality or 'sharing'

Children's confidentiality

3.40 A range of guidance exists for professionals who receive confidences from mature children. This may be in connection with those children in the course of their work and specifically in relation to court proceedings. For example, this comes from *Working Together 2018*[29] (guidance for 'sharing' information concerning

26 *Sharland v Sharland* [2015] UKSC 60, [2015] 2 FLR 1367.

27 *Vernon v Bosley* [1995] 2 FCR 78, *Times* 5 August 1994, Sedley J.

28 As explained in Chapter 4.

29 *Working Together to Safeguard Children*: A Guide to Inter-agency Working to Safeguard and Promote the Welfare of Children July 2018 (London: HMSO, 2018). Available at: https://assets.publishing.service.gov.uk/government/uploads/system/uploads/attachment_data/file/729914/Working_Together_to_Safeguard_Children-2018.pdf); Children Act 2004 s 11.

work with children); *GMC Guidance on Confidentiality* for treating children;[30] and the common law as outlined in *Gillick v West Norfolk and Wisbech AHA* ('*Gillick*'),[31] especially for doctors. It includes legal advice privilege, which protects confidences of mature children in their discussions with lawyers. Each of these creates different legal principles.

3.41 Alongside this variety of guidance and law is the fact that differences of professional culture may lead to differences of approach to the legal principles and of their application[32] as between (say) the absolute privacy accorded to a lawyer's advice privilege as against the 'sharing' principle – which can be the antithesis of confidentiality – required by guidance, but not necessarily the common law, of professionals who work with and for children and as required by the statutory guidance in *Working Together 2018*.

3.42 The terminology and rationale behind *Gillick* remain central to assessment of the 'understanding' – a word taken directly from the opinions in *Gillick* – of a mature child. That understanding then dictates the extent to which a doctor must treat as entirely confidential information provided by a child (subject to any overriding public interest duty[33] of the doctor to pass on information[34]). How far do the confidentiality principles on which *Gillick* is based apply to all professionals who work with children? If *Gillick* is inconsistent with *Working Together 2018*, how much is this so; and which – *Gillick* or *Working Together 2018* – should guide or direct the professional?

3.43 *Gillick* principles apply the same rules for the doctor as for any other professional given confidential information by a mature child; and this is despite what may be said to the contrary in *Working Together 2018*. If there is a clash of professional cultures between 'sharing' under *Working Together 2018* and confidentiality in *Gillick*, then the common law as it now stands puts *Gillick* before departmental guidance where a child's privacy and their Article 8 rights are concerned.

Confidentiality of the mature child

Confidentiality: a definition

3.44 The principle of confidentiality, especially in relation to children proceedings, is the source of the privacy in which most family proceedings under

30 Available at: www.gmc-uk.org/guidance/ethical_guidance/children_guidance_contents.asp.

31 [1985] UKHL 7, [1986] 1 AC 112, [1986] 1 FLR 224; see Chapter 2, Part 4.

32 The contrast between the various professional rules is considered in outline in David Burrows 'Child Confidentiality: A Clash of Professional Rules' (2017) 47(6) *Family Law* 638–644.

33 *GMC Guidance on Confidentiality*: '47 A disclosure is in the public interest if the benefits which are likely to arise from the release of information outweigh both the child or young person's interest in keeping the information confidential and society's interest in maintaining trust between doctors and patients.'

34 *GMC Guidance*. Available at: www.gmc-uk.org/guidance/ethical_guidance/children_guidance_47_50_public_interest.asp paras 47–50; *W v Egdell* [1989] EWCA Civ 13, [1990] Ch 359, [1990] 2 WLR 471.

FPR 2010 are heard.[35] Indeed, in *Clibbery v Allan*,[36] Dame Elizabeth Butler-Sloss P used private in a context where now it is treated as synonymous with hearings in 'secret' and the proceedings 'remain confidential':

> [19] ... I am driven to recall Humpty Dumpty: "When I use a word – it means just what I choose it to mean – neither more nor less."
>
> [20] I would therefore suggest that there are three categories of case, those heard in open court, those heard in private and those heard in secret where the information disclosed to the court and the proceedings remain confidential.

3.45 Confidentiality is fundamental to a doctor's relationship with a patient, subject to the public interest exception considered later.[37] In the case of a mature child, confidentiality defines the ability of children under 16 to consent to medical treatment (as decided in *Gillick*). The importance of confidentiality in relation to treatment of a patient is stressed by *GMC Guidance* to doctors (see below). This defines 'Principles of confidentiality' in relation to children as:

> 42 Respecting patient confidentiality is an essential part of good care; this applies when the patient is a child or young person as well as when the patient is an adult. Without the trust that confidentiality brings, children and young people might not seek medical care and advice, or they might not tell you all the facts needed to provide good care.

Gillick *and* Roddy*: consent of a child under 16*

3.46 *Gillick* defines the circumstances in which a child under 16 may consent to treatment. The case also regulates the relationship between mature children and the professionals dealing with them. Munby J explained this in *Re Roddy (A Child) (Identification: Restriction on Publication)*[38] ('*Roddy*'). In the later case, Angela Roddy was 16. Her child had been taken into care and she herself had been made the subject of a care order when she was 13. She wanted to tell her story to the press, but it was assumed she needed court permission.[39]

3.47 Munby J said[40] of Angela Roddy and of older children generally, that the general principles for decisions as to her choice as to privacy and release of her confidentiality depended on the varying extent to which parental control could legitimately be exercised over them. Finding a definition of those principles started with Lord Fraser in *Gillick* where he said:[41]

---

35 Administration of Justice Act 1960 s 12(1); FPR 2010 r 27.10; and see eg, *Allan v Clibbery* [2002] EWCA Civ 45, [2002] Fam 261 sub nom *Clibbery v Allan* [2002] 1 FLR 565.

36 [2002] EWCA Civ 45, [200] Fam 261, [2002] 1 FLR 565.

37 See Part 6 of this chapter.

38 *Re Roddy (A Child)(Identification: Restriction on Publication)* [2003] EWHC 2927, [2004] 2 FLR 949 per Munby J.

39 The *Roddy* case is considered fully in Chapter 5.

40 Quoted by Munby J at [50].

41 [1986] 1 FLR 224 at 236.

> … Moreover, the degree of parental control actually exercised over a particular child does in practice vary considerably according to his understanding and intelligence and it would, in my opinion, be unrealistic for the courts not to recognise these facts. Social customs change, and the law ought to, and does in fact, have regard to such changes when they are of major importance.

3.48 Munby J cited Lord Scarman:[42]

> The law relating to parent and child is concerned with the problems of the growth and maturity of the human personality. If the law should impose upon the process of "growing up" fixed limits where nature knows only a continuous process, the price would be artificiality and a lack of realism in an area where the law must be sensitive to human development and social change … The underlying principle of the law … is that parental right yields to the child's right to make his own decisions when he reaches a sufficient understanding and intelligence to be capable of making up his own mind on the matter requiring decision.

Reality: judge's sensitivity to a child's developmental change

3.49 In the context of a mature child who wanted to tell her story to the press Munby J emphasised the importance of judges and public bodies generally facing 'reality'. A person of Angela's 'understanding and maturity' must be permitted to make her own decisions:

> [56] The courts must face reality. We must, as Lord Scarman said, be sensitive to human development and social change. Angela may not yet be quite 17 years old but she is a young woman with a mind of her own and, as her solicitor B has said, a mature and articulate young person. We no longer treat our 17-year-old daughters as our Victorian ancestors did, and if we try to do so it is at our – and their – peril. Angela, in my judgment, is of an age, and has sufficient understanding and maturity, to decide for herself whether that which is private, personal and intimate should remain private or whether it should be shared with the whole world.

3.50 Angela, he said was seeking 'to tell her story to the world – a right, and it is nothing less, securely founded in Articles 8 and 10'.[43] So what were Angela's rights and on what jurisprudence were they based? If she was competent then she was entitled to make her own decisions on her own confidentiality. Save to the extent that it affected anyone else's rights – in that case there was the father of Angela's child, the father and the child's adoptive family – then the court had no power to interfere with her private rights.

---

42 Ibid at 250, quoted by Munby J at [51].

43 Ibid at [47].

A mature child as patient

GMC Guidance to doctors

3.51 Where does this leave a medical professional who is working with a mature child? *Gillick* refers specifically to the practice of doctors; but what it says has been applied to practice in a variety of fields where dealing with mature children, including lawyers. The GMC has issued Guidance ('*GMC Guidance*'). It deals with doctors and their treatment of children as a subject which spans children of all ages.: *0–18 years guidance*.[44] The subjects which arise here are dealt with in the *GMC Guidance* as follows:

- Principles of confidentiality (paras 42 and 43).
- Sharing information with the consent of a child or young person (para 44).
- Sharing information without consent (paras 45–46).
- 'Public interest' and passing on of information (paras 47–50).
- Sources of law on confidentiality, data protection and privacy.[45]

3.52 The first paragraph of the *GMC Guidance* on 'The ethical and legal duties of confidentiality'[46] asserts the important role of confidentiality in the role of the doctor: 'Trust is an essential part of the doctor–patient relationship and confidentiality is central to this.' In relation to children – that is, all children between 0 and 18 – the *GMC Guidance* goes on to explain circumstances in which information sharing – that is the passing on of information, and thus the breaching of a patient's confidentiality (eg, including the passing on information to colleagues and nursing staff, for research or where a child might be at risk).

3.53 In particular, the *GMC Guidance* stresses the importance of a practitioner being required to pass on information where this is required by law or the public interest demands it.[47] This section will consider the *GMC Guidance* generally, followed in the next section by a review of the public interest and other legal exceptions to confidentiality.

3.54 If a doctor is required to treat details of a child patient's treatment confidential or to have – or to override – a child patient's consent, the *GMC Guidance* summarises the process of assessment of the child's capacity:

44 The link to the contents page is www.gmc-uk.org/guidance/ethical_guidance/children_guidance_contents.asp

45 Available at: www.gmc-uk.org/guidance/ethical_guidance/30627.asp.

46 Available at: www.gmc-uk.org/guidance/ethical_guidance/30591.asp.

47 See eg, *W v Egdell* [1989] EWCA Civ 13, [1990] Ch 359, where the Court of Appeal said a doctor was justified in passing on information to the Home Office about a prisoner-patient whom he regarded to be a threat to the community if he was released from prison; considered at Chapter 10 Part 5.

Young people who have capacity[48]

> 29 You should encourage young people to involve their parents in making important decisions, but you should usually abide by any decision they have the capacity to make themselves (see paragraphs 30 to 33[49] and paragraphs 46 to 52) …

Confidentiality: sharing medical information with and without consent

3.55 Patient trust applies as much if the patient is a child as it does if the patient is an adult; and the same duties arise for the child as for the adult. The *GMC Guidance* defines 'Principles of confidentiality'[50] in relation to children as:

> 42 Respecting patient confidentiality is an essential part of good care; this applies when the patient is a child or young person as well as when the patient is an adult. Without the trust that confidentiality brings, children and young people might not seek medical care and advice, or they might not tell you all the facts needed to provide good care.

3.56 The *GMC Guidance* explains when information as to a child or young person can be shared: with and without consent of the patient. First the Guidance, under the heading 'Sharing information with the consent of a child or young person' states the following:[51]

> 44 Sharing information with the right people can help to protect children and young people from harm and ensure that they get the help they need. It can also reduce the number of times they are asked the same questions by different professionals. By asking for their consent to share relevant information, you are showing them respect and involving them in decisions about their care.
>
> 45 If children and young people are able to take part in decision-making, you should explain why you need to share information, and ask for their consent. They will usually be happy for you to talk to their parents and others involved in their care or treatment.

---

48 Available at: www.gmc-uk.org/guidance/ethical_guidance/children_guidance_29_capacity_to_consent.asp.

49 '30 Respect for young people's views is important in making decisions about their care. If they refuse treatment, particularly treatment that could save their life or prevent serious deterioration in their health, this presents a challenge that you need to consider carefully.
31 Parents cannot override the competent consent of a young person to treatment that you consider is in their best interests. But you can rely on parental consent when a child lacks the capacity to consent.'

50 Available at: www.gmc-uk.org/guidance/ethical_guidance/children_guidance_42_43_principles_of_confidentiality.asp.

51 Available at: www.gmc-uk.org/guidance/ethical_guidance/children_guidance_44_45_consent_of_young_person.asp.

3.57 'Sharing information without consent' in the *GMC Guidance* deals with the question of 'disclosure'[52] – passing on of information – as a matter of public interest or of law:[53]

> 46 If a child or young person does not agree to disclosure there are still circumstances in which you should disclose information:
>
> (a) when there is an overriding public interest in the disclosure
>
> (b) when you judge that the disclosure is in the best interests of a child or young person who does not have the maturity or understanding to make a decision about disclosure
>
> (c) when disclosure is required by law.

3.58 Paragraph 46(b) leaves the doctor in a very similar position to that of the lawyer confronted with the decision of whether a child is of understanding to proceed with a court application.[54] The doctor, like the lawyer, is required to make the judgment as to the child's level of 'maturity or understanding'.

'Sharing' of information: Working Together 2018

Guidance for professionals working with children

3.59 Since the Cleveland Report[55] successive versions of guidance have been issued for those working with children. The latest version is *Working Together to Safeguard Children*[56] ('*Working Together 2018*'). The difference of approach to the confidences of a mature child as between *Working Together 2018* and, respectively the *GMC guidance* and the *Gillick* case must now be considered.

3.60 *Working Together 2018* is 'a guide to inter-agency working to safeguard and promote the welfare of children'. Amongst its 'key principles' is 'a child-centred and coordinated approach to safeguarding' of children. Children Act 2004

---

52 Of the term 'disclosure' in this context it is worth noting, in passing, the following:
(1) The disparaging comment of MacDonald J in *AS v TH (False Allegations of Abuse)* [2016] EWHC 532 Fam, MacDonald J: '[33] ... I pause to note that despite the fact that the use of the term "disclosure" to describe a statement or allegation of abuse made by a child has been deprecated since the Cleveland Report due to it precluding the notion that the abuse might not have occurred (see para 12.34(1)), *every* professional who gave evidence in this case (except the Children's Guardian) used the term "disclosure" to describe what the children had said to them'; and
(2) That to a lawyer (see eg in Chapters 9 and 10) the terms disclosure has a specific meaning applied to informing other parties to the case that documents and information are held by one party, as in 'privilege from disclosure' (see Chapter 5).

53 Available at: www.gmc-uk.org/guidance/ethical_guidance/children_guidance_46_sharing_info_without_consent.asp.

54 FPR 2010 r 16.6(3)(b).

55 *Report of the Inquiry into Child Abuse in Cleveland 1987* Cm 412 (London: HMSO, 1988).

56 *Working Together to Safeguard Children. A Guide to Inter-agency Working to Safeguard and Promote the Welfare of Children* (London: Department of Education, 2017). Available at: www.gov.uk/government/uploads/system/uploads/attachment_data /file/419595/Working_Together_to_Safeguard_Children.pdf ('*Working Together*').

section 11 places duties to safeguard children and to promote their welfare on specified public bodies including local authorities, health authorities and the police (CA 2004 s 11(1)). Each of these bodies are required to 'make arrangements for ensuring that their functions are discharged having regard to the need to safeguard and promote the welfare of children' and to make arrangements to promote co-operation between the agencies concerned with children.

3.61 CA 2004 section 11(4) requires any body to which section 11(1) applies, to discharge their duty under the section in such a way as to 'have regard to any guidance' issued by the Department of Education:

> (4) Each person and body to whom this section applies must in discharging their duty under this section have regard to any guidance given to them for the purpose by the Secretary of State.

Working Together *and confidentiality*

3.62 *Working Together 2018* is the guidance issued under section 11(4). It applies to a child defined by CA 2004 section 65(1) as in CA 1989 as 'a person under the age of eighteen'. It deals with guidance over safeguarding, help and assessment for all ages of children. The guidance strongly advocates the need to listen to a child's views. It urges the sharing of information concerning children. There is no clear reference to dealing with the confidences of the mature child, as *Gillick* requires. For any professional who deals with mature children – treating them, teaching them, advising them, mediation – this provision as to 'sharing' information raises the question of confidentiality of mature children.

3.63 *Working Together 2018* does not consider the subject of 'confidentiality' in any specific or clear way; though guidance is provided to its opposite, 'sharing' of information in *Information sharing: Advice for practitioners providing safeguarding services* etc.[57] *Working Together 2018* explains the 'early sharing of information' as being 'the key to providing effective early help where there are emerging problems'. If child protection – as distinct from their confidences – is the only criterion, this must surely be right? But 'Fears about sharing information cannot be allowed to stand in the way of the need to promote the welfare and protect the safety of children' says paragraph 24 of *Working Together 2018*.

Role and function of statutory guidance

3.64 Guidance, such as *Working Together 2018* – even though provided for by statute – cannot alter the common law.[58] Only express statutory provision, or the Supreme Court, can do that and the principles outlined in *Gillick* are already

---

57 *Information Sharing Advice for Practitioners Providing Safeguarding Services to Children, Young People, Parents and Carers* (London: HMSO, 2015). Available at: www.gov.uk/government/uploads/system/uploads/attachment_data/file/419628/Information_sharing_advice_safeguarding_practitioners.pdf).

58 See Chapter 1.

well embedded in family law.[59] The ambit of confidentiality and the extent to which it is regarded as in the public interest is summarised by Lord Goff in *Attorney General v Guardian Newspapers Ltd (No 2)*.[60] The common law which asserts that confidentiality principles can apply to children of age and understanding is set out in *Gillick*.[61]

3.65 Lord Scarman explained his view of the common law position in *Gillick* as follows:[62]

> Although statute has intervened in respect of a child's capacity to consent to medical treatment from the age of 16 onwards, neither statute nor the case law has ruled on the extent and duration of parental right in respect of children under the age of 16. More specifically, there is no rule yet applied to contraceptive treatment, which has special problems of its own and is a late-comer in medical practice. It is open, therefore, to the House to formulate a rule.

3.66 He and Lord Fraser then went on to explain their views of the law, generally, as to the rights of mature children – of 'intelligence and understanding' – and of the right of such children to confidentiality in particular. So, said Lord Scarman, of the extent to which the law – in relation to a mature child's confidentiality – must adjust itself according to the facts of each individual case:[63]

> If the law should impose upon the process of "growing up" fixed limits where nature knows only a continuous process, the price would be artificiality and a lack of realism in an area where the law must be sensitive to human development and social change ... Unless and until Parliament should think fit to intervene, the courts should establish a principle flexible enough to enable justice to be achieved by its application to the particular circumstances proved by the evidence placed before them.

Information sharing and a mature child's confidentiality

3.67 Privacy and rights of a mature child engage the European Convention 1950 Article 8 (respect for family life). This creates a tension between the law (based on *Gillick*) and the departmental guidance in *Working Together 2018*. What right to confidentiality does the mature child have when caught in this conflict?

3.68 A mature child's right to privacy was considered by Keehan J in *PD v SD & Anor*.[64] (PD was a gender change 16-year-old who sought an order in wardship that no information should be given by the local authority, in whose care he was,

59 See recently *Re RD (Deprivation or Restriction of Liberty)* [2018] EWFC 47 per Cobb J.
60 [1990] 1 AC 109, [1988] UKHL 6, [1987] 1 WLR 776, (*Spycatcher case*); see 3.7.
61 [1985] UKHL 7, [1986] 1 AC 112, [1986] 1 FLR 224; as affirmed in *R (Axon) v The Secretary of State for Health and anor* [2006] EWHC 37 (Admin), [2006] 2 FLR 206 per Silber J.
62 [1986] 1 FLR 224 at 250.
63 Ibid at 249.
64 [2015] EWHC 4103 (Fam), Keehan J.

to his adoptive parents.) Keehan J held that the Article 8 rights of each of the child and of his parents were engaged. He held further the rights of PD prevailed over his parents: [23] …'Where there is a tension between the Article 8 rights of the child, on the one hand, and the parents, on the other, the rights of the child prevail, he must follow *Yousef v The Netherlands (Application No 33711/96).*'[65] The European Court of Human Rights said in that case:

> [66] … If there was any clash of Art 8 rights between a child and its father, the interests of the child should always prevail …
>
> [73] The court reiterates that in judicial decisions where the rights under Art 8 of parents and those of a child are at stake, the child's rights must be the paramount consideration. If any balancing of interests is necessary, the interests of the child must prevail (see *Elsholz v Germany* (2002) 34 EHRR 58, [2000] 2 FLR 486, para 52 and *TP and KM v United Kingdom* (2002) 34 EHRR 2, [2001] 2 FLR 549, para 72).

3.69 The court must focus, said Keehan J, on the competing Article 8 rights of P and of his parents; and he did so, in the first instance, by referring[66] to the view of Lord Scarman in *Gillick* as to the limits of parental responsibility:

> The rights of a parent exist primarily to enable the parent to discharge his duty of maintenance, protection and education until he reaches such an age as to be able to look after himself and make his own decisions.

3.70 As did the common law in *Gillick*, so in *PD v SD*, the rights of the mature child have priority over parental responsibility. It is likely that if the same balance were struck as between private rights and the guidance in *Working Together 2018*, in respect of confidential information in respect of a mature child, the same respect for a child's confidentiality at common law would prevail. This is emphasised by Lord Goff's comment in *Spycatcher* (above): that there is always 'a public interest in the maintenance of confidences' equally for a *Gillick*-competent child as for an adult.

'Sharing' as against confidentiality

Guidance over safeguarding in the context of a child's confidentiality

3.71 *Working Together 2018* deals with guidance over safeguarding.[67] It is intended to assist professionals with assessment for children of all ages. The

65 (2003) 36 EHRR 20, [2003] 1 FLR 210, ECtHR.

66 Ibid at [26].

67 Cobb J stressed the importance of 'safeguarding' children in *AZ, BZ and CZ v Kirklees Council (Human Rights Claim: Costs)* [2017] EWFC 11 in relation to a HRA 1998 claim in the following general terms: '[1] Local authorities responsible for safeguarding children carry a heavy obligation to ensure that they perform their statutory duties at all times in a manner which is compatible with the rights of the individuals and their families who they are assigned to help, specifically the rights which individuals enjoy under the *European Convention on Human Rights (ECHR) – Article 6* and *Article 8*. Any violation of these *Convention* rights is of course unlawful (*section 6 Human Rights Act 1998 'HRA 1998'*); when such an alleged violation occurs, those affected are entitled to bring claims under *sections 7* and *8* of the *HRA 1998* for relief, including declarations and/or damages' (judge's italics).

intention here is to review the guidance from the point of view of a mature child. Thus, the way *Working Together 2018* considers such a child's views will dictate how its statutory guidance treats confidentiality.

3.72 *Working Together 2018* strongly advocates the need to listen to a child's views; but it also urges the sharing of information concerning children, without any overt reference to *Gillick* and the needs for the confidential information from mature children to be respected. This will create a tension between the law and the guidance in *Working Together 2018* where the wishes and feelings and any confidential information of a mature child have been passed on by that child to, say, a teacher or social worker.

Confidentiality and 'myth-busting'

3.73 References to 'confidentiality' and confidence (in the sense under discussion here) are very few. On page 20, under the heading 'Myth-busting guide to information sharing' comes the comment from *Working Together 2018*:

> The common law duty of confidence and the Human Rights Act 1998 prevent the sharing of personal information?
>
> No – this is not the case. In addition to the Data Protection Act 2018 and GDPR, practitioners need to balance the common law duty of confidence and the Human Rights Act 1998 against the effect on individuals or others of not sharing the information.

3.74 No legal authority is cited for this comment. It is true only so far as it goes. It does not apply to the mature child who does not want his or her confidence breached, unless there is another right in issue which overrides the mature child's right to respect for their private life in accordance with *Gillick*, Article 8 and *Yousef* (above).[68] The entitlement of a mature child to respect for his or her confidences is absolute, subject only to any overriding right.

3.75 Any guidance as to 'sharing' of information about a mature child is, to that extent, wrong. It is overridden by *Gillick*.

Information 'sharing'

3.76 *Working Together 2018* requires all professionals who work with children[69] and who have a role in early identification of problems which may be suffered by them, to 'share information with other professionals'. This is stated in *Working Together 2018* as follows:[70]

---

68 *Gillick v West Norfolk and Wisbech AHA* [1985] UKHL 7, [1986] 1 AC 112, [1986] 1 FLR 224; *Yousef v The Netherlands (Application No 33711/96)* (2003) 36 EHRR 20, [2003] 1 FLR 210, ECtHR.

69 See eg, the list in CA 2004 s 10(4) at n to 3.80.

70 *Working Together* Ch 1 para 3 p 12.

3 Local agencies should have in place effective ways to identify emerging problems and potential unmet needs for individual children and families. This requires all professionals, including those in universal services and those providing services to adults with children, to understand their role in identifying emerging problems and to share information with other professionals to support early identification and assessment.

3.77 This provision as to 'sharing' information immediately raises the question of the confidentiality of mature children. Government advice – *Information sharing advice*[71] – does not differentiate the consequences in terms the law on confidentiality as between the rights of a mature child and those of a dependent child. Particular care must be exercised where a mature child thinks his/her confidentiality can be guaranteed by a professional; but where the duties of the professional are treated (eg, by advice in *Working Together*) as being overridden.[72]

3.78 As ever, in a consideration of whether to override the confidentiality of a mature child, the professional will need to consider the public interests under *W v Egdell* and also reasons for interference with the child's rights.[73] The lawyer who gives legal advice will need to be clear as to whether advice privilege adds another dimension or layer of privacy to any decision as to whether to override confidentiality.

3.79 The emphasis in *Working Together 2018* is that professionals should work for prompt passing on of information amongst those covered by its guidance. In the vast majority of cases of dependent children this will be justified from the point of view their welfare. They will be treated as not being in a position to have confidences. However, once a child is of age and understanding about the issue concerned, that child will be entitled to claim privacy for confidential information; he or she is entitled to have those confidences respected.

Children Act 2004: *Working Together* and the duty to safeguard

Promoting the welfare of children

3.80 Children Act 2004 section 11 places the duties to safeguard children and to promote their welfare on specified public bodies including local authorities, health authorities and the police.[74] Each of these bodies are required to 'make arrangements for ensuring that their functions are discharged having regard to the need to safeguard and promote the welfare of children'.[75] CA 2004 section 10 requires each local authority to 'make arrangements to promote co-operation

71 *Information sharing Advice for practitioners providing safeguarding services to children, young people, parents and carers,* July 2018 HM Government. Available at: https://assets.publishing.service.gov.uk/government/uploads/system/uploads/attachment_data/file/721581/Information_sharing_advice_practitioners_safeguarding_services.pdf.

72 See eg, *Re A (A Child)* [2012] UKSC 60.

73 See Chapter 10 Part 5.

74 CA 2004 s 11(1).

75 Ibid s 11(2)(a).

between' the agencies concerned with children: within the local authority, 'the authority's relevant partners'[76] and any other body they consider appropriate.[77]

3.81 These arrangements are to be made to improve 'the well-being of children in the authority's area', including in relation to 'physical and mental health and emotional well-being [and] protection from harm and neglect'. CA 1989 section 47, for example, places on a local authority the duty to investigate in response to a report under these sections. It has a duty to investigate and to establish whether the child in question requires local authority 'action to safeguard or promote [the child's] welfare'.[78]

Overriding a child's confidentiality

The confidentiality of a mature child

3.82 If confidentiality is to be overridden on the decision of a professional, including social workers, lawyers and doctors, steps which must be taken by the individual professional, and minuted as they are taken (or immediately afterwards) are set out below. What follows is a variation on Lord Kerr's 'sequencing' in the *H(H)* case where a decision is to be made to infringe a child's rights.[79]

3.83 Lord Kerr held that, once the subject child or children have been identified, a sequencing test should be applied to assess or define a child's rights (including

76 CA 2004 s 10(4) defines 'relevant partner' as:
- (a) where the authority is a county council for an area for which there is also a district council, the district council;
- (b) the local policing body and the chief officer of police for a police area any part of which falls within the area of the local authority;
- (c) a local probation board for an area any part of which falls within the area of the authority;
- (ca) the Secretary of State in relation to his functions under sections 2 and 3 of the Offender Management Act 2007, so far as they are exercisable in relation to England;
- (cb) any provider of probation services that is required by arrangements under section 3(2) of the Offender Management Act 2007 to act as a relevant partner of the authority;
- (d) a youth offending team for an area any part of which falls within the area of the authority;
- (e) a Strategic Health Authority and Primary Care Trust for an area any part of which falls within the area of the authority;
- (f) a person providing services in pursuance of section 68 of the Education and Skills Act 2008 in any part of the area of the authority;
- (fa) the governing body of a maintained school that is maintained by the authority ...;
- (fb) the proprietor of a school approved by the Secretary of State under section 342 of the Education Act 1996 and situated in the authority's area;
- (fc) the proprietor of a city technology college, city college for the technology of the arts or Academy situated in the authority's area;
- (fd) the governing body of an institution within the further education sector the main site of which is situated in the authority's area; ...

77 CA 2004 s 10(1).

78 CA 1989 s 47(1).

79 See *H(H) v Deputy Prosecutor of the Italian Republic, Genoa (Official Solicitor Intervening)* [2012] UKSC 25, [2013] 1 AC 338: '[144] ... This calls for a sequencing of, first, consideration of the importance to be attached to the children's rights (by obtaining a clear-sighted understanding of their nature), then an assessment of the degree of interference and finally addressing the question whether extradition justifies the interference ...'

rights to privacy and confidentiality). As appropriate, Lord Kerr's test has been adapted into the following sequence:

(1) The child or children whose confidentiality is in issue or who are otherwise thought to be at risk of harm must be identified individually. Each will be assessed separately.

(2) If they are mature (ie, of age and understanding), but under (say) 16, why does the assessing professional (eg, doctor, lawyer, social worker) think they are mature? This will also depend on definition of the issue(s) relevant to their case(s) (see (3) below).

(3) What is the issue, or issues, on which it may lead to a breach of the child's confidentiality (ie to interfere with his/her Article 8(1) rights)?

(4) What rights of the child are engaged (ie Art 8(1) rights to confidentiality) derived from the issue(s) defined at (3)?[80]

(5) Is any interference with the confidentiality (ie Art 8 rights) of the child(ren) by the person carrying out the assessment?

(6) What is the importance of the child's rights, relative to rights of others (including any public interest) engaged by the particular confidentiality issue(s)? This may include the rights of another adult, mature or dependent child.

(7) What is the degree of any proposed interference with the child's Article 8(1) rights (and see per Lord Steyn pointed out in *Re S*, paragraph [25], it is 'necessary to measure the nature of the impact ... on the child' of what is in prospect[81])?

3.84 If these steps are followed and minuted as they are taken, the record of why confidentiality is to be breached (if that is the decision of the professional concerned) and the justification for a breach of confidentiality can be explained in the case of each individual child

3.85 It is clear that the approaches of the law and of clinical practice to a child's confidentiality on the one hand and that of *Information sharing advice* on the other is appreciably different, in that the guiding principles or priorities of each are different. The first emphasises that in each case, each child must be judged according to general principles applied to the individual; whereas it may be thought that *Information sharing* starts from the – entirely laudable, perhaps – general principle that the end is child protection only.

80 Examples of the way these rights can be defined are provided by Lady Hale in *Re A (Sexual Abuse: Disclosure)* [2012] UKSC 60, [2013] 1 FLR 948 at [1] and by Munby J in *Re Roddy (A Child) (Identification: Restriction on Publication)* [2003] EWHC 2927, [2004] 2 FLR 949.

81 I particular the review of the importance of child's interest in *PJS v News Group Newspapers Ltd* [2016] UKSC 26, [2016] AC 1081, [2016] 2 FLR 251, [2016] 2 WLR 1253 as discussed in Chapter 2.

Differences of professional cultures

3.86 What is the position in relation to confidentiality if a child of understanding – the *Mabon*[82] boys (for example) – wants to discuss the child's personal circumstances and concerns in relation to (say) court proceedings between their parents. They want what they say to be on terms of absolute confidentiality between them and anyone they talk to; and on terms that what they say will not be passed on to third parties, save with their permission. That is a clear pre-condition of their discussion with any professional: lawyer, doctor, social worker, teacher or anyone else.

3.87 Their confidence will be protected absolutely if they speak with a lawyer where he or she considers that the boys can give instructions in proceedings.[83] It is likely, if they are regarded by a doctor as being of 'sufficient understanding' (ie, *Gillick*-competent) that they can speak confidentially to that doctor. Their confidences will be protected if there is no public interest in them being overridden.[84]

3.88 On *Gillick* principles, the same rules apply for a doctor as to any other professional given confidential information by a mature child, despite what may be said to the contrary in *Working Together 2018*. If there is a clash of professional cultures between 'sharing' under *Working Together 2018* and confidentiality in *Gillick*, then the common law, as it now stands, puts *Gillick* before departmental guidance where a child's privacy and their Article 8 rights are concerned.

5 CONFIDENTIALITY AND SOLICITORS

Confidentiality: solicitor and client

Solicitors' Regulation Authority Code

3.89 Requirements of confidentiality have long been essential to the way in which the solicitor's profession operates. It is an absolute rule that what is said by a client to his or her lawyer is said in complete confidence. This practice principle is asserted in, for example, the *Solicitors' Regulation Authority Code 2011*.[85] Principle 4 of the *Code* says that a solicitor should always 'observe [the solicitor's] duty of confidentiality to the client'. This is elaborated upon in Chapter 4 of the *Code* under the heading 'Confidentiality and disclosure'.

3.90 The *Code* is written in a *faux* informal style where the 'you' is a solicitor reading it; though, of course, lay people who have instructed a solicitor will also be concerned to read the *Code* and they are entitled to expect that their relationship with their solicitor will be regulated by it. Chapter 4 states, early on, that:

82 *Mabon v Mabon* [2005] EWCA Civ 634, [2005] Fam 366, [2005] 2 FLR 1011.
83 FPR 2010 r 16.6(3).
84 *GMC Guidance* at paras 47–50.
85 Available at: www.sra.org.uk/solicitors/handbook/code/content.page.

> Protection of confidential information is a fundamental feature of your relationship with clients. It exists as a concept both as a matter of law and as a matter of conduct. This duty continues despite the end of the retainer and even after the death of the client.

3.91 The duty of confidentiality which is owed to all clients must be reconciled with a parallel professional duty of disclosure to existing clients. The duty of disclosure, says the *Code*,[86] is limited to information of which the solicitor is aware which is material to the client's case. Where a solicitor 'cannot reconcile these two duties, then the protection of confidential information is paramount'. The solicitor should not continue to act for a client. The conflict between confidentiality and the duty to disclose information can be shown in the *Bolkiah* case explained below.

Duty of confidentiality

3.92 Rules in relation to confidentiality exist for the protection of the client and that client's information. The solicitor must protect that information from being used in any way against the client's interests. In *Bolkiah v KPMG*[87] Lord Millett defines the solicitor's duty of confidentiality as follows:

> A solicitor is under a duty not to communicate to others any information in his possession which is confidential to the former client. But the duty extends well beyond that of refraining from deliberate disclosure. It is the solicitor's duty to ensure that the former client is not put at risk that confidential information which the solicitor has obtained from that relationship may be used against him in any circumstances.

3.93 A conflict does not arise solely because a solicitor or the solicitor's firm have acted for a particular client (B) previously. The conflict turns on whether the solicitor or the solicitor's firm has information which is, or may be, contrary to the interests of the B if, later, the firm are asked by A to act against B, or if B may have a contrary interest of any sort to A.

3.94 Thus, if the firm of solicitor X acted for a husband and wife, H and W, in a routine conveyancing matter three years before, and W then approaches the same firm when subsequently her marriage breaks down it is unlikely that the firm would have information contrary to H's interests which would prevent it acting for W; or if he so alleged, H would have to prove it. However, if the firm was small (ie, only one or two solicitors were available to act for W) and, at the time of the conveyance it had been necessary for H to discuss his financial affairs with the conveyancer in some detail (ie, it was not a routine transaction) then it is quite likely that, even three years later, the firm could have information which might be contrary to H's interest, and it should not act for his wife in their subsequent divorce.

86 See Chapter 4.

87 [1998] UKHL 52, [1999] 2 AC 222.

Disclosure and confidentiality

3.95 The conflict of the same firm acting for two clients with conflicting interests can be illustrated by *Re Z (Restraining Solicitors from Acting)*.[88] A husband Z had instructed Mrs F some nine years before the events giving rise to his application to restrain her from later acting for his wife. Mrs F, now senior partner of F & Co, had represented Mr Z in connection with an application by his wife (Y) for a freezing order in relation to £12 million in his bank account. Mrs F became, according to Z, a friend and confidante of his. By 2009 a reconciliation between the Z and Y had failed. Y instructed one of Mrs F's partners in Mrs F's newly founded firm. The couple's assets now exceed £18 million, it seems. At this point when the matter was raised with her, Mrs F said she did not remember Z ('though ... the name sounded familiar'[89]). The case was allocated to a partner who had not been employed by F & Co at the earlier time.

3.96 F & Co offered various undertakings to promote confidentiality. Despite these undertakings and her assurance that Mrs F did not remember him, Z applied for an injunction for removal of F & Co from the court record as acting for Mrs Z.

Conflict of public interests

3.97 In his judgment Bodey J starts from the proposition that a case of this sort 'creates a tension between two public interests': there must be 'no risk or perception of risk' that confidential information might be disclosed and there must be freedom for a client to instruct a solicitor of their choice:

> [20] Situations like this create a tension between two public interests: first, there is the interest of the client in being able to have the fullest confidence in the solicitor whom he instructs, for which purpose there should be no risk or perception of risk that confidential information would be disclosed to anyone else. Second, there is the interest in the freedom of the solicitor to be able to take instructions from any member of the public, together with the interest of members of the public to be able to instruct solicitors of their choice whenever there is no real need for constraint: see in *Re A Firm of Solicitors, Re* [1997] Ch 1, [1995] 3 All ER 482, per Lightman J at 9 and 488 respectively, who there noted that "... there must be good and sufficient reason to deprive a client of the solicitor or the solicitor of the client of his choice".

3.98 That said, 'every case in this sphere is fact-specific';[90] though only two of the cases cited to the judge were family cases[91] (and in altogether different circumstances to *Re Z*).

88 [2009] EWHC 3621 (Fam), [2010] 2 FLR 132, Bodey J.
89 Ibid at [12].
90 Ibid at [28].
91 *Davies v Davies* (below); *Re L (Minors) (Care Proceedings: Solicitors)* [2001] 1 WLR 100, [2000] 2 FLR 887, Wilson J.

3.99 As in *Bolkiah v KPMG* (above and discussed further below) the *Z* case turned on the solicitor's unqualified 'duty to preserve confidentiality'.[92] The burden rested on the solicitor to establish that there was 'no risk of information confidential to the client being unwittingly or inadvertently passed on' to a new client with a contrary interest.[93]

3.100 In his discussion of the arguments before him, Bodey J discussed first the burden upon the husband to assert his claim that Mrs F's firm should not act – a burden, it will be recalled, which Lord Millett described as 'not heavy'. Bodey J started from the proposition that subconscious memories can be unexpectedly triggered. He explained this as follows:

> [38] … Some recollections, albeit vague and patchy, do, therefore, seem to have made their way back [into Mrs F's memory]. But leaving that aside, it is well recognised in the authorities that things may happen, perhaps unexpectedly, which reawaken subconscious memories. We have all had such experience of retrieving information unexpectedly after some trigger. Neuberger J recognised as much in *Halewood* when he said:
>
> > "… I have not overlooked the fact that [the former solicitor] says that he cannot recall anything specific in relation to the [particular litigation]. There is no challenge to his good faith, but memories can change and matters could come back to his mind particularly if he was prompted by hearing or seeing what was going on in [his new firm's] offices …;"
>
> and he repeated Lightman J's comment in *Re a Firm of Solicitors*, that:
>
> > "… common sense requires recognition that confidential information acquired by a solicitor will remain in the mind of the solicitor or be susceptible of being triggered as a recollection after a lapse after a period of time".

3.101 Bodey J decided that it was for F & Co to show him that there were sufficient safeguards in place to enable them to act. They failed to do so. Subject to an issue on costs[94] Z succeeded to his application. He did so on grounds of his concerns as to the ability of the memory as to confidential matters to be triggered unexpectedly; and on the *Bolkiah* test for intervening: that the risk of this was a real risk 'not merely fanciful or theoretical. But it need not be substantial':[95]

> [42] … So, on an overview of all the factors, I have come to the conclusion that the husband has satisfied the burden of proof on him that Mrs F is in possession of information (in the 'triggerable' sense, discussed above) which is confidential to him, which will or may be relevant to the present litigation and which would or could compromise the

92 Per Lord Millet, quoted by Bodey J at para [22].

93 Ibid at [25].

94 The husband's delay in making up his mind to bring the application caused him to have to pay Mrs Z's costs for a five-week period.

95 Per Lord Millett in *Bolkiah*.

> fairness of the process if it leaked out. Further, I am of the view that this risk, although modest, is a real one. It is clearly not substantial, but it does not need to be. It is, I find, a risk which is not merely fanciful nor theoretical.

Confidentiality and court proceedings

Bolkiah v KPMG

3.102 *Bolkiah v KPMG*[96] was described by Bodey J as the case which provided the key to the decision he had to make. *Bolkiah* concerned litigation support given by accountants to Prince Bolkiah where they were instructed by another firm run by another family within the prince's family. The question arose as to whether the protection which they erected within the firm was sufficient to absolve them from any possible breach of confidentiality to Prince Bolkiah. Lord Millett, who gave the main opinion in the House of Lords, stressed his view as to the absolute nature of confidentiality. He summarised his starting point as follows:

> I consider that the nature of the work which a firm of accountants undertakes in the provision of litigation support services requires the court to exercise the same jurisdiction to intervene on behalf of a former client of the firm as it exercises in the case of a solicitor. The basis of that jurisdiction is to be found in the principles which apply to all forms of employment where the relationship between the client and the person with whom he does business is a confidential one. A solicitor is under a duty not to communicate to others any information in his possession which is confidential to the former client.

3.103 However, said Lord Millett, the duty goes further. It is not merely a duty to protect confidential information. It is also a duty to ensure that there is no 'risk' that confidential information possessed by the solicitor may be used in any way against the former client. It is that future risk which was in issue in *Bolkiah* and which arises when a new client (or a former client who has instructed a firm jointly with one or more others eg, a husband and wife) approaches a firm with new instructions. Lord Millett explained the future risk as follows:

> But the duty extends well beyond that of refraining from deliberate disclosure. It is the solicitor's duty to ensure that the former client is not put at risk that confidential information which the solicitor has obtained from that relationship may be used against him in any circumstances.

Challenge by a former client

3.104 *Bolkiah* turned on whether the litigation services provided by KPMG were in the same category as work done by lawyers (to which the House answered: yes) and whether or not new work taken on by KPMG infringed their duty of

96 [1998] UKHL 52, [1999] 2 AC 222.

confidentiality owed to Prince Bolkiah. In the course of giving his opinion, Lord Millett dealt with the approach to be adopted by the court where a solicitor was no longer acting for a former client and who was instructed in proceedings against that former client. Was there an issue as to confidentiality; and if so how should the courts deal with it?

3.105 There could not be actual conflict, since the retainer between the solicitor and his client was at an end.

> Thereafter the solicitor has no obligation to defend and advance the interests of his former client. The only duty to the former client which survives the termination of the client relationship is a continuing duty to preserve the confidentiality of information imparted during its subsistence.

3.106 Thus, if a former client was validly to object to his former solicitor acting for another client, he must establish that:

(1) the solicitor has confidential information which he has not agreed to the solicitor disclosing; and

(2) the information is, or may be, relevant to the new case and that that the interest of the new client is or may be adverse to that of the former client.

3.107 It is for the former client to establish these factors but the burden 'is not a heavy one' says Lord Millett:

> Whether a particular individual is in possession of confidential information is a question of fact which must be proved or inferred from the circumstances of the case.

Solicitor's duty in relation to use of information

3.108 Lord Millett then considered the extent of the solicitor's duty.[97] He explained that this was 'unqualified'.

> It is a duty to keep the information confidential, not merely to take all reasonable steps to do so. Moreover, it is not merely a duty not to communicate the information to a third party. It is a duty not to misuse it, that is to say, without the consent of the former client to make any use of it or to cause any use to be made of it by others otherwise than for his benefit. The former client cannot be protected completely from accidental or inadvertent disclosure. But he is entitled to prevent his former solicitor from exposing him to any avoidable risk; and this includes the increased risk of the use of the information to his prejudice arising from the acceptance of instructions to act for another client with an adverse interest in a matter to which the information is or may be relevant.

97 Ibid at 235 and 225 respectively.

3.109 When or in what circumstances should the court intervene? Lord Millett answered this question by suggesting a simple test. The court should intervene unless there is 'no risk of disclosure':

> Many different tests have been proposed in the authorities. These include the avoidance of "an appreciable risk" or "an acceptable risk". I regard such expressions as unhelpful: the former because it is ambiguous, the latter because it is uninformative. I prefer simply to say that the court should intervene unless it is satisfied that there is no risk of disclosure. It goes without saying that the risk must be a real one, and not merely fanciful or theoretical. But it need not be substantial.

Risk of the memory being triggered

3.110 In *Davies v Davies*,[98] the question had been whether a solicitor could act for a husband where, some seven years previously, he (the solicitor) had had one consultation with the wife. The case was resolved for other reasons, but Johnson J ordered that the husband should pay the costs of the wife on issuing her application. The reported case is on a costs decision in the Court of Appeal. In dealing with costs, Jonson J had said he considered that there was a real, as opposed to a fanciful, risk of information in the mind of the husband's solicitor having some impact upon the conduct of the case.

3.111 The wife's summons had been properly issued, said the Court of Appeal. The husband should pay the wife's costs. As Bodey J points out in *Re Z*, the Court of Appeal had commented on the complexity of memory and of how recollection can be triggered:

> [40] Aldous LJ observed (at 50) that: "... the memory is a complex phenomenon. Recall may be conscious or subconscious. That has been recognised in copyright cases where courts recognise that conscious and unconscious copying can take place ...". The important distinguishing feature of the *Davies* case [said Bodey J] compared with this one is that there it was the very solicitor himself who had formerly advised the wife and who was now acting for the husband; whereas here, it is not Mrs F herself who is acting for the wife, but Mr A.

98 [2000] 1 FLR 39, CA.

4

DISCLOSURE AT COMMON LAW

1 INTRODUCTION

Statement that a document exists

4.1 Formally, the term 'disclosure' in civil proceedings, as in family proceedings, consists of stating that a document relevant to the proceedings in question exists or is available to the disclosing party.[1] Inspection follows procedurally from disclosure and requires the disclosing party to enable another party to look at disclosed material. Civil Procedure Rules 1998 (CPR 1998) Part 31 deals with procedure for disclosure in civil proceedings. In more modest terms, Family Procedure Rules 2010 (FPR 2010) Part 21 deals with aspects of disclosure in family proceedings; though the main part of disclosure in family proceedings is a matter of common law as defined by CPR 1998 (mostly Part 31).

4.2 Gwyneth Knowles J explained this in *Lancashire County Council v A, B and Z (A Child: Fact Finding Hearing: Police Disclosure)*[2] as (judge's italics):

> [8] Part 21 of the FPR "*Miscellaneous Rules About Disclosure and Inspection of Documents*" makes provision for the disclosure and inspection of documents against persons who are not parties to the proceedings. Within family proceedings, disclosure is taken to mean the production of copies of documents though this is, strictly speaking, a means of providing for the inspection of documents. Rule 21.1(1) of the FPR states that: "*A party discloses a document by stating that the document exists or has existed.*" The next logical step in the process is the inspection of a document by a party when that document has been disclosed by another person [Rule 21.1(2)] …

4.3 In practice 'disclosure' is a much-misused term. Indeed, the rule to which Gwyneth Knowles J was ultimately to refer, FPR 2010 r 21.2,[3] uses 'disclosure' – as in 'disclosure against a person not a party' when it means production of material. The Cleveland report cautions strongly against 'disclosure' – in a very different context – as used by social workers and others of what children say to them.

1 CPR 1998 r 31.2; FPR 2010 r 21.1(1).
2 [2018] EWHC 1819 (Fam).
3 Considered fully in Chapter 11, Part 5.

MacDonald J drew attention to this 30 years later in in *AS v TH (False Allegations of Abuse)*.[4]

Privilege from disclosure

4.4 Privilege from disclosure means that a document is exempt from inspection or production in court, though its existence should still be stated (a rule which is only rarely followed by parties to family proceedings[5]). Privilege and the separate, though related, public interest immunity (eg, FPR 2010 r 21.3) are dealt with elsewhere in this book as follows:

- Legal professional privilege, as legal professional privilege (Chapter 5)
- Litigation privilege (Chapter 6)
- Self-incrimination privilege (Chapter 7)
- Without prejudice rule immunity (Chapter 8)
- Public interest immunity (Chapter 16).

4.5 This chapter proceeds as follows:

- Part 2 explains the right to disclosure and production of relevant evidence and the rules which regulate this in FPR 2010 Part 21.
- Part 3 sets out how the family proceedings rules are supplemented by CPR 1998, which must be treated as a representation of the common law for family proceedings purposes.
- Part 4 deals with 'standard disclosure', a subject taken from CPR 1998, but which has a role in family proceedings.
- Part 5, based in part on CPR 1998 r 31.11, explains the duration of disclosure over the course of proceedings.
- Part 6 explains how the practice in relation to bundles is affected by a Practice Direction and by rules of disclosure.

2 DISCLOSURE

Disclosure and a fair trial

4.6 Disclosure is an essential component of a fair trial and has been for many years. It is now a fundamental element of a fair trial in terms of Article 6(1) of

4 [2016] EWHC 532 Fam at [33] '... I pause to note that despite the fact that the use of the term "disclosure" to describe a statement or allegation of abuse made by a child has been deprecated since the Cleveland Report due to it precluding the notion that the abuse might not have occurred (see para 12.34(1)), *every* professional who gave evidence in this case (except the Children's Guardian) used the term "disclosure" to describe what the children had said to them'.

5 *Tchenguiz-Imerman v Imerman* [2012] EWHC 4047 (Fam), [2014] 1 FLR 232 Moylan J.

the European Convention 1950. It is essential – it is the right of individual parties (subject to exceptions) that all materials relevant to a case are considered by them and by the court and that a judge and all parties where possible – privilege is an important exception to this – see the same material.

4.7 In the extreme circumstance of closed material procedures Lord Neuberger in *Bank Mellat v Her Majesty's Treasury (No 1)*[6] commented as follows:

> [3] … Fundamental to any justice system in a modern, democratic society is the principle of natural justice, whose most important aspect is that every party has a right to know the full case against him, and the right to test and challenge that case fully. A closed hearing is therefore even more offensive to fundamental principle than a private hearing. At least a private hearing cannot be said, of itself, to give rise to inequality or even unfairness as between the parties …

Disclosure and Family Procedure Rules 2010 Part 21

4.8 Part 21 of the Family Procedure Rules 2010 is the only part of the rules which is dedicated to dealing with the subject of 'disclosure'. The Civil Procedure Rules 1998 (CPR 1998) devote 23 rules to the subject. In contrast, Part 21 deals with aspects of disclosure in three rules under the heading 'Miscellaneous rules about inspection of documents'. All are derived from CPR 1998, but the aspects of disclosure chosen for regulating family proceedings is haphazard, namely:

- a definition of the terms 'disclosure' and 'inspection' (r 21.1);
- disclosure against a person not a party (r 21.2); and
- a claim to withhold disclosure or inspection of a document (r 21.3).

4.9 Part 21 by no means deals with all procedural aspects of the subject. It crops up in other parts of FPR 2010 (eg, FPR 2010 r 5.2, documents to be attached to a form which a party is required to file[7]), expressly or by implication in the text of the rules. It is therefore necessary to refer to the common law to define how disclosure is regulated.[8] Mostly the common law is codified in CPR 1998 Part 31, such as:

---

6 [2013] UKSC 38, [2014] AC 700.

7 *5.2 Documents to be attached to a form*
Subject to any rule or practice direction, unless the court directs otherwise, a form must have attached to it any documents which, in the form, are –
(a) stated to be required; or
(b) referred to.

8 When asked about a redraft of FPR 2010 Pt 21 to extend and clarify the existing three rules on disclosure to bring the subject into line with CPR 1998, the Family Procedure Rules Committee replied in December 2013: 'After careful consideration the Committee concluded that the Family Procedure Rules in relation to disclosure provide as much as is needed. The Committee had not wanted to provide for open-ended disclosure by list, so had included only those provisions that were necessary. The rules in Pts 9 (Applications for a Financial Remedy) and 21 (Miscellaneous Rules about Disclosure and Inspection of Documents) were not restrictive and did not undermine the common law duty of disclosure. It was considered that this was a training issue rather than one that required rule amendment.'

- period over which duty of disclosure continues (CPR 1998 r 31.11);
- 'use' of disclosed documents (the 'implied undertaking') (CPR 1998 r 31.19); and
- specific disclosure (see eg, *Tchenguiz-Imerman v Imerman* (below)).

4.10 This reliance of family proceedings on CPR 1998 was noted by Moylan J in *Tchenguiz-Imerman v Imerman*[9] when he commented:

> [10] There is no specific rule in [FPR 2010] which governs the issue of privilege. The general rule is that parties are required, after the preliminary exchange of documents, to make such disclosure as may be required by the court. I have, therefore, for guidance, been referred to the Civil Procedure Rules 1998 (CPR) and other documents, including extracts from textbooks ...

4.11 In that case he went on to deal with 'standard disclosure', which will be explained later.[10]

Disclosure: defined terms

4.12 FPR 2010 r 21.1 states:

> **21.1 Interpretation**
>
> (1) A party discloses a document by stating that the document exists or has existed.
>
> (2) Inspection of a document occurs when a party is permitted to inspect a document disclosed by another person.
>
> (3) For the purposes of disclosure and inspection –
>
> (a) "document" means anything in which information of any description is recorded; and
>
> (b) "copy" in relation to a document, means anything onto which information recorded in the document has been copied, by whatever means and whether directly or indirectly.

4.13 Though disclosure is formally of documents, it can be taken to include any information or other material relevant to an issue in the proceedings.[11] Disclosure in financial relief represents a duty to the court, as well as to other parties.[12]

---

9 [2012] EWHC 4047 (Fam), [2014] 1 FLR 232.

10 See 4.18.

11 *Imerman v Tchenguiz and ors* [2010] EWCA Civ 908, [2010] 2 FLR 814 para [25] per Lord Neuberger MR: 'At the outset it may be helpful to distinguish between three things which, before recent changes, were more clearly distinguished as a matter of terminology: the *disclosure* of relevant facts and matters; the *discovery* of relevant documents; and the *evidence* required to establish the relevant facts.'

12 The Matrimonial Causes Act 1973 s 25 as explained in *Livesey (formerly Jenkins) v Jenkins* [1985] AC 424, [1985] FLR 813.

4.14 Documents covered by any form of privilege must be disclosed, in that other parties must be notified of their existence: the privilege applies to inspection and production in court. Despite what is stated in r 21.1(1), there is no formal or proscribed disclosure statement in family proceedings; though FPR 2010 r 5.2 (see above) imposes a duty on parties to include with forms filed at court such documents as a rule may prescribe.

Disclosure and inspection

4.15 Disclosure gives the party to whom disclosure is provided a right to inspect, with certain exceptions such as in relation to privilege and public interest immunity[13] or where a document is no longer in the control of the disclosing party.[14] Inspection is the process whereby a party is provided with access to disclosed documents (eg, by their being photocopied and sent to that other party).[15] 'Specific disclosure' is provided for in the practice direction to FPR 2010 Part 21.[16]

3 DISCLOSURE, FAMILY PROCEEDINGS AND THE CIVIL PROCEDURE RULES 1998

(1) Family proceedings and the Civil Procedure Rules 1998

4.16 Civil proceedings rules (ie Civil Procedure Rules 1998) formally do not apply in family proceedings.[17] However, as explained above,[18] the Family Procedure Rules Committee considers that the common law dictates much of what is to be gleaned of disclosure for family proceedings.

4.17 For example, in *Tchenguiz-Imerman v Imerman*[19] Moylan J was dealing with financial relief proceedings where a variation of trusts was claimed on the basis that they were post-nuptial settlements. The beneficiaries of the settlements were the husband's three adult children from a previous relationship, his parents, the 10-year-old child of the parties and one of the husband's grandchildren. W applied for disclosure of certain documents in relation to the trusts. The husband claimed common interest privilege (legal professional privilege to which he said he was entitled jointly with other beneficiaries) in respect of the documents.

4.18 To resolve the impasse and to enable the court to consider the privilege question, the judge directed H to provide a list of documents falling within the category of documents requested with the dates of those communications. The

13 Legal advice privilege and public interest immunity are explained respectively in Chapters 5 and 16. A claim to privilege or public interest immunity is made under FPR 2010 r 21.3 as explained in Chapter 11.
14 CPR 1998 r 31.3(1).
15 CPR 1998 r 31.15. Inspection may be ordered under CPR 1998 r 31.12.
16 *PD21A* para 2.4; and see FPR 2010 r 4.1(3)(b) (court's case management powers).
17 CPR 1998 r 2.1(2).
18 See 4.9.
19 [2012] EWHC 4047 (Fam), [2014] 1 FLR 232.

judge's intention was to follow the practice set out in CPR 1998 r 31.10. The main part of r 31.10 reads as follows:

Procedure for standard disclosure

(2) Each party must make and serve on every other party, a list of documents in the relevant practice form.

(3) The list must identify the documents in a convenient order and manner and as concisely as possible.

(4) The list must indicate –

(a) those documents in respect of which the party claims a right or duty to withhold inspection; and

(b) (i) those documents which are no longer in the party's control; and

(ii) what has happened to those documents.

(Rule 31.19(3) and (4)[20] requires a statement in the list of documents relating to any documents inspection of which a person claims he has a right or duty to withhold.)

4.19 The list must include a 'statement' and that 'disclosure statement' must state the extent of search a party has made to identify all documents which are required to be disclosed.[21]

Claim for privilege

4.20 So far as a claim for privilege was made in respect of any document or class of documents, or a part of a document, then – said Moylan J – it must be stated in writing that there was such a right and the grounds on which that right was claimed.[22] The grounds on which the right was claimed must be sufficient to enable the wife to determine whether the right might, or could, be challenged.[23] The judge said that what was required was sufficient elaboration of the grounds to enable the wife, as advised, to determine whether or not the claim for privilege should, or could, be challenged.

4.21 The procedure for the court to decide whether privilege (or any other reason for material to be withheld from inspection) is at FPR 2010 r 21.3 (as explained in Chapter 10) and the procedure for testing privilege proposed by Beatson J in *West London Pipeline and Storage Ltd v Total UK Ltd*.[24]

20 CPR 1998 r 31.19(3) and (4) are in the same terms as FPR 2010 r 21.3(3) and (4).
21 CPR 1998 r 31.10(5) and (6).
22 As a matter of fact this is what is required already in FPR 2010 r 21.3(3), to which the judge does not appear to have been referred.
23 See Chapter 11 on withholding disclosure (FPR 2010 r 21.3).
24 [2008] EWHC 1729 (Comm) and see Chapter 11.

'Standard disclosure' and the Civil Procedure Rules 1998 Part 31

4.22 The first part of CPR 1998 Part 31 deals with 'standard disclosure' as follows:

(1) Disclosure gives the other party ('B') or parties the right to inspect any disclosed document, with certain exceptions (including that A no longer has the document or that A asserts it is covered by privilege).[25]

(2) If ordered to provide disclosure, A is required only to give 'standard disclosure'[26] of documents within A's control.[27]

(3) Standard disclosure imposes on A a duty to search for relevant documents.[28]

(4) The procedure for standard disclosure requires service of a list in appropriate court form, and that it include a disclosure statement.[29]

(5) B can apply to the court for an order against A for specific disclosure or inspection.[30]

(6) Disclosure continues until the conclusion of the proceedings.[31] (The question of when the duty arises is considered later in this chapter.)

(7) Information or clarification of a matter in issue may be requested by one party of another, which, if refused or not adequately dealt with, may be the subject of an order;[32] and the court may make an order requiring clarification or additional information on its own initiative.[33] This is dealt with in Chapter 25.

4.23 Specific disclosure, if applied for by a party, is a matter of case management. On an unsuccessful appeal against a judge's order for specific disclosure, it has been said by the Court of Appeal:[34]

> [42] Disclosure under CPR 1998 a continuing process. It is part of case management. It is always open to a court to revisit an earlier procedural order. If the judge's order is upheld and the appellants fail to comply with it, it would be open to them to put evidence before the court to explain their reasons for non-compliance. In particular, it would be open to them to produce further evidence in order to cast a different light on their relationship with the trustees. A judge's discretion in the exercise of case management powers is wide and it was well within the

---

25 CPR 1998 r 31.3(1).
26 Ibid, r 31.5; 'standard disclosure' is defined by r 31.6.
27 Ibid, r 31.8.
28 Ibid, r 31.7.
29 Ibid, r 31.10 and see CPR 1998 *PD31* para 4 (which explains further what is to be included in a disclosure statement).
30 Ibid, r 31.12 and see CPR 1998 *PD31* para 5 (which provides further requirements for the application for specific disclosure).
31 Ibid, r 31.11; *Livesey (formerly Jenkins) v Jenkins* [1985] AC 424, [1985] FLR 813.
32 CPR 1998 r 18.1.
33 CPR 1998 r 3.3(1) (general powers of the court to make orders on its own initiative); see similar powers in FPR 2010 r 4.3(1).
34 *North Shore Ventures Ltd v Anstead Holdings Inc* [2012] EWCA Civ 11.

> proper exercise of the judge's discretion to make the order which and when he did.

4.24 As can be seen, in connection with disclosure, the Court of Appeal takes the view that orders for disclosure are a matter of case management and thus of the court's discretion.

Right of inspection

4.25 Under CPR 1998 r 31.3(1) a party has a right of inspection of a disclosed document where it has been disclosed save where a party no longer has 'control' of it or that party has a 'right to withhold inspection' (ie, privilege or other form of confidentiality):

> (a) the document is no longer in the control of the party who disclosed it;
>
> (b) the party disclosing the document has a right or a duty to withhold inspection of it; ...

4 STANDARD DISCLOSURE

Standard disclosure: case management

4.26 FPR 2010 r 4.1(3)(e) enables the court, as part of its case management powers, to 'make such order for disclosure and inspection' as may be thought appropriate. In civil proceedings an order to provide disclosure is to give 'standard disclosure'.

4.27 Standard disclosure is defined by CPR 1998 r 31.6 as follows:

> **31.6 Standard disclosure – what documents are to be disclosed**
>
> Standard disclosure requires a party to disclose only –
>
> (a) the documents on which he relies; and
>
> (b) the documents which –
>
> (i) adversely affect his own case;
>
> (ii) adversely affect another party's case; or
>
> (iii) support another party's case; and
>
> (c) the documents which he is required to disclose by a relevant practice direction.

4.28 In *Shah & Anor v HSBC Private Bank (UK) Ltd*[35] the Court of Appeal (Pill LJ with Munby LJ) explained the meaning of standard disclosure as follows:

35 [2011] EWCA Civ 1154.

> The obligation is of course more limited than under [pre-CPR 1998 rules] test but the rationale for a rule as to disclosure, including the present rule, remains that stated by Sir Thomas Bingham MR in *Taylor v Anderton* [1995] 1 WLR 447, at page 462. It is whether the party "suffers no litigious disadvantage by not seeing [the document] and will gain no litigious advantage by seeing it." Curiosity about the contents of a document, as Sir Thomas Bingham added, was of no importance. The expressions "adversely affects his own case" and "support another party's case" in the rule can be applied in the light of that.

4.29 The new rules were designed to limit expense on disclosure and extensive enquiry; further rules are now under review to save over-enquiry, especially in relation to electronic documents. The proportionality aspect of the overriding objective was intended to support this. The same principle will be applied in family proceedings but will be balanced against the need to secure disclosure in that minority of cases where a party seeks to deny the existence of or to hide assets, and to hide relevant information and documents about those assets.

4.30 Disclosure must be seen in the light of the various attempts by the President of the Family Division and the rule-makers to limit court bundles, which might be though also to limit disclosure. This is considered below.

Documents in a party's control

4.31 Disclosure is limited to documents in a party's possession or control. CPR 1998 r 31.8 defines 'documents ... in a party's control' as follows:

> **31.8 Duty of disclosure limited to documents which are or have been in a party's control**
>
> (1) A party's duty to disclose documents is limited to documents which are or have been in his control.
>
> (2) For this purpose a party has or has had a document in his control if –
>
> (a) it is or was in his physical possession;
>
> (b) he has or has had a right to possession of it; or
>
> (c) he has or has had a right to inspect or take copies of it.

4.32 The meaning of 'control' in this context and in the comparable context of the enforcement provisions of CPR 1998 r 71.2[36] were considered by the Court of Appeal in *North Shore Ventures Ltd v Anstead Holdings Inc.*[37] The defendants had borrowed around $50 million from the claimants (NSV, respondents to the appeal). The loan was guaranteed by the appellants, F and P. NSV secured a judgment against F and P for around $20 million. An order for production of documents was

36 That a debtor can be ordered to attend court and to produce there 'documents in his control which are described in the [court's] order' (CPR 1998 r 71.2(6)(b)). FPR 2010 r 33.23 applies CPR 1998 Pt 71 to family proceedings.

37 [2012] EWCA Civ 11.

made against them, including a variety of documents which related to trusts set up by each of them for the benefit of their respective families. The court was told that the appellants had not kept copies of the documents. The judge doubted this;[38] and the Court of Appeal was suspicious of the way the trusts had been set up and the reason for their creation.[39]

4.33 But was this sufficient for the court to say the appellants had 'control' of the trust documents; or, more generally, would it be sufficient to say that documents in the physical possession of a third party are still under the 'control' of a party to proceedings? This will depend on what is, as a matter of fact, 'the true nature of the relationship' between the third party and the party in the proceedings. In *North Shore Ventures Ltd v Anstead Holdings Inc*,[40] Toulson LJ explained this as follows:

> [40] ... In determining whether documents in the physical possession of a third party are in a litigant's control for the purposes of CPR 31.8, the court must have regard to the true nature of the relationship between the third party and the litigant ... Even if there were on a strict legal view no "right to possession", for example, because the parties to the arrangement caused the documents to be held in a jurisdiction whose laws would preclude the physical possessor from handing them over to the party at whose behest he was truly acting, it would be open to the English court in such circumstances to find that as a matter of fact the documents were nevertheless within the control of that party within the meaning of CPR 31.8(1). CPR 31.8(2) states that for the purpose of CPR 31.8(1) a party has or has had a document in his control if the case falls within paragraphs (a) to (c). It does not state that a party has or has had a document in his control if *but only if* the case falls within one of those paragraphs.

Right to possession

4.34 Toulson LJ took a similar view of the 'right to possession' provision in CPR 1998 r 31.8(2)(b). Documents may be in the actual possession of an employee or professional person (eg, solicitor or accountant of the litigant); but for the purposes of production the position would be the same as if the litigant had actual physical possession:

> [40] ... The concept of "right to possession" in CPR 31.8(2)(b) covers a situation where a third party is in possession of documents as agent for a litigant. The same would apply in my view if the true nature of the relationship was that the litigant was to be the puppet master in the handling of money entrusted to him for the specific purpose

38 Quoted by Toulson LJ at [20]: '[22] ... But I think [counsel for NSV] is right that in practice if such an order is made it is reasonable to suppose that Mr Fomichev and Mr Peganov will be able to comply with it. I am told that the beneficiaries of the trust are their wives and their children. If that is the position, then it seems to me to be wholly unrealistic to suppose that if Mr Fomichev does not keep copies of these documents himself then there is no way in which he would be able to obtain copies.'

39 See eg, per Toulson LJ at [38].

40 [2012] EWCA Civ 11.

of defeating the claim of a creditor. The situation would be akin to agency.

4.35 Where a party has the right, or by custom is able, to copy documents of a third party, such as a company of which he is a director, these would be disclosable and can be ordered to be produced. For reasons of confidentiality there is a possibility that they might be exempt from inspection; though the court can make an order which restricts or prohibits use of any documents which are disclosed.[41]

Sole ownership: fact specific; 'reasonable search'

4.36 In *North Shore Ventures Ltd v Anstead Holdings Inc*,[42] Toulson LJ was unwilling to provide a general definition of when an order for production might be made where documents were not in the physical possession of a party, but where that party might be said to have 'control', de facto possession, or where a party is treated as a 'one-man company'. Each case is fact specific:

> [35] If one asks the question what "different considerations" may apply in the case of the one-man company, the answer lies in the fact that a person with such domination over a company has or is likely to have the real say whether to produce the document. To obtain the "consent" of the company requires obtaining the consent of himself and no one else ...[43]
>
> [37] Whether Floyd J had jurisdiction to make the order which he did in this case depends on what conclusion he was properly entitled to draw on the material before him as to the true nature of the relationship between the appellants and the trustees. In paragraph 22 of his judgment he referred to the relationship between the appellants and the beneficiaries of the trust, i.e. their wives and their children, but the way in which North Shore put its application was wider than that.

4.37 In providing standard disclosure it is required of parties that they conduct a 'reasonable search for documents falling within r 31.6(b) and (c)',[44] unless to do so would be 'unreasonable'.[45] What is a 'reasonable search' is defined in terms of proportionality: the complexity of the case; the expense of retrieval and the 'significance' of any document likely to be found.[46]

---

41 CPR 1998 r 31.22(2) (and cf the former implied undertaking as to confidentiality.

42 [2012] EWCA Civ 11.

43 For example, as Toulson LJ points out in *North Shore Ventures Ltd v Anstead Holdings Inc* at para [29] that the owner of a one-man company could have control of documents, and that in *Lohnro v Shell* [1980] 1 QB 358 at 371 Lord Denning MR emphasised that, though each case depended on its own facts: '... A great deal depends on the facts of each individual case. For instance, take the case of a one-man company, where one man is the shareholder – perhaps holding 99% of the shares, and his wife holding 1% – where perhaps he is the sole director. In those circumstances, his control over that company may be so complete – his "power" over it so complete – that it is his alter ego ...'

44 CPR 1998 r 31.7(1).

45 Ibid, r 31.7(3).

46 Ibid, r 31.7(2).

Disclosure and non-parties

4.38 In Chapter 11, Part 2 the extent to which these rules in CPR 1998 as to specific disclosure may be applicable in cases where non-parties are required by statute, namely the Senior Courts Act 1981 section 34(2),[47] to produce documents into family proceedings (especially by police into care proceedings).

5 DURATION OF DISCLOSURE

Duty of disclosure: from when does the duty run?

4.39 In family proceedings, at what pointdoes the duty of disclosure arise? The answer is not as clear as it might be in civil litigation generally. The answer seems to depend on the type of proceedings (financial relief or other cases) and for how long they continue.

4.40 In this Part the subject of how long the duty of disclosure continues will be considered in three contexts:

(1) proceedings settled after mediation or other forms of negotiation (eg, assisted by lawyers);

(2) matrimonial financial relief cases where proceedings are issued under FPR 2010 Part 9; and

(3) proceedings which continue to appeal.

Duty of disclosure: financial relief, mediation and settlement

4.41 The common law as to the period over which disclosure runes is best explained by the House of Lords in *Livesey (formerly Jenkins) v Jenkins*.[48] In that case, the couple agreed terms and there was a consent order without issue of proceedings. The wife was to receive an outright transfer to her of the couple's former matrimonial home in full settlement of all her financial claims, including for periodical payments for herself. However, she failed to tell her former husband or the court that soon after the transfer she intended to remarry. The House of Lords held that she was under a duty to have done so. This failure lead to their holding that the order should be set aside for lack of material disclosure on the wife's part.

4.42 The extent to which a party must provide disclosure – 'full and frank disclosure' – was put beyond doubt by Lord Brandon in that case:[49]

> ... Unless a court is provided with correct, complete and up-to-date information on the matters to which, under s. 25(1), it is required to have

47 Especially the Senior Courts Act 1981 s 34(2)(a).

48 [1985] AC 424, [1985] FLR 813.

49 [1985] FLR 813 at 823.

> regard, it cannot lawfully or properly exercise its discretion in the manner ordained by that subsection. It follows necessarily from this that each party concerned in claims for financial provision and property adjustment (or other forms of ancillary relief not material in the present case) owes a duty to the court to make full and frank disclosure of all material facts to the other party and the court. This principle of full and frank disclosure in proceedings of this kind has long been recognized and enforced as a matter of practice.

4.43 There is no question but that, in cases which are settled after negotiation, the duty of disclosure arises from the earliest opportunity and continues until the case has settled and a consent order is made.

Disclosure in financial relief proceedings after Imerman

4.44 Meanwhile, in *Imerman v Tchenguiz and ors,*[50] the Court of Appeal considered the parties' position as to disclosure where the parties – as they must do if proceedings are to be issued – follow the procedure now provided for under FPR 2010 Part 9: filing of Form A, Form E and questionnaires. Giving the judgment of the court (himself, Munby and Moses LJJ) Lord Neuberger MR said:

> [33] In relation to these rules we make two general observations. First, that the rules do not provide for any disclosure of information or disclosure (discovery) of documents until a spouse has lodged his Form E. Second, and even more significantly, that the process of disclosure (discovery) of documents both then and thereafter is closely regulated by the rules and, in accordance with the rules, by the court. Although there is a general and continuing duty to make full disclosure of all relevant information, there is, despite the duty imposed on the court by s 25 of the 1973 Act, no duty of general disclosure (discovery) of documents of the kind required in ordinary civil proceedings by the CPR ...

4.45 As can be seen the court did not reflect on what may be the common law position, apart from FPR 2010 Part 9 or where parties settle financial issues in mediation or following negotiations between solicitors. They asserted that 'no duty of general disclosure' arose as under CPR 1998 until at the appropriate time under the Part 9 procedure. This assertion is based on what the rule-makers say, not on what the common law provides.

4.46 On this logic, if a case is settled, a consent order drafted (but not filed) and then further facts are disclosed which render the agreement unsatisfactory to one party, the consent order becomes redundant. The dissatisfied party files Form A to start financial relief proceedings. On the logic of *Imerman,* the duty of disclosure, it seems, disappears underground and does not emerge again until five or six months later. This, it is submitted, is unlikely to be the law.

---

50 [2010] EWCA Civ 908, [2011] Fam 116, [2010] 2 FLR 814.

4.47 It can, perhaps, be said that successful mediation, the common law and MCA 1973, section 25 (as explained by Lord Brandon in *Livesey v Jenkins* (above)) all dictate that standard disclosure should take place at as early a stage as reasonably possible. Rules and a court form (ie, Form E) cannot override this requirement. Beyond that, once a duty to disclose has arisen, the further from the crystallisation of that duty to the date when relevant information is discovered unlawfully, the greater the likelihood that the court will order that relevant information be admitted at trail.

4.48 Further, it is trite law that there cannot be settlement of a case, whether in mediation, between lawyers or between the parties themselves without full relevant disclosure; and that if there is not full disclosure any settlement risks becoming unravelled.[51]

Duty of disclosure: until 'proceedings are concluded'

4.49 At common law,[52] the duty of disclosure and of production of documents (where relevant), continues throughout the proceedings. CPR 1998 r 31.11 affirms this as follows:

> **31.11 Duty of disclosure continues during proceedings**
>
> (1) Any duty of disclosure continues until the proceedings are concluded.
>
> (2) If documents to which that duty extends come to a party's notice at any time during the proceedings, he must immediately notify every other party.

4.50 In *Vernon v Bosley (No 2)*,[53] Stuart Smith LJ held that the law is that any duty of disclosure 'continues until the proceedings are concluded'. In late 1996, CPR 1998 r 31.11 was then in draft; but Stuart Smith LJ regarded it as a 'restatement of the law'. In *Livesey v Jenkins* the position in financial relief proceedings and the need to keep the court informed as to up-to-date information was stated by Lord Brandon (as mentioned above) by reference also to MCA 1973 section 25.

4.51 *Vernon v Bosley* emphasises the continuing disclosure principle starkly. Mr Vernon (V) had been involved in lengthy personal injury proceedings in which, it was claimed, his mental health had a substantial effect on his measure of damages. In parallel family proceedings, in which he sought residence orders in respect of his children, he – supported by psychiatric evidence – told the county court that his health had considerably improved. He was represented in each set of proceedings by different lawyers, but each court received evidence from the same psychiatrists: namely medical witnesses who had treated him as well as reported as expert witnesses.

---

51 See *Livesey v Jenkins* (above).

52 *Vernon v Bosley (No 2)* [1999] QB 18, [1998] 1 FLR 304, CA per Stuart Smith LJ at and see *Livesey v Jenkins* (above).

53 [1998] 1 FLR 304; [1996] EWCA Civ 1217.

4.52 The defendant appealed on quantum of damages. On the first appeal hearing the change in the psychiatric evidence was not mentioned by Mr Vernon and his advisers to the defendants or to the Court of Appeal. It was only revealed when a report from the children proceedings came into the possession of counsel for the defendants. The Court of Appeal reheard the appeal. In doing so they admitted fresh evidence from the psychiatrists and permitted one of them to be cross-examined.[54]

4.53 Stuart Smith LJ held that there is a continuing duty to disclose documents and of information.[55] He considered the then draft of CPR 1998 r 31.11 and held it to be restatement of the then existing law:

> Finally, [counsel for Mr Vernon] contrasted the existing [RSC] Ord 24 with Lord Woolf's proposed draft Civil Proceedings Rules, r 7.12 [now CPR r 31.11] of which provides that the duty of standard disclosure continues until the proceedings are concluded. For my part I do not regard this as a change to the existing law but a restatement.

4.54 The judge explained his reasons for reaching this conclusion by the following steps. Emergence of fresh information or documents may, as a matter of fact, alter a party's case; and the court should be made aware of this. Failure to inform the court risks the court being misled as to a party's true case. The court in any event has an inherent power to order disclosure and the provision of further information.[56] Denying the existence of a continuing duty, would result in frequent pre-trial applications for disclosure. This being the case, said Stuart Smith LJ, the duty of continuing disclosure must subsist as follows:

> If there is a continuing obligation to disclose after-acquired documents, up till what point of time does the obligation extend? Clearly in my view it must extend up to the close of the evidence; in most cases where judgment follows shortly afterwards, this in practice will no doubt suffice. But I can see no logical reason to take that as a cut-off point rather than the conclusion of the proceedings, as expressly provided in Lord Woolf's draft rules. If the party to whom discovery of the after-acquired document is disclosed has closed his case, or the evidence as a whole is concluded, he will have to obtain the leave of the judge to recall relevant witnesses or to reopen the case.

54 Stuart Smith LJ explained the admission of further evidence as follows: 'In *Mulholland v Mitchell (by his next friend Hazel Doreen Mitchell)* [1971] AC 666 the House of Lords held that the exercise by the Court of Appeal of its discretion to admit fresh evidence as to matters arising after the date of the trial was largely a matter of discretion and degree. The principle that there should be finality in litigation should be borne in mind and evidence could not be admitted of every change which might have occurred since trial.'

55 See *Livesey v Jenkins* (above).

56 See now CPR 1998 r 3.3 and FPR 2010 r 4.3.

6 BUNDLES

Disclosure and family proceedings

4.55 There follows here a note on court bundles in family proceedings since this has an effect on production of relevant material to the court. A real problem for courts dealing with family cases is that parties treat disclosure in the lay sense: of producing a document for inspection (ie, photocopying all documents which seem relevant to the proceedings). No attempt is made merely to list relevant documents as CPR 1998 Part 31 requires and as FPR 2010 r 21.1(1) appears to require. Court offices and judges are consequently faced with untamed varieties of documents which have not be combed through by the parties to ensure that only though documents are produced at trial which are relevant to the issues, and which – if possible – are the documents which the parties agree together are those which are relevant to the issues for trial (ie, are those which the documents which the court needs to try the issues which the parties agree are those for trial).

4.56 The result of this has been – especially for care proceedings – that Practice Directions which seek to regulate what is to go before the court have been successively issued by the President of the Family Division. FPR 2010, *PD27A*, paragraphs 4 and 5 has been amended with effect from 31 July 2018. Thus, for example, the maximum length of specific documents (eg, statements, skeleton arguments, experts reports) is prescribed (para 5.1) with the result that:

> **5.2A.1 Format of the bundle**
>
> Unless the court has specifically directed otherwise, being satisfied that such direction is necessary to enable the proceedings to be disposed of justly, the bundle (if a paper bundle) shall be contained in one A4 size ring binder or lever arch file limited to no more than 350 sheets of A4 paper and 350 sides of text and (if an electronic bundle) shall be limited to 350 pages of text.

All relevant material before the court

4.57 There is a danger that this direction cuts across the rule of law – touched upon by FPR 2010, *PD27A*, paragraph 4.1[57] – that all relevant evidence

57 The bundle shall contain copies of only those documents which are relevant to the hearing and which it is necessary for the court to read or which will actually be referred to during the hearing. In particular, copies of the following classes of documents must not be included in the bundle unless specifically directed by the court:
(a) correspondence (including letters of instruction to experts);
(b) medical records (including hospital, GP and health visitor records);
(c) bank and credit card statements and other financial records;
(d) notes of contact visits;
(e) foster carer logs;
(f) social services files (with the exception of any assessment being relied on by any of the parties); and
(g) police disclosure.
This does not prevent the inclusion in the bundle of specific documents which it is necessary for the court to read or which will be referred to during the hearing.

(documents, information and other relevant material) must be before a court if it is to make a decision. For example – and in the extreme circumstance created by closed material procedures – Lord Neuberger in *Bank Mellat v Her Majesty's Treasury (No 1)*[58] commented on Lord Dyson's judgment in *Al Rawi & Ors v The Security Service & Ors* [2011] UKSC 34 [2012] AC 531, [2011] 3 WLR 388 (that the common law generally could not create its own procedures (outside CPR 1998 Pt 82) for closed materials) as follows:

> [3] .... Fundamental to any justice system in a modern, democratic society is the principle of natural justice, whose most important aspect is that every party has a right to know the full case against him, and the right to test and challenge that case fully. A closed hearing is therefore even more offensive to fundamental principle than a private hearing. At least a private hearing cannot be said, of itself, to give rise to inequality or even unfairness as between the parties. But that cannot be said of an arrangement where the court can look at evidence or hear arguments on behalf of one party without the other party ("the excluded party") knowing, or being able to test, the contents of that evidence and those arguments ("the closed material"), or even being able to see all the reasons why the court reached its conclusions.

4.58 This goes to the relevance of evidence and a fair trial; but there is no doubt that parties to family proceedings might comply more correctly with disclosure rules if parties were required to exchange lists (rather than produce all their documents onto the court file); and if those lists and the resulting trial bundle could be more scrupulously tested for relevance before a bundle is prepared.

58 [2013] UKSC 38, [2014] AC 700; and see Chapter 14 for closed material procedures.

5

LEGAL ADVICE PRIVILEGE

1 INTRODUCTION

Exclusion of information in court proceedings

5.1 Chapter 4 explained the main legal principles of disclosure in family proceedings. It is a common law principle of all civil litigation that both parties must provide disclosure to each other of all documents and other material relevant to issues before the court. This chapter considers the exceptions to disclosure rules represented by a parties' right to claim legal professional privilege (LPP) for certain forms of documents and other information and the principles on which that right is decided.

5.2 This will involve a review of the legal sources of LPP and its main branch, legal advice privilege (LAP). Chapter 5 will consider the separate sub-branch of LPP, namely litigation privilege (LP). Self-incrimination privilege (Chapter 6 and without prejudice rule immunity (also called 'privilege': see Chapter 7). Each comprise different aspects of what may be excluded from production in court, but which are based on legal principles separate from LPP.

5.3 Privilege is further considered:

- In Chapter 8: in what 'relevant legal context' does LPP apply? When is contact with a lawyer not a 'legal context'?
- In Chapter 9: waiver, or otherwise discarding, of privilege.
- In Chapter 10: the 'iniquity exemption' or the circumstances in which, though advice may be given, LPP did not apply in the first place because of the 'iniquity' of the individuals receiving the advice.
- In Chapter 11: procedural aspects of resolving issues as to the existence of privilege and how these are resolved by the court (FPR 2010 r 21.3).

5.4 This chapter proceeds as follows:

- Part 2 looks at the origins of LPP and especially at its importance to the administration of justice.

- Part 3 explains the fact that LPP enables a party to proceedings to withhold relevant evidence and at how this is explained by the common law, especially the *Derby Magistrates'* case.
- Part 4 considers the 'inception of advice' and the solicitor's retainer, from which time LPP will apply to the dealings of a lawyer and the client.
- Part 5 deals with the variety of ways in which privilege may be waived, or lost; and explains the difference between the two:
  - (a) After an introduction to the subject;
  - (b) The main ways in which privilege may be impliedly waived are discussed;
  - (c) CPR 1998 r 31.14 and what happens when a privileged document is mentioned in a pleading is explained;
  - (d) Partial or conditional loss of privilege, and how it can be redeemed, at common law is discussed;
  - (e) What happens when privileged or confidential documents are passed to family or friends.
  - (f) And, finally in this Part, what happens where privileged documents are released to another party by mistake? The answer is discussed in the light of CPR 1998 r 31.20.
- Part 6 deals with a child's right to privilege and that this must not be overridden by a judge in children proceedings.

2 ORIGIN OF LEGAL PROFESSIONAL PRIVILEGE

Common law and legal professional privilege

5.5 Legal professional privilege is a 'single integral privilege, whose sub-heads are legal advice privilege and litigation privilege'.[1] It prevents communications between a lawyer (solicitor, legal executive and barrister) and client being seen by anyone – especially, in the present context, in court proceedings – save where:

- the client agrees (ie, 'waives' privilege);
- statute otherwise expressly provides (see eg, Police and Criminal Evidence Act 1984 section 10(2) referred to by Lord Goff below[2]);
- the document was 'prepared for, or in connection with, a nefarious purpose'[3] in which case it may also be said that the privilege did not anyway exist in the first place;[4] or

1 Lord Carswell in *Three Rivers District Council and ors v Governor and Company of the Bank of England (No 6)* [2004] UKHL 48, [2004] 3 WLR 1274, HL.

2 See 5.9.

3 *R (Prudential plc and anor) v Special Commissioner of Income Tax* [2013] UKSC 1, [2013] 2 AC 185 per Lord Neuberger at [17].

4 See 'iniquity exemption' in Chapter 10.

- in a small number of instances where privilege is otherwise lost (eg, in a probate case where the validity of a will is contested, an example singled out by Lord Neuberger in the *Prudential* case (below)).

5.6 Circumstances in which LPP may be lost or may be said not to have existed in the first place, are explained in Chapter 10.

Towards a definition

5.7 The concept of LPP (LAP and LP) is derived entirely from the common law.[5] On occasion, attempts have been made by statute to define LAP. For example, the Police and Criminal Evidence Act 1984 section 10(1) describes 'legal privilege' as follows:

(1) ... in this Act "items subject to legal privilege" means—

(a) communications between a professional legal adviser and his client or any person representing his client made in connection with the giving of legal advice to the client;

(b) communications between a professional legal adviser and his client or any person representing his client or between such an adviser or his client or any such representative and any other person made in connection with or in contemplation of legal proceedings and for the purposes of such proceedings; and

(c) items enclosed with or referred to in such communications and made—

(i) in connection with the giving of legal advice; or

(ii) in connection with or in contemplation of legal proceedings and for the purposes of such proceedings,

when they are in the possession of a person who is entitled to possession of them.

5.8 Section 10(1) provides a definition of LAP which has been held authoritatively to be intended to give effect to the common law. Of section 10(1) in *R v Central Criminal Court exp Francis & Francis*[6] Lord Griffiths said:[7]

> The definition [in s 10(1)] corresponds closely with the established common law principles that govern the existence of legal privilege. Section 10(1) sets out the scope of legal privilege in terms that would be instantly recognised by any lawyer as covering the position at common law.

---

5 As explained in *Prudential* (above).
6 [1989] AC 346.
7 Ibid at 384.

5.9 In the same case Lord Goff said:[8]

> If I turn to subsection (1), I find that the words "items subject to legal privilege" are there defined. They relate (consistently with the common law position, to which the subsection must therefore be presumed to be intended to give effect) to (a) certain communications made in connection with the giving of legal advice, (b) certain communications made in relation to legal proceedings, and (c) items enclosed or referred to in such communications and made in connection with the purposes referred to in (a) and (b). It is the making of communications in the specified circumstances (or of enclosures with or references in such communications) which confers legal privilege. Subsection (2) is concerned to negative the legal privilege which would otherwise be so conferred. By far the most likely moment when it would operate to negative such privilege is at the time when the relevant communication is made — which, in the case of a solicitor, will be the time when it comes into his possession, either through delivery to him by his client or by coming into existence in his own office. It follows that, if legal privilege is negatived under section 10(2), this is the point of time when that will occur.

Administration of justice

5.10 The reasons for LPP were made clear judicially in the nineteenth century (though the existence of the privilege had been recognised at least in the sixteenth century[9]). The primary justification for LPP is its importance to the administration of justice: that an individual should have the right (ie, not strictly a 'privilege', but a right) privately to 'make a clean breast' of a matter to a legal adviser (*Anderson v Bank of British Columbia* (1876) 2 Ch D 644), as explained by Sir George Jessel MR at 649:

> The object and meaning of the rule is this: that as, by reason of the complexity and difficulty of our law, litigation can only be properly conducted by professional men ... [That being so it is necessary that a client] should be able to make a clean breast of it to the gentleman whom he consults ...; that he should be able to place unrestricted and unbounded confidence in the professional agent, and that the communications he so makes to him should be kept secret, unless with his consent (for it is his privilege, and not the privilege of the confidential agent), that he should be enabled properly to conduct his litigation. That is the meaning of the rule.

5.11 The privilege is that of the client, not of the lawyer; and only the client (subject to the lawyer's agency on the client's behalf) can waive the privilege. As Bingham LJ said in *Ventouris v Mountain*,[10] the expression 'legal professional privilege' is 'unhappy' in so far as it suggests that the privilege is that of the legal

8 Ibid at 392.

9 A history of the legal professional privilege case law is provided by Lord Taylor in *R v Derby Magistrates' Court exp B* [1995] UKHL 18, [1996] 1 AC 487, [1996] 1 FLR 513.

10 [1991] 1 WLR 607 at 611.

profession. It is 'the client who enjoys the privilege' not his or her lawyer. Lord Hoffmann expressed the point in *R v Special Commissioner and anor exp Morgan Grenfell & Co Ltd* [11] '... if the client chooses to divulge the information, there is nothing the lawyer can do about it'.

A fundamental right

5.12 In *Prudential* (below) Lord Neuberger defined LAP as follows:

> [17] Where legal professional privilege ("LPP") attaches to a communication between a legal adviser and a client, the client is entitled to object to any third party seeing the communication for any purpose, unless (i) the client has agreed or waived its right, (ii) a statute provides that the privilege can be overridden, (iii) the document concerned was prepared for, or in connection with, a nefarious purpose, or (iv) one of a few miscellaneous exceptions applies (eg, in a probate case where the validity of a will is contested) ...
>
> [19] LAP applies to all communications passing between a client and its lawyers, acting in their professional capacity, in connection with the provision of legal advice, i.e. advice which "relates to the rights, liabilities, obligations or remedies of the client either under private law or under public law" – *Three Rivers (No 6)* paragraph [38], per Lord Scott.

5.13 Lord Neuberger continued his judgment by praising the explanation of the 'development and rationale' of LAP[12] provided by Lord Sumption (who was in the minority in the Supreme Court). In *R (Prudential plc and anor) v Special Commissioner of Income Tax*[13] the issue before the court was whether advice on law given by accountants was legal advice such that legal advice privilege applied to it.

5.14 The Supreme Court held that that the privilege was a creature of the common law which that court was not in a position to change; largely because of the uncertainty which such a change might develop were any legal advice, by whomsoever, should be sought to attract advice privilege. That is, only Parliament could alter the definition of LPP. The Court concluded that the question was not whether privilege attached to legal advice; but whether it should attach where legal advice was given other than by lawyers. By a majority they decided that privilege should attach only where legal advice was given by qualified lawyers, and, as specifically sanctioned by statute, to patent attorneys, trade mark agents and licensed conveyancers.[14]

11 [2002] UKHL 21, [2003] 1 AC 563, [2002] 2 WLR 1299 at para [37].

12 Ibid at [115]–[121].

13 [2013] UKSC 1.

14 Per Lord Neuberger at para [35]: '... there are the statutory extensions of LAP to patent attorneys, to trade mark agents and to licensed conveyancers – see respectively s 280 of the Copyright, Designs and Patents Act 1988, s 87 of the Trade Mark Act 1994 (as amended by the Legal Services Act 2007), and s 33 of the Administration of Justice Act 1985.'

Administration of justice

5.15 The rationale for the privilege is that it is an essential component of the administration of justice. In the *Derby Magistrates'* case[15] Lord Taylor asserted that LAP was 'a fundamental condition on which the administration of justice as a whole rests':

> [58] The principle which runs through all these cases, and the many other cases which were cited, is that a man must be able to consult his lawyer in confidence, since otherwise he might hold back half the truth. The client must be sure that what he tells his lawyer in confidence will never be revealed without his consent. Legal professional privilege is thus much more than an ordinary rule of evidence, limited in its application to the facts of a particular case. It is a fundamental condition on which the administration of justice as a whole rests.

5.16 In the same case Lord Nicholls explained the same principle as follows:

> [72] Legal professional privilege is concerned with the interaction between two aspects of the public interest in the administration of justice. The public interest in the efficient working of the legal system requires that people should be able to obtain professional legal advice on their rights and liabilities and obligations. This is desirable for the orderly conduct of everyday affairs. Similarly, people should be able to seek legal advice and assistance in connection with the proper conduct of court proceedings. To this end communications between clients and lawyers must be uninhibited …

Adverse inferences from a claim for privilege

5.17 If LPP is claimed the court may not draw inferences against the party who claims it.[16] The Court of Appeal has re-affirmed this principle, for example, in *Sayers v Clarke Walker (a firm)*[17] in the following terms:

> [16] ... Ever since *Wentworth v Lloyd* (1864) 10 HLC 589 the courts have refused to permit a party to draw adverse inferences from the refusal by the other party to waive privilege in respect of the legal advice he has received. Brooke LJ applied this principle recently in his judgment in *Oxford Gene Technology v Affymetrix Inc* (CAT 23 November 2000: unreported save for a summary in The Times 5 December 2000), with which Aldous and Sedley LJJ agreed ...

15 *R v Derby Magistrates' Court exp B* [1995] UKHL 18, [1996] 1 FLR 513.
16 *Wentworth v Lloyd* (1864) 10 HL Cas 589 at 591–592.
17 [2002] EWCA Civ 910 per Brooke LJ at [16].

3 A RIGHT TO WITHHOLD RELEVANT EVIDENCE

The withholding of relevant evidence: R v Derby Magistrates' Court

5.18 LAP provides an absolute right to confidentiality as between a lawyer and the client. Once the privilege applies it gives the client an absolute right to withhold relevant evidence from any third party or the court. This is so, despite the possibility that the exclusion of privileged, but otherwise relevant, evidence may cause real unfairness to third parties. The *Derby Magistrates'* case (below) provides an example of a case where injustice to third parties may follow where LAP is insisted upon, but despite this, such injustice may be permitted by application of LAP principles.

5.19 In *R v Derby Magistrates' Court exp B,*[18] B, the applicant in the judicial review proceedings, had been charged with the murder of a young girl. He originally told the police he had killed the girl, but later changed his story. He said that his stepfather (S) had killed her. B was tried and acquitted. S was charged with the murder. At his committal for trial,[19] B was called as a prosecution witness. Cross-examined for S he was asked to tell the court the version of events he had given to his solicitors and in his original account of what had taken place. He refused to waive privilege so that the court and the defence would be able to see what he had said to his solicitor.

5.20 On application by S the stipendiary magistrate issued a witness summons requiring B's solicitor to produce all attendance notes and proofs of evidence disclosing B's instructions on the murder charge. (He was not required to reveal the advice given to him by his lawyers.) B applied successfully in judicial review for the witness summons to be quashed. As Lord Millet said later in *B v Auckland District Law Society*:[20] 'The public interest in overriding the privilege [in the *Derby Magistrates'* case] could scarcely have been higher', but LAP was firmly upheld by the House of Lords.

Wasted costs

5.21 In *Medcalf v Weatherill*[21] the question of a defendant's right to claim LAP arose where their leading and junior counsel, acting on instructions, made serious allegations of fraud against the claimant, Mr Medcalf (M), in pleadings, their skeleton argument and at the hearing of the appeal. The Court of Appeal dismissed Weatherill's appeal. M applied for a wasted costs order[22] against the defendants' counsel on the ground that he had drafted pleadings contrary to the Code of Conduct of the Bar, paragraph 606. That Code required a barrister to have

18 [1996] 1 AC 487, [1996] 1 FLR 513.

19 Procedure then was that evidence could be heard by magistrates when they were asked to commit a trial to the Crown Court.

20 *B & ors v Auckland District Law Society (New Zealand)* [2003] UKPC 38, [2003] 2 AC 736.

21 [2002] UKHL 27, [2003] 1 AC 120.

22 Senior Courts Act 1981 s 51(7).

before him or her 'reasonably credible material' which established a prima facie case of fraud; and this could not have been the case in the case of counsel for the defendants against M. The claimant sought to recover the costs of investigating and rebutting the allegations.

5.22 The defendants refused to waive privilege. Consequently, their counsel was unable to place before the court privileged and confidential material which showed exactly what was included in their instructions so as to demonstrate whether or not they had had credible material when they prepared their case. In the absence of the material covered by privilege, the Court of Appeal held that counsel's conduct had been improper and made the wasted costs order applied for by M.

5.23 On the barristers' appeal to the House of Lords and on the issue of LAP, the appeal was allowed. Advocates must be entitled to defend themselves against the making of the orders by placing before the court, without restriction, all material which was relevant to the issue as to whether they had before them 'reasonably credible material' which established a prima facie case of fraud. However, because the defendants claimed their right to advice, privilege counsel had been unable to do this. A wasted costs order should not have been made, unless – proceeding with extreme care – the court could say that it was satisfied that there was nothing that counsel could have said to resist the order if the privileged information had been available. In the absence of the full facts, due to the defendants' refusal to waive privilege, the court was not entitled to speculate and infer that there could not have been any material upon which counsel could have been justified in making the allegations of fraud. The benefit of the doubt should be conceded to the barristers and the wasted costs orders set aside. In the absence of the material covered by privilege, M was unable to recover his costs. He was unable to secure a fair outcome to the case where he had, in all legal respects, been successful.

Legal advice privilege: an absolute right

5.24 Once established, LPP is absolute. It is not a matter judicial discretion as to whether it applies. No judicial balance need be struck. A person has a right to have advice given to them confidentially. That advice and the information on which it is based must kept confidential, unless the confidentiality is waived. In *R v Derby Magistrates' Court exp B*,[23] the absolute nature of the privilege was explained by Lord Taylor as follows:

> [65] But it by no means follows that because a balancing exercise is called for in one class of case [ie public interest immunity], it may also be allowed in another. Legal professional privilege and public interest immunity are as different in their origin as they are in their scope. Putting it another way, if a balancing exercise was ever required in the case of legal professional privilege, it was performed once and for all in the 16th century, and since then has applied across the board in every case, irrespective of the client's individual merits ... It is in the wider

23 [1995] UKHL 18, [1996] 1 FLR 513.

> interests of all those hereafter who might otherwise be deterred from telling the whole truth to their solicitors. For this reason I am of the opinion that no exception should be allowed to the absolute nature of legal professional privilege, once established.

5.25 Once the privilege was established 'a judicial balancing exercise' was out of the question, said Lord Nicholls, in the same case. Any blurring of boundaries could reduce confidence in the soundness of the right:

> [81]: … the prospect of a judicial balancing exercise in this field is illusory, a veritable will-o'-the wisp. That in itself is a sufficient reason for not departing from the established law. Any development in the law needs a sounder base than this. This is of particular importance with legal professional privilege. Confidence in nondisclosure is essential if the privilege is to achieve its raison d'être. If the boundary of the new incursion into the hitherto privileged area is not principled and clear, that confidence cannot exist.

Conflict of public interests

5.26 LAP (like any other form of privilege or immunity) deprives the courts of otherwise relevant evidence. The onus therefore rests on the person who claims the right to prove that it applies (see below). It calls for two public interests to be balanced. First, that an individual should be able to consult a lawyer without fear that the content of any discussion or advice may be passed on by the lawyer (subject to the separate 'iniquity exemption' question). Balanced against that is that justice depends on cases being tried with all relevant evidence before the court.

5.27 In the *Derby Magistrates' case*[24] Lord Nicholls explained the balancing of these principles as follows:

> [LPP] is concerned with the interaction between two aspects of the public interest in the administration of justice. The public interest in the efficient working of the legal system requires that people should be able to obtain professional legal advice on their rights and liabilities and obligations. This is desirable for the orderly conduct of everyday affairs. Similarly, people should be able to seek legal advice and assistance in connection with the proper conduct of court proceedings. To this end communications between clients and lawyers must be uninhibited. But, in practice, candour cannot be expected if disclosure of the contents of communications between client and lawyer may be compelled, to a client's prejudice and contrary to his wishes. That is one aspect of the public interest. It takes the form of according to the client a right, or privilege as it is unhelpfully called, to withhold disclosure of the contents of client-lawyer communications …

24 [1995] UKHL 18, [1996] 1 AC 487, [1996] 1 FLR 513 at [1996] 1 AC 487 at 510.

5.28 However, in relation to the need for all relevant material to be before the court, Lord Nicholls continued:[25]

> The other aspect of the public interest is that all relevant material should be available to courts when deciding cases. Courts should not have to reach decisions in ignorance of the contents of documents or other material which, if disclosed, might well affect the outcome ... Subject to recognised exceptions, communications seeking professional legal advice, whether or not in connection with pending court proceedings, are absolutely and permanently privileged from disclosure even though, in consequence, the communications will not be available in court proceedings in which they might be important evidence.

4 INCEPTION OF ADVICE

Retainer: the starting point

5.29 The solicitor's retainer will be the starting point for a definition of the relevant context for the application of advice privilege. The solicitor's *SRA*[26] *Code of Conduct 2011* at Chapter 1 dealing with 'client care' comes nearest in the code to requiring definition of a retainer. It asserts that the solicitor–client relationship is 'contractual' which carries with it 'legal, as well as conduct, obligations'. This retainer would define the 'legal context' in the narrow sense of precisely what the lawyer had undertaken to do; but not in the wider sense envisaged by Taylor LJ in *Belabel.*[27]

5.30 The retainer will define a narrow view of the lawyer's advice; but advice privilege will often apply to a wider spectrum of the lawyer's work. The nature of the retainer contract was explained in the Court of Appeal (in the context of its termination) by Lord Esher MR in *Underwood, Son v Piper Lewis*:[28]

> When one considers the nature of a common law action, it seems obvious that the law must imply that the contract of the solicitor upon a retainer in the action is an entire contract to conduct the action till the end. When a man goes to a solicitor and instructs him for the purpose of bringing or defending such an action, he does not mean to employ the solicitor to take one step, and then give him fresh instructions to take another step, and so on; he instructs the solicitor as a skilled man to act for him in the action, to take all the necessary steps in it, and to carry it on till the end. If the meaning of the retainer is that the solicitor is to carry on the action to the end, it necessarily follows that the contract of the solicitor is an entire contract – that is, a contract to take all steps which are necessary to bring the action to a conclusion.

25 [1996] 1 AC 487 at 510.
26 Solicitors' Regulation Authority.
27 *Balabel v Air India* [1988] Ch 317, CA; and explained further in Chapter 8.
28 [1894] 2 QB 306 at 309.

5.31 LAP cannot apply to a narrower area of legal context work than that which is defined by the retainer contract; and in practice it may apply to a range of work which is wider than the retainer. It may extend sometimes to advice on factors outside the scope of the immediate issue for which the solicitor or other lawyers are taken on. Though the fact that certain aspects of advice or documents in relation to it are on the solicitor's file and are perhaps outside the original retainer is irrelevant. In the wider frame, the 'context' in which the assistance is given by the lawyer is what is likely to define the scope of the work to which privilege will apply.

5.32 A document, once covered by confidentiality in the context of a solicitor/client relationship, remains confidential for all time, subject to that confidentiality being waived or lost in some other way.[29] The same applies with even more force to documents covered by privilege which come under the general rule which arises in connection with a solicitor's client confidentiality: that the confidence continues indefinitely whilst there remains scope for conflict[30] unless the client agrees not to rely upon it.

5 WAIVER AND LOSS OF PRIVILEGE

Introduction

Loss of legal professional privilege

5.33 In this Part it will be important to distinguish between where privilege is waived (the first section of this Part), and where it is lost but not gone for ever (the privilege cat may be out of the bag, but it can be put back in again, and it can this be revived or retained[31]). This aspect of LPP will be explained in the latter part below.

5.34 In *Prudential*, Lord Neuberger defined, in broad terms and as set out above, the circumstances in which LPP may be lost.[32] Further, the court may find[33] that privilege was wrongly claimed in the first place[34] or that what is said by the person who claims to be privileged is not covered by any privilege at all.[35] The court may even find proceedings to be non-adversarial and that therefore LPP, as litigation privilege, does not apply at all.[36]

29 See Chapters 8 and 9.
30 *Bolkiah v KPMG* [1998] UKHL 52, [1999] 2 AC 222.
31 *B & ors v Auckland District Law Society (New Zealand)* [2003] UKPC 38, [2003] 2 AC 736; see 5.61 et seq.
32 See 5.12.
33 Application to test whether privilege applies is by CPR 1998 r 31.19.
34 *Waugh v British Railways Board* [1980] AC 521 (see Chapter 6).
35 *Parry-Jones v Law Society* [1969] 1 Ch 1, [1968] 2 WLR 397, CA per Diplock LJ.
36 *Re L (Police Investigation: Privilege)* [1997] AC 16, [1996] 1 FLR 731.

5.35 To balance questions of waiver or loss of privilege, the words of Lord Taylor in the *Derby Magistrates'* case[37] must be borne in mind throughout all that follows in this Part:

> ... a document protected by privilege continues to be protected so long as the privilege is not waived by the client: once privileged, always privileged ... the privilege is the same whether the documents are sought for the purpose of civil or criminal proceedings, and whether by the prosecution or the defence, and that the refusal of the client to waive his privilege, for whatever reason, or for no reason, cannot be questioned or investigated by the court.

5.36 Privilege may be waived for a limited purpose.[38] As part of a mediation or collaborative law process it would be possible to release documents and to waive privilege only in respect of those documents and for the purpose of mediation. The documents, if covered by LPP, would be withdrawn if the mediation or collaborative law process failed; and no party could then refer to the documents or other information in them in subsequent court proceedings.

Loss of confidentiality

5.37 A pre-requisite of a claim for LPP is that the document or information is confidential.[39] Lord Bingham CJ explained the requirement for confidentiality in *Paragon Finance v Freshfields*[40] as follows:

> The nature and basis of legal professional privilege have been often and authoritatively expounded, most recently in *R v Derby Magistrates' Court exp B*. At its root lies the obligation of confidence which a legal adviser owes to his client in relation to any confidential professional communication passing between them.
>
> If the document loses its confidentiality it cannot be covered by privilege. It is therefore necessary to summarise the law on loss of confidentiality in this context.

Loss of privilege

5.38 Loss of privilege will now be considered in the following contexts in the remaining sections of this Part:

- Waiver of privilege and implied waiver: section (2).
- Document covered by privilege mentioned in a court document (including in an expert's report): section (3).

---

37 *R v Derby Magistrates' Court exp B* [1995] UKHL 18, [1996] 1 AC 487 at 503.

38 *B & ors v Auckland District Law Society (New Zealand)* [2003] UKPC 38, [2003] 2 AC 736.

39 For consideration of confidentiality and a definition in *Attorney-General v Guardian Newspapers Ltd (No 2)* [1988] UKHL 6, [1990] 1 AC 109, [1987] 1 WLR 776 (*Spycatcher* case) at 3.7.

40 [1999] 1 WLR 1183 at 1188.

- Partial or conditional waiver: section (4)
- Disclosure of privileged information to family or friends: section (5)
- Disclosure by mistake: section (6)

Waiver and implied waiver

Waiver of legal professional privilege

5.39 It is the client only, not that client's lawyer (save as agent with implied authority of the client) who can waive privilege. Waiver may be intentional or it may occur impliedly. Express waiver may also be partial or conditional. Where waiver is intended (ie, express waiver) it will normally be clear and little further comment is needed here.

5.40 Thus, waiver can only be by the beneficiary of the privilege, namely the client. However, the implied authority accorded to solicitors and counsel in the conduct of litigation on a client's behalf extends to the waiver of privilege.[41] It may be appropriate, for example, for a solicitor to set out to the solicitor for the other party what that solicitor's client has been advised in the context of a case. Save where this is done in the course of 'without prejudice' correspondence or mediation, privilege will be waived in respect of that advice. Reference to part only of advice contains its own hazards explained below.[42]

5.41 Privilege is lost where a document or information is deliberately released by the person entitled to the privilege to an opponent in litigation; or the document or information is otherwise intentionally made public by him or her. If a document is deliberately released, then privilege will only be lost if the intention was to waive privilege. If the document was released to a jointly instructed expert with the expressed intent that the expert prepares a report, the privilege will generally remain with the party entitled to it, even if the document is passed on to the other party by the expert.

Implied waiver

5.42 Implied waiver may occur where a party refers to or otherwise specifically relies upon a document otherwise covered by privilege but does not produce the original in the course of proceedings. This could happen, for example, where an advocate cross-examines by specific reference to a specialist's report; but the report is neither produced in court nor included in the court bundle. In each case a material document is relied upon as to part of it, at a final hearing by one party, but is not produced in evidence. The same could happen where a party refers to the advice of counsel to bolster their case. Privilege would be lost in the case of

41 See eg, Lord Denning MR in *Causton v Mann Egerton (Johnsons) Ltd* [1974] 1 WLR 162 at 167.
42 See 5.42.

each document. (This example of waiver is separate from that which applies where a document is mentioned in statement of case. This is dealt with in section (3).)

5.43 In *Re D (A Child)*[43] a mother in care proceedings had included in her statement, prepared by solicitors, reference to notes she had prepared during meetings with her solicitor and counsel, in which she wrote down what she said had happened to the couple's child. In particular, this note explained a substantial change in her evidence, showing a 'paradigm shift' in her evidence between what she had said initially and what she said later and after she and the father of the child had separated. She exhibited the note but no more information as to the interview to her statement. His Honour Judge Barnett, the judge case managing the care proceedings, ordered disclosure of hitherto privileged documents in the following terms, said Ward LJ:

> [8] ... that the mother should serve all contemporaneous notes made by counsel during the conferences with the mother and all contemporaneous notes which were made by her solicitor during their meetings [dates provided], such disclosure to include any notes made by her solicitor during the conferences with counsel.

5.44 Ward LJ started from the premise that conferences between a client and counsel and solicitors are confidential and that consequently they attract LPP:

> [12] ... This confers on the client a substantive absolute right of fundamental importance to the administration of justice as a whole. It can only be waived by the person, the client, entitled to it. Whereas litigation privilege may have no part to play in proceedings under the Children Act 1989,[[44]] legal professional privilege is as applicable to these proceedings as it is to ordinary civil or criminal proceedings.

5.45 The question which then arose was whether privilege in *Re D* had been impliedly waived by the mother. Implied privilege raised questions of fairness as between the parties. A court, confronted with an application to imply that privilege had been waived, must balance any breach of the confidentiality of the party entitled to it against what was fair to the applicant for its breach. Ward LJ summarised the question as follows:

> [23] ... The undesirability of breaching confidentiality must be balanced against the unfairness to the father if the cloak that ordinarily concealed the discussions with her lawyers was not lifted.

Fairness and implied waiver

5.46 Elias LJ sat with Ward LJ (and Rimer LJ) in *Re D*, and Ward LJ referred to a decision of Elias LJ to emphasise the fairness point:

43 [2011] EWCA Civ 684, [2011] 2 FLR 1183.

44 *Re L (Police Investigation: Privilege)* [1997] AC 16, [1996] 1 FLR 731; and see 6.18.

> [19] [This] appeal turns on the 'fundamental question', as my Lord, then Elias J, expressed it in *Brennan v Sunderland City Council* [45]: 'whether, in the light of what has been disclosed and the context in which disclosure has occurred, it would be unfair to allow the party making disclosure not to reveal the whole of the relevant information because it would risk the court and the other party only having a partial and potentially misleading understanding of the material.'

5.47 The judge, faced with an application to find that privilege has been impliedly waived, must decide on the facts of an individual case whether it would be unfair to the applicant for production not to order it in respect of documents otherwise covered by legal professional privilege. Ward LJ explained this further in *Re D*:

> [13] Fairness lies at the heart of waiver and its consequences. It mattered not whether the mother intended to waive privilege: viewed objectively she clearly did so in respect of the matters contained in her statement of 23 February. As the judge eloquently put it: 'She need not have mentioned anything beyond the fact that conferences were held on particular dates. However, not only has the mother taken the other parties and the Court to the doors of the conference room, she has taken the reader of her statement into that room. And the journey has been undertaken more than once.'
>
> [14] For the judge the real issue was, therefore, whether as a consequence of that waiver, the application of the principle of fairness demanded disclosure of the material which the father sought so as to prevent the court and the party's adversary being given only a partial picture: the court should not allow cherry picking.
>
> [15] In my paraphrase of his conclusion, he held that fairness did inevitably lead to the need for full disclosure because without producing the whole pie, it would be impossible to decide whether or not the mother, cornered as she was, had simply behaved like little Jack Horner, pulled out a plum, and said, 'What a good girl am I' …

5.48 So, said Ward LJ, the only fair way to meet the father's concern in the particular case was to order production as had been ordered by the judge so that the change of the mother's account could be explained:

> [15] … Having an unexpurgated account of how the witness statement evolved was the only fair way to meet the father's concern that the mother may have been led by her lawyers into saying things to please them.

Practice: warning for parties against implied waiver

5.49 Ward LJ ended with a direction as to practice, both for lawyers and for judges, to guard against privilege being waived in statements or in evidence at trial. First, for lawyers:

45 [2009] ICR 479 at [63].

[24] ... Counsel and solicitors will be aware (or ought to be aware) of the fact that advice may have been given to prompt the change of heart or change of attitude and they should be on guard to protect their client from revealing that advice either in the written evidence or when giving oral evidence to the court ...

5.50 And for judges:

[24] ... Judges must also be astute to anticipate an unintentional observation which results in privilege being waived and must be ready to warn a witness of any such danger ...

Professional negligence and waiver

5.51 An aspect of implied waiver which will be touched on only here is the rule that where a former client sues that client's solicitor or barrister the client waives privilege. In *Lillicrap v Nalder & Son*,[46] this was explained by Dillon LJ as follows:[47]

... A client who sues his solicitor invites the court to adjudicate the dispute and thereby in my judgment, waives privilege and confidence to the extent that is necessary to enable the court to do so fully and fairly in accordance with the law including the law of evidence ...

5.52 In *Paragon Finance plc v Freshfields*[48] Lord Bingham CJ (with Brooke and Chadwick LJJ) gave the judgment of the court. He explained the rationale for the waiver. The public nature of the proceedings means that by starting proceedings the client relieves the lawyer from duties of confidence.[49] However, the client may not pick and choose which confidential documents to rely on and which to keep 'from forensic scrutiny':

When a client sues a solicitor who has formerly acted for him, complaining that the solicitor has acted negligently, he invites the court to adjudicate on questions directly arising from the confidential relationship which formerly subsisted between them. Since court proceedings are public, the client brings that formerly confidential relationship into the public domain. He thereby waives any right to claim the protection of [LPP] in relation to any communication between them so far as necessary for the just determination of his claim; or, putting the same proposition in different terms, he releases the solicitor to that extent from the obligation of confidence by which he was formerly bound. This is an implication of law, the rationale of which is plain. A party cannot deliberately subject a relationship to public scrutiny

46 [1993] 1 WLR 94, CA (alleged negligence arising from a conveyancing transaction, where solicitors wished to rely – and were permitted by the Court of Appeal to do so – on other files where they had acted for the particular clients).

47 Ibid at 99 considered in *Paragon* below at 1189.

48 [1999] 1 WLR 1183, CA (where lawyers were sued, waiver did not extend to the files of the solicitors who replaced them and concluded the action on behalf of the original solicitors).

49 Ibid at 1188.

and at the same time seek to preserve its confidentiality ... He cannot attack his former solicitor and deny the solicitor the use of materials relevant to his defence.

Mention of a privileged document in court documents

Documents mentioned in pleadings

5.53 Under the heading 'Documents referred to in statements of case etc', CPR 1998 r 31.14 provides as follows:

(1) A party may inspect a document mentioned in –

(a) a statement of case;

(b) a witness statement;

(c) a witness summary; or

(d) an affidavit[GL] ...

(2) Subject to rule 35.10(4), a party may apply for an order for inspection of any document mentioned in an expert's report which has not already been disclosed in the proceedings.

(Rule 35.10(4) makes provision in relation to instructions referred to in an expert's report.)

5.54 In a rule which deals with the contents of an expert's report, CPR 1998 r 35.10(4) provides as follows:

(4) The instructions referred to in paragraph (3)[50] shall not be privileged[GL] against disclosure but the court will not, in relation to those instructions –

(a) order disclosure of any specific document; or

(b) permit any questioning in court, other than by the party who instructed the expert,

unless it is satisfied that there are reasonable grounds to consider the statement of instructions given under paragraph (3) to be inaccurate or incomplete.

5.55 There is no equivalent to CPR 1998 r 31.14 in FPR 2010, so the applicability of CPR 1998 Pt 31 to family proceedings applies here.[51] FPR 2010 r 25.14 (which deals with the contents of an expert's report) is limited to the assertion that the instructions to an expert are not privileged from disclosure. The matters which arise from the remainder of CPR 1998 r 35.10(4) are not specifically dealt with in FPR 2010.

50 CPR 1998 r 35.10(3) states: '(3) The expert's report must state the substance of all material instructions, whether written or oral, on the basis of which the report was written.'

51 As explained in Chapter 4.

Mention of document covered by privilege

5.56 Rule 31.14 refers only to the mention of a document in a statement of case etc, without specific reference to the confidential – or otherwise – status of the document mentioned. There is no question but that mention of a document covered by privilege (eg, an expert's report which is not intended to be disclosed, counsel's opinion or other evidence of legal advice) will raise questions as to whether it should be produced for inspection and therefore whether privilege has been waived.

5.57 This issue was considered *obiter* in *Lucas v Barking, Havering and Redbridge Hospitals NHS Trust.*[52] There Waller LJ suggested that the right to inspect may need to be read in conjunction with rules in relation to the right to inspect in CPR 1998 r 31.3 and 31.15 (right to inspect documents: also not reproduced in express terms in FPR 2010); in particular in connection with r 31.3(1)(b) which gives a party a right to object to inspection on grounds that although the existence of a document must be disclosed, that party 'has a right [to claim] a right or a duty to withhold inspection of'[53] the document. Waller LJ explained his view as follows:

> [25] It is possible that on a proper construction of CPR 31.15 there is a right to refuse inspection on the grounds of privilege even if documents are referred to in a statement of case, a witness statement, a witness summary or an affidavit. CPR 31.15 appears in broad terms to refer to a party's right to inspect without any right to refuse so to do but in parenthesis at the end of the rule it says: "(Rules 31.3. and 31.14 deal with the right of party to inspect documents.) By bringing in CPR 31.3 at that stage it is possible that the draughtsmen contemplated that a party may be able to refuse disclosure on the grounds that it has "a right" to do so under CPR 31.3(1)(b) allowing for the matter then to be argued out as to whether reference to the document or deployment of its contents has waived privilege."

5.58 Application of the principles in CPR 1998 rr 31.3, 31.14 and 31.15 was not specifically alluded to in *Re D*; but Waller LJ's point was dealt with, in effect, by Ward LJ in that later case.

Partial or conditional loss of privilege

Conditional loss of legal professional privilege

5.59 LPP may be dispensed with conditionally and for restricted purposes or in relation to particular documents. This is not a waiver but temporary or conditional loss of privilege. Only the person entitled to the privilege can dispense with it and thus cause it to be waived in this way. For example, in the course of mediation or the collaborative law process a party may refer to advice on valuation which

52 [2003] EWCA Civ 1102, [2003] 1 WLR 220.

53 The claim to withhold inspection is dealt with in CPR 1998 r 31.19 and is dealt with in similar terms in FPR 2010 r 21.3 (see 11.37).

has been received, but only for the purposes of alternative dispute resolution. If this fails, information discussed or any document seen in mediation cannot be mentioned in court. The valuation would be covered by litigation privilege and that privilege will revive as explained below. Normally the conditional dispensing with privilege will be in express terms; though it can be implied by the actions of the person entitled to it (eg, because information was discussed only in mediation).

5.60 Similarly, an applicant for legal aid might send documents or statements which are subject to LPP. For the limited purposes of the application for legal aid and their reference to the Legal Aid Agency privilege in the documents might be said to be lost. Any privilege would only be lost conditionally and for the legal aid application, not for any other purpose (eg, for any of the documents to be sent to another government department).[54] As between the client and the Legal Aid Agency the client's 'cat can be put back in the bag'.[55]

B v Auckland District Law Society

5.61 Conditional loss of LPP occurred in *B & Ors v Auckland District Law Society (New Zealand)*.[56] In that case the Privy Council considered a claim by New Zealand solicitors concerning documents which they had released by them to leading counsel for their law society, for the purposes of an inquiry by the society. Privilege in the documents remained with the solicitors' clients (for legal advice to particular clients). The clients agreed that the documents could be produced on terms that (as they wrote to their law society): 'privilege is not waived, and that the documents will not be further copied by [counsel for the Law Society].'

5.62 The arrangement broke down when the law society's original counsel had to hand over the inquiry to another barrister and that barrister did not agree to the same terms as to privilege. The judge at first instance agreed that the documents were privileged, the New Zealand Court of Appeal disagreed by a majority. The Privy Council restored the judge's original order.

5.63 Lord Millet explained the Board's view of privilege where it had been dispensed with on a conditional basis. Privilege was not waived; but could it be said that it was 'lost' (see italicised words in paragraph [68] below)? Lord Millet considered that it could not be completely lost, even though documents had been released wholesale to the Auckland Law Society and their original counsel:

> [68] The Society's argument, put colloquially, is that privilege entitles one to refuse to let the cat out of the bag; once it is out of the bag, however, privilege cannot help to put it back. Their Lordships observe that this arises from the nature of privilege; it has nothing to do with waiver. It does not follow that privilege is waived generally because a privileged document has been disclosed for a limited purpose only:

54 See eg, *R v Snaresbrook Crown Court ex p Director of Public Prosecutions* [1988] 1 QB 532.
55 See per Lord Millet in *B & ors v Auckland District Law Society (New Zealand)* [2003] UKPC 38, [2003] 2 AC 736 at [69], cited at 5.64.
56 [2003] UKPC 38, [2003] 2 AC 736.

> see *British Coal Corporation v Dennis Rye Ltd (No 2)* [1988] 1 WLR 1113: *Bourns v Raychem Corporation* [1999] 3 All ER 154. *The question is not whether privilege has been waived, but whether it has been lost* [emphasis added]. It would be unfortunate if it were. It must often be in the interests of the administration of justice that a partial or limited waiver of privilege should be made by a party who would not contemplate anything which might cause privilege to be lost, and it would be most undesirable if the law could not accommodate it.

5.64 As Lord Millet then explained, the result of the conditional release of the papers was that they were the same documents and the protection of privilege still applied to them:

> [69] The Society argued that, once the documents were produced to [their counsel], they ceased to be privileged. Their Lordships consider that this is playing with words. It confuses the nature of the documents with the rights to which the arrangements with [counsel] gave rise. The documents are privileged because they were created for the purpose of giving or receiving legal advice. If they are not produced voluntarily, production cannot be compelled. If they are produced voluntarily, the right to withhold production no longer attaches to them. In that sense the privilege may be said to be lost. But they are the same documents, and it is not inappropriate to describe them as privileged. Their inherent characteristics are the same. The policy which protected them from unauthorised disclosure is the same. The cat is still a cat. It can be put back in the bag.

5.65 It is the nature of the documents and the reason for their being created which creates the privilege, not the fact that they have been released on terms which the recipient of the documents seeks later to alter. The valuation referred to in mediation or the report read and discussed in (say) collaborative law is still the same information or report; if mediation fails, the privilege which relates to it remains. The document or other information discussed in alternative dispute resolution can be 'put back in the [privilege] bag' if court proceedings resume.

Privileged information passed to family or friends

Confidences between husband and wife and others living together

5.66 In *Imerman v Tchenguiz and ors,*[57] Lord Neuberger MR, giving the judgment of the court (with Moses and Munby LJJ) explained the court's view of confidentiality as between a husband and wife, when they are living together as a couple, as follows:

> [82] The notion that a husband cannot enjoy rights of confidence as against his wife in respect of information which would otherwise be confidential as against her if they were not married, seems to us to

57 [2010] EWCA Civ 908, [2010] 2 FLR 814.

be simply unsustainable. The idea that a husband and a wife should be regarded as a single unit in law was a fiction which the law has been abandoning for a long time. Thus, more than two centuries ago, in *Barwell v Brooks* (1784) 3 Doug 371, page 373, Lord Mansfield CJ said that "[t]he fashion of the times has introduced an alteration, and now husband and wife may, for many purposes, be separated, and possess separate property, a practice unknown to the old law." ...

[84] So, and not least in relation to financial matters, English law recognises that although marriage may be a partnership of equals there is nonetheless a sphere in which each spouse has, within and as part of the marriage, a life separate and distinct from the shared matrimonial life. This, after all, is what one would expect. It is, moreover, implicit in the protection which article 8 affords each spouse in relation to his or her personal and individual private life, in contrast to their shared family life.

5.67 Though each case depended on its individual facts, in principle at least there was no reason why the same rules as to confidentiality should not apply as between husband and wife, as between any other two individuals living together. In turn, the nature of confidentiality between them would depend on their relationship:

[88] The question must, inevitably, depend on the facts of the particular case. Thus, if a husband leaves his bank statement lying around open in the matrimonial home, in the kitchen, living room or marital bedroom, it may well lose its confidential character as against his wife. The court may have to consider the nature of the relationship and the way the parties lived, and conducted their personal and business affairs. Thus, if the parties each had their own study, it would be less likely that the wife could copy the statement without infringing the husband's confidence if it had been left by him in his study rather than in the marital bedroom, and the wife's case would be weaker if the statement was kept in a drawer in his desk and weaker still if kept locked in his desk. But, as we have already said, confidentiality is not dependent upon locks and keys. Thus the wife might well be able to maintain, as against her husband, the confidentiality of her personal diary or journal, even though it was kept visible and unlocked on her dressing table.

[89] But it is important to emphasise that the relationship between the parties and the circumstances in which the information or document is obtained is relevant only to the question as to whether the information or document is to be cloaked with confidentiality. Once it is determined that the document is properly to be regarded as confidential to one spouse but not to the other, the relationship has no further relevance in relation to the remedy for breach of that confidentiality.

5.68 The same principles would apply as between husband and wife or cohabitants in respect of information or documents covered also by [LPP]. The question then must be: does the sharing of documents covered by [LPP] as between husband and wife, or man and woman, or two partners living together, create a waiver of privilege while they are married or cohabiting which is lost if they separate or otherwise become involved in negotiations for separation? No thought will have been given to the point whilst the couple are together, but if they separate, the issue may arise (eg, if legal advice[58] has been given to one spouse as to estate-planning or on other tax-avoidance this will be covered by legal professional privilege). Does that privilege revive or is it permanently lost?

Production of a privileged document by mistake

Inspection of a privileged document allowed inadvertently

5.69 In modern times and despite judicial efforts, the variety and quantity of documents in individual cases proliferate. This includes electronic documents. It is perhaps inevitable that, from time to time, documents covered by LPP (or which should be withheld under public interest immunity rules) will be released to other parties in litigation where they should have remained undisclosed. What happens to the privilege then?

5.70 There is no rule to cover this in FPR 2010. The common law position can be treated as defined in CPR 1998 Part 31. Under the heading 'Restriction on use of a privileged document inspection of which has been inadvertently allowed' CPR 1998 r 31.20[59] states:

> 31.20 Where a party inadvertently allows a privileged[GL] document to be inspected, the party who has inspected the document may use it or its contents only with the permission of the court.

5.71 Rule 31.20 does not say by whom application for permission of the court should be made; though in practice it has been beneficiaries of the privilege (ie who have allowed documents covered by legal professional privilege to be inspected or released to other parties) who have applied to restrain use of documents disclosed by mistake, rather than the recipients who have applied for permission. Resolution of whether use of documents mistakenly released should be prevented from use or whether they should be inspected and remain available for production.

No rule for return: equitable principles apply

5.72 There is no clear rule that a document produced for inspection by mistake must be returned to the party whose privilege has been breached and that privilege therefore remains lost. Each case depends on its own facts; and equitable principles come into play. The background to the present legal position is informed by the

58 It will be recalled that only legal advice can be behind the veil of privilege (*R (Prudential plc and anor) v Special Commissioner of Income Tax* [2013] UKSC 1; see 5.12); not, eg, valuation advice on planning matters or an accountant's tax advice (though this advice in both cases is likely to be confidential).

59 See Chapter 4 for discussion as to the extent to which CPR 1998 Pt 31 applies to family proceedings.

rule in *Calcraft v Guest*,[60] namely that a party, to whom a document is released mistakenly, can use it in litigation. This is balanced by the rule of equity that the beneficiary of the privilege who has released the document is entitled to apply for the protection of an injunction.

5.73 The grant of an injunction is not guaranteed. Grant of an injunction remains an equitable remedy. Each case is fact specific. In the final analysis, rules in relation to confidentiality will apply; and in that case, public interest may override the stricter rules which would have applied in relation to LPP.[61] This was explained by Lawrence Collins J in *Istil Group Inc & Anor v Zahoor & Ors*: [62]

> [93] … there is nothing in the authorities which would prevent the application of the rule that confidentiality is subject to the public interest. In this context, the emergence of the truth is not of itself a sufficient public interest. The reason why the balancing exercise is not appropriate is because the balance between privilege and truth has already been struck in favour of the former by the establishment of the rules concerning legal professional privilege: see … *R v Derby Magistrates Court, ex parte B* [1996] AC 487 at 508.

5.74 He then went on to explain the effect of iniquity, or fraud, on a plea for relief in equity on grounds of confidentiality. The subject of the iniquity exemption will be dealt with in Chapter 10, where – it may be said – privilege does not, in any event, arise in the first place.

6 PRIVILEGE: CHILDREN AND VULNERABLE INDIVIDUALS

Rights of the child or vulnerable individual

5.75 The rights of a child or other vulnerable individual, as client, are precisely the same as for any adult client. In *Re E (A Child)(Family Proceedings: Evidence)*[63] the Court of Appeal was critical of the way the judge dealt with confidential evidence in the proceedings. The oldest child's solicitor (S) was criticised for failing properly to respect the confidentiality, that is LAP, of the oldest child (A, born in 2001). In the Court of Appeal McFarlane LJ started from the premise that:

> [90] … A, as a party to the proceedings who is represented by his own solicitor, must be entitled to the same protection afforded to all other individuals who undertake communications with their lawyers. No suggestion was made in the hearing of this appeal that any different standard or approach should be taken to A either because he is a child or because he may lack the capacity to instruct his solicitor directly.

60 *Calcraft v Guest* [1898] 1 QB 759, CA.
61 As explained at 10.40.
62 [2003] EWHC 165 (Ch).
63 [2016] EWCA Civ 473, [2017] 1 FLR 1675, [2016] 4 WLR 105.

5.76 McFarlane LJ went on to cite[64] what Lord Taylor had said in *R v Derby Magistrates' Court exp B*[65] as follows:

> The principle which runs through all these cases, and the many other cases which were cited, is that a man must be able to consult his lawyer in confidence, since otherwise he might hold back half the truth. The client must be sure that what he tells his lawyer in confidence will never be revealed without his consent. Legal professional privilege is thus much more than an ordinary rule of evidence, limited in its application to the facts of a particular case. It is a fundamental condition on which the administration of justice as a whole rests.

5.77 The particular meeting with the solicitor occurred in relation to a visit by S and A's guardian and the confidentiality arose in the following way:

> [91] The express purpose of [the visit] was to go through the evidence against him for the purposes of the forthcoming hearing. It is not apparent from the guardian's statement or any other material that we have seen that the question of legal professional privilege was considered or discussed with A. The following day the fact that the visit had occurred was made known to the court and the judge directed the guardian to file a statement giving an account of it. There is no indication that that direction was contested or that the solicitor and guardian expressly purported to waive A's legal professional privilege on his behalf … The result was that the full details of A's meeting with his solicitor to discuss these allegations, such as it was, became fully known to the court.

5.78 McFarlane LJ made a number of criticisms of the interview, but of the LPP aspect he says (continuing at [91]), first:

> [91] … It is obviously most important that, in the case of a vulnerable young person, those who are instructed to act on his behalf where he or she is facing serious factual allegations are utterly clear as to their professional responsibilities and astute to ensure that their young client's rights are properly acknowledged and protected.

Privilege and the child's rights under the European Convention 1950 Article 6

5.79 He then went on to criticise the judge for not having taken account of the extent to which LAP had been breached and how this affected A's rights under Article 6 of the European Convention 1950. He thought the order the judge had made for filing evidence by the guardian as to the meeting with A was 'highly unusual':

> [97] … Whilst the judge may have been correct that the mere formulation of aspects of the existing evidence into a more detailed threshold

64 Ibid at [90].

65 [1995] UKHL 18, [1996] 1 FLR 513.

document was not a breach of A's rights under Article 6, her judgment does not engage with the processes adopted by the social worker, guardian and solicitor in the context of those rights. That this is so is not altogether the fault of the judge, as no party seems to have been aware of that aspect of the case during the hearing. Nevertheless the judge did make an order requiring a party's representative to file a statement setting out what transpired at a meeting expressly established to elicit that party's instructions to his lawyers on serious allegations of abuse. That is a significant and highly unusual order to make and, irrespective of the position of the parties, the judge ought to have questioned the basis of the proposed order and been aware of the need to protect A's Art 6 rights and his entitlement to legal professional privilege.

5.80 Amongst the court's seven numbered reasons for allowing the appeal[66] was: '(v) A's right under ECHR, Article 6 to a fair trial and his right to the protection of legal professional privilege were breached to a substantial degree'. By this route McFarlane LJ brought this aspect of the case back to the administration of justice starting point to which he had referred from Lord Taylor's speech in *R v Derby Magistrates' Court exp B*.[67]

Child's privilege overridden

5.81 It is tempting to wonder whether LPP was merely overridden or overlooked by the court in *Wolverhampton City Council v JA & Ors*.[68] In that case, Keehan J dealt with a care case which involved allegations of sexual abuse of two young girls. They were aged 13 (X) and 12 (Y) at the time of his judgment. The proceedings are continuing. There were a variety of allegations against the children's father and two male friends of the mother dating back nearly ten years. Keehan J summarised his conclusion on the facts he had found during the 17-day hearing that the girls had been subjected to 'sustained and prolonged sexual abuse' over a number of years by their father and the two males (YQ and ZK); to physical abuse by their father; and their immediate family – their mother and maternal grandmother – had failed to protect them ([288]).

5.82 The children were originally represented by a solicitor (SN; though Keehan J ordered that her name should be included in the judgment) and a children's guardian, described only as AB. Keehan J records that ten weeks into the care proceedings they went to see X:

> [173] During the course of this interview X is recorded as having made a number of disclosures relating to her having been sexually abused.
>
> [174] On 6 September 2016 AB and Ms Noel paid a similar visit to Y.
>
> [175] At an advocates' meeting the disclosures made by X in her interview on 30 August were revealed. It became apparent that no referral in respect

66 Ibid at [98].

67 [1995] UKHL 18, [1996] 1 FLR 513; see passage cited at 5.24.

68 [2017] EWFC 62.

of those disclosures had been made to the local authority nor to the police. The advocates' meeting was immediately terminated and an urgent directions hearing was sought before the then allocated judge.

[176] The children's guardian and the children's solicitor were ordered to disclose their notes on both interviews with the children and to file and serve witness statements.

[177] On 30 September 2016 the appointment of the children's guardian and the children's solicitor were terminated and a new guardian and solicitor were appointed for the children ...

Privilege and the advocates' meeting

5.83 The meeting with X arose, explained Keehan J (at [186]), at his request 'to establish X's views about giving evidence'. The solicitor took the lead in the interview (an interview described in detail by the judge at [172]– [212]). AB said, however, that she did not refer the information about sexual abuse from X to the police because SN had said she needed to discuss the matter with the barrister then instructed for the child. AB and SN visited Y a week later.

5.84 The advocates' meeting ([175] above) took place two weeks later. This was attended, it must be assumed, by the barrister for X, retained by SN. On the subject of confidentiality, this series of events raises the following questions:

(1) Confidentiality and advice privilege: Did SN have the authority of both X and Y to pass on information at the advocate's meeting?

(2) LPP: If not, why did SN say anything before she had consulted with her professional body (eg, SRA) as to her duties both to her clients and the court?

(3) Why was the judge asking the solicitor to make inquiries (see [186] referred to above) where the evidence, if it were to be given in court, would be part of the local authority's case?

(4) Was the solicitor warned as to her entitlement to self-incrimination privilege?[69]

5.85 It is not possible to tell from the judgment whether SN had the authority of both of her child clients – explained by her to them in terms which X and Y would understand – to breach their confidentiality; but it seems probable that she did not have such authority. Authority or not, she seems to have breached their confidentiality at the advocates' meeting recorded at paragraph [175] (above). Self-incrimination privilege was not mentioned by the judge when he said what he did at paragraph 1(i) of his order; though it looks as though a warning would have been appropriate.

69 See Chapter 7.

Confidentiality and legal professional privilege

5.86 In contrast with confidentiality, LPP is absolute.[70] The children's guardian is in a quite different position to the lawyer. No question of privilege applies to her, though what she learns from the children is confidential. If information was given to her in confidence by X and Y, she should have explained to them straightaway that she probably could not respect that confidence. Her duty is to the court and to 'safeguard their interests' (CA 1989 s 41(2)(b)). She is bound by the guidance in *Working Together 2018*.[71]

5.87 In the *Wolverhampton* case the judge made an order[72] for the filing of evidence by SN (not dissimilar to the order criticised by the Court of Appeal in *Re E*[73]) and after the advocates' meeting where information was given by or on her behalf to other parties. Keehan J's order was that X and Y's new solicitor:

> 1(i) … shall write to the appropriate manager at [ ] Solicitors informing her that [SN], the former children's solicitor, employed by them is likely to be a witness of fact in these proceedings and is likely to be the subject of criticism as to her professional conduct; …

5.88 What was said by the children to SN, unless the children authorised SN as a lawyer to reveal what was said by them (ie, that they specifically waived privilege) is covered by LAP in exactly the same way as for any adult client assuming that each are *Gillick*-competent.[74] The entitlement of a child to confidentiality and privilege was explained by McFarlane LJ in *Re E* as set out above in paragraph [90] of his judgment.

5.89 The children in each case – A (in *Re E*), and X and Y in the *Wolverhampton* case – are likely to have been of comparable vulnerability and intelligence. All three were entitled to have their views respected. In terms of *Gillick* it is likely that they would be entitled to expect confidentiality and advice privilege. This was certainly accorded to A by McFarlane LJ as his paragraph [90] (above) shows.

5.90 In the *Wolverhampton* case it may be easy to understand the judge's reservations as to SN's interview (see especially [191]–[206]); but the question remains as to whether evidence about that interview should have been before the court in the way it was, unless the children's LAP had been specifically been waived by them. In law and in the absence of a waiver of privilege from X and Y, was the evidence covered by the child's 'absolute right' to LPP (as explained by Lords Taylor and Nicholl in the *Derby Justices'* case) lawfully disclosed to the court? As McFarlane LJ makes clear in *Re E,* children are as much entitled to respect for their confidences and thus their right to privilege, as adults.

---

70 *R v Derby Magistrates' Court exp B* [1995] UKHL 18, [1996] 1 AC 487, [1996] 1 FLR 513.

71 Explained further in Chapter 13.

72 *Wolverhampton City Council v JA & Ors* at [20].

73 Considered at 5.75.

74 *Gillick v West Norfolk and Wisbech AHA* [1985] UKHL 7, [1986] 1 AC 112, [1986] 1 FLR 224; see Chapter 13.

6

LITIGATION PRIVILEGE

1 INTRODUCTION

Litigation privilege

6.1 The second sub-branch of legal professional privilege (LPP) is litigation privilege (LP). Unlike legal advice privilege (LAP), LP can only arise in connection with actual or proposed litigation. In that case, any communication between a lawyer and the lawyer's client or between any of them and a third party (such as a witness or expert witness) where the sole or dominant purpose of the communication is the litigation, is covered by the privilege. Thus, a party to actual or pending proceedings can interview witnesses (and prepare proof of their evidence) or obtain expert evidence[1] in connection with court proceedings without having to disclose the result of the researches to other parties or to the court.

6.2 Once established, LP has all the main features of LPP. It is an absolute right protected in the same way. It cannot be overridden save by statute or by consent of the person entitled to it. In *S County Council v B* [2] Charles J defined it in relation to children proceedings as follows:

> … litigation privilege covers two areas, namely: (a) communications between a solicitor (or a lawyer) and third parties which come into existence after litigation is contemplated, or commenced, and made with a view either to obtaining or giving advice in relation to it, or of obtaining or collecting evidence to be used in it, or obtaining information which may lead to the obtaining of such evidence (see *Anderson v Bank of British Columbia* (1876) 2 Ch D 644, 650, and (b) communications between the client (or a non-lawyer) and third parties, the dominant purpose of which is to obtain legal advice, or to conduct or aid in the conduct of litigation in reasonable prospect (see, for example, *Waugh v British Railways Board* [1980] AC 521).

1 Subject to what is said about *Re L (Police Investigation: Privilege)* [1997] AC 16, [1996] 1 FLR 731 below; see 5.34.

2 [2000] Fam 76, [2000] 2 FLR 161; *S County Council v B* is considered further at 6.2.

Legal advice privilege and litigation privilege

6.3 Many communications between a lawyer and client in relation to litigation will be covered by advice privilege as well as by litigation privilege. The essence of LP, separate from LAP, is that it enables a lawyer to communicate with third parties (eg, a witness or expert) in connection with litigation. Such communication will be covered by LP.

6.4 As with any form of privilege, the privilege is that of the client. It can be waived only by the client or where it can be overridden. The burden rests on the person claiming the privilege to assert it and for the person seeking to override it to apply to do so; application to court (if need be) to seek inspection of documents for which the privilege is claimed is set out in Chapter 10.

6.5 This chapter proceeds as follows:

- Part 2 explains the 'dominant purpose' test in assessment of whether LP applies.
- Part 3 examines the question of to what extent LP applies in children proceedings especially after *Re L (Police Investigation: Privilege)*.[3]
- Part 4 provides a short introduction to the subject of materials for litigation 'privilege' to which litigants in person may be entitled.

2 LITIGATION PRIVILEGE: DOMINANT PURPOSE

Legal advice and the 'dominant purpose' test

6.6 Litigation privilege is a part of LPP. In *Re L (Police Investigation: Privilege)*,[4] Lord Nicholls (who was in the minority in *Re L* in the House of Lords) explained the interrelation of the two forms of privilege comprised in LPP:

> [LPP] is sometimes classified under two subheadings: [LAP] and [LP]. The former, covering communications between a client and his legal adviser, is available whether or not proceedings are in existence or contemplated. The latter embraces a wider class of communications, such as those between the legal adviser and potential witnesses. These are privileged only when proceedings are in existence or contemplated … The two subheadings are integral parts of a single privilege. In the context of court proceedings, the purpose of legal advice privilege would be frustrated if the legal adviser could not approach potential witnesses in confidence before advising the client. This is as much true in family proceedings as any other.

3 [1997] AC 16, [1996] 1 FLR 731.
4 Ibid, Ibid at 744–745.

6.7 The definition of litigation privilege derives from *Waugh v British Railways Board*.[5] In that case, a widow sought damages from the Board following the death of her husband in a railway accident. She sought disclosure of an internal inquiry report prepared for the Board in relation to the accident and which included statements of witnesses. The question for the Lords was whether the sole purpose of the report was for litigation or whether it was something other than that. Was the prospect of litigation the 'dominant purpose' for obtaining the report; or was litigation subsidiary or one of a number of purposes which led to the report being obtained?

6.8 Lord Wilberforce defined his view of the 'dominant purpose' test as follows:[6]

> It appears to me that unless the purpose of submission to the legal adviser in view of litigation is at least the dominant purpose for which the relevant document was prepared, the reasons which require privilege to be extended to it cannot apply. On the other hand to hold that the purpose, as above, must be the sole purpose would, apart from difficulties of proof, in my opinion, be too strict a requirement, and would confine the privilege too narrowly …

6.9 Lord Edmund-Davies explained the same point as follows:[7]

> After considerable deliberation, I have finally come down in favour of the test propounded by Barwick C.J. in *Grant v Downs* 135 CLR 674 [in the High Court of Australia], in the following words, at p 677: "Having considered the decisions, the writings and the various aspects of the public interest which claim attention, I have come to the conclusion that the court should state the relevant principle as follows: a document which was produced or brought into existence either with the *dominant* purpose of its author, or of the person or authority under whose direction, whether particular or general, it was produced or brought into existence, of using it or its contents in order to obtain legal advice or to conduct or aid in the conduct of litigation, at the time of its production in reasonable prospect, should be privileged and excluded from inspection." (Italics added.)
>
> *Dominant* purpose, then, in my judgment, should now be declared by this House to be the touchstone [Lord Edmund-Davies's italics]. It is less stringent a test than "sole" purpose, for, as Barwick C.J. added, at 677: "… the fact that the person … had in mind other uses of the document will not preclude that document being accorded privilege, if it were produced with the requisite dominant purpose."

6.10 The House allowed Mrs Waugh's appeal and ordered, in that case, that the dominant purpose of the report was other than litigation. Its main purpose had

---

5 [1980] AC 521.

6 Ibid at 533.

7 Ibid at 543–544.

been for the defendants to deal with safety issues. LP could not, therefore, apply and Mrs Waugh was entitled to see the report.

'Proceedings reasonably in prospect'

6.11 Whether the privilege can attach depends on whether litigation is 'reasonably in prospect' and, if so, whether the dominant purpose of obtaining the document is that of seeking legal advice in any subsequent proceedings. For example, in *R v Snaresbrook Crown Court ex p Director of Public Prosecutions*[8] a question arose concerning LP in relation to documents held by the legal aid authorities (at that time legal aid was administered by The Law Society). A had been arrested and charged with assault. He pleaded guilty, but later complained through his solicitors that at the time of his arrest he had been assaulted by the police. He applied for legal aid to bring an action for assault, but subsequent police inquiries revealed that his nose had been broken two days before the arrest. A was charged with attempting to pervert the course of justice and the prosecution requested production by The Law Society of A's legal aid application form.

6.12 Glidewell LJ, in the Divisional Court, explained his view of the relationship of The Law Society, the client and the documents concerned:[9]

> [A] is the client of a professional legal adviser. The application for legal aid, on the face of it, is a communication between him and another person, namely, the area officer of The Law Society. Clearly it was made in contemplation of and for the purpose of legal proceedings. On the face of it the material does come within the definition of items subject to legal privilege in section 10(1) of the 1984 Act.[10]

6.13 He then explained his view that the absolute truthfulness, or not, of the statement of a client or witness was not the criterion for deciding whether some form of dishonesty would exclude privilege from applying to the document (per *R v Cox and Railton*[11]):[12]

> ... litigants in civil litigation may not be believed when their cases come to trial, but that is not to say that the statements they had made to their solicitors pending the trial, much less the applications which they made if they applied for legal aid, are not subject to legal privilege. The principle to be derived from *Reg v Cox and Railton,* applies in my view to circumstances which do not cover the ordinary run of case such as this is.

8 [1988] 1 QB 532.

9 Ibid at 736.

10 Police and Criminal Evidence Act 1984 s 10 states: (1) Subject to subsection (2) below, in this Act 'items subject to legal privilege' means – ... (b) communications between a professional legal adviser ... or his client ... and any other person made in connection with or in contemplation of legal proceedings and for the purposes of such proceedings; ... (2) Items held with the intention of furthering a criminal purpose are not items subject to legal privilege.

11 *R v Cox and Railton* (1884) 14 QBD 153, Stephen J; see further at 10.5.

12 Ibid at 537–538.

6.14 The Divisional Court held that LP applied to the documents held by the Law Society for legal aid application purposes and refused to quash the decision by the Society's area director not to release them to the DPP.

Litigation privilege after SFO v ENRC

6.15 The importance of LP in a large organisation – perhaps a local authority – was stressed in *Serious Fraud Office (SFO) v Eurasian Natural Resources Corp Ltd.*[13] The case was an appeal from Andrews J. ENRC were anticipating some form of enforcement raid by the SFO. They were carefully considering self-reporting under SFO guidelines as a result of allegations of criminality on the part of certain African companies it was seeking to acquire. ENRC set in motion extensive enquiries as to the background and mostly involving members of their own staff by, amongst others, Dechert, a firm of solicitors.

6.16 SFO finally decided to 'accept ENRC for criminal investigation' (ie, to pursue their enquiries further). ENRC asserted LPP (ie, advice privilege and LP) in relation to documents which had arisen in their internal enquiry. SFO replied with an application, heard ultimately by Andrews J, that there be a declaration that ENRC must disclose three categories of document.

- The first category was notes taken by Dechert of the evidence given to them by individuals (including employees and former employees or officers of ENRC and of its subsidiary companies) when asked about the events being investigated.
- Next ('Category 2') was of the 'books and records of Forensic Risk Alliance (FRA), a firm of forensic accountants and of reviews they carried out.
- Finally, 'Category 4' comprised 17 documents referred to in a letter dated 22 August 2014 sent to the SFO by a barrister's chambers.

6.17 Andrews J held that none of these were covered by privilege. The Court of Appeal held that all, save a couple of e-mails, were covered by LP.

3 LITIGATION PRIVILEGE AND CHILDREN PROCEEDINGS

Privilege in 'non-adversarial' proceedings

6.18 In *Waugh v British Railways Board*[14] the exact meaning of the word 'litigation' was not defined. In 1980, perhaps this was thought to be unnecessary. However, in *Re L (Police Investigation: Privilege)*[15] the House of Lords held that

13 [2018] EWCA Civ 2006.
14 [1980] AC 521.
15 [1997] AC 16, [1996] 1 FLR 731.

litigation privilege does not apply to reports obtained in care proceedings (CA 1989 Pt 4). The House said that this was because of the 'non-adversarial' nature of such proceedings derived – as the House held – from the fact that children proceedings under CA 1989 are modelled on non-adversarial wardship proceedings:[16]

> ... in these proceedings which are primarily non-adversarial and investigative as opposed to adversarial the notion of a fair trial between opposing parties assumes far less importance.[17] In the latter case the judge must decide the case in favour of one or other party upon such evidence as they choose to adduce however much he might wish for further evidence on any point. In the former case the judge is concerned to make a decision which is in the best interest of the child in question and may make orders which are sought by no party to the proceedings ... The court is seeking to reach a decision which will be in the best interests of someone who is not a direct party and is granted investigative powers to achieve that end. In these circumstances I consider that care proceedings under Part IV of the Act are so far removed from normal actions that *litigation privilege has no place in relation to reports* obtained by a party thereto which could not have been prepared without the leave of the court to disclose documents already filed or to examine the child (emphasis added).

6.19 Lord Jauncey's opinion was that LP could not apply, but only to two categories of reports (ie, the majority of reports which are prepared in care proceedings) where permission from the court is required to instruct an expert witness:

(1) to produce documents to the expert to enable the report to be prepared; or

(2) to have a child medically or psychiatrically examined for production of a report.[18]

6.20 All reports and other evidence which would otherwise be covered by LP would, on this formula, remain privileged. They need not be inspected or produced to the court, save by order. The protection for this evidence would remain the same as for any other documents covered by LPP. However, documents within Lord Jauncey's two categories in care proceedings would not be subject to privilege.

The issue in *Re L*

6.21 The issue for the House of Lords in *Re L* was whether LP applied to a medical report which was obtained in connection with care proceedings (CA 1989 Pt 4). The child of two drug addicts became seriously ill after ingesting methadone.

16 [1996] 1 FLR 731 at 738–739.

17 This is not the place to debate concepts of 'fairness' in care proceedings; nor the extent to which – especially at the proof stage – proceedings are adversarial (in the sense understood by European Court and English jurisprudence).

18 As now under CFA 2014 s 13(3).

The mother's case was that this ingestion had been accidental. The local authority obtained an interim care order. On the application of both parents, the district judge made an order giving them leave to disclose the court papers to a medical expert to obtain a report on the frequency of the consumption of methadone by the child. The report when filed was to be available for inspection by any party to the proceedings.

6.22 The mother's solicitors instructed an expert, whose report concluded that there was no evidence of the child being habituated to methadone; but the report cast doubts on the mother's account of accidental ingestion. The police heard of the existence of the report at a case conference and applied for copies for the purpose of investigating criminal offences. Bracewell J, at first instance, held that she had a discretion as to whether to order production of the report to non-parties. She considered that her discretion should be exercised in favour of release of the report to the police.

6.23 The mother appealed on grounds as follows:

(1) that the report was protected by LP;

(2) that its disclosure would infringe her privilege against self-incrimination; and

(3) that the judge had exercised her discretion wrongly.

6.24 The Court of Appeal dismissed the mother's appeal. They held that the report was covered by LP, but that they had power to override it. On the mother's appeal to the House of Lords, Lord Jauncey said that the concept of LP was an aspect of adversarial proceedings only. In care proceedings the court is seeking to reach a conclusion in the interests of a child, who is not 'a direct party' to the proceedings (formally they are, of course, a party[19]). Care proceedings are so far from 'normal actions' that LP has no part in such proceedings, said Lord Jauncey:[20]

> The better view [of the case] is that litigation privilege never arose in the first place rather than that the court has power to override it. It is excluded by necessary implication from the terms and overall purpose of the Act.

6.25 The source of Lord Jauncey's assumptions on wardship is Lord Scarman in a wardship appeal case. Lord Jauncey explains his reference to wardship as follows:[21]

---

19 CA 1989 s 41.

20 *Re L (Police Investigation: Privilege)* [1996] 1 FLR 731 at 739.

21 Ibid at 738.

> Lord Scarman in *Re E (A Minor) (Wardship: Court's Duty)* [1984] FLR 457 pointed out at 488F–G[22] that a court in wardship proceedings was not exercising an adversarial jurisdiction and that: 'Its duty is not limited to the dispute between the parties: on the contrary, its duty is to act in the way best suited, in its judgment, to serve the true interest and welfare of the ward. In exercising wardship jurisdiction, the court is a true family court. Its paramount concern is the welfare of its ward. It will, therefore, sometimes be the duty of the court to look beyond the submissions of the parties in its endeavour to do what it judges to be necessary.'

Litigation privilege and a fair hearing

6.26 There were only two reasoned speeches in *Re L*. Lords Lloyd and Steyn agreed with Lord Jauncey. Lord Mustill agreed with Lord Nicholls, whose was the only other speech. Lord Nicholls sets out his reasoning on the application of LP in more detail than did Lord Jauncey. He explains how he sees the law on LP and its role in a fair trial. In the central passage of his speech he says:

> I can see no reason why parties to family proceedings should not be as much entitled to a fair hearing having these features and safeguards as are parties to other court proceedings. Indeed, it must be doubtful whether a parent who is denied the opportunity to obtain legal advice in confidence is accorded the fair hearing to which he is entitled under Art 6(1), read in conjunction with European Convention 1950 Art 8 ...
>
> Parents and other parties should be entitled to such a hearing notwithstanding the special role of judges in family proceedings. If this is not to be, Parliament should say so expressly.[23] Legal professional privilege is part of the established framework within which judges discharge their special role in family proceedings ... The judges' special role is to be discharged within this framework, not outside it. The paramountcy principle must not be permitted to become a loose cannon, destroying all else around it.

---

22 What Lord Scarman had said was – unusually, perhaps – in the context of an exercise of their discretion by the House of Lords: 'Neither party directed any attention in their submissions to the possibility of a trial period of access [between the father appellant and the ward] before reaching a final decision between the courses of adoption or father's resumption of parental control ... A court exercising jurisdiction over its ward must never lose sight of a fundamental feature of the jurisdiction that it is exercising, namely that it is exercising a wardship, not an adversarial, jurisdiction. Its duty is not limited to the dispute between the parties: on the contrary, its duty is to act in the way best suited, in its judgment, to serve the true interest and welfare of the ward. In exercising wardship jurisdiction, the court is a true family court. Its paramount concern is the welfare of its ward. It will, therefore, sometimes be the duty of the court to look beyond the submissions of the parties in its endeavour to do what it judges to be necessary. When a local authority or a parent persuades the court that it should make a child its ward, the court takes over the ultimate responsibility for the child. No doubt, it will only be in exceptional cases that the court decides upon a course not advocated by any party to the proceedings. Nevertheless, exceptional cases, however rarely, do arise.'

23 This represents the form of words by which changes in the law, including – as here – the common law as explained by the House of Lords in the later *R v Secretary of State for the Home Department, exp Simms* [1999] UKHL 33, [2000] 2 AC 115, [1999] 3 WLR 328.

6.27 Under the heading 'litigation privilege' Lord Nicholls then goes on to explain why principles which attach to legal professional privilege apply equally to its second component litigation privilege – 'integral parts of a single privilege' – and their part in assuring a fair trial.[24] He concludes by pointing out that there is no reason why proceedings – as indeed is the case with care proceedings – should not have both inquisitorial and adversarial features:[25]

> In this context the contrast between inquisitorial and adversarial needs handling with care, for at least two reasons. First, the contrast suggests that proceedings are either wholly adversarial or wholly inquisitorial. They partake wholly of the one character or wholly of the other. This is not always so. Proceedings may possess some adversarial features and some inquisitorial features. Family proceedings are an example.

Reports obtained with permission only excluded from litigation privilege

6.28 The passage by Lord Jauncey, which represents the ratio of *Re L* is as follows:[26]

> In these circumstances I consider that care proceedings under Part IV of the Act are so far removed from normal actions that *litigation privilege has no place in relation to reports* obtained by a party thereto which could not have been prepared without the leave of the court to disclose documents already filed or to examine the child (emphasis added).

6.29 As can be seen from the italicised passage, above, Lord Jauncey emphasises the limits of the extent to which the House of Lords was saying LP 'has no place' in children proceedings. That is, the ratio applied only to reports for which court permission is required. All other communications covered by LP are excluded from inspection (as with any document covered by privilege). For example, if there is contact with a witness, and a proof is prepared, or there are other enquiries made by a party's lawyers in relation to the case, these will be covered by litigation privilege, as they would be in any other litigation.[27]

6.30 Reports in children proceedings may only be obtained with permission from the court;[28] and children may only be examined, for the preparation of a

---

24 Ibid at 744.

25 Ibid at 743.

26 *Re L (Police Investigation: Privilege)* [1997] AC 16, [1996] 1 FLR 731 per Lord Jauncey at 738–739.

27 To this extent *Children Law and Practice* is misleading, so far as it states (at para C[3014]): 'Litigation privilege does not apply to proceedings under CA 1989 as it is excluded by necessary implication from the terms and overall purpose of the 1989 Act [here citing *Re L* and *Vernon v Bosley (No 2)* (above)]. As a result, where the court has given leave for the relevant papers to be disclosed to an expert witness, the resulting report of the expert must be disclosed to the court and to the other parties to the proceedings.' The first sentence puts the point too widely; the second is a correct summary of the law.

28 Children and Families Act 2014 s 13(1).

report, with permission from the court.[29] As with any expert evidence in civil proceedings it can only be placed before the report with permission.[30]

Permission for expert evidence

6.31 The difference between children proceedings and other civil proceedings is that in the latter there is no need to obtain permission to commission the report. The limit only is on whether a party may use it in court. In children's proceedings, at least nominally, a party may not instruct any expert without permission from the court. However, CFA 2014 section 13 implies a statutory let-out for this restriction. It enables a person who has obtained a report, without CFA 2014 section 13(1) permission, to apply – after the event – for permission to be granted. The fact of having obtained the report – covered by LP in all other civil and criminal proceedings – is that in children proceedings no privilege arises: it must be produced for inspection whichever way it goes as far as the client is concerned and even if there would have been no intent to rely upon it.

6.32 LAP remains, in all respects, for children cases (as confirmed by Lord Jauncey at the end of the short passage quoted below).[31] As far as expert reports are concerned only, LAP does not arise because of what the House of Lords held to be the 'non-adversarial' nature of care proceedings.

6.33 The principle in relation to LP in *Re L*, it has been said, applies to all children proceedings.[32] In *Vernon v Bosley (No 2)* Stuart Smith LJ explained the point as follows:[33]

> [Counsel for Mr Vernon] submits that the reports of Mr Mackay and Dr Lloyd are subject to litigation privilege. I do not agree. These were reports obtained from experts in Children Act proceedings and such reports are not privileged: *In re L. (A Minor) (Police Investigation: Privilege)* [1997] A.C. 16. The ratio decidendi of that case is not confined to wardship and care proceedings.

6.34 This assertion is difficult to reconcile with what was said by Lord Jauncey. He said in terms that he was concerned 'that care proceedings under [Children Act 1989 Pt 4] are so far removed from normal actions that litigation

---

29 Ibid s 13(3).

30 FPR 2010 r 25.4(2); CPR 1998 r 35.4(1).

31 For further confirmation of this see eg, Ward LJ in *Re D (A Child)* [2011] EWCA Civ 684, [2011] 2 FLR 1183 at para [12].

32 *Vernon v Bosley (No 2)* [1999] QB 18, [1998] 1 FLR 304, CA per Stuart Smith LJ at [1998] 1 FLR 319: [Counsel for Mr Vernon] submits that the [medical reports on Mr Vernon in the children proceedings] are subject to litigation privilege. I do not agree. These were reports obtained from experts in Children Act Proceedings and such reports are not privileged: *Re L (A Minor) (Police Investigation: Privilege)* [(above)]. The *ratio decidendi* of that case is not confined to wardship and care proceedings. A document which does not attract legal professional privilege does not do so simply because, if it had been brought into existence in other circumstances, it would have done so. Nor does a document not entitled to privilege become privileged merely because it is handed to a solicitor for the purposes of litigation: *Ventouris v Mountain, The Italia Express* [1991] 1 WLR 607, CA.

33 *Vernon v Bosley (No 2)* at 35–36.

privilege has no place in relation to reports'. What was said was strictly limited to care proceedings. In *Vernon v Bosley*, the question was whether reports from other children proceedings (ie, Mr Vernon's CA 1989 Pt 2 (residence order) proceedings) attracted LP. However, whether LP covered the reports in the *Vernon* proceedings was not in issue. Whether the reports could be covered by privilege in the damages proceedings could have been the only issue in relation to the reports on the appeal. It is difficult to see how a *Re L* question could therefore have arisen in the *Vernon v Bosley* appeal.

Three Rivers (No 6) and Re L

6.35 In *Three Rivers District Council and ors v Governor and Company of the Bank of England (No 6)*,[34] the House of Lords touched on litigation privilege; and, inconclusively, they considered their earlier decision in *Re L*. The issue was the extent of privilege which attached to documents produced by the Bank of England to the Bingham inquiry. Lord Scott explained his view of *Re L* and privilege in non-adversarial proceedings. He concluded that the subject of litigation privilege and *Re L* needed review but not in *Three Rivers (No 6)*.[35] He concluded:

> [53] In *In re L (A Minor)(Police Investigation: Privilege)* [1997] AC 16 your Lordships' House held, Lord Mustill and Lord Nicholls of Birkenhead dissenting, that proceedings under Part IV of the Children Act 1989 were "investigative" rather than "adversarial" in nature and that litigation privilege was therefore excluded by necessary implication ... [In this case] it is unnecessary to analyse more fully the characteristics of those kinds of proceedings which do attract litigation privilege. In his dissenting speech in *In re L* Lord Nicholls of Birkenhead sounded a note of caution against basing any such analysis simply on the distinction between "adversarial" and "inquisitorial" proceedings: [1997] AC 16, 31G–32D. In the meantime those cautionary words have gained force since, for the purposes of the Human Rights Act 1998, one of the characteristics of a fair trial under article 6 is that the proceedings should be "adversarial": eg *Lobo Machado v Portugal* (1996) 23 EHRR 79, para 31.[36] The ethos of

34 [2004] UKHL 48, [2004] 3 WLR 1274.

35 *Three Rivers District Council and ors v Governor and Company of the Bank of England (No 6)* 29.

36 In *Lobo Machado v Portugal* an industrial tribunal application appeal was dealt with by the Portuguese Supreme Court solely on written documents, in private; and on the basis of an opinion from their Deputy Attorney-General without the appellant being given an opportunity to reply to the opinion. The European Court concluded: '[31] Regard being had, therefore, to what was at stake for the applicant in the proceedings in the Supreme Court and to the nature of the Deputy Attorney-General's opinion, in which it was advocated that the appeal should be dismissed the fact that it was impossible for Mr Lobo Machado to obtain a copy of it and reply to it before judgment was given infringed his right to adversarial proceedings. That right means in principle the opportunity for the parties to a criminal or civil trial to have knowledge of and comment on all evidence adduced or observations filed, even by an independent member of the national legal service, with a view to influencing the court's decision ([see eg, *McMichael v United Kingdom*, 24 February 1995, Series A no. 307-B, pp. 53–54, para. 80]). The Court finds that this fact in itself amounts to a breach of Article 6(1).' And *McMichael* at para [80] includes: '... as a matter of general principle the right to a fair – adversarial – trial means the opportunity to have knowledge of and comment on the observations filed or evidence adduced by the other party'.

the new system of civil procedure in England and Wales, and of the more limited changes in civil procedure in Scotland, may also have a bearing on the question. Consideration of the issue must, however, await a case where the matter arises for decision.

4 'MATERIALS FOR LITIGATION ' PRIVILEGE

Materials for evidence

6.36 Legal professional privilege, of which LP is part, applies because of the relationship between a lawyer and his client. But what of the case where a litigant has no lawyer, or is assisted in proceedings by a 'McKenzie friend'? In its technical sense LP cannot apply.[37] It is an aspect of LPP which can only apply to assistance from lawyers. That said, a form of privilege akin to LP may apply where a litigant has no lawyer acting for him or her in court proceedings, or in preparation for such proceedings.

6.37 The term 'materials for evidence' privilege (derived from mid-twentieth-century editions of the Rules of the Supreme Court 1965 *Annual Practice* (the 'White Book')) has been adopted in this context so far. It describes a form of privilege which attaches to documents obtained by an unrepresented party for litigation. Such documents should be protected by privilege independently of their having been obtained by lawyers. A litigant in person should not be hindered in preparation of a case if that litigant decides to deal with the case without instructing a lawyer (or does so because his or her means do not permit it). That litigant should enjoy the same immunities in terms of privilege as that enjoyed by the litigant who employs a lawyer.

Privilege and the litigant in person

6.38 A view of the point can be found in *R (Kelly) v Warley Magistrates Court & Anor.*[38] In that case Laws LJ stated his opinion that LP was not a 'sub-class' of LPP and that it can arise without their being a legal adviser instructed by the litigant concerned. He explained this as follows:

> [18] ... it is clear that [litigation privilege] can arise without the involvement of any legal adviser. A litigant in person enjoys it. It was described by Lord Rodger of Earlsferry in *Three Rivers DC* [2005] AC 610, [2004] 3 WLR 1274 as follows: "[52] Litigation privilege relates to communications at the stage when litigation is pending or in contemplation. It is based on the idea that legal proceedings take the form of a contest in which each of the opposing parties assembles his own body of evidence and uses it to try to defeat the other, with the

37 As explained in *R (Prudential plc and anor) v Special Commissioner of Income Tax* [2013] UKSC 1, [2013] 2 AC 185; and see further at 5.12.

38 [2007] EWHC Admin 1836, [2008] 1 WLR 2001 (QB Divisional Court).

> judge or jury determining the winner. In such a system each party should be free to prepare his case as fully as possible without the risk that his opponent will be able to recover the material generated by his preparations. In the words of Justice Jackson in *Hickman v Taylor* (1947) 329 US 495, 516, 'Discovery was hardly intended to enable a learned profession to perform its functions either without wits or on wits borrowed from the adversary'."

6.39 So, the argument goes, if a lawyer's client has protection from LP, why should not a litigant in person have the same protection? The common law has not yet developed a clear view on this possible aspect of privilege. As an increasing number of individuals no longer have access to lawyers (with the decline in legal aid availability after the coming into operation of the Legal Aid Sentencing and Punishment of Offenders Act 2012) materials for litigation privilege preserves a right for an individual to prepare his or her case with the immunity provided by LP.

7

SELF-INCRIMINATION PRIVILEGE

1 INTRODUCTION

Origins of self-incrimination privilege

7.1 The concept of self-incrimination privilege (SIP) developed in the late seventeenth century following the abolition of the Star Chamber (associated as it was with Charles I's autocratic rule (1625–1642)) and as a reaction to the abuses practised by that court (often by seventeenth century associated with confessions under torture). It derives from the law's distaste for the possibility of anyone being required to provide evidence against himself or herself, and upon threat of punishment (as had been common in the Star Chamber). It represents, it might be said, the law's way of telling a party to proceedings to mind their own business, and where the questioner is not entitled to an answer which tends to incriminate.[1]

7.2 In family proceedings it occurs most prominently in Children Act 1989 (CA 1989) proceedings. CA 1989 section 98 provides a special relief from self-incrimination privilege to encourage frankness in parties involved in care proceedings.

7.3 This chapter proceeds as follows:

- Part 2 provides a definition of the subject of SIP.
- Part 3 looks at SIP and children proceedings, especially CA 1989 section 98.
- Part 4 considers briefly the subject of SIP and search orders.

2 SELF-INCRIMINATION PRIVILEGE DEFINED

Right to silence

7.4 Self-incrimination privilege is based on the proposition that no-one can be required to make a case against himself. In *Reg v Director of Serious Fraud Office, ex p Smith*,[2] Lord Mustill identified six 'rights of silence' as follows:

1 *Reg v Director of Serious Fraud Office, exp Smith* [1993] AC 1 at 30–31, [1992] 3 WLR 66 per Lord Mustill.
2 [1993] AC 1 at 30–31, [1992] 3 WLR 66 at 74.

(1) A general immunity from being compelled 'on pain of punishment' to answer questions put to one individual (or body) by another (also described by Lord Mustill as a 'reflection of the common view that one person should so far as possible be able to tell another person to mind his own business').

(2) A general immunity from being compelled 'on pain of punishment' to answer questions which may incriminate.

(3) A specific immunity for anyone under suspicion of a crime, whilst being questioned by police, to refuse to answer questions.

(4) A specific immunity from answering questions in the dock or being compelled to give evidence.

(5) A specific immunity for persons charged with an offence, from having questions asked by police officers concerning matters material to the charge.

(6) A specific immunity from having adverse inferences drawn at trial arising from a refusal to answer questions or give evidence.

7.5 This right and the associated self-incrimination privilege may be overridden by statute or at common law. CA 1989 section 98 – where there is a balancing amnesty (up to a point) for evidence in care proceedings is provided – is an example of a statutory exception. If there is to be any question of self-incrimination privilege being overridden at common law (or in accordance with European Convention 1950 principles) it must be by statute or justified by a court on public policy grounds.[3]

Compulsion to produce evidence

7.6 Where there is a requirement to provide evidence to the court then, subject to any higher public interest, self-incrimination privilege will apply. In *R v K*,[4] the Court of Appeal considered the question of a spouse being required to answer questions about that spouse's means in Form E. The husband (K) filed his Form E and disclosed various bank accounts and investment portfolios in Switzerland and Liechtenstein. In replies to the wife's questionnaire he made statements which tended to show that he had failed to pay tax. Meetings were also held at which K made admissions; though these are not directly relevant to this chapter.

7.7 An informer supplied the Inland Revenue with copies of K's Form E and his answers to the questionnaires. He was charged with tax evasion. In the course of a preparatory hearing the Crown sought permission to adduce K's Form E, his answers to the questionnaires and certain open admissions made by him in the financial relief proceedings.

7.8 When he swore Form E and replied to the questionnaire K had been unable – as was the case – to invoke self-incrimination privilege. By complying

3 *Brown v Stott* [2001] 2 WLR 817, PC: public interest in safety on the roads overrode Mrs Brown's right not to incriminate herself for drunken driving.

4 [2009] EWCA Crim 1640, [2010] QB 343, [2010] 1 FLR 807.

with the requirement to complete Form E he had exposed himself to a risk of prosecution. If the evidence thus obtained were adduced against him, he would be denied the right to a fair trial on the tax evasion charges to which he was entitled under Article 6 of the European Convention 1950. The judge held that K could have invoked SIP at the time of swearing Form E and answering questions, but that he had failed to do so.

7.9 On appeal, that part of the appeal which related to evidence in the financial relief proceedings was allowed. K was required by law to provide information to enable the court to make orders under MCA 1973 section 25 and under FPR 2010 Part 9. He could not, therefore, invoke SIP to withhold information in Form E and in replies to the questionnaire. It was therefore covered by SIP and immune from production in his criminal trial. The rules 'must have been intended to have abrogated the privilege' (see italicised passage below). As a result, the information was provided under compulsion. This is in contrast to the normal civil proceedings disclosure rules in CPR 1998 Part 31.

7.10 In financial relief proceedings a spouse was therefore entitled to claim SIP (emphasis supplied):

> [31] … The argument in the present case, however, is, and must be, that the rules [then Family Procedure Rules 1991 now FPR 2010], which are contained in secondary legislation and have the approval of Parliament, *must have been intended to have abrogated the privilege*, since the court could not discharge the duty imposed on it by Matrimonial Causes Act 1973 s 25 unless the parties were required to disclose all relevant information, even if tending to incriminate them.
>
> [32] … It follows that in our view the information contained in K's form E and his answers to Mrs K's questionnaires was obtained under compulsion.

7.11 The privilege applies equally in European Convention 1950 jurisprudence where it is equated with preventing a fair trial under Article 6(1).[5]

Self-incrimination privilege: referral of a solicitor to the Solicitors' Regulation Authority

7.12 An awkward question mark hangs over the right to privilege of the solicitor (SN) in *Wolverhampton City Council v JA & Ors*,[6] where Keehan J made an order[7] for the filing of evidence by SN after the advocates' meeting, where information as to what she had been told by the children in the case was given by or on her behalf to other parties. Keehan J's order was that the children's solicitor who replaced SN:

5 See eg, *Funke v France* (1993) 16 EHRR 297: legislation which prevented a taxpayer from withholding bank statements which were suspected of indicating tax evasion was said to prevent a fair trial on grounds equivalent to self-incrimination privilege.

6 [2017] EWFC 62.

7 Ibid at [20].

> 1(i) … shall write to the appropriate manager at [ ] Solicitors informing her that Sinead Noel, the former children's solicitor, employed by them is likely to be a witness of fact in these proceedings and is likely to be the subject of criticism as to her professional conduct; …

7.13 Keehan J makes it clear in his order that SN is 'likely to be the subject of criticism as to her professional conduct'. It is the case that the concept of SIP is associated more with criminal prosecution. However, *R v K*[8] makes it clear that any information which is 'obtained under compulsion' – in *Wolverhampton* SN was ordered to file her evidence – in any forensic context is covered by the privilege.

7.14 As far as can be deduced, SN was not warned of her right not to incriminate herself by the filing of the statement. If that is the case, in any professional misconduct proceedings – if the Solicitors' Regulation Authority pursues such proceedings – they may have difficulty using evidence filed by SN in the children proceedings. It would have been open to Keehan J to override SIP on public interest grounds (*Brown v Stott (Procurator Fiscal, Dunfermline) and another*[9]); but this must be the subject of specific findings as to the extent of that public interest by him.

3 CHILDREN PROCEEDINGS

Incriminating evidence and children proceedings

7.15 The Children Act 1989 section 98 provides a form of SIP which is special to proceedings under CA 1989 Parts 4 and 5 (care, interim care and emergency protection proceedings). The aim of section 98 is to encourage frankness in parties to public law children proceedings. This is encouraged by preventing the use or admissibility of evidence given in the proceedings in subsequent criminal proceedings (other than criminal proceedings for perjury in the children proceedings).

7.16 That said, it does not prevent the evidence which emerges either in the proceedings or in connection with them being used in any criminal investigations arising as a result; nor does it prevent a prosecution based on the evidence of the children proceedings. It merely ensures that the evidence actually provided in the children proceedings is not admissible (ie, it cannot be used) in any later proceedings.

7.17 Children Act 1989 section 98 is as follows:

> **98 Self-incrimination**
>
> (1) In any proceedings in which a court is hearing an application for an order under Part IV or V, no person shall be excused from –

8 [2009] EWCA Crim 1640, [2010] QB 343, [2010] 1 FLR 807 (above).
9 [2000] UKPC D3, [2003] 1 AC 681.

(a) giving evidence on any matter; or

(b) answering any question put to him in the course of his giving evidence,

on the ground that doing so might incriminate him or his spouse or civil partner of an offence.

(2) A statement or admission made in such proceedings shall not be admissible in evidence against the person making it or his spouse or civil partner in proceedings for an offence other than perjury.

7.18 The immunity given by section 98(2) is in respect of 'a statement or admission' made, and of its subsequent use in 'proceedings for an offence'. This does not prevent a judge from permitting disclosure of the evidence to third parties (as will be explained below). It only prevents the evidence itself being used later against him or her. It does not prevent the same case being made against the parent or witness, which they will have to defend again in another court (or in some other forum[10]). It will then be a matter for the judge at any subsequent criminal trial as to whether the content of that interview was admissible under CA 1989 section 98(2) in the later trial.

Disclosure of confidential material

7.19 *Re EC (Disclosure of Material) (Re C (A Minor) (Care Proceedings: Disclosure)*[11] provides the test for deciding how the court should deal with evidence covered by section 98(2). The case applies whether application is made in the course of proceedings or a subsequent application for release is made to the court for release of the children proceedings evidence to the police or for any of the other types of reason outlined above.

7.20 As explained by Swinton Thomas LJ in *Re EC*, a court must start from the premise that the judge should consider any application for disclosure as balancing the desirability of privacy and the protection of SIP in children proceedings on the one hand, as against the public interest in making information available for a criminal trial on the other:[12]

> [That is] between the importance of maintaining confidentiality in family cases and the public interest in making available material information for the purposes of a criminal trial, taking into account the purpose for which the information was required, its weight and significance ... and the gravity of the offence.

7.21 *Re EC* concerned care proceedings in respect of a child aged three, whose baby sister had been injured and had died. There were five members of the child's

10 See eg, the doctor in *A County Council v W and Others (Disclosure)* [1997] 1 FLR 574.

11 [1997] Fam 76, [1997] 2 WLR 322, sub nom *Re EC (Disclosure of Material)* [1996] 2 FLR 725, CA.

12 Ibid at 732.

family who came under suspicion for killing the sister. Each gave evidence at the care proceedings hearing and each was told of the effects of section 98(2). Swinton Thomas LJ explained his understanding of the meaning and effect of CA section 98(2) and of its irrelevance to the confidentiality of the proceedings:[13]

> The proceedings themselves are confidential but subject to the power of the judge, in appropriate circumstances, to order disclosure. Nothing in s 98 detracts from that power. Section 98(2) gives protection only against statements being admissible in evidence in criminal proceedings except for an offence of perjury. *Accordingly, the judge could not give any guarantee for all time as to confidentiality, even had he wished to do so because the law makes no provision which would enable him to do so.* It may well be that in fairness to persons giving evidence in these circumstances judges may wish to point this out to a witness to whom the warning is given and, almost certainly, a legal adviser should do so (emphasis added).

Test for release of confidential information

7.22 Swinton Thomas LJ suggested a list of factors to be taken into account where application is made to the court – by the police or a local authority, say – for permission to be given by the court for the release of confidential information, and where that may be said to be covered by the CA 1989 section 98(2) privilege:[14]

(1) The welfare and interests of the child or children concerned in the care proceedings. If the child is likely to be adversely affected by the order in any serious way, this will be a very important factor.

(2) The welfare and interests of other children generally.

(3) The maintenance of confidentiality in children cases.

(4) The importance of encouraging frankness in children's cases. All parties to this appeal agree that this is a very important factor and is likely to be of particular importance in a case to which section 98(2) applies. The underlying purpose of section 98 is to encourage people to tell the truth in cases concerning children, and the incentive is that any admission will not be admissible in evidence in a criminal trial. Consequently, it is important in this case. However, the added incentive of guaranteed confidentiality is not given by the words of the section and cannot be given.

(5) The public interest in the administration of justice. Barriers should not be erected between one branch of the judicature and another because this may be inimical to the overall interests of justice.

(6) The public interest in the prosecution of serious crime and the punishment of offenders, including the public interest in convicting those who have been guilty of violent or sexual offences against children. There is a strong public

13 Ibid.
14 Ibid at 733.

interest in making available material to the police which is relevant to a criminal trial. In many cases, this is likely to be a very important factor.

(7) The gravity of the alleged offence and the relevance of the evidence to it. If the evidence has little or no bearing on the investigation or the trial, this will militate against a disclosure order.

(8) The desirability of co-operation between various agencies concerned with the welfare of children, including the social services departments, the police service, medical practitioners, health visitors, schools, etc. This is particularly important in cases concerning children.

(9) In a case to which section 98(2) applies, the terms of the section itself, namely, that the witness was not excused from answering incriminating questions and that any statement of admission would not be admissible against him in criminal proceedings. Fairness to the person who has incriminated himself and any others affected by the incriminating statement and any danger of oppression would also be relevant considerations.

(10) Any other material disclosure which has already taken place.

Tension: frankness against public interest in prosecution

7.23 In *Re AB (Care Proceedings: Disclosure of Medical Evidence to Police),*[15] Wall J was confronted by an application by the police for evidence from care proceedings. He described the difficulties for the court as follows:

> This case raises in an acute and unusual form the well-recognised tension in care proceedings between, on the one hand, the desirability of encouraging frankness on the part of parents suspected of killing or injuring their children and, on the other, the public interest in the prosecution of serious crime and the punishment of offenders, including the public interest in convicting those who have been guilty of violent or sexual offences against children.

7.24 In *Re AB* a mother had been advised by the lawyers instructed by her in criminal proceedings to restrict the basis on which she would be willing to be seen by a doctor. The doctor, Professor David, objected strongly that the mother – as he saw it – had been put in this position, to protect herself in criminal proceedings at the cost of frankness in the interests of her own child. Wall J felt he was bound by the Court of Appeal decision in *Re EC* and could not override the police request for any evidence arising from the interview with the doctor.

7.25 Wall J summarised the position in *Re AB,* at the end of a long and careful judgment, as follows:

> [134] The principal messages resulting from this judgment are, I think, the following:

15 [2002] EWHC 2198 (Fam) [2003] 1 FLR 579.

(1) Cases involving disclosure to the police of confidential material generated by care proceedings fall to be decided by carrying out the discretionary balancing exercise laid down by *Re C*.

(2) There is no presumption in favour of disclosure to the police in 1989 Act cases. Each case falls to be judged on its merits according to the guidelines laid down in *Re C*. Equally, *Re C* does not give any one factor a pre-determined importance, and the list of factors set out in *Re C* is not exhaustive.

(3) The provisions of s 98(2) of the 1989 Act apply to any statement or admission which a parent gives to an expert witness.

(4) Prior to being interviewed by an expert witness, parents should have the terms and the purpose of s 98(2) explained to them by their lawyers.

(5) It may be that the extent and effect of the protection given by s 98(2) are currently being underestimated by family lawyers. Section 98 gives substantial protection to any parent who wishes to be frank, and who makes a self-incriminating statement either to an expert witness or in the witness-box.

4 SEARCH ORDER PROCEEDINGS

Search orders

7.26 SIP may be claimed in part in connection with search orders.[16] *C Plc v P & Anor*[17] is authority for the proposition that although SIP applies to disclosure of documents which are produced by the search, it does not extend to material which is collected in the course of the search. In that case, in advance of execution of a search order, P claimed SIP in respect of anything 'which might be produced by the search'. Certain computers were handed to the supervising solicitor who passed them to W, an employee of C Plc (independent computer experts). In the course of imaging the contents of the computer W 'uncovered highly objectionable images of children' on one of them. W was a retired police officer, he knew that it can be an offence to be found in possession of such material and he had been involved with prosecutions for such offences. Could the computer material be covered by P's claim to SIP?

7.27 Longmore LJ analysed a variety of English, European and US jurisprudence on the subject, before concluding that of the documents and other material released by the search, SIP could not apply:

> [36] ... I would, therefore, conclude in the present case that, although the offending material had to be disclosed to the supervising solicitor and

16 *Anton Piller* orders (*Anton Piller KG v Manufacturing Processes Ltd & Ors* [1975] EWCA Civ 12, [1976] Ch 55).

17 [2007] EWCA Civ 493, [2007] 3 WLR 437.

> the computer experts by virtue of the order originally granted by Peter Smith J, there is no privilege in the offending material itself which is material which existed independently of the order.

7.28 Whilst documents which were recovered by the search could be subject to a claim which would be assessed under principles which apply to SIP, the material recovered by the order was not in the same category. It could not have protection in the same way. There can be no SIP in the offending material itself; for it is material which existed independently of the order. This was so, even though the material was nothing to do with the issues which arose in the litigation. It was material which was, on the face of it, connected with criminal activity and it should therefore be passed on to the police.

8

WITHOUT PREJUDICE IMMUNITY

1 INTRODUCTION

Negotiation immunity

8.1 Without prejudice rule immunity – or without prejudice privilege – is based on the principle that documents and information that are generated by negotiations between parties to a dispute are immune (or privileged) from production in court if settlement is not achieved and if a case then goes to trial. The immunity is based, first, on public policy: that parties should be encouraged to settle their disputes without going to trial;[1] secondly, it is a term, implied between the parties, that they agree that admissions made against interest by either or any of them, will not be disclosed by the other (unless both or all parties agree to waiver).[2] This was explained by Robert Walker LJ in *Unilever v Proctor & Gamble*:[3]

> [35] … the without prejudice rule is founded partly in public policy and partly in the agreement of the parties.

8.2 To this end, this chapter refers to without prejudice immunity and the without prejudice rule and attempts to make no reference to the term 'privilege'. Its inclusion in the book is justified on grounds that, as between the parties, negotiations for settlement are confidential as between the parties and may be confidential between them and any mediator.

8.3 The negotiations must be reasonably 'proximate' to any litigation if the immunity is to apply to the material (eg, letters and proposals) generated by them.[4]

8.4 Documents involved in the negotiation may be headed 'without prejudice'. Often this will be the case; but such a heading is not essential if negotiation documents are to be treated as immune from production. There are a number of exceptions to this immunity (summarised in *Unilever plc v The Procter &*

1 *Cutts v Head* [1984] Ch 290, Oliver J.

2 *Unilever plc v The Procter & Gamble Co* [2000] 1 WLR 2436, CA; and see 8.32.

3 [2000] 1 WLR 2436, CA.

4 *Framlington Group Ltd & Anor v Barnetson* [2007] EWCA Civ 502, [2007] 1 WLR 2443; see Part 4.

Gamble Co[5]) where documents or information, otherwise covered by the rule, may be adduced in evidence if the court so orders.

Privilege from inspection and production

8.5 Documents covered by the without prejudice rule are described as 'privileged'. However, the immunity is closer to a form of confidentiality between parties to a particular dispute or litigation. The only sense in which 'privilege' arises is that material covered by the without prejudice rule is immune – 'privileged' in a loose sense of the word – from production in court. That is the limit of their similarity with other forms of privilege considered in this book.

8.6 Without prejudice rule immunity, though it may also be termed 'privilege', is quite different from legal professional privilege, for example, in that, by definition, that privilege in that sense depends on only one party – or jointly with one or more other parties – having access to documents; whereas material covered by the without prejudice rule is, by definition (since it is part of negotiations) common to all parties to the particular dispute. This was explained by Jacobs LJ in *Reed Executive plc and another v Reed Business Information Ltd and others* as follows:[6]

> [19] [It is submitted] that the exclusion of "without prejudice" negotiations is a rule of evidence not a privilege, relying on *Rush & Tompkins Ltd v Greater London Council* [1989] AC 1280. That case was not actually concerned with the difference. Nor, as I see, does it matter what label is attached to it. It is a rule of law. Normally "privilege" attaches to the rights of a single party, for instance a party has, and can waive, legal professional privilege. The detail of "without prejudice" negotiations has some analogy, the difference being that it is admissible if both parties "waive" their rights to non-disclosure …

8.7 This chapter proceeds as follows:

- Part 2 defines the rule and its operation where there are genuine settlement negotiations between parties to litigation, or incipient litigation.
- Part 3 looks at the requirement that for the rule to apply litigation must be in prospect.
- Part 4 considers admissions in negotiations.
- Part 5 considers the termination of the immunity.
- Part 6 considers exceptions to the rule:
  - The *Unilever* list and where without prejudice rule immunity may be overridden; and some specific examples from that list.
  - Where without prejudice correspondence may be looked at to determine if there was an agreement in that correspondence.

5 See n 2; and see 8.32.

6 [2004] EWCA (Civ) 887, [2004] 1 WLR 3026.

- Overriding the immunity where without prejudice correspondence can show that it is being used to 'cloak perjury, blackmail or other unambiguous impropriety'.
- To what extent can without prejudice rule correspondence be used in separate proceedings?
- *Calderbank* correspondence, which automatically overrides the without prejudice rule where appropriate and on an issue of costs.
- The *Oceanbulk* exception: to use evidence from the parties' negotiations to explain terms of their agreement.

• Section 7 considers briefly the subject of waiver of the immunity.

2 THE WITHOUT PREJUDICE RULE

Genuine settlement negotiations

8.8 Without prejudice immunity depends on the existence of genuine settlement negotiations. In that case the immunity will attach to documents and other relevant material arising from those negotiations. Use of words such as 'without prejudice' on correspondence or at the outset of a meeting does not dictate whether a document or meeting is covered by the rule. The immunity can only apply if there are genuine negotiations. Lord Hope explained this in *Ofulue v Bossert*:[7]

> [2] Sometimes letters get headed "without privilege" in the most absurd circumstances, as Ormrod J observed in *Tomlin v Standard Telephones & Cables Ltd* [1969] 1 WLR 1378, 1384. But where the letters are not headed "without prejudice" unnecessarily or meaninglessly, as he went on to say at p 1385, the court should be very slow to lift the umbrella unless the case for doing so is absolutely plain …

8.9 In *Williams v Hull*,[8] Arnold J echoed the comments of Ormrod LJ and Lord Hope above: if a letter is in fact headed 'without prejudice' there is a rebuttable presumption that it will be treated as being covered by the without prejudice rule:

> [18] It is well established that a communication which is not expressed to be "without prejudice" may nevertheless be protected by the rule, and that a communication which is expressed to be "without prejudice" may nevertheless not be protected by the rule. In *South Shropshire District Council v Amos* [1986] 1 WLR 1271 at 1277 Parker LJ said that, where a letter was marked "without prejudice": 'This prima facie means that it was intended to be a negotiating document.' He went on to make it clear that that did not mean that the marking was conclusive. It may be, in the light

7 [2009] UKHL 16.

8 [2009] EWHC 2844 (Ch).

> of the observations of Lord Mance in *Bradford & Bingley plc v Rashid* [2006] UKHL 37 at [84]–[87], that this slightly overstates the position. Nevertheless, I think it is correct to say that, if a letter is expressly stated to be "without prejudice", that gives rise to a rebuttable presumption that the communication is a without prejudice communication within the meaning of the rule unless it is clear that the expression has been used with some other meaning or purpose.

Immunity for admissions in negotiations

8.10 The without prejudice rule entitles a party not to disclose to the court details of negotiations in relation to litigation, or anticipated litigation. It protects statements or offers made in the course of negotiations for settlement of a case from being put before the court as admissions against interest.

8.11 The rule was described by Lord Clarke (with whom the other law lords agreed) in *Oceanbulk Shipping & Trading SA v TMT Asia Ltd and ors*)[9] ('*Oceanbulk*') as follows:

> [19] The approach to without prejudice negotiations and their effect has undergone significant development over the years. Thus the without prejudice principle, or, as it is usually called, the without prejudice rule, initially focused on the case where the negotiations between two parties were regarded as without prejudice to the position of each of the parties in the event that the negotiations failed. The essential purpose of the original rule was that, if the negotiations failed and the dispute proceeded, neither party should be able to rely upon admissions made by the other in the course of the negotiations. The underlying rationale of the rule was that the parties would be more likely to speak frankly if nothing they said could subsequently be relied upon and that, as a result, they would be more likely to settle their dispute.

(a) The public policy element

8.12 What is regarded as the public policy element to the rule is that it is intended to encourage parties to speak frankly in the hopes that they will settle their litigation. This was explained by Lord Griffiths in *Rush & Tomkins Ltd v Greater London Council*:[10]

> [23] ... The "without prejudice" rule is a rule governing the admissibility of evidence and is founded upon the public policy of encouraging litigants to settle their differences rather than litigate them to a finish. It is nowhere more clearly expressed than in the judgment of Oliver LJ in *Cutts v Head* [(above) at] 306: 'That the rule rests, at least in part,

9 [2010] UKSC 44.
10 [1989] 1 AC 1280.

> upon public policy: ... that parties should be encouraged so far as possible to settle their disputes without resort to litigation and should not be discouraged by the knowledge that anything that is said in the course of such negotiations (and that includes, of course, as much the failure to reply to an offer as an actual reply) may be used to their prejudice in the course of the proceedings ... The public policy justification, in truth, essentially rests on the desirability of preventing statements or offers made in the course of negotiations for settlement being brought before the court of trial as admissions on the question of liability ...'

(b) Contractual element

8.13 The contractual basis of the rule rests on the implied agreement of the parties that communications in the course of their negotiations should not be admissible in evidence if, despite their negotiations, a contested hearing ensues. In *Unilever plc v The Procter & Gamble Co*,[11] Robert Walker LJ considered the general application of the rule, first as to public policy and then as to its contractual qualities, as follows:

> Its other basis or foundation is in the express or implied agreement of the parties themselves that communications in the course of their negotiations should not be admissible in evidence if, despite the negotiations, a contested hearing ensues.

Waiver of without prejudice privilege

8.14 The agreement may be waived by the parties (whether expressly or impliedly) but waiver can only be by both or all the parties jointly (any mediator's assent to this joint agreement is not needed[12]). In the case of *Calderbank* correspondence,[13] the express waiver by one party is accepted as part of a position treated by both as excluding the privilege, uniquely in respect of the specific correspondence on costs and the outcome of the case.

3 LITIGATION IN PROSPECT

Court proceedings or litigation in prospect

8.15 The without prejudice rule attaches only where there are court proceedings in existence or proceedings are anticipated. The principle is that there must be a dispute and an attempt by negotiations to resolve it; though there is no need for

11 [2000] 1 WLR 2436 at 2442.

12 *Farm Assist Ltd v Secretary of State for the Environment, Food and Rural Affairs (No 2)* [2009] EWHC 1102 (TCC), Ramsey J.

13 After *Calderbank v Calderbank* [1976] Fam 93.

actual litigation to have started. This was explained by Lord Mance in *Bradford & Bingley Plc v Rashid*:[14]

> [81] ... The existence of a dispute and of an attempt to compromise it are at the heart of the rule whereby evidence may be excluded (or disclosure of material precluded) as "without prejudice". This is clear from the passage ... from Lord Griffiths' speech in *Rush & Tompkins Ltd v Greater London Council* [(above) and there quoted in full]: ... The rule does not of course depend upon disputants already being engaged in litigation. But there must as a matter of law be a real dispute capable of settlement in the sense of compromise ...

8.16 In what circumstances can it be said that proceedings are genuinely anticipated? When can it be said that there is a 'real dispute capable of settlement' and therefore of engaging the rule? Sometimes this will be obvious. Two people who have hitherto lived together as a couple in more-or-less harmonious existence, do not normally meet and discuss their future financial arrangements with a mediator or take on solicitors to negotiate about their relationship, unless at that stage one or both of them think their relationship or marriage is at an end.

8.17 Formal mediation or other professional involvement is not a pre-requisite to a finding that without prejudice immunity applies; but where either are present, the likelihood is that proceedings are proximate.

8.18 If a mediator is not involved the question of proximity of any proceedings may be critical. In *BE v DE*,[15] Bodey J considered whether a 'post-pre-nuptial' (the husband's term) agreement was part of a negotiation for settlement of an incipient matrimonial dispute; but where the wife said the document was presented to her at a dinner where she thought she was meeting her husband to discuss reconciliation. (She wanted to be able to use the document as evidence that she was resident in England.) The document was held not to be covered by privilege.

8.19 *SC v YD*[16] was an appeal from a district judge's case management decision in linked Trusts of Land and Appointment of Trustees Act 1996 and Children Act 1989 Schedule 1 proceedings, where Roberts J refused permission to appeal.[17] The case related to a document produced by SC (the man) to YD as a proposal to settle; though neither was, at that stage, involved in litigation. Litigation was held not to be sufficiently proximate for the without prejudice rule to apply.

---

14 [2006] UKHL 37, [2006] 1 WLR 2066.

15 [2014] EWHC 2318 (Fam). Both parties – unknown to each other – had filed what they called 'protective' divorce petitions in different jurisdictions.

16 [2014] EWHC 2446 (Fam).

17 In refusing permission to appeal, the judge made a series of what might be regarded as findings. Strictly speaking they are only persuasive because permission to appeal was refused. Given the important discussion conducted by the judge on law it is perhaps disappointing that she did not give permission and then dismiss the appeal.

Framlington v Barnetson: *litigation, how proximate?*

8.20 In *Framlington Group Ltd & Anor v Barnetson,*[18] the question was: How proximate was litigation to the parties' negotiations?[19] Mr Barnetson (B) claimed damages against Framlington for wrongful dismissal from its employment as its chief operating officer and for other alleged breaches of his contract of employment. Information as to the course of negotiations which preceded and followed the dismissal was detailed in B's statement in later court proceedings. Framlington sought to have this information excluded so far as it contained details of the parties' negotiations.

8.21 The outcome of the negotiations, as Auld LJ held, was that the truth of the parties' positions was that 'they were already well and truly at odds as to [B's] contractual entitlement'. What followed 'amounted to wrangling over the terms of that entitlement, not discussions as to variation of them' as the judge below had found. The Court of Appeal was therefore confronted by:

> [38] ... negotiations arising out of a dispute as to Mr Barnetson's contractual entitlement on his early dismissal, all against the backcloth of potential litigation if they could not resolve the dispute by compromise.

8.22 The claim for pre-issue privilege cannot 'turn on purely temporal considerations'. Proximity must depend also on the nature and subject matter of the dispute; and on whether the parties anticipated litigation if they could not agree:

> [34] The critical feature of proximity for this purpose, it seems to me, is one of the subject matter of the dispute rather than how long before the threat, or start, of litigation it was aired in negotiations between the parties. Would they have respectively lowered their guards at that time and in the circumstances if they had not thought or hoped or contemplated that, by doing so, they could avoid the need to go to court over the very same dispute? On that approach, which I would commend, the crucial consideration would be whether in the course of negotiations the parties contemplated or might reasonably have contemplated litigation if they could not agree.

8.23 The 'crucial consideration', as Auld LJ explained, was the extent to which the parties 'contemplated or might reasonably have contemplated litigation if they could not agree'.

The life of an offer

8.24 The continued life of the negotiations and thus the continuance of application of the without prejudice rule raises a separate point. For example,

18 [2007] EWCA Civ 502, [2007] 1 WLR 2443.

19 For a review of the applicable law on proximity the applicable law was helpfully reviewed in the Employment Appeal Tribunal in *Portnykh v Nomura International plc* [2013] UKEAT 0448-13-0511 HHJ Hand QC.

in *Brown v Rice and anor*,[20] Mr Stuart Isaacs QC (sitting as a deputy High Court judge in the Chancery Division) pointed out that offers made in mediation 'are commonly left on the table after conclusion of the formal mediation'. That is to say, they have a life beyond the mediation. This might enable the parties to reflect on proposals they had discussed. He took the view that acceptance of an offer in these circumstances is as capable of forming a valid acceptance, as if it was made in mediation.[21]

4 ADMISSIONS IN NEGOTIATIONS

Admissions in the course of proceedings

8.25 Admissions against the interest of the party making them are the main rationale for the rule. It enables a party to litigation or anticipated litigation to make admissions which cannot later be put forward as evidence in the court proceedings by the party to whom the admission was made. Making such admissions immune from production in court is intended to encourage settlement of cases.

8.26 The importance of the freedom to make admissions against interest in the without prejudice rule is stressed by Robert Walker LJ in *Unilever plc v The Procter & Gamble Co*[22] (emphasis added):

> [35] ... the without prejudice rule is founded partly in public policy and partly in the agreement of the parties. *They show that the protection of admissions against interest is the most important practical effect of the rule.* But to dissect out identifiable admissions and withhold protection from the rest of without prejudice communications (except for a special reason) would not only create huge practical difficulties but would be contrary to the underlying objective of giving protection to the parties ... to speak freely about all issues in the litigation ...
>
> [36] Parties cannot speak freely at a without prejudice meeting if they must constantly monitor every sentence, with lawyers ... sitting at their shoulders as minders.

5 TERMINATION OF THE IMMUNITY

Termination or exception of privilege

8.27 Other than by waiver, when does without prejudice immunity and any confidentiality arising from the immunity come to an end? The privilege from disclosure of without prejudice documents operates only as against the court

20 [2007] EWHC Ch 625.

21 Ibid at [63].

22 [1999] EWCA Civ 3027, [2000] 1 WLR 2436.

and in respect of deployment in any proceedings which may arise following or alongside the negotiation. Two questions follow from this:

(1) Once the entirety of the proceedings are at an end, then as between the parties and the court it could be argued that there is no longer any question of privilege from production. To what extent does the confidentiality in the documents remain following conclusion of the proceedings by a court order, so that others can still be prevented from seeing them? This question is considered in this section.

(2) The privilege or immunity may also come to an end in a number of specific circumstances, considered in Part 6 of this chapter.

8.28 Lord Griffiths considered termination of the immunity in *Rush & Tompkins Ltd v Greater London Council*.[23] Does the conclusion of the proceedings or other dispute dispose also of the privilege? Lord Griffith explained his view as follows:

> I cannot accept the view of the Court of Appeal that *Walker v Wilsher* (1889) 23 QBD 335 is authority for the proposition that if the negotiations succeed and a settlement is concluded the privilege goes, having served its purpose. In *Walker v Wilsher* the Court of Appeal held that it was not permissible to receive the contents of a "without prejudice" offer on the question of costs and no question arose as to the admissibility of admissions made in the negotiations in any possible subsequent proceedings. There are many situations when parties engaged upon some great enterprise such as a large building construction project must anticipate the risk of being involved in disputes with others engaged on the same project. Suppose the main contractor in an attempt to settle a dispute with one subcontractor made certain admissions it is clear law that those admissions cannot be used against him if there is no settlement. The reason they are not to be used is because it would discourage settlement if he believed that the admissions might be held against him. But it would surely be equally discouraging if the main contractor knew that if he achieved a settlement those admissions could then be used against him by any other subcontractor with whom he might also be in dispute. The main contractor might well be prepared to make certain concessions to settle some modest claim which he would never make in the face of another far larger claim.

8.29 Lord Griffiths bases his findings as to continuance of the privilege where it arises in a set of proceedings with more than one party. A can settle on terms that the correspondence between A and another party (B) can remain confidential between both of them and that the correspondence is immune from disclosure to another party (C). The correspondence then remains privileged from disclosure to the court in the continuing proceedings between A and C (this was the position in *Rush & Tompkins*) and confidential to A and B as against C.

---

23 [1989] AC 1280 at 1300.

8.30 By contrast where there are separate proceedings between A and D (as in *Muller v Linsley*[24]) if A raises an issue which is answered by something arising in the negotiations and settlement of a claim between A and B (assertions as to the reasonableness of their earlier settlement of company law proceedings, in the separate professional negligence case of *Muller v Linsley*) then the confidentiality of the negotiations and their without prejudice immunity goes.

A rationale

8.31 If there is no finalisation of the proceedings in which the privilege arises, then, unless waived, it continues to bind the parties to its joint confidentiality. Once proceedings are concluded, says Lord Hope, any protection from without prejudice immunity 'ceases to have any purpose'.[25] In logic, it can be said: once there is a court order then – as with a concluded agreement arising from without prejudice correspondence – the privilege is at an end. The terms of the negotiations can be looked at to determine whether an agreement can be constructed from the correspondence.[26]

6 EXCEPTIONS TO WITHOUT PREJUDICE PRIVILEGE

The Unilever list

Without prejudice privilege: 'the ability to speak freely'

8.32 In *Unilever plc v The Proctor & Gamble Co*[27] Robert Walker LJ sets out what he describes as the 'most important instances' where the without prejudice rule may be lost, or it may otherwise be held that the rule does not apply. Relevant evidence, otherwise thought to be immune from production, will then be admissible in subsequent proceedings where examples in this list apply and the privilege has been lost. The *Unilever* list was cited with approval by the House of Lords/Supreme Court in both *Ofulue v Bossert* and in *Oceanbulk*.[28]

8.33 The full list follows; and then four instances relevant to family proceedings will be considered in more detail:

(1) Where the issue is whether without prejudice communications have resulted in a concluded compromise agreement, those communications are admissible (see eg, *Tomlin v Standard Telephones and Cables*[29]).

24 *Muller & anor v Linsley & Mortimer* [1994] EWCA Civ 39, [1996] PNLR 74.
25 *Ofulue v Bossert* [2009] UKHL 16, [2009] 1 AC 990.
26 *Tomlin v Standard Telephones* [1969] 1 WLR 1378.
27 [1999] EWCA Civ 3027, [2000] 1 WLR 2436.
28 *Oceanbulk Shipping & Trading SA v TMT Asia Ltd and ors* [2010] UKSC 44.
29 [1969] 1 WLR 1378.

(2) Evidence of the negotiations is admissible to show that an agreement arising from negotiations 'should be set aside on the ground of misrepresentation, fraud or undue influence'.

(3) Even if no compromise results 'a clear statement which is made by one party to negotiations, and on which the other party is intended to act and does in fact act, may be admissible as giving rise to an estoppel' (see eg, Neuberger J in *Hodgkinson & Corby v Wards Mobility Services*[30]).

(4) One party may be allowed to give evidence of what the other said or wrote in without prejudice negotiations if the exclusion of the evidence would act as a cloak for perjury, blackmail or other 'unambiguous impropriety' (see eg, *Williams v Hull* (below)).

(5) 'Evidence of negotiations may be given (for instance, on an application to strike out proceedings for want of prosecution) in order to explain delay or apparent acquiescence.'

(6) In *Muller & anor v Linsley & Mortimer*[31] one of the issues between the parties was whether the claimant, in an action against his former solicitors, had acted reasonably to mitigate his loss in his conduct and conclusion of other negotiations and compromise of proceedings. Hoffmann LJ treated that issue as one unconnected with the truth or falsity of anything stated in the negotiations, 'and as therefore falling outside the principle of public policy protecting without prejudice communications.'

(7) The exception for an offer expressly made 'without prejudice except as to costs' was clearly recognised by this court in *Cutts v Head*, and by the House of Lords in *Rush & Tomkins*, as based on an express or implied agreement between the parties.

8.34 To this list must be added the *Oceanbulk* exception,[32] considered at (5) below.

Correspondence as evidence of agreement

Without prejudice correspondence: evidence of agreement

8.35 Where one party asserts that correspondence, otherwise covered by the without prejudice rule, is evidence of an agreement then – if that party is correct – the immunity from production of the evidence to the court goes (*Tomlin v Standard Telephones and Cables* (above)). The correspondence, formerly immune from production, becomes the evidence (or part of it) for the agreement between the parties.

8.36 The alleged agreement in *Tomlin v Standard Telephones* was that in correspondence – all marked 'without prejudice' – the parties had agreed that,

30 [1997] FSR 178 at 191.

31 [1994] EWCA Civ 39, [1996] PNLR 74.

32 *Oceanbulk Shipping & Trading SA v TMT Asia Ltd and ors* [2010] UKSC 44.

whatever the outcome of the damages claim in terms of quantum, the plaintiff should receive 50 per cent. A hesitant Court of Appeal (Ormrod LJ dissenting) held that this is what had been agreed. Dankwerts LJ (with whom Sir Gordon Wilmer agreed) reasoned the agreement point as follows:[33]

> The judge quoted a statement by Lindley LJ which ... seems to me to have great force and to be of great importance with regard to the present case. This was in *Walker v Wilsher* (1889) 23 QBD 335. When the case is looked at, it appears that, in fact, the decision was that the letters in question should not have been looked at for the purpose of the case at all and consequently the judge in the court below had been at fault in relying upon them for the purpose of depriving the party of his costs. In the course of his judgment, however, Lindley LJ said at 337: 'What is the meaning of the words "without prejudice"? I think they mean without prejudice to the position of the writer of the letter if the terms he proposes are not accepted. If the terms proposed in the letter are accepted a complete contract is established, and the letter, although written without prejudice, operates to alter the old state of things and to establish a new one.'
>
> That statement of Lindley LJ is of great authority and seems to me to apply exactly to the present case if, in fact, there was a binding agreement, or an agreement intended to be binding, reached between the parties, and, accordingly, it seems to me that not only was the court entitled to look at the letters, though they were described as "without prejudice" but it is quite possible (and, in fact, the intention of the parties was) that there was a binding agreement contained in that correspondence.

8.37 In *Muller v Linsey* (below) Hoffman LJ explained the same point as follows:

> Thus, when the issue is whether without prejudice letters have resulted in an agreed settlement, the correspondence is admissible because the relevance of the letters has nothing to do with the truth of any facts which the writers may have expressly or impliedly admitted. They are relevant because they contain the offer and acceptance forming a contract which has replaced the cause of action previously in dispute.

Without prejudice used to cloak perjury, blackmail or other unambiguous impropriety

Documents as a cloak for impropriety

8.38 Evidence of otherwise privileged documents cease to be immune from production if they are established to be being used a 'cloak for ... impropriety'. The *Unilever* list[34] describes this heading as:

33 Ibid at 1382–1383.
34 Ibid at 2444.

Apart from any concluded contract or estoppel, one party may be allowed to give evidence of what the other said or wrote in without prejudice negotiations if the exclusion of the evidence would act as a cloak for perjury, blackmail or other "unambiguous impropriety" (the expression used by Hoffmann LJ in *Forster v Friedland* (unreported), 10 November 1992; Court of Appeal (Civil Division) Transcript No. 1052 of 1992).

8.39 This allegation was raised, unsuccessfully, by the applicant (who was herself a solicitor) as a preliminary issue in *Williams v Hull*.[35] The primary claim was by former cohabitants who sought a declaration from the court as to their beneficial interests in their jointly owned property under the Trusts of Land and Appointment of Trustees Act 1996. Their contributions to the purchase price had been such that Ms Williams (W) had paid appreciably more than Mr Hull (H). The couple had signed a TR1 (transfer of title) which appeared to have been altered after its execution by them. This document might be treated as defining their beneficial entitlements.

8.40 W sought an order that without prejudice immunity did not attach to a letter written to her by H. This letter was one in a series of three written by the couple to each other before the issue of proceedings. W sought to rely on the second letter in the series, headed by H: 'Subject to Contract and Without Prejudice.' In the letter H made specific reference to his then estimate of the valuation of his share in the property. W sought to bring H's letter within the *Unilever* exception as 'cloaked in perjury'. She argued that H's pleaded case – that he was entitled to an equal share in the property with her – contradicted what was in his letter.

8.41 Arnold J held that there might be inconsistencies between H's pleaded case and what was asserted in the letter, and this might lead ultimately to an allegation of perjury at a later date. However, such an allegation at a preliminary stage in the proceedings was not enough to override the immunity provided by the without prejudice rule and thus to prevent production of the letter at this stage.

Whether privilege can apply in separate proceedings

Reasonableness of settlement in earlier proceedings

8.42 In *Muller & anor v Linsley & Mortimer*,[36] one of the issues between the parties was whether the claimant, in an action against his former solicitors, had acted reasonably to mitigate his loss in his conduct and conclusion of earlier negotiations and compromise of proceedings arising from work the solicitors had done on their behalf. In the subsequent professional negligence proceedings, the Mullers claimed that the terms of the settlement between them and their former employers/fellow shareholders was reasonable; but they refused to allow

35 [2009] EWHC 2844 (Ch) per Arnold J; the judge discusses the impropriety heading fully at [45]–[55].

36 [1994] EWCA Civ 39, [1996] PNLR 74.

inspection of the documents – which they claimed were covered by without prejudice privilege – to confirm or deny this.

8.43 Hoffman LJ gave the main judgement. He found that the documents should be disclosed in the second and separate proceedings, mostly on the basis that the defendants – the solicitors who were being sued in negligence – were not parties to the negotiations giving rise to the settlement. The issue giving rise to the solicitors' claim for disclosure had been raised by the Mullers themselves (ie, the reasonableness of the settlement and the extent to which they had mitigated their loss). He excluded the public policy element, which he saw as directed 'solely to admissions'. The solicitors were not a party to the earlier proceedings.

8.44 Where the solicitor defendants were not parties to the negotiations 'there can be no other basis for the privilege'. The issue with which the correspondence was concerned was the plaintiffs' assertion of their reasonableness. The correspondence goes to that issue, not to the truth or otherwise, of any admissions made by the Mullers:

> ... the without prejudice correspondence forms part of that conduct and its relevance lies in the light it may throw on whether the Mullers acted reasonably in concluding the ultimate settlement and not in its admissibility to establish the truth of any express or implied admissions it may contain ...

Calderbank correspondence

Without prejudice correspondence and costs

8.45 In *Muller & anor v Linsley & Mortimer,*[37] Hoffman LJ explained the logic of the rule which enables without prejudice correspondence to be used alongside a claim for costs (*Calderbank* correspondence) and by reference to Oliver J in *Cutts v Head* [38] as follows:

> So, in *Cutts v Head* the rule that one could not rely upon a without prejudice offer on the question of costs after judgment was held not to be based upon any public policy. It did not promote the policy of encouraging settlements because as Oliver LJ said: "As a practical matter, a consciousness of a risk as to costs if reasonable offers are refused can only encourage settlement ..." It followed that the only basis for excluding reference to a without prejudice offer on costs was an implied agreement based on general usage and understanding that the party making the offer would not do so. Such an implication could be excluded by a contrary statement as in a *Calderbank* offer.

37 Ibid.
38 [1984] Ch 290 at 306.

8.46 In *Calderbank v Calderbank*,[39] Cairns LJ (with whom Scarman LJ and Sir Gordon Willmer agreed) in the Court of Appeal explained what has become the basis for the *Calderbank* offer, as follows:

> There are various other types of proceedings well known to the court where protection has been able to be afforded to a party who wants to make a compromise of [proceedings] and where payment-in is not an appropriate method. One is in proceedings before the Lands Tribunal where the amount of compensation is in issue and where the method that is adopted is that of a sealed offer which is not made without prejudice but which remains concealed from the tribunal until the decision on the substantive issue has been made and the offer is then opened when the discussion as to costs takes place. Another example is in the Admiralty Division where there is commonly a dispute between the owners of two vessels that have been in collision as to the apportionment of blame between them. It is common practice for an offer to be made by one party to another of a certain apportionment. If that is not accepted no reference is made to that offer in the course of the hearing until it comes to costs, and then if the court's apportionment is as favourable to the party who made the offer as what was offered, or more favourable to him, then costs will be awarded on the same basis as if there had been a payment in.
>
> I see no reason why some similar practice should not be adopted in relation to such matrimonial proceedings in relation to finances as we have been concerned with.

8.47 Thus, a party to proceedings can specifically give advanced notice that otherwise privileged correspondence will be able to lift the without prejudice immunity and open without prejudice correspondence for consideration of the court (where applicable) on an issue as to costs.

8.48 That the *Calderbank* letter is also applicable outside family proceedings was confirmed by Oliver LJ in *Cutts v Head*:[40]

> I think that it must now be taken to be established that the *Calderbank* formula suggested by Cairns LJ is not restricted to matrimonial proceedings but is available in all cases where what is in issue is something more than a simple money claim in respect of which a payment into court would be the appropriate way of proceeding.

Costs without the Calderbank *formula: the 'wholly "without prejudice" basis'*

8.49 The position where costs are claimed on the basis of without prejudice correspondence, but no *Calderbank* formula – 'without prejudice save as to costs' – is used was considered by the Court of Appeal in *Reed Executive plc and another*

39 [1976] Fam 93, (1975) FLR Rep 123.

40 [1984] Ch 290 at 312.

v Reed Business Information Ltd and others [41] where Jacob LJ said of cases which are argued on a 'wholly "without prejudice" basis':

> [21] But generally, parties who have negotiated on a wholly "without prejudice" basis have always done so in the faith and expectation that what they say cannot be used against them even on the question of costs. As long ago as 1889 this court held, in *Walker v Wilsher* (1889) 23 QBD 335 that, in the words of the headnote: "Letters or conversations written or declared to be 'without prejudice' cannot be taken into consideration in determining whether there is good cause for depriving a successful litigant of costs." I shall call that "the rule in Walker v Wilsher".

***Oceanbulk*: construction of terms of agreement**

Oceanbulk Shipping*: facts and the interpretation exception*

8.50 *Oceanbulk*[42] provides an exception to the without prejudice rule, explained by Lord Phillips, as to assist when the construction of the terms of a contract is in issue in proceedings:

> [48] ... evidence of facts within their common knowledge is admissible where those facts have a bearing on the meaning that should be given to the words of the contract. This is so even where the knowledge of those facts is conveyed by one party to the other in the course of negotiations which are conducted "without prejudice".

8.51 The exclusion exception to the without prejudice rule is described by Lord Clarke, who gave the lead speech and with whom all the other Supreme Court judges agreed, as making admissible factual evidence of what was communicated between the parties to settlement negotiations, in any subsequent dispute as to the terms of their agreement. The limit of the exception to the rule is that it applies to factual information only which assists in construction of what may be the meaning of the settlement terms.[43] This exception, said Lord Clarke, 'should be recognised as an exception to the without prejudice rule' (para [46]).

8.52 A substantial debt was due from the appellants and was the subject of an agreement between them and their creditor, the respondent. The issue before the Court related to forward freight agreements by which the parties bet on the value of market rates for freight moving by sea, the result of which was that they owed the respondent substantial sums of money which they had failed to repay. Terms were settled between them, and both parties accepted that their settlement terms were accurately recorded in the written settlement agreement. The issue which divided the parties was as to the 'true construction of one of the terms of the agreement'. Was it therefore permissible 'to refer to anything written or said in

41 [2004] EWCA (Civ) 887, [2004] 1 WLR 3026.

42 *Oceanbulk Shipping & Trading SA v TMT Asia Ltd and ors* [2010] UKSC 44, [2011] 1 AC 662.

43 Ibid, see especially [40] and [41].

the course of the without prejudice negotiations as an aid to the interpretation of the agreement' (para [6]).

8.53 After reviewing the law on without prejudice privilege and the exceptions set out in *Unilever* Lord Clarke addressed the question: 'Should the interpretation exception be recognised as an exception to the without prejudice privilege rule?' In his answer he deals with construction of contracts. It will be submitted in the next section that the same principles can be applied to an agreement between parties to a mediation or to a court consent order.

8.54 Lord Clarke's short answer to the question is 'yes'.[44] His main reason was, by reference to Lord Hoffmann in *Chartbrook Ltd v Persimmon Homes Ltd*:[45]

> [37] ... Every case in which the interpretation of the language used in the contract is in issue, the question is what a reasonable person having all the background knowledge which would have been available to the parties would have understood them to be using the language in the contract to mean ...

8.55 Lord Clark continued:

> [40] In these circumstances, I see no reason why the ordinary principles governing the interpretation of a settlement agreement should be any different regardless of whether the negotiations which led to it were without prejudice. The language should be construed in the same way and the question posed by Lord Hoffmann should be the same, namely what a reasonable person having all the background knowledge which would have been available to the parties would have understood them to be using the language in the contract to mean. That background knowledge may well include objective facts communicated by one party to the other in the course of the negotiations. As I see it, the process of interpretation should in principle be the same, whether the negotiations were without prejudice or not. In both cases the evidence is admitted in order to enable the court to make an objective assessment of the parties' intentions.

8.56 Thus, facts communicated in the negotiations, but not part of the formal agreement document can be used to construct the meaning of the terms agreed between the parties.

Application of Oceanbulk *in construction of a consent order*

8.57 The same, it is submitted, applies where the negotiations lead to a consent order in family proceedings. If a term is not clear – for example what was agreed about interest on a lump sum – then the fact that 'facts communicated by

44 Ibid at [36].

45 [2009] UKHL 38, [2009] AC 1101 at [14].

one party to the other in the course of [without prejudice] negotiations'[46] should not prevent them being used to construct the meaning and terms of a – later – disputed consent order.

7 WAIVER OF WITHOUT PREJUDICE IMMUNITY

8.58 An issue as to waiver of privilege attaching to without prejudice negotiations will be unusual; since (save in rare examples) both parties to any litigation will have been parties to the negotiations in which the question of immunity arises. The immunity can only be waived by them jointly. An exception to this assertion occurs, for example, where the party seeking sight of the privileged documents is, separately, a party to proceedings where settlement had been achieved by other parties.[47]

8.59 Without prejudice immunity is joint as between the parties to the negotiation. It can only be waived by them jointly (save in the case of the *Calderbank* reservation on costs, where the right to refer to negotiation can be retained: privilege can be unilaterally waived on that issue alone). As between the client (the parties to the mediation) and the mediator, the privilege is always that of the parties to the dispute.

8.60 If there is a negotiated agreement, the terms of that and background facts on which it is based or to determine whether it is an agreement can be adduced in evidence a subsequent trial: in that sense immunity cannot apply where that is the issue before the court.[48]

46 Per Lord Clark in *Oceanbulk* above.

47 This happened eg, in *Rush & Tompkins Ltd v Greater London Council* [1989] AC 1280.

48 *Brown v Rice and anor* [2007] EWHC Ch 625, Stuart Isaacs QC sitting as a deputy judge of the High Court.

9

RELEVANT LEGAL CONTEXT

1 INTRODUCTION

Context of legal advice

9.1 This chapter belongs to the subject of legal professional privilege (LPP). It is easy to think that any steps taken by a lawyer for a client involves legal advice and that, therefore, advice privilege attaches. That is not necessarily the case. It is only that part of the lawyer's work for a client which involves legal advice, and which occurs in a 'relevant legal context',[1] which attracts LPP, though other work (eg, managing investments, fixing insurance etc) may involve confidentiality.

9.2 It is not the advice on law which makes it legal advice. It is only advice on law where that advice is given by lawyers. For present purposes, a lawyer is a solicitor or a barrister. Advice on law given by others (eg, accountants)[2] is not advice in a legal context for the purpose of LPP.

9.3 The mediation process, though it will be confidential as between the parties, cannot provide a 'legal context'; it is unlikely to attract any form of advice privilege (not least perhaps because advice is rarely given by the mediator).

9.4 This chapter proceeds as follows:

- Part 2 defines the 'relevant legal context' and considers it in the case law where it arises.
- Part 3 looks at the circumstances where a solicitor is working for a client but not as legal adviser.
- Part 4 considers circumstances where involvement of a lawyer may not give rise to privilege because the work done by the lawyer is not in a 'relevant legal context'.

1 Taylor LJ in *Balabel v Air India* [1988] Ch 317, CA (below).
2 *R (Prudential plc and anor) v Special Commissioner of Income Tax* [2013] UKSC 1, [2013] 2 AC 185.

2 RELEVANT LEGAL CONTEXT

Context of the advice

9.5 *Balabel v Air India*[3] remains the lead authority on the context in which LPP applies.[4] In that case the plaintiffs brought an action seeking specific performance of an agreement for an underlease. They sought discovery (disclosure) of certain documents: (1) communications between the defendant and its solicitors other than those seeking or giving legal advice; (2) drafts, working papers, attendance notes and memoranda of the defendant's solicitors relating to the proposed new underlease; and (3) internal communications of the defendant other than those seeking advice from the defendant's Indian legal advisers. The master upheld the defendant's claim to privilege. A circuit judge allowing the plaintiffs' appeal in respect of specified documents and held that documents which simply recorded information, transactions or meetings were not privileged.

9.6 On appeal by the defendant to the Court of Appeal, Taylor LJ explained the court's view that the purpose of LPP is to enable legal advice to be sought and given in confidence. A document was covered by privilege if it had been made confidentially for the purposes of legal advice; and such advice included as to what should prudently and sensibly be done in a 'relevant legal context'. He explained this as follows:[5]

> ... In most solicitor and client relationships, especially where a transaction involves protracted dealings, advice may be required or appropriate on matters great or small at various stages. There will be a continuum of communication and meetings between the solicitor and client. The negotiations for a lease such as occurred in the present case are only one example. Where information is passed by the solicitor or client to the other as part of the continuum aimed at keeping both informed so that advice may be sought and given as required, privilege will attach.

Legal professional privilege and 'appropriate advice'

9.7 It follows, said Taylor LJ, that in many solicitor–client relationships LPP will be presumed. In such relationships the tendering of legal advice by the lawyer to the client will be readily implied:[6]

> A letter from the client containing information may end with such words as "please advise me what I should do". But, even if it does not, there will usually be implied in the relationship an overall expectation that the solicitor will at each stage, whether asked specifically or not, tender appropriate advice. Moreover, legal advice is not confined to telling the client the law; it

3 [1988] Ch 317, CA.

4 See eg, *Z v Z (Legal Professional Privilege: Fraud Exception)* [2018] EWCA Civ 307, [2018] 4 WLR 52.

5 Ibid at 331.

6 Ibid.

must include advice as to what should prudently and sensibly be done in the relevant legal context.

9.8 In view of the increased range of assistance given by solicitors to their clients, not all solicitor and client communications were privileged, but in a conveyancing transaction, communications passing in the handling of that transaction were privileged even though they did not incorporate a specific piece of advice provided that their aim was to obtain appropriate legal advice and that, accordingly, the defendant's claim to privilege for the documents should have been upheld

9.9 Taylor LJ was critical of the judge's approach which he described as 'too restrictive. It suggests that a communication only enjoys privilege if it specifically seeks or conveys advice'.[7] Taylor LJ went on to explain the breadth which should be allowed to the term 'documents conveying legal advice':[8]

> Although originally confined to advice regarding litigation, the privilege was extended to non-litigious business. Nevertheless, despite that extension, the purpose and scope of the privilege is still to enable legal advice to be sought and given in confidence. In my judgment, therefore, the test is whether the communication or other document was made confidentially for the purposes of legal advice. Those purposes have to be construed broadly. Privilege obviously attaches to a document conveying legal advice from solicitor to client and to a specific request from the client for such advice. But it does not follow that all other communications between them lack privilege. In most solicitor and client relationships, especially where a transaction involves protracted dealings, advice may be required or appropriate on matters great or small at various stages. There will be a continuum of communication and meetings between the solicitor and client.

9.10 Taylor LJ had already explained his view that documents may be part of an exchange of information; and 'of which the object is the giving of legal advice as and when appropriate'. Finally, said Taylor J, in his definition of legal advice:[9]

> ... legal advice is not confined to telling the client the law; it must include advice as to what should prudently and sensibly be done in the relevant legal context.

Lawyers and the case for an inquiry

9.11 An important aspect of their Lordships consideration of LAP in *Three Rivers District Council and ors v Governor and Company of the Bank of England (No 6)*[10] (*'Three Rivers No 6'*) was the context in which legal advice had been provided to the Bank of England, following the collapse of the bank, Bank of Credit and Commerce

7 [1988] Ch 317 at 332.
8 Ibid at 330.
9 Ibid.
10 [2004] UKHL 48, [2004] 3 WLR 1274.

International (BCCI). Freshfields, the lawyers concerned, had assisted the Bank of England in their presentation of their case for the inquiry, set up under Bingham LJ, into its failure. The question was whether the information prepared by the bank's officials for their lawyers was covered by legal advice privilege. Tomlinson J at first instance and then the Court of Appeal had both said not.[11]

9.12 The relatively narrow issue in *Three Rivers (No 6)*, led the House of Lords to consider the justification for advice privilege which had come into question in the Court of Appeal. Two issues of principle arose on appeal to the House of Lords, both of which will be of concern to family lawyers: first, whether, for LPP purposes, communications from an employee for his or her employer and a lawyer are to be treated in the same way as a communication between a client and a lawyer; secondly, is communication where no immediate litigation is in prospect covered by privilege?[12] Conduct of an inquiry, it was suggested to their lordships, was not necessarily litigation.

9.13 These questions may be of relevance to a family lawyer. The first point raises questions as to the status of communications between social workers and other local authority employees in care or other public law proceedings with local authority lawyers. As to the inquiry question: this raises the issue of adversarial, as against inquisitorial, proceedings which may arise in a number of family proceedings, but which – for the present – can be side-stepped here, since the House of Lords made light of dismissing it (as will be seen).

9.14 In its discussion of the principles relevant to these two questions the House started from the principle, which attaches to all consideration of what defines advice privilege: namely that it is essential to take account of the context in which the discussions with a lawyer took place. It will therefore be appropriate to review the context question first and then to return to the specific points which arose in *Three River (No 6)*.

3 SOLICITOR WORKING NOT IN A 'LEGAL CONTEXT'

Solicitor: not acting as a lawyer

9.15 In *Minter v Priest*,[13] the respondent, Mr Priest, was a solicitor. However, his relationship with two men who had approached him was such that the House of Lords considered that he was not acting as a lawyer. The two men had approached Mr Priest essentially as a mortgage broker. At his meeting with the men he had slandered the plaintiff/appellant (a land agent who was the owner of the land proposed to be charged by the men). Thus, said Lord Buckmaster LC, because

11 Per Lord Scott: [19] 'The judgment (*Three Rivers (No. 6)*) made clear the view of the Court of Appeal that for legal advice privilege purposes the advice being sought from the lawyers must be advice as to legal rights or liabilities. Advice as to how the Bank should present its case to the Inquiry so as to lead to a conclusion as favourable to the Bank as possible did not qualify for privilege.'

12 See Lord Scott at [21] and [29].

13 [1930] AC 558.

clients have a conversation with a solicitor, does not mean automatically that it is covered by any form of privilege:[14]

> The conversation to secure this privilege must be such as, within a very wide and generous ambit of interpretation, must be fairly referable to the relationship, but outside that boundary the mere fact that a person speaking is a solicitor, and the person to whom he speaks is his client affords no protection.

9.16 It therefore followed, said Lord Buckmaster:[15]

> ... in my opinion, the cloak of privilege is stripped off the whole conversation and, as the learned judge said, the respondent "is responsible in the same way as if the words had been uttered on any other occasion".

9.17 In *Three Rivers (No 6)*,[16] Lord Carswell cited extensively from *Balabel v Air India*[17] and then affirmed that what had been said there and in the earlier *Minter v Priest*[18] remains the law in relation to legal professional privilege and its context:

> [111] ... I agree with the view expressed by Colman J in *Nederlandse Reassurantie Groep Holding NV v Bacon & Woodrow Holding* [1995] 1 All ER 976 at 982 that the statement of the law in *Balabel v Air India* does not disturb or modify the principle affirmed in *Minter v Priest*, that all communications between a solicitor and his client relating to a transaction in which the solicitor has been instructed for the purpose of obtaining legal advice will be privileged, notwithstanding that they do not contain advice on matters of law or construction, provided that they are directly related to the performance by the solicitor of his professional duty as legal adviser of his client.

9.18 Legal professional privilege, whether as LAP or as LP, cannot exist in the absence of a legal issue or context in which it operates. Legal advice or pending litigation is the oxygen which feeds it. It is not therefore necessary that only litigation is pending for the advice to qualify for protection from privilege.[19] It is the legal advice which qualifies it for LPP. Conversely, the mere fact of speaking with a lawyer does not guarantee protection.

---

14 Ibid at 568.

15 Ibid at 570; even if a relationship of solicitor and client had been found in *Minter v Priest*, the facts might have justified a claim that the 'iniquity exemption' applied so that legal professional privilege might have been excluded from the outset.

16 [2004] UKHL 48, [2004] 3 WLR 1274.

17 [1988] Ch 317.

18 [1930] AC 558.

19 *Greenough v Gaskell* (1833) 1 My & K 98.

Legal professional privilege: 'within justifiable bounds'

9.19 Taylor LJ touches upon the 'ordinary business' point in *Balabel.*[20] The term 'ordinary business of a solicitor' was one which was changing. LPP could only apply to the legal advice aspect. Its extent must therefore be kept under review.

> It follows from this analysis that those dicta in the decided cases which appear to extend privilege without limit to all solicitor and client communication upon matters within the ordinary business of a solicitor and referable to that relationship are too wide. It may be that the broad terms used in the earlier cases reflect the restricted range of solicitors' activities at the time. Their role then would have been confined for the most part to that of lawyer and would not have extended to business adviser or man of affairs. To speak therefore of matters "within the ordinary business of a solicitor" would in practice usually have meant the giving of advice and assistance of a specifically legal nature. But the range of assistance given by solicitors to their clients and of activities carried out on their behalf has greatly broadened in recent times and is still developing. Hence the need to re-examine the scope of legal professional privilege and keep it within justifiable bounds.

Litigation not a pre-requisite

9.20 The context need not be litigious for legal advice privilege to apply. *Balabel v Air India*[21] related to a conveyancing transaction, just as in *C v C (Privilege)*,[22] the court was dealing with an application by a wife to see a lawyers' conveyancing file. In the second case, a wife asserted that registered land conveyancing was mostly a mechanical process,[23] but the husband replied that it was 'plainly ... legal context'; and Munby J agreed.[24] His context for doing so, after a short survey of the case law on LPP, was as follows:

> [25] ... legal professional privilege is not merely a fundamental principle of the English common law. It is also a principle of European Community law and a right protected by Art 8 of the European Convention for the Protection of Human Rights and Fundamental Freedoms 1950.[[25]] ...

---

20 *Balabel v Air India* at 331–332.

21 [1988] Ch 317, CA.

22 [2006] EWHC 336 (Fam), [2008] 1 FLR 115 Munby J.

23 The response of Munby J to this submission was: '[29] No doubt, as its architects planned and hoped, the system of registered conveyancing is in many respects much simpler than the traditional system of conveyancing. But the sale and purchase even of registered land is, of its very nature, infinitely more technical and complex, and more demanding of professional assistance, than the sale and purchase of a tin of peas in a supermarket or even the sale and purchase of a motor car ...

[31] A solicitor is instructed in a conveyancing transaction because – whatever other reasons there may also be – the client requires the technical skill and advice which comes from someone with legal expertise. One does not, after all, employ a rude mechanical – a plumber or carpenter – to do one's conveyancing, any more than one would employ a solicitor to do one's plumbing or carpentry ...'

24 Paras [32] and [33].

25 Per Munby J: see *General Mediterranean Holdings SA v Patel* [2000] 1 WLR 272, at 288–291 for a discussion by Toulson J of the relevant authorities.

[26] As a matter of first impression and, dare I say it, as a matter of common sense, it would seem obvious on this approach that privilege attaches to communications between a solicitor and his client (and vice versa) in the course of a conveyancing transaction in which the solicitor is retained by his client to act in that capacity. If authority is required [see] Taylor LJ's judgment in *Balabel and Another v Air India* [[26]]

[27] Some doubt was thrown upon this by the observations of Lord Phillips of Worth Matravers MR in *Three Rivers District Council and Others v Governor and Company of the Bank of England (No 6)* [2004] EWCA Civ 218, [2004] QB 916, at para [39] questioning why privilege should attach to 'matters such as the conveyance of real property or the drawing up of a will' and saying 'It is not clear why it should'. But this view was repudiated in the House of Lords,[[27]] in particular by Lord Rodger, at para [55]:

> Despite its long pedigree the Court of Appeal in this case appear to have been less than enthusiastic about the very notion of legal advice privilege. In particular, they thought that it was not clear why it should attach to matters such as the conveyance of real property or the drawing up of a will: see [2004] QB 916, 935, para 39, per Lord Phillips MR. I do not share these doubts.

9.21 More recently, the sensational – in terms of the lump sum awarded – judgment of Haddon-Cave J of *AAZ v BBZ & Ors* [2016] EWHC 3234 (Fam), Haddon-Cave J contains its 'iniquity' aspect. In the absence of a Russian husband, Haddon-Cave J (sitting in the Family Division) awarded a former wife £453 million. This sum included a modern art collection (estimated value: around £90 million). In a slightly later judgment (*Z v Z and others (Legal Professional Privilege: Fraud Exemption)*[28]) Haddon-Cave J considered the extent to which the solicitor for Z (now known as Kerman with the husband as Akhmedova (see further below)) could claim LAP in his dealings with insurance of the art collection.

9.22 Haddon-Cave J held that the arranging of insurance was not covered by privilege: it was not a 'relevant *legal* context' (see Taylor LJ in *Balabel v Air India* [1988] Ch 317, CA: emphasis added). So far as it was relevant to issues, such as enforcement of the judgment and recovery of assets, S was required to give evidence.

[16] In my view, the arranging of insurance is something that a "man of business" would do for a client rather than qua solicitor. Arranging insurance is a fairly routine matter, involving instructing brokers. It would not generally involve giving legal advice. In this regard, it is more

26 [1988] Ch 317 at 331: '... the "purpose of legal advice" test will result in most communications between solicitor and client in, for example, a conveyancing transaction being exempt from disclosure, either because they are privileged or because they are immaterial or irrelevant.'

27 In *Three Rivers District Council and ors v Governor and Company of the Bank of England (No 6)* [2004] UKHL 48, [2004] 3 WLR 1274.

28 [2016] EWHC 3349 (Fam), [2017] 4 WLR 84.

> akin to the prosaic matters referred to Brooke LJ in *USA v Philip Morris Inc*[29] at [80] (eg, advice or assistance in collecting and collating, listing, spring-cleaning, storing, transporting and warehousing documents), or the buying of air tickets for a client (see *Hollander on Documentary Evidence*, (2015) 12th ed, p 262). I am not persuaded by Mr Warshaw QC that the possibility that a client might have asked a lawyer "what to do" with a valuable asset necessarily cloaks the mere arranging of insurance with a "relevant legal context".

9.23 The solicitor appealed against the *Z v Z* decision (*Kerman v Akhmedova* [2018] EWCA Civ 307). The Court of Appeal upheld Haddon-Cave J: the lawyer here was a 'person of business' and that, so far as it was relevant to issues (such as enforcement of the judgment and recovery of assets) it was permissible for the court to require Mr Kerman to give evidence. The solicitor-witness's appeal on any LAP point was dismissed. In so doing, the Court of Appeal restated the approach of Haddon-Cave J; and added – crucially, perhaps – that (at [47]) if Mr Akhmedov had been at the trial (which he had evaded) he could not have relied on privilege. His own lawyer could not be in a different or better position.

No nit-picking or hiving off[30]

9.24 Taylor LJ devotes a part of his judgment to balancing two aspects of the legal context. First, he says, is the need to be as clear as possible as to what is not covered by privilege in the variety of communication between solicitors and the firm's client. Secondly, where the solicitor-client communications are relatively extensive, to avoid the need for a narrow approach to what should and should not be available for inspection.

9.25 In *R v Manchester Crown Court exp Rogers*,[31] Mr Rogers (R) sought to use an alleged appointment with solicitors as an alibi. He refused to answer questions at a police interview. The police, seeking to establish whether the applicant had been present at and left the scene of the incident at the material time to visit solicitors, applied[32] for an order for production by his solicitors of any record or log recording his arrival time at their offices on the date in question. The judge made the order and then a further order to confirm that it included any record of appointment as to the time R was to attend or any attendance note showing whether he had attended. R sought judicial review of the judge's orders including on grounds that these records were protected from production by legal professional privilege. His application was heard by the Queen's Bench Divisional Court.

9.26 R secured part of the order he sought, on technical grounds.[33] Lord Bingham reminded himself of the purpose of LAP (that a client is able to seek

29 [2004] EWCA Civ 330.

30 The words used by Mervyn Davies J in *Re Sarah C Getty Trust* [1985] QB 956 cited by Taylor LJ in *Balabel* at 327.

31 [1999] 1 WLR 832, QBD Div Ct.

32 Police and Criminal Evidence Act 1984 s 9 Sch 1.

33 Though the Crown was encouraged to make a further application for the correct order.

advice secure in the knowledge that nothing will be passed on by his adviser without his consent); that 'a narrow or nit picking approach to documents must be avoided';[34] but:[35]

> It is none the less true that legal professional privilege applies, and applies only, to communications made for the purpose of seeking and receiving legal advice.

9.27 Thus, so far as it can easily be extracted from a file, it may be the case that simple factual information does not attract privilege. *Ex p Rogers* (above) is an example of this. Notes of conversations with administrative staff will rarely involve legal advice (though over-generalisation here may be dangerous). The date of separation of parties may be critical in a divorce case. A asserts that he told his solicitor of the date at the time of separation, but now wants to argue for an earlier date. The letter, record of an e-mail or telephone attendance note which provides evidence of the conversation which records this date, especially if A changes solicitors, may be ordered to be disclosed for inspection.

9.28 By contrast, in *R (Kelly) v Warley Magistrates Court & Anor,*[36] the Queen's Bench Divisional Court dealt with a magistrates' court order for production of information about addresses from a defendant's solicitor's file to the CPS. The main issue, said Laws LJ, was whether (1) the district judge's direction requires the claimant to produce material covered by LPP or litigation privilege; and if so (2) did the district judge have the necessary legal authority to override that privilege? LP, he said, was not a 'sub-class' of LPP[37] and can arise without the involvement of any legal adviser.

9.29 He thus returned to the point in issue before him and the question of the information on the solicitors' file:[38]

> ... it is clear that litigation privilege attaches to the identity and other details of witnesses intended to be called in adversarial litigation, civil or criminal, whether or not their identity is the fruit of legal advice ... [A] party may plainly have a strong interest – "legitimate" from his point of view – in keeping his powder dry. The practical availability of the witness may in some circumstances depend upon his doing so.

LPP applied to the information which Mr Kelly had been ordered to produce. The Divisional Court quashed the order of the magistrates' deputy district judge accordingly.[39]

---

34 *Balabel v Air India* as explained at 9.5–9.10.
35 Ibid at 839.
36 [2007] EWHC Admin 1836, [2008] 1 WLR 2001, QB Divisional Court.
37 Ibid at [18].
38 Ibid at [20].
39 Ibid at [35].

Order for release of file where client had forfeit 'any right to legal privilege'

9.30 By contrast and with respect to the judge concerned, the decision in *Kimber v Brookman Solicitors*[40] is not easy to explain on principled terms. The solicitor for Mr Kimber (K) was ordered to produce his entire file to K's wife's solicitors because they sought his address and to know the whereabouts of the parties' matrimonial assets. The judge considered that he had a discretion to order that a party 'has forfeited any right to the protection of legal privilege' and he made the order asked for because K was 'in breach of orders of the court'.[41]

9.31 No representation was heard on behalf of K; nor any submissions as to his right to privilege (if he was entitled to privilege) heard. (If it be suggested that this could be an aspect of the 'iniquity exemption' to privilege, this was not so found by the judge; and the facts of this case alongside the normal run of iniquity cases are not easy to reconcile.)

40 [2004] 2 FLR 221.

41 Ibid at [19].

10

EXCEPTIONS FROM PRIVILEGE AND CONFIDENTIALITY

1 INTRODUCTION

Privilege does not apply

10.1 There are instances where it may be said that legal advice does not attract privilege from the outset because of the dishonesty of the reason for the advice being sought:[1] the 'nefarious purpose' referred to by Lord Neuberger in *R (Prudential plc and anor) v Special Commissioner of Income Tax*.[2] This chapter looks at the subject of confidentiality and privilege from the points of view either that one or other did not exist at all or that it can be overridden:

10.2 This chapter proceeds as follows:

- Part 2 defines and considers the 'iniquity exemption' (and especially *R v Cox and Railton*[3]); that privilege cannot be said to exist where the relationship with a lawyer is for purposes of criminal or other wrong-doing; or where there is a fear that the privilege, if allowed, may be abused.
- Part 3 explains the special difficulties of pleading fraud or iniquity.
- Part 4 considers particular issue in relation to the 'iniquity exemption' in the context of advice in children proceedings.
- Part 5 explains the rare circumstances in which privilege and other pro fessional confidentiality may be overridden, especially in the light of *W v Egdell*.[4]

1 *R v Cox and Railton* (1884) 14 QBD 153, Stephen J.
2 [2013] UKSC 1, [2013] 2 AC 185 at [17]: see quote at 5.12.
3 (1884) 14 QBD 153 per Stephen J.
4 [1989] EWCA Civ 13, [1990] Ch 359, [1990] 2 WLR 471.

2 FRAUD AND OTHER INIQUITY

Communications before commission of crime: not privileged

10.3 The basis for refusing privilege to Messers Cox and Railton[5] arose from the fact that they tried to endorse a dishonest date on a document. They had been in partnership as publishers. To avoid enforcement of a judgment in libel (on the application of Mr Munster) against Railton, they sought advice from a solicitor who, not knowing of their intent to misrepresent the date on a deed, advised on the date on which they could dissolve their partnership. They then purported to dissolve their partnership and endorsed their partnership deed with note stating that. They dated the endorsement with a date earlier than Mr Munster's judgment.

10.4 They were prosecuted for conspiring to defraud Mr Munster. The prosecutor wanted to adduce evidence of Cox and Railton's discussions with their solicitor. When the defendants pleaded that what had passed between them and their lawyer was excluded from being adduced in evidence because covered by LPP, the criminal court heard the evidence but referred the question of whether it was properly received was reserved to the Court of Crown Case Reserved.

10.5 Stephen J in that Court held that LPP did not apply in the first place, in a case of this nature, since it is not part of 'a solicitor's business to further any criminal object':

> ... In order that [LPP] may apply there must be both professional confidence and professional employment, but if the client has a criminal object in view in his communications with his solicitor one of these elements must necessarily be absent. The client must either conspire with his solicitor or deceive him. If his criminal object is avowed, the client does not consult his adviser professionally, because it cannot be the solicitor's business to further any criminal object. If the client does not avow his object he reposes no confidence, for the state of facts, which is the foundation of the supposed confidence, does not exist. The solicitor's advice is obtained by a fraud.

10.6 As will be seen shortly, this definition – 'any criminal object' – may conceivably be capable of being widened to any behaviour which is considered by the court 'sufficiently iniquitous for public policy'[6] to interfere; though such a wide application is open to doubt.

'Fraud' at common law

10.7 To define what may be meant by 'fraud' in civil proceedings a definition can be found in *Derry v Peek*.[7] In that case the House of Lords tried to narrow the

5 *R v Cox and Railton* per Stephen J.

6 *Barclays Bank plc v Eustice* [1995] 1 WLR 1238, CA, [2006] EWHC 336 (Fam), [2008] 1 FLR 115.

7 [1889] UKHL 1, (1889) 14 App Cas 337.

ambit of the term 'fraud' in relation to the tort of deceit. Defendants had naively issued a prospectus setting out a state of affairs which they assumed would occur, but which did not. They failed to secure approval of a transport scheme from the Board of Trade. The plaintiffs had brought shares in the defendant company and sued in deceit.

10.8 Lord Hershell considered whether inaccuracy was enough to amount to fraud. No, he said: there must be a deliberate, or knowing, misstatement if a person is to be said to be responsible for fraud:

> ... The prospectus was therefore inaccurate. But that is not the question. If they believed that the consent of the Board of Trade was practically concluded by the passing of the Act, has the plaintiff made out, which it was for him to do, that they have been guilty of a fraudulent misrepresentation? I think not. I cannot hold it proved as to any one of them that he knowingly made a false statement, or one which he did not believe to be true, or was careless whether what he stated was true or false. In short, I think they honestly believed that what they asserted was true, and I am of opinion that the charge of fraud made against them has not been established.

10.9 As will be seen, it has been held that other iniquitous behaviour, such as deliberately setting up a transfer at an undervalue, may be sufficient to ensure that LPP does not apply and legal advice on the subject is open to inspection.[8] For this purpose, the issue of fraud goes wider than criminal or other illegal intent.

Other iniquitous or dishonest intent

10.10 In *C v C (Privilege)*,[9] Munby J was confronted by an interim application by a wife (W) that she be permitted to have produced[10] for inspection the conveyancing files of the solicitors for a Lichtenstein Anstalt whom, the wife alleged, was the *alter ego* of her former husband. The Anstalt was joined in the proceedings and a further date was fixed for argument – ultimately between W and the Anstalt – as to whether LPP applied to the files.

10.11 Munby J was unimpressed by the extent to which the wife had failed to plead her claim, but in the process of his judgment he drew attention to the fact that in *Barclays Bank plc v Eustice*,[11] the Court of Appeal held that there was no privilege in the case of a transaction caught by the Insolvency Act 1986 section 423. Section 423 invalidates a transaction by someone 'at an undervalue'[12] if the court is satisfied[13] that it was entered into by him, explained Munby J:[14]

---

8 See *Barclays Bank plc v Eustice* (above).

9 [2006] EWHC 336 (Fam), [2008] 1 FLR 115.

10 As was then the procedure Family Proceedings Rules 1991 r 2.62.

11 *Barclays Bank plc v Eustice* [1995] 1 WLR 1238, CA.

12 Insolvency Act 1986 s 423(1).

13 Ibid at s 423(3).

14 Ibid at [39].

for the purpose—

(a) of putting assets beyond the reach of a person who is making, or may at some time make, a claim against him, or

(b) of otherwise prejudicing the interests of such a person in relation to the claim which he is making or may make.

10.12 Munby J then pointed out that the Matrimonial Causes Act 1973 (MCA 1973) section 37 'catches transactions where the court is satisfied[15] that a spouse is about to make, or has made, a disposition' and that this disposition is '... with the intention of defeating the [other spouse's] claim for financial relief' namely, by section 37(1), with the intention of '... preventing financial relief from being granted ... or reducing the amount of any financial relief which might be ... granted, or frustrating or impeding the enforcement of any order which might be or has been made'.

10.13 From this, Munby J concluded, *obiter*, that LPP might not attach to transactions caught by MCA 1973 section 37:

> [42] By parity of reasoning with both *Williams v Quebrada Railway Land and Copper Co* [1895] 2 Ch 751[16] and *Barclays Bank plc v Eustice* [1995] 1 WLR 1238, and consistently with the line of cases stretching from *R v Cox and Railton* (1884) 14 QBD 153 to Derby & Co Ltd and Others v Weldon and Others (No 7) [1990] 1 WLR 1156, a transaction within [MCA 1973 s 37] is, in my judgment, one to which legal professional privilege does not attach.

Barclays Bank v Eustice

10.14 The decision in *Barclays Bank v Eustice* (above) may prove to be controversial. In *Re McE (Northern Ireland)*[17] Lord Neuberger said in passing:

> [109] ... The right to privilege in respect of communications has thus always been subject to the so-called iniquity exception: see *R v Cox and Railton* (1884) 14 QBD 153, 167, and, more recently, *Barclays Bank plc*

---

15 MCA 1973 s 37(2).

16 At [38] Munby J explained this case as follows: In *Williams v Quebrada Railway Land and Copper Co* [1895] 2 Ch 751, Kekewich J had to consider a transaction involving (see the description by Vinelott J in *Derby & Co Ltd and Others v Weldon and Others (No 7)* [1990] 1 WLR 1156, at 1167) the execution by a failing company of a charge. The charge had been created when the cesser of business by the company was inevitable and in order to remove the assets from the scope of a pre-existing floating charge before it crystallised; in other words, to defeat or delay the rights of the company's debenture holders under the floating charge. The claim, which for technical reasons could not be brought as a statutory claim under the fraudulent preference provisions then contained in s 164 of the Companies Act 1862 (compare now Insolvency Act 1986 s 239), was, however, analogous to a claim to set aside a transaction for fraudulent preference. Kekewich J, expressing himself in trenchant terms, held that there was no legal professional privilege. His decision has often been cited and never been doubted.

17 [2009] UKHL 15, [2009] AC 908.

> *v Eustice* [1995] 1 WLR 1238, 1249 (although, for my part, I would leave open the question of whether the latter case was rightly decided) ...

10.15 The *Eustice* case related to a farming family who wished to raise funds to buy further land and then to raise further funds. The farmers were in financial difficulties and the Inland Revenue distrained on goods at the farm. Within the family the borrowers then assigned their interests in the farm for a nominal consideration and a rent to be paid annually in arrears. The bank sought a declaration that the assignment should be avoided as at an undervalue and the first instance judge agreed. He concluded that, as a result, the defendant farmers should make disclosure of documents held by their solicitors, as explained by Scheimann LJ, as follows:[18]

> ... does legal professional privilege attach to documents containing or evidencing communications between the transferor and his legal advisers relating to transactions entered into by the transferor at an undervalue for the purpose of prejudicing the interest of persons making a claim against him?

10.16 He took the view that there was a 'strong prima facie case' that an Insolvency Act 1976 section 423 order should be made. He analysed the rationale behind the public interest in legal professional privilege, and concluded, on the authorities which he cited, that '"fraud" is in this context used in a relatively wide sense'.[19] The dominant purpose of the family's transaction was to 'stop the bank from interfering with the defendants' use of what they regarded as family assets'. The court analysed what had happened in terms of public policy, as defined by the court and in the light of authority:[20]

> Various words other than "dishonest" have been used in the course of the cases in which privilege has been in issue. However to me the most important consideration is that we are here engaged not in some semantic exercise to see what adjective most appropriately covers the debtor's course of conduct but in deciding whether public policy requires that the documents in question are left uninspected.

10.17 So, said Scheimann LJ:[21]

> ... We start here from a position in which, on a prima facie view, the client was seeking to enter into transactions at an undervalue the purpose of which was to prejudice the bank. I regard this purpose as being sufficiently iniquitous for public policy to require that communications between him and his solicitor in relation to the setting up of these transactions be discoverable.

10.18 In *C v C (Privilege)* (above), as already explained, Munby J held that the position in insolvency law was equivalent to that under MCA 1973 section

18 Ibid at 1241.
19 Ibid at 1249.
20 Ibid at 1250.
21 Ibid at 1252.

37(2) but that Mrs C failed in her interim application because of the fact that her allegations were not properly pleaded (as considered further in Part 3).

Iniquity or man of business

10.19 The case of *Kerman v Akhmedova*[22] (on appeal from *Z v Z and others (Legal Professional Privilege: Fraud Exemption)*[23]) at first instance had held, not only that the involvement of the husband's solicitor, Mr Kerman, was not a 'relevant legal context' where he arranged insurance but, said Haddon-Cave J, that he was entitled to 'lift' LPP.[24] Haddon-Cave followed *Barclays Bank plc v Eustice.*[25] Once he had held that the insurance arrangement was not legal advice he need not consider the iniquity exemption: he could say that no question of LAP arose in the first place.

10.20 As considered already, the solicitor appealed against the *Z v Z* decision.[26] The Court of Appeal upheld Haddon-Cave's decision that the lawyer here was a 'person of business' and that, so far as it was relevant to issues (such as enforcement of the judgment and recovery of assets), Mr Kerman could be required by the court to give evidence. The solicitor–witness's appeal on any LAP point was dismissed.

3 DEFINING AND PLEADING INIQUITY AND FRAUD

Pleading fraud

10.21 In *C v C (Privilege)*,[27] Munby J, after citing the cases referred to in the remainder of this Part, described the wife's application and its failure to discharge the burden on her to allege fraud as follows:

> [62] [W has] failed to make good the "prima facie case ... resting on solid grounds" to which Lord Wrenbury[28] referred. There is suspicion and assumption. There is surmise and conjecture, some of it founded on mere rumour. But there is not, at least at present, the strong evidence for which Lord Denning MR called. There is not, in my judgment, sufficiently compelling evidence, either that the Anstalt is the husband's alter ego or creature or that the transaction is one caught by s 37 of the 1973 Act, to justify going behind the Anstalt's privilege on the ground of "fraud". On the contrary, there is uncertainty. The wife, in

22 [2018] EWCA Civ 307.

23 [2016] EWHC 3349 (Fam), [2017] 4 WLR 84Haddon-Cave J.

24 With respect to the judge, that was perhaps a misunderstanding – perhaps of no real import. If the 'iniquity' exemption applies (*R v Cox and Railton* (above)) no question of confidentiality, and therefore none of privilege, arises in the first place. Even if a judge can 'lift privilege' there would be none to 'lift'.

25 [1995] 1 WLR 1238, CA.

26 *Kerman v Akhmedova* [2018] EWCA Civ 307.

27 [2006] EWHC 336 (Fam), [2008] 1 FLR 115 (above).

28 In *O'Rourke v Darbishire* [1920] AC 581.

> my judgment, has failed to satisfy the heavy burden which rests upon anyone who in a case such as this seeks to go behind privilege on the ground of 'fraud'.

10.22 A review of the cases on which allegations of fraud must be based and the care with which it must be pleaded follows.

A definition of iniquitous conduct

10.23 So, what is fraud or iniquitous conduct for purposes of dealing with or negating LPP? It exists on a spectrum from clear dishonesty by the lawyer in taking part – intentionally or, most likely, not – in the intended crime (or, more likely, the honest lawyer being used to advise so that a crime can be committed[29]) to, at the other extreme, advice on 'sharp practice'.[30]

10.24 In all cases, and in the interests of the administration of justice, the courts will be concerned to preserve LPP where it exists. In a case cited by Vinelott J in *Derby v Weldon (No 7)*,[31] Goff LJ expressed the point thus:

> Where you draw the line in the infinite gradation of good and evil… I do not attempt to say, … the court must in every case, of course, be satisfied that what is prima facie proved really is dishonest, and not merely disreputable or a failure to maintain good ethical standards and must bear in mind that legal professional privilege is a very necessary thing and is not lightly to be overthrown, but on the other hand, the interests of victims of fraud must not be overlooked. Each case depends on its own facts.

10.25 Much of the post-1990 case law on the iniquity exemption cites the summary of the law provided by Vinelott J in *Derby & Co Ltd v Weldon (No 7)*.[32] This case, with a number of those cited by Vinelott J – his survey of the law on the iniquity exemption to LPP runs from [1167] to [1173] – stresses that in the final analysis, each case depends on its individual facts. For himself, Vinelott J summarised the position:[33]

> There is a continuous spectrum and it is impossible to, as it were, calibrate or express in any simple formula the strength of the case that the plaintiff must show in each of these categories. An order to disclose documents for which legal professional privilege is claimed lies at the extreme end of the spectrum. Such an order will only be made in very exceptional circumstances …

---

29 *R v Cox and Railton* (1884) 14 QBD 153 (above).

30 *Barclays Bank plc v Eustice* [1995] 1 WLR 1238, CA; or as 'very widely defined' by Kekewich J in *Williams v Quebrada Railway, Land and Copper Co* [1895] 2 Ch 751 (considered by Vinelott J in *Derby v Weldon (No 7)* (below) at 1167 as: 'where there is anything of an underhand nature or approaching to fraud, especially in commercial matters, where there should be the veriest good faith, the whole transaction should be ripped up and disclosed in all its nakedness to the light of the court …'

31 *Derby v Weldon (No 7)* at [1171] namely *Gamlen Chemical Co (UK) Ltd v Rochem Ltd* (unreported) 7 December 1979; Court of Appeal (Civil Division) Transcript No 777 or 1979.

32 [1990] 1 WLR 1156.

33 Ibid at 1173.

10.26 Where inspection of privileged documents is requested, the court treads the line between protecting privilege and the public policy on which it is based, on the one hand; and, on the other, on ensuring that dishonesty – or, perhaps, other nefarious behaviour – is not allowed to override privilege. Vinelott J summarised this balance as follows:[34]

> In all the cases I have cited what is stressed is that every case must be judged on its own facts. In any given case, the court must weigh, on the one hand, the important considerations of public policy on which legal professional privilege is founded — the necessity that the citizen should be able to make a clean breast of it to his legal adviser (*see Anderson v. Bank of British Columbia*[[35]]) — and, on the other, the gravity of the charge of fraud or dishonesty that is made.

10.27 Vinelott J likens the task of the judge in seeking the balance between the right to privilege and iniquity with the grant of an interlocutory injunction.[36] He concluded with the passage quoted at the start of this section.

Pleading fraud or other serious misconduct

10.28 The substantial caveat in all this is that merely to allege fraud or other iniquitous conduct, the party – or his or her lawyer – who pleads it must have clear grounds for so doing.[37] The point was explained by Lord Wrenbury in *O'Rourke v Darbishire*:[38]

> Before professional "confidence can be broken you must have some definite charge either by way of allegation or affidavit or what not".[39] If I may venture to express this in my own words I should say that to obtain discovery on the ground of fraud the plaintiff must show to the satisfaction of the Court good ground for saying that prima facie a state of things exists which, if not displaced at the trial, will support a charge of fraud. This may be done in various ways — admissions on the pleadings of facts which go to show fraud — affidavits in some interlocutory proceedings which go to show fraud —

34 Ibid.

35 (1876) 2 ChD 644 649 per Sir George Jessel MR considered at 5.10.

36 *Derby v Weldon (No 7)* at 1173: 'There are many contexts in which the court similarly has to strike a balance between the need to do justice to the plaintiff, on the one hand, and, on the other, the extent to which interlocutory relief may result in an unjustified interference with the defendant's property and his right to privacy. The point at which the balance is struck must depend on the extent to which the relief sought may unjustifiably invade the defendant's rights. So if a plaintiff can show that he has a fairly arguable case and if the defendant can be fully protected by a cross-undertaking in damages, the court in granting or refusing a purely negative injunction will be primarily concerned with a balance of convenience. More is required (in ascending order of importance) if the plaintiff seeks a mandatory injunction or a negative injunction which, in the words of Hoffmann J "may have intrusive effect," or if the plaintiff seeks Mareva relief or an Anton Piller order or the disclosure of confidential banking documents.'

37 See eg, Munby J cited at 10.21.

38 [1920] AC 581.

39 Per Lord Halsbury in *Bullivant and ors v The Attorney-General for Victoria* [1901] AC 196.

possibly even without admission or affidavit allegations of facts which, if not disputed or met by other facts, would lead a reasonable person to see, at any rate, a strong probability that there was fraud, may be taken by the Court to be sufficient. Every case must be decided on its merits: [*R v Cox and Railton*]. The mere use of the word "fraud" or the prefix of the adverb "fraudulently" from time to time throughout the narrative will not suffice.

10.29 Munby J made the same point in *C v C (Privilege)*,[40] in an exchange with counsel. He quotes this exchange in his judgment.[41] Counsel for the wife was seeking, in unspecific terms – and, in the event, unsuccessfully – the file of a firm of solicitors which acted for the Anstalt in the case (as explained above[42]):

> [50] … Munby J: "I am sorry, that is the world of Humpty Dumpty … It is for plaintiffs to establish their case, or at least to put forward a prima facie case. We do not work on a system by and large where the plaintiff simply asserts and says, 'well, unless and until the defendant produces evidence to disprove our bald assertion, our bald assertion holds the field'."

Bar Standards Board guidance

10.30 The Bar Council, now the Bar Standards Board, has reviewed its *Guidance on pleading fraud* (eg, including a pleading that a spouse had been fraudulent in respect of disclosure in financial relief proceedings); the *Guidance* applies to other allegations against a party of serious misconduct. Fresh guidance in March 2003, which was further reviewed in 2008, recalled that in *Medcalf v Weatherill*, [43] the House of Lords rejected their earlier interpretation of a pleader's duty in relation to allegations of fraud. Lord Bingham, with whom the other law lords agreed, said:

> … the requirement is not that counsel should necessarily have before him evidence in admissible form but that he should have material of such a character as to lead responsible counsel to conclude that serious allegations should properly be based upon it.

10.31 So, says the Bar Professional Standards Committee: 'there is no litmus test for determining whether it is proper to allege fraud'. The pleader must exercise professional judgment whether it is in all circumstances proper to lend the pleader's name to any serious allegation according to the facts of each individual case. And, if any serious allegation, such as fraud, is to be alleged it must be fully pleaded with the evidence properly available to the pleader.

40 [2006] EWHC 336 (Fam), [2008] 1 FLR 115.

41 As will be seen (see 10.12) the wife had shown that if MCA 1973 s 37(2) could be established, iniquitous conduct might be in question; but the absence of a 'definite charge' ensured that in the particular case the argument failed.

42 See 10.10.

43 [2002] UKHL 27, [2003] 1 AC 120.

4 INIQUITY AND THE WELFARE OF THE CHILD

Confidentiality and the whereabouts of a child

10.32 The Family Law Act 1986 section 33(1) and (2) and CA 1989 section 48(1) gives power to the Family Court to order information as to the whereabouts of a child; and CA 1989 section 50(3) implies a similar order into a recovery order under CA 1989 section 50. Where a solicitor has information as to the whereabouts of an abducted child or as to a possible address for a child in need of emergency protection[44] then what is the extent of any privilege attaching to that confidential information?

10.33 In *Ramsbotham v Senior*,[45] Sir R Malins V-C, sitting in the Court of Chancery, dealing with the address of a ward, held – when it was argued that information as to the address of the ward's mother held by a solicitor – that the information was not covered by privilege, akin to the exception in the later case of *R v Cox and Railton*,[46] that is, not that privilege is 'overridden', but that it did not arise in the first place.[47] Of the 'rule' in relation to legal professional privilege the Vice-Chancellor said:

> The rule has no application to the case of concealing the residence of a ward, which may lead to the utter ruin or destruction of that ward. My decided opinion is, that those authorities have no application to the present case, and I am of opinion that I made the right order in *Burton v Earl of Darnley*,[48] when I directed the solicitor, who did know the address of another lady who is keeping a ward out of the way of the court, to answer the question where she was ... [In this case the solicitor] does not know [the ward's address], but he is in possession of documents which may by possibility lead to its being ascertained. Those documents, for the reasons I have already stated, I am clearly of opinion he is bound to produce. The order must be made according to the summons.

10.34 It may also be asked whether any privilege attaches to the fact of where a person is living (such as a solicitor's client who is the parent of a child being searched for). The information is confidential; but, as such, it would probably not be difficult to override the confidentiality if the welfare of a child thought to be at risk demanded it. In *Re T (Wardship: Impact of Police Intelligence)*,[49] McFarlane J made it clear that he assumed that the court had power – perhaps inherent power – to order information as to whereabouts. In the absence of a

44 CA 1989 s 48(1).

45 (1869) FLR Rep 591 at 593.

46 (1884) 14 QBD 153, Stephen J and see 10.5.

47 This decision is in line with *Re T (Wardship: Impact of Police Intelligence)* [2009] EWHC 2440 (Fam), [2010] 1 FLR 1048 where McFarlane J was clear that the court had power to make an order for disclosure as to a child's whereabouts; but that without the order a solicitor did not necessarily have a duty to produce information.

48 (1869) LR 8 Eq 576.

49 [2009] EWHC 2440 (Fam), [2010] 1 FLR 1048; more fully considered at [20].

court order it was a matter for each individual solicitor to decide whether, in a given case, it was appropriate for that solicitor to override a client's entitlement to confidentiality:

> [102] … I am fully satisfied that there is no general duty, absent of a court order, requiring solicitors to disclose information as to the whereabouts of a ward in breach of the duty of confidentiality that is owed to their client.

10.35 McFarlane LJ then went on to say that he agreed with counsel's submission that where a child had been abducted by a client for over two years, in breach of longstanding wardship orders then:

> [103] … a solicitor should consider whether or not those facts amount to the "exceptional circumstances" described in the guidance to the Solicitors' Code of Conduct amount to "abuse" of the child which involves "a threat to the child's life or health, both mental and physical, [which] is sufficiently serious to justify a breach of the duty of confidentiality".
>
> [104] I would endorse that submission. It must be a matter for the individual solicitor to determine on a case by case basis. General guidance on the point by this court, however carefully it may be phrased, may well cause more confusion than clarity. I would, however, point to the devastating effect that the father's actions have had in the present case on the life of young TS. I found in the course of the substantive judgment that the father's actions "must have caused TS significant emotional harm". A solicitor who knew the circumstances as I have now found them to be might well conclude that this was a case which was sufficiently serious to justify a breach of the duty of confidentiality. But, I stress, it is a matter for the judgment of the individual solicitor in each individual case.

10.36 It is not easy to identify, under the current Solicitors' Regulation Authority *Code of Practice*, what is now the principle to which McFarlane J refers. Chapter 4 of the *Code*[50] includes the following:

> Protection of confidential information is a fundamental feature of your relationship with clients. It exists as a concept both as a matter of law and as a matter of conduct. This duty continues despite the end of the retainer …

10.37 In the terminology of the 'outcomes focused' *Code*, a solicitor complies with this requirement if that solicitor achieves the following outcome: that the solicitor keeps 'the affairs of clients confidential unless disclosure is required or permitted by law or the client consents'. The likelihood that that outcome as to confidentiality would be achieved if there were a court order or within the terms of CA 1989 section 50(3)(c) where disclosure is implied by the making of the order.

50 Available at: www.sra.org.uk/solicitors/handbook/code/part2/rule4/content.page.

5 OVERIDING CONFIDENTIALITY

Confidentiality and professional relationships

10.38 Confidentiality may arise as between a client or patient and a professional (eg, doctor, lawyer, banker etc). If the professional is a lawyer, LPP will generally apply and be superimposed on that confidentiality. The question, then, is: are there circumstances in which confidentiality or even privilege can be overridden in the circumstances of the case (separate from the child's address point mentioned in the previous Part)? For example: if a lawyer is told by a client that a criminal offence is to be committed, such as child abduction or child abuse or a client acts abusively towards a small child in the presence of a lawyer and whilst the client is seeking legal advice (say in connection with care proceedings) does privilege override any other duty to report to others the lawyer may think applies? (It must be open to question whether any of those examples relate to a matter of 'advice in a legal context' anyway; and if not given in a legal context, legal advice privilege cannot apply in any event.)

10.39 A client's right to privilege is absolute.[51] There is a public interest in anyone who receives a confidence, in whatever relationship, keeping that confidence private.[52] There is, therefore, a heavy duty on a professional person to maintain confidence; and this duty is particularly relevant to medical professionals.[53]

Confidentiality and *W v Egdell*

10.40 The question of whether confidentiality can be overridden for anyone who receives confidential information in a professional capacity was considered by the Court of Appeal in *W v Egdell*.[54] This is likely to be the case which provides any professional, including lawyers and LPP, with the criteria by which they judge whether confidentiality should be overridden.

10.41 In *Egdell*, W had shot and killed five people and seriously wounded two others. He pleaded guilty to manslaughter on the ground of diminished responsibility. He was in a special hospital where he remained at the time of the appeal. In 1984, a tribunal recommended steps to lead to W's eventual release. The Home Secretary did not accept the advice for transfer. W instructed solicitors to apply to a tribunal for a review of his case. Dr Egdell (E), a well-known consultant psychiatrist, was instructed prepare a report. E considered that features of W's personality (eg, a long-standing interest in explosives) had previously been insufficiently appreciated. He did not favour W's transfer at that stage and

51 *R v Derby Magistrates' Court exp B* [1995] UKHL 18, [1996] 1 AC 487, [1996] 1 FLR 513; and see Chapter 5.

52 *Attorney-General v Guardian Newspapers Ltd (No 2)* [1988] UKHL 6, [1990] 1 AC 109, [1987] 1 WLR 776; and see Chapter 3.

53 GMC ethical guidance on *Confidentiality* (2009). Available at: www.gmc-uk.org/guidance/ethical_guidance/confidentiality.asp.

54 [1989] EWCA Civ 13, [1990] Ch 359 Sir Stephen Baker P, Bingham LJ and Sir John May.

so reported to W's solicitors. W withdrew his application to the tribunal but did not want anyone to see the report. E wanted his report sent to W's hospital. The solicitors refused in view of their instructions.

10.42 When E sent a copy of his report to the Home Office, W issued a breach of confidence claim. He was restrained from communicating the contents of the report save to W or with W's authority. The first instance judge discharged the restraining injunction. W appealed against that discharge. Bingham LJ, who gave the most authoritative judgment, approached the question of any restraint on E as one of contract and depended on what the court ruled. In law, the position turned on how the court approached the public interest in confidences being kept in the individual case:[55]

> Where, as here, the relationship between doctor and patient is contractual, the question is whether the doctor's disclosure is or is not a breach of contract. The answer to that question must turn not on what the doctor thinks but on what the court rules. But it does not follow that the doctor's conclusion is irrelevant. In making its ruling the court will give such weight to the considered judgment of a professional man as seems in all the circumstances to be appropriate.
>
> The parties were agreed, as I think rightly, that the crucial question in the present case was how, on the special facts of the case, the balance should be struck between the public interest in maintaining professional confidences and the public interest in protecting the public against possible violence. Mr. Robertson submitted that on the facts here the public interest in maintaining confidences was shown to be clearly preponderant.

Public interest in overriding privilege

10.43 In the final analysis, said Bingham LJ, where a professional person – in this case a consultant psychiatrist – considers that a person with whom he has a confidential relationship poses a public risk, then he is entitled to breach confidentiality and to take reasonable steps to pass on that information 'to the responsible authorities' (see italicised passage below):

> There is one consideration which in my judgment, as in that of the judge, weighs the balance of public interest decisively in favour of disclosure. It may be shortly put. Where a man has committed multiple killings under the disability of serious mental illness, decisions which may lead directly or indirectly to his release from hospital should not be made unless a responsible authority is properly able to make an informed judgment that the risk of repetition is so small as to be acceptable. A consultant psychiatrist who becomes aware, even in the course of a confidential relationship, of information which leads him, in the exercise of what the court considers

55 See opinion of Lord Goff in *Attorney-General v Guardian Newspapers Ltd (No 2)* [1988] UKHL 6, [1990] 1 AC 109, [1987] 1 WLR 776 considered at 3.7.

> a sound professional judgment, to fear that such decisions may be made on the basis of inadequate information and with a real risk of consequent danger to the public is entitled *to take such steps as are reasonable in all the circumstances to communicate the grounds of his concern to the responsible authorities*. I have no doubt that the judge's decision in favour of Dr Egdell was right on the facts of this case [emphasis added].

10.44 In assessing the balance to be weighed where a decision on public interest is concerned, Bingham LJ drew attention to European Convention 1950 rights (not then formally part of English law): that Article 8 applied, but that these might be overridden in the interests of 'public safety or the interest of crime'.

> No reference was made in argument before us (nor, so far as I know, before the judge J to the European Convention of Human Rights, but I believe this decision to be in accordance with it. I would accept that Article 8(1) of the Convention may protect an individual against the disclosure of information protected by the duty of professional secrecy. But Article 8(2) envisages that circumstances may arise in which a public authority may legitimately interfere with exercise of that right in accordance with the law and where necessary in a democratic society in the interests of public safety or the prevention of crime. Here there was no interference by a public authority. Dr Egdell did, as I conclude, act in accordance with the law. And his conduct was in my judgment necessary in the interests of public safety and the prevention of crime.

Confidentiality and children

10.45 If the interests of children are in issue, there interests predominate where a privacy balance falls to be decided:[56]

> [73] The court reiterates that in judicial decisions where the rights under Art 8 of parents and those of a child are at stake, the child's rights must be the paramount consideration. If any balancing of interests is necessary, the interests of the child must prevail (see *Elsholz v Germany* (2002) 34 EHRR 58, [2000] 2 FLR 486 at para [52] and *TP and KM v United Kingdom* (2002) 34 EHRR 2, [2001] 2 FLR 549 at para [72]). This applies also in cases such as the present.

10.46 It remains to be seen whether a similar loss of privilege – if it arose in the first place[57] – may arise where children are concerned. For example, it might be said that the welfare of a child created a public interest which was in a different category to any other in this chapter. The public interest in the welfare and protection of a child might be said to override litigation privilege (as has been the

---

56 *Yousef v The Netherlands* (Application No 33711/96), [2003] 1 FLR 210; and see *ZH (Tanzania) v Secretary of State for the Home Department* [2011] UKSC 4, [2011] 1 FLR 2170; *H(H) v Deputy Prosecutor of the Italian Republic, Genoa (Official Solicitor intervening)* [2012] UKSC 25, [2013] 1 AC 338 concerning children's 'interests' and European Convention 1950 decisions.

57 See discussion of *Ramsbotham v Senior* (1869) FLR Rep 591 at 10.33.

case where care proceedings are concerned). In an appropriately extreme case, as McFarlane J mentions in *Re T (Wardship: Impact of Police Intelligence)*,[58] it may be appropriate for a lawyer to decide override his or her client's confidentiality where the welfare of children is engaged.

10.47 That said, the person who is considering overriding a child's confidentiality must assess that child's age and understanding, as the doctor was – hypothetically – required to do in *Gillick v West Norfolk and Wisbech AHA*.[59] What is the extent of the child's understanding? If that child opposes passing on of information, is the child old enough and of sufficient understanding – as with the *Gillick* child – to oppose overriding of his or her confidentiality?[60]

10.48 In cases of urgency a lawyer or other professional may have to make a decision quickly and proceed accordingly (eg, prompt contact with the police or a children's department). In other cases, as with *W v Egdell*, there may be time to give notice of the intention to breach confidentiality and then for the professional to await a court order restraining breach of confidence if the client or patient applies.

58 [2009] EWHC 2440 (Fam), [2010] 1 FLR 1048.
59 [1985] UKHL 7, [1986] 1 AC 112, [1986] 1 FLR 224.
60 Considered fully in Chapter 14.

11

PROCEDURE: PUBLIC INTEREST IMMUNITY, PRIVILEGE AND NON-PARTY DISCLOSURE

1 INTRODUCTION

Disclosure rules

11.1 The very modest disclosure rules for family proceedings in FPR 2010 – limited three rules in FPR 2010 Part 21; and of those only two have specific functions (r 21.1 does little more than provide a short definition of 'disclosure'):

- Rule 22.2: orders for 'disclosure' (properly production) against 'a person not a party' (ie, against a third party or non-party), where this is permitted by statute; and
- Rule 21.3: claims to withhold inspection or disclosure of a document.

11.2 Even these two rules are overlooked by practitioners and puisne judges (see eg, per Roberts J in *Local Authority X v HI and Others*[1] and Gwyneth Knowles J – partially overlooked – in *Lancashire County Council v A, B and Z (A Child: Fact Finding Hearing: Police Disclosure)*;[2] and in *Tchenguiz-Imerman v Imerman*[3] Moylan J seems not to have been referred to r 21.3 which might have short-circuited the specific disclosure issue he was dealing with.

11.3 Disclosure has already been dealt with in Chapter 3; aspects of privilege are dealt with in Chapters 4 to 7; and public interest immunity (PII) is covered in Chapter 16. The existence of r 21.2 is discussed here to the extent that it may be relied upon in family proceedings to seek confidential information for non-parties which may raise important questions as between the court and the individual who

1 [2016] EWHC 1123 (Fam), [2017] 1 FLR 1362.
2 [2018] EWHC 1819 (Fam).
3 [2012] EWHC 4047 (Fam), [2014] 1 FLR 232.

is the subject of any order. Reference to police information is included since it is the obverse of the *Protocol*[4] provisions in Chapter 16.

Rules derived from Civil Procedure Rules 1998 Part 31

11.4 As with most procedural rules in relation to evidence, FPR 2010 rr 21.2 and 21.3 are derived from the Civil Procedure Rules 1998 (CPR 1998), in this case respectively rr 31.17 and 31.22. They repeat each rule almost word for word; so cases which explain the CPR 1998 versions of each rule can helpfully be cited to explain the FPR 2010 version. On occasion the civil proceedings jurisprudence could usefully be used to operate the family proceedings rules: see, for instance, *West London Pipeline and Storage Ltd v Total UK Ltd*[5] and the procedure suggested there to determine whether a document was covered by privilege or other confidentiality.[6]

11.5 This chapter will explain the law which underlies FPR 2010 rr 21.2 and 21.3 and will examine their procedural consequences for the parties in using the rules. The chapter will then consider the rather different aspect of this rule: production to the family courts (especially in care proceedings) by police.

11.6 This chapter proceeds as follows:

- Part 2 considers the various means whereby information can be required to be placed before or produced to family courts, in particular under FPR 2010 r 21.2.
- Part 3 explains FPR 2010 r 21.3, and in particular its first limb: dealing with testing whether a document is covered by legal professional privilege or whether it is confidential and if so, should it be produced for inspection (per the procedure under *West London Pipeline and Storage Ltd v Total UK Ltd*[7]).
- Part 4 deals with the procedure for adjudication on a public interest immunity claim under FPR 2010 r 21.3.
- Part 5 considers the specific aspect of non-party production of material between the police and local authorities in relation to care and parallel criminal proceedings; introduces the 2013 *Protocol and Good Practice Model: Disclosure of information in cases of alleged child abuse and linked criminal cases*; and questions to what extent family judges are dealing with this in accordance with statute (ie Senior Courts Act 1981 (SCA 1981) s 34(2) and FPR 2010 r 21.2).

---

4 *Protocol and Good Practice Model Disclosure of information in cases of alleged child abuse and linked criminal and care directions hearings* October 2013 (published by, amongst others, Crown Prosecution Service, President of the Family Division, Welsh Government).

5 [2008] EWHC 1729 (Comm) Beatson J.

6 See, by contrast, *Local Authority X v HI and Others* [2016] EWHC 1123 (Fam), [2017] 1 FLR 1362, Roberts J discussed at 11.49.

7 [2008] EWHC 1729 (Comm) Beatson J.

2 OBTAINING INFORMATION FROM NON-PARTIES

Production into family proceedings

Disclosure from a 'person not a party'

11.7 FPR 2010 r 21.2 (derived directly from CPR 1998 r 31.17) enables a party to proceedings to obtain a court order for disclosure of material from a non-party in circumstances defined by statute. (It is called 'disclosure'; but strictly what is sought under r 21.2 is first, disclosure by list, then production of documents or information by the non-party (as appropriate).) Outside the powers (mostly statutory) considered here there is no general rule that a Family Court can require non-parties – such as the police – to produce documents or other material into family proceedings.[8]

11.8 A non-party can be required to produce material into family proceedings in the following ways:

(1) FPR 2010 r 21.2: where statute permits the court to make an order against a non-party (r 21.2(1)).

(2) A witness summons which requires production of documents[9] (formerly a subpoena *ad duces tecum*).

(3) An application for information as to the whereabouts of a child under FLA 1996 section 33 and CA 1989 sections 48 and 50.

(4) An order (very rare in family proceedings) under the *Norwich Pharmacal*[10] jurisdiction.

Non-party production into family proceedings 'under an Act'

11.9 The main operative part of FPR 2010 r 21.2 provides as follows:

> **21.2 Orders for disclosure against a person not a party**
>
> (1) This rule applies where an application is made to the court under any Act for disclosure by a person who is not a party to the proceedings.
>
> (2) The application –
>
> (a) may be made without notice; and
>
> (b) must be supported by evidence.
>
> (3) The court may make an order under this rule only where disclosure is necessary in order to dispose fairly of the proceedings or to save costs.

8 But see *Lancashire County Council v A, B and Z (A Child: Fact Finding Hearing: Police Disclosure)* [2018] EWHC 1819 (Fam), Gwyneth Knowles J, considered at 11.59.

9 FPR 2010, r 24.2(1)(b).

10 *Norwich Pharmacal v Commissioners of Customs and Excise* [1974] AC 133, HL.

11.10 The only statutes of immediate relevance in family proceedings (in addition to those dealing with children's whereabouts[11]) where application under this rule might be made are:

- the Senior Courts Act 1981 section 34 (and the parallel County Courts Act 1984 section 53); and
- the Bankers Book Evidence Act 1879.

Senior Courts Act 1981 section 34

11.11 The Senior Courts Act 1981 section 34(2) provides, in respect of all civil (including family) proceedings, as follows:

(2) On the application, in accordance with rules of court, of a party to any proceedings to which this section applies, the High Court shall, in such circumstances as may be specified in the rules, have power to order a person who is not a party to the proceedings and who appears to the court to be likely to have in his possession, custody or power any documents which are relevant to an issue arising out of the said claim—

(a) to disclose whether those documents are in his possession, custody or power; and

(b) to produce such of those documents as are in his possession, custody or power to the applicant or, on such conditions as may be specified in the order—

(i) to the applicant's legal advisers; or

(ii) to the applicant's legal advisers and any medical or other professional adviser of the applicant; or

(iii) if the applicant has no legal adviser, to any medical or other professional adviser of the applicant.

11.12 Disclosure against a non-party under section 34(2) is dealt with procedurally as an interim order under FPR 2010 r 20.2(1)(i). FPR 2010 r 20.2(1) does not provide the remedy. It provides the means whereby the remedy (ie, under section 34(2)) can be exercised. Thus r 20.2(1) includes:

20.2 Orders for interim remedies

(1) The court may grant the following interim remedies – …

(i) an order under section 34 of the Senior Courts Act 1981 or section 53 of the County Courts Act 1984 (order in certain proceedings for disclosure of documents or inspection of property against a non-party);

11 As explained at 11.24.

11.13 As can be seen, section 34 provides the court with the means by which a party to proceedings to apply for production. It is for the court in its discretion to decide, first, whether its discretion is to be exercised to order disclosure – that is, that the non-party makes a list of what the non-party has in his or her possession or control (s 34(2)(a)); and, subject to that, secondly, that the non-party produce any of the documents to any of the individuals in section 34(2)(b).

11.14 It should be stressed that section 34(2) uses the correct language of the disclosure rules (ie, 'disclosure' to say what documents are in the non-party's possession and 'production' for release of the documents to a party to the proceedings). Practice under section 34(2) and CPR 1998 Part 31 (there is no equivalent disclosure process prescribed by FPR 2010) is as follows:

(1) Application is in the High Court.

(2) The person or body (eg, the police or a health department) which has the documents must prepare 'a list of documents' (s 34(2)(a); and in accordance with CPR 1998 r 31.10(2)); and see CPR 1998 r 31.10(3) and (4) as to the content of the list.[12]

(3) If one or more parties requires any documents of the non-party, those documents shall be produced to a limited range of individuals set out in section 34(2)(b), subject to the usual rules as to relevant to the issues in the case.

11.15 The extent to which SCA 1981 section 34(2) is complied with in family proceedings will be discussed in Part 5.

Bankers' Book Evidence Act 1879 section 7

11.16 In the case of the Bankers' Book Evidence Act 1879 section 7, procedure at a court hearing is simplified by enabling evidence from bank accounts to speak for themselves in court rather than evidence being called from a bank employee to come to court with the entries.

11.17 Evidence from a non-party's bank account goes to an extreme of an individual's confidential information. Making any order must be regarded as an extreme step and must be justified by the extent of how the information is

12 *31.10 Procedure for standard disclosure*

(1) The procedure for standard disclosure is as follows.

(2) Each party must make and serve on every other party, a list of documents in the relevant practice form.

(3) The list must identify the documents in a convenient order and manner and as concisely as possible.

(4) The list must indicate –

(a) those documents in respect of which the party claims a right or duty to withhold inspection; and

(b) (i) those documents which are no longer in the party's control; and

(ii) what has happened to those documents.

relevant to proceedings.[13] For example, a spouse must show very good reason why a cohabitant's means, and therefore sight of his or her bank account(s), can truly be said to be relevant to a financial issue before the court;[14] but perhaps Mrs Young might have required information under the Bankers Book Evidence Act 1879 from the 'friends' of Mr Young who, he said, had supported him during his claimed insolvency.[15]

Witness summons to produce documents

Witness summons under FPR 2010 Part 24

11.18 FPR 2010 r 24.2 deals with witness summonses. As relevant FPR 2010 r 24.2 provides:

> **24.2 Witness summonses**
>
> (1) A witness summons is a document issued by the court requiring a witness to –...
>
> (b) produce documents to the court ...
>
> (5) The only documents that a summons under this rule can require a person to produce before a hearing are documents which that person could be required to produce at the hearing.

11.19 The witness referred to in r 24.2(1) is, by definition, not a party to proceedings. So, for example, if medical records are required by the court, a summons could be addressed to a suitable person who holds health authority records.

11.20 Only documents which could be required at the final hearing can be ordered to be produced.[16] Documents covered by confidentiality, especially by privilege, would be excluded from production. The question of testing whether confidentiality applies is dealt with under FPR 2010 r 21.3 (see Part 3 of this chapter). Only documents which are relevant to the issues in the particular case will be ordered to be produced.

Setting aside a witness summons

11.21 A non-party as witness who is summonsed to produce documents is able to apply to the court to 'set aside or vary a witness summons',[17] so that the witness does not have to produce the documents which the summons ordered. The court

---

13 See eg, *Williams and ors v Summerfield* [1972] 2 QB 512, QBD Divisional Court where police sought access to the bank accounts of alleged criminals and their wives in connection with their prosecution.

14 *Frary v Frary* [1993] 2 FLR 696, CA.

15 *Young v Young* [2013] EWHC 34 (Fam), [2014] 1 FLR 269 Moor J.

16 FPR 2010 r 24.2(5).

17 Ibid r 24.3(4).

has a discretion to say, for example, that production would be oppressive, not relevant to an issue before the court or otherwise not necessary to its 'fair disposal'.[18]

11.22 In *Morgan v Morgan*,[19] Watkins J defined the test for setting aside a witness summons (subpoena) issued to the wife's father. He was being required to produce information as to his assets and testamentary intentions: highly confidential. He applied to set aside the subpoena. Watkins J said the court must balance the need to have the information necessary to get the answer as near as possible right in the case concerned (financial relief for the daughter and the amount of any lump sum); as against the 'rights of the citizen ... to keep to himself ... details of his wealth and what he intends to do with it'.

11.23 Put in terms of the European Convention 1950, following introduction by HRA 1998, this translates – and for modern purposes can be translated – as: that the rights of the husband to a fair trial of his claim for a lump sum (European Convention 1950 Art 6), must be balanced against the Article 8 (right to respect for private life) of the father to keep his personal information confidential. The need for disclosure to secure a fair trial for Mr Morgan can be balanced against the right of a non-party witness to privacy. If the witness is a child, and especially if the child is a party, his interests are likely to override those of any other party (such as his parents).[20]

Information as to a child's whereabouts

Whereabouts of a child: recovery of children

11.24 The statutory jurisdiction to order non-parties to produce documents is limited to provision under FLA 1986 and CA 1989. Where recovery of children is concerned, the family courts have an inherent power to order information to be provided from third parties. The court has statutory powers also. Both aspects of the family courts' jurisdiction must now be explained.

11.25 The inherent jurisdiction to order third parties to provide information Munby LJ[21] in *Re HM (Vulnerable Adult: Abduction)*[22] said of the High Court's inherent jurisdiction concerning children and information from third parties:

> [36] It has long been recognised that, quite apart from any statutory jurisdiction (for example under s 33 of the Family Law Act 1986 or s 50 of the Children Act 1989), the Family Division has an inherent jurisdiction to make orders directed to third parties who there is reason to believe may be able to provide information which may lead

---

18 See *South Tyneside Borough Council v Wickes Building Supplies Ltd* [2004] EWHC 2428 (Comm) for what is 'necessary for the fair disposal' of a case.

19 [1977] Fam 122, (1976) FLR Rep 473.

20 *Yousef v The Netherlands (Application No 33711/96)* (2003) 36 EHRR 20, [2003] 1 FLR 210, ECtHR; *Local Authority X v HI and Others* [2016] EWHC 1123 (Fam), [2017] 1 FLR 1362, Roberts J; and see further at 11.49.

21 Sitting as a judge of the Family Division.

22 [2010] EWHC 870 (Fam), [2010] 2 FLR 1057.

> to the location of a missing child. Thus orders can be made against public authorities (for example, Her Majesty's Revenue and Customs, the Benefits Agency, the DVLA, local authorities or local education authorities, etc, etc) requiring them to search their records with a view to informing the court whether they have any record of the child or the child's parent or other carer. Similar orders can be directed to telephone and other IT service providers, to banks and other financial institutions, to airline and other travel service providers – the latter with a view to finding out whether the missing child has in fact left the jurisdiction and, if so, for what destination – and to relatives, friends and associates of the abducting parent …

Statutory provisions

11.26 Examples of statutory provision for production of information in relation to children exist in FLA 1986 section 33 and CA 1989 section 48. Applications under these statutory provisions are covered procedurally by FPR 2010 r 21.2;[23] but will be considered separately here from other statutory provisions referred to in that rule.

11.27 FLA 1986 gives power to the Family Court to order information as to the whereabouts of a child who is the subject of proceedings under the 1986 Act be produced. Section 33(1) and (2) is as follows:

> **33 Power to order disclosure of child's whereabouts**
>
> (1) Where in proceedings for or relating to a Part I order[24] in respect of a child there is not available to the court adequate information as to where the child is, the court may order any person who it has reason to believe may have relevant information to disclose it to the court.
>
> (2) A person shall not be excused from complying with an order under subsection (1) above by reason that to do so may incriminate him or his spouse of an offence; but a statement or admission made in compliance with such an order shall not be admissible in evidence against either of them in proceedings for any offence other than perjury.

11.28 An order under section 33(1) can be addressed to individuals who are not parties to the proceedings including the manager of a women's refuge, a person's doctor[25] or the police, as well as relatives or friends of a person who may be keeping the child. The person's access to information as to a child's whereabouts is the critical factor.

---

23 Text at 11.09.

24 Defined by FLA 1986 as any one of a number of children orders, including CA 1989 s 8, Adoption and Children Act 2002 orders for contact.

25 This may be subject to a doctor's claim of confidentiality; but this may be required to be balanced against the welfare of a child in the proceedings.

11.29 CA 1989 sections 48 and 50 both provide the family courts with powers to order that information be provided as to the whereabouts of children who may be in need of emergency protection or who, it is thought, have been abducted and in respect of whom the court has ordered recovery. In each case the orders for providing information are ancillary to existing children proceedings; and require third parties who have information to provide it direct to the 'applicant', that is the local authority which is taking the care proceedings. To give effect to this, CA 1989 section 48(1) provides:

(1) Where it appears to a court making an emergency protection order[26] that adequate information as to the child's whereabouts –

(a) is not available to the applicant for the order; but

(b) is available to another person,

it may include in the order a provision requiring that other person to disclose, if asked to do so by the applicant, any information that he may have as to the child's whereabouts.

11.30 CA 1989 section 50(1) gives power to the court to make a 'recovery order' where a child has been taken away unlawfully, has run away or is missing. By CA 1989 section 50(3)(c) the making of a recovery order 'requires any person who has information as to the child's whereabouts to disclose that information, if asked to do so, to a constable or an officer of the court'. By definition, such a person will not be a party to the proceedings.

Norwich Pharmacal orders

11.31 An order made under the *Norwich Pharmacal* rule[27] will be only very rare in family proceedings. Mostly, where information is needed, proceedings are under way. In that case one of the other means of obtaining information explained in this Part (eg, witness summons) is available. However where, say, a former wife suspected her former husband had not disclosed information she could issue an application under the rule under FPR 2010 Part 19 (ie, as a claim arising the earlier financial relief proceedings, but in separate parallel proceedings) against his accountants or a company who might have that information. The accountants or company would be the respondents to the *Norwich Pharmacal* proceedings.

11.32 *Norwich Pharmacal* concerned a company whose patent had been breached; and where the defendants to the disclosure (discovery) application, HM Customs and Excise, had in their records – as disclosed by them in their list of documents – information as to whom it was who had tortiously infringed Norwich Pharmacal's patent.

26 CA 1989 s 44.

27 *Norwich Pharmacal v Commissioners of Customs and Excise* [1974] AC 133.

11.33 Lord Morris in the House of Lords summarised the issue before the House as follows:[28]

> In my view, it would be reasonable, and in a broad sense of the term just, if the desired information could be supplied ... It will be unfortunate not only from the point of view of the plaintiffs but also of that of the public if the wrongdoers cannot be challenged. In this situation two questions arise: (1) Is it within the power of the court to assist the plaintiffs or is the law powerless? (2) If the court has power to make the desired order — would it be against the public interest to make it?

11.34 The House uniformly held that the answer to both these questions was affirmative; and the order sought by the patent owners was made. The questions to be asked by a would-be applicant for an order are:

(1) Has a wrong been committed or on the face of it carried out by a wrong-doer.

(2) The applicant intends to assert rights against the wrong-doer.

(3) An order is needed to enable an application to be made against the wrong-doer; or to identify the wrong-doer where there is no other source of information.

(4) The respondent is in some way – perhaps innocently (as in the case of HM Customs and Excise) – involved in the wrong-doing.

(5) That only the respondent has the information.

3 PROCEDURE FOR WITHHOLDING INSPECTION

Disclosure and a fair trial

Disclosure: part of the right to a fair trial

11.35 FPR 2010 r 21.3 is derived from CPR 1998 r 31.19 and deals with procedures for two perceptually different forms of disclosure or inspection of documents:

- an application for documents to be withheld on grounds of public interest immunity (PII); and
- for the withholding of documents on other grounds such as privilege and other forms of confidentiality.

11.36 The general rule is that a fair trial demands that a court decide a case on all relevant material being available – that is, disclosed and, where necessary, produced – to the parties and to the court. There are exceptions to this, such as privilege and PII, which have been considered elsewhere in this book. If privilege, confidentiality or PII apply, and were normal civil proceedings disclosure rules to

28 Ibid at 178A.

apply to family proceedings, all documents which a party seeks to withhold – because of, for example, privilege – should still be disclosed[29] (ie, other parties should be told of the existence of such documents).

Claim to withhold inspection

11.37 FPR 2010 r 21.3 is taken directly from CPR 1998 r 31.19 and is as follows:

Claim to withhold inspection or disclosure of a document

(1) A person may apply, without notice, for an order permitting that person to withhold disclosure of a document on the ground that disclosure would damage the public interest.

(2) Unless the court otherwise orders, an order of the court under paragraph (1) –

(a) must not be served on any other person; and

(b) must not be open to inspection by any other person.

(3) A person who wishes to claim that he has a right or a duty to withhold inspection of a document, or part of a document, must state in writing –

(a) that he has such a right or duty; and

(b) the grounds on which he claims that right or duty.

(4) The statement referred to in paragraph (3) must be made –

(a) *in the list in which the document is disclosed; or*

(b) *if there is no list*, to the person wishing to inspect the document.

(5) A party may apply to the court to decide whether a claim made under paragraph (3) should be upheld.

(6) For the purpose of deciding an application under paragraph (1) (application to withhold disclosure) or paragraph (3) (claim to withhold inspection) the court may –

(a) require the person seeking to withhold disclosure or inspection of a document to produce that document to the court; and

(b) invite any person, whether or not a party, to make representations.

(7) An application under paragraph (1) or paragraph (5) must be supported by evidence.

11.38 The italicised words appear in CPR 1998 r 31.19(4); (but have been left out of FPR 2010 r 21.3(4)). The rule-maker accepts that in family proceedings lists of documents are only very rarely used. In theory, at least, this rule does not override a parties' duty to provide to other parties' information that that party has

29 FPR 2010 r 21.1(1).

material covered by privilege, or other right or duty;[30] and the reasons why that party says he or she has the right or duty withhold that which is claimed should be withheld.[31]

11.39 As can be seen, the rule breaks down thus:

(1) *Public interest immunity* – Rule 21.3(1) and (2) deals with PII and the steps to be taken to establish the immunity.

(2) *Privilege and confidentiality* – Rule 21.3(3)–(5) requires that a claim for privilege or confidentiality – namely 'a right or a duty to withhold inspection' – be made in writing to anyone who wishes to see the document; and that any such claim be made by the person claiming confidentiality or privilege to apply to the court.

(3) *Procedure* – Rule 21.3(6) and (7) deals with procedural matters: production to the court; representations by others to the court; and evidence by affidavit.

Procedure for claiming privilege

The application for immunity

11.40 The burden of establishing that material can be withheld from disclosure rests on the party who claims to withhold, say on grounds of confidentiality or legal professional privilege. In the conclusion to his judgment in *West London Pipeline and Storage Ltd v Total UK Ltd*[32] (*WLP*) Beatson J summarised his understanding of the law on the burden of establishing that material should be withheld (in *WLP* it was a question of litigation privilege) as follows:

> [86] The burden of proof is on the party claiming privilege to establish it ... A claim for privilege is an unusual claim in the sense that the party claiming privilege and that party's legal advisers are, subject to the power of the court to inspect the documents, the judges in their or their own client's cause. Because of this, the court must be particularly careful to consider how the claim for privilege is made out and affidavits should be as specific as possible without making disclosure of the very matters that the claim for privilege is designed to protect: *Bank Austria Akt v Price Waterhouse* (unreported 16 April 1997 Neuberger J) *Sumitomo Corp v Credit Lyonnais Rouse Ltd* [2001] 151 NLJ 272 [Andrew Smith J].

11.41 In *WLP* Beatson J surveyed recent case law on the subject of claims for privilege and considered the procedure for claiming that material should be withheld; and in that case, the court's options where privilege is claimed. The claim was for litigation privilege arising from the litigation following the explosion and fire at Buncefield Oil Terminal in December 2005. The procedure proposed by Beatson

30 FPR 2010 r 21.3(4)(a).
31 Ibid r 21.3(4)(b).
32 [2008] EWHC (Comm) 1729 Beatson J.

J would cover any claim by a party – such as HI in the *HI* case, for example[33] – for material to be withheld under FPR 2010 r 21.3(3). That said, it must be recalled that in proceedings under FPR 2010, including all children proceedings, the silence in Part 21 is such that there is no standard disclosure; and that the only reference to a requirement for disclosure of information and of asserting a right to privilege are respectively in rr 21.1(1) and 21.3(4).

11.42 A party to proceedings who claims privilege must be sensitive to the fact that the court is being asked to make an order on their assertions as to the content of the documents; unless – as in *HI* – a separate judge is deputed to try the withholding question as a preliminary issue (and apparently without regard to r 21.3 and *WLP*). Other parties will not see the documents (unless the claim to privilege or confidentiality is not allowed); and it is possible – likely even – that they will be suspicious of the assertions of the party claiming the confidentiality. It follows that any challenge to the claim will be made without the underlying evidence being seen by the respondent to the application and, probably, by the court. (A quite separate procedure for closed material is explained in Chapter 15.)

11.43 Rule 21.3(7) requires that the application 'be supported by evidence'. This rule and the duties it dictates is explained fully by Beatson J. The affidavit should comply with the following:

> [53] … Affidavits claiming privilege whether sworn by the legal advisers to the party claiming privilege as is often the case, or, as in this case, by a Director of the party, should be specific enough to show something of the deponent's analysis of the documents or, in the case of a claim to litigation privilege, the purpose for which they were created. It is desirable that they should refer to such contemporary material as it is possible to do so without making disclosure of the very matters that the claim for privilege is designed to protect …
>
> [54] Notwithstanding these threshold requirements, and the care the court must show, once it is established that a communication was made when litigation was contemplated or pending and for the dominant purpose of obtaining legal advice, the privilege cannot be overridden by another public interest.

Procedure for withholding inspection: legal professional privilege (LPP)

11.44 Based on the procedure under CPR 1998 r 31.19 as explained by Beatson J in *WLP*, and subject to what happened in *HI* (where neither Holman nor Roberts JJ seems to have had their attention drawn to (1) r 21.3, (2) *WLP* or (3) to the cases considered below which deal with parties lawyers only seeing documents), an application under FPR 2010 r 21.3(3) is likely to proceed as a preliminary issue as follows:

33 *Local Authority X v HI and Others* [2016] EWHC 1123 (Fam), [2017] 1 FLR 1362, Roberts J and see 11.49.

(1) A party (A) who seeks to withhold inspection on grounds of LPP (mostly either legal advice privilege (LAP) or litigation privilege (LP)) must provide disclosure (ie, to say that A has the document (eg, a medical or valuation report covered by LP, or the variety of attendance notes and (as appropriate) advices on evidence or other notes from counsel, including emails which record legal advice etc). Documents can be described as a group: 'various emails and letters recording legal advice; counsel's notes etc'. In such statement (r 21.3(3) and (4)) A must state (1) that he or she objects to inspection and (2) why A says privilege applies or that documents are confidential (letters from a doctor or from a child's school, perhaps).[34]

(2) If another party (B) wants to see the document, B can apply to the court for inspection (r 21.3(5)) using the FPR 2010 Part 18 procedure and as set out in *WLP*.

(3) The burden of establishing that the privilege applies is on the party claiming it;[35] though the parties and the court must be wary as to how affidavits seeking privilege are drafted (eg, to avoid later recusal by the judge who has been allowed or caused to read privileged material). A must assume that a mere statement of the existence privilege may not be determinative.

(4) An affidavit setting out the basis for a claim will be required of A or of A's legal adviser. This is likely to be determinative, unless it is otherwise clear from the affidavit that further questions are required (*WLP* at [86](3)).

(5) If the judge is still uncertain as to the adequacy of the affidavit the court may (*WLP* at [86](4)):

- reject the claim for privilege;
- call for further affidavit evidence;
- 'as a last resort' look at the documents;
- order that the maker of the affidavit canbe cross-examined.

11.45 If the court is uncertain whether on the basis of the affidavit evidence that the claim to withhold has been made out, it may consider it necessary to go behind the affidavit. In these circumstances,[36] says Beatson J, the options for the court are as follows:

(a) It may be held that there is no right to withhold, so that the passing on of the information, or filing of the evidence, is ordered.

(b) A further affidavit may be ordered by the court to deal with matters which the earlier affidavit does not cover or on which it is unsatisfactory.

---

34 LPP is established the right to withhold a document is absolute (*R v Derby Magistrates' Court exp B* [1995] UKHL 18, [1996] 1 AC 487, [1996] 1 FLR 513; *Re E (A Child)(Evidence)* [2016] EWCA Civ 473, [2017] 1 FLR 1675, [2016] 4 WLR 105). It cannot be overridden by another public interest (*Three Rivers District Council and ors v Governor and Company of the Bank of England (No 6)* [2004] UKHL 48, [2004] 3 WLR 1274).

35 *WLP* at [86](1).

36 Ibid at [86](4).

(c) The court may look at the documents as anticipated by FPR 2010 r 21.3(6)(a). Inspection by the court should be a solution of last resort; and should only be undertaken if there is credible evidence that those claiming privilege have either misunderstood their duty, or are not to be trusted with the decision making, or there is no reasonably practical alternative.[37]

11.46 If the court has had to proceed as at (c) – the solution of last resort – then the judge who has read the documents cannot be the judge who deals finally with the case (though he or she may still be involved in case management).

Confidential information: application to withhold disclosure

11.47 The above procedure in r 21.3 applies equally to material covered by privilege (as was the case in the *WLP* case) and by confidentiality. So, for example, what is to happen if 'Amelia', a 13-year-old – who in this instance is treated as *Gillick*-competent and is subject to care proceedings – has discussed confidential (to her) matters with a school teacher? Under the rule in *Gillick v West Norfolk and Wisbech AHA*[38] – but perhaps not under the principle in *Working Together 2018*[39] – her confidential material may not be released to third parties on ordinary confidentiality principles.[40] However, if it is relevant evidence (say, a statement by Amelia as to improper and sexualised behaviour (short of sexual intercourse) by her step-father) the fact of the confidential information (ie, that it exists) must be disclosed, that is, its existence must be stated by the local authority – 'stated in writing'[41] – to other parties.[42] So far as it is confidential its detail can be withheld unless the court orders – if it does so – that the confidential information be produced for inspection by other parties.

11.48 It is then open to another party – say, Amelia's parents – to apply to the court to decide whether the claim by the local authority to withhold the evidence 'should be upheld'.[43] An affidavit should be filed by the local authority explaining in outline why the information is confidential, and why Amelia's confidentiality should not be overridden; but not stating any detail as to what the confidential information is. This affidavit will be considered by the judge. This is the conventional, common law and rules-based approach, which does not call for a separate judge and a preliminary issue hearing.[44] It is an approach is based on r 21.3 drawn from Beatson J's common law procedure set out in the *WLP* case.

37 *National Westminster Bank plc v Rabobank Nederland* (above); *Atos Consulting Ltd v Avis plc (No 2)* [2007] EWHC TCC 233, Ramsay J.
38 [1985] UKHL 7, [1986] 1 AC 112, [1986] 1 FLR 224; considered at 3.47.
39 See discussion at 3.59.
40 See eg, *Local Authority X v HI and Others* (above).
41 FPR 2010 r 21.3(3).
42 Ibid r 21.1(1).
43 Ibid r 21.3(5).
44 As happened in *Local Authority v HI*.

Withholding disclosure and Local Authority X v HI

11.49 What is not permissible,[45] it is submitted, is that confidential evidence is seen only the parties' lawyers, to the exclusion of the parties themselves.[46] This is, in effect, a form of closed material procedure which can only be dealt with by order of the High Court with the assistance of special advocates (as explained later[47]) not by the parties own lawyers.

11.50 Thus, in *Local Authority X v HI and Others*,[48] it was open to Holman J, for example and in accordance with r 21.3, on receiving an application from HI's guardian (r 21.3(5)) to have directed that on behalf of HI an affidavit was filed, as required by r 21.3(7). The affidavit would explain in outline why HI did not want documents considered by his father and step-mother: perhaps by explaining the effects which such disclosure would, or might, have on him. In the context of the particular case it would have been important not to be specific as to the content of the material. If this is correct there would have been no need for a separate hearing with disclosure to advocates only, before Roberts J.

Withholding inspection and Article 6 rights

11.51 *European Convention 1950 rights* – The Article 8 rights of the parents could not take precedence over HI's Article 8 rights which were paramount. The judge explained this: 'As *Yousef* makes clear, the child's rights are the paramount consideration in any balancing of competing Art 8 rights.'[49] As to the parents' Article 6 rights: Roberts J had the jurisprudence discussed by Lord Bingham and Lady Hale in *MB* [50] and by Munby J in *Re B* in mind when she said:

> [58] ... The [parents'] rights to a fair trial are, of course, absolute but, as Hale LJ acknowledged in *Re X*,[51] in deciding how to conduct a fair trial, it is perfectly reasonable to take account of the facts and circumstances of the particular case with which the court is dealing.

45 Despite what was ordered in *Local Authority X v HI and Others* (above), and see 11.59.

46 *Somerville and others v Scottish Ministers (HM Advocate General for Scotland intervening)* [2007] UKHL 44, [2007] 1 WLR 2734; *Browning v The Information Commissioner & Anor* [2014] EWCA Civ 1050, [2014] 1 WLR 3848.

47 See Chapter 15.

48 [2016] EWHC 1123 (Fam), [2017] 1 FLR 1362, Roberts J.

49 Ibid at [57]; *Yousef v The Netherlands* (Application No 33711/96) (2003) 36 EHRR 20, [2003] 1 FLR 210, ECHR.

50 *Secretary of State for the Home Department v MB* [2007] UKHL 46 [2008] 1 AC 440, [2007] 3 WLR 681.

51 *Re X (Adoption: Confidential Procedure)* [2002] EWCA Civ 828, [2002] 2 FLR 476: a case where prospective adopters, who were known to the natural parents, nevertheless wanted their adoption to be anonymous. Of the fair trial aspect, Hale LJ said: '[13] Unlike the right to respect for family and private life in Art 8, the right to a fair trial in Art 6 is absolute and unqualified. But the content of a fair trial in any particular case is more flexible and depends upon the context: as Lord Bingham of Cornhill said in *Brown v Stott (Procurator Fiscal, Dunfermline) and Another* [2001] 2 WLR 817, at 824: "What a fair trial requires cannot, however, be the subject of a single unvarying rule or collection of rules. It is proper to take account of the facts and circumstances of particular cases, as the European Court has consistently done." Departures from the usual requirements of an adversarial trial must, of course, be for a legitimate aim and proportionate to that aim. Protecting the welfare of these very vulnerable children is undoubtedly a legitimate aim.'

> The concept of a fair trial is inviolable but the *content* (including the evidence) which is placed before the court is flexible and depends upon context and the issues with which the court is dealing. Whilst I accept that any departure from the usual requirements in relation to the disclosure of evidence in an adversarial trial must be for a legitimate aim and proportionate to that aim, the Court of Appeal has held that protecting the welfare of vulnerable young persons is a specific and undoubtedly a legitimate aim.

11.52 Thus, the procedure for the fair trial will normally depend on the facts of the particular case; and the procedure adopted must be proportionate to its aims. The right to a fair trial was absolute, but denying the father and step-mother access to the information here – even so far as it was relevant – would not deprive them of a fair trial. The harm which would be caused to HI would, said Roberts J, be 'wholly disproportionate to any legitimate forensic purposes served'.[52]

11.53 In *X and Y (Children)*[53] Knowles J considered placement order proceedings in respect of two teenage girls whose father was serving a sentence of imprisonment for his severe sexual and other abuse of them. Over his objection the local authority was given permission not to consult with him or to disclose information to him about the girls.

11.54 In considering the European Convention 1950 balance, as between his Article 6 rights, and the girls' Article 8 rights, the judge also weighed the girl's Article 3 rights (not to be subjected to inhuman and degrading treatment: [30]; and see per Lady Hale in *Re A (Sexual Abuse: Disclosure)* [2012] UKSC 60, [2013] 2 AC 66, [2013] 1 FCR 69 at [60]). Of the father's Article 6 rights she recalled the limits which the court may put on restricting a party's sight of documents (*Re B (Disclosure to Other Parties)* [2001] 2 FLR 1017, [2002] 2 FCR 32 Munby J).

4 WITHHOLDING PRODUCTION ON GROUNDS OF PUBLIC INTEREST IMMUNITY

Withholding disclosure on ground of public interest

11.55 Public interest immunity (PII) is explained in Chapter 16. Its modern origins derive from *R v Chief Constable of the West Midlands, ex p Wiley*.[54] The procedure by which the courts deal with an application for a certificate that material be withheld on grounds of PII is defined by a combination of *ex parte Wiley* and FPR 2010 r 21.3.

11.56 As relevant to withholding on PII grounds r 21.3 sets out the procedure by which application should be made. As with seeking an order that production be denied on grounds of privilege, evidence must be supported by an affidavit:

52 Ibid at [59].
53 [2018] EWHC 451 (Fam).
54 [1994] UKHL 8, [1995] AC 274.

Claim to withhold inspection or disclosure of a document

(1) A person may apply, without notice, for an order permitting him to withhold disclosure of a document on the ground that disclosure would damage the public interest.

(2) Unless the court orders otherwise, an order of the court under paragraph (1) –

(a) must not be served on any other person; and

(b) must not be opened to inspection by any other person …

(6) Where the court is deciding an application under paragraph (1) or (5) it may –

(a) require the person seeking to withhold disclosure or inspection of a document to produce that document to the court; and

(b) invite any person, whether or not a party, to make representations.

(7) An application under paragraph (1) or (5) must be supported by evidence.

(8) This Part does not affect any rule of law which permits or requires a document to be withheld from disclosure or inspection on the ground that its disclosure or inspection would damage the public interest.

11.57 In *Re C (A Child) (Application for Public Interest Immunity)*,[55] Pauffley J reminded herself of the three steps required for a decision as to whether PII should be ordered in accordance with *R v Chief Constable of the West Midlands, ex p Wiley*:[56]

> [29] There are three required steps when the SSHD considers whether to make a claim for PII. First, whether the material is relevant and passes the threshold test for disclosure in the applicable proceedings – (certificate, para 11). Secondly, if the threshold test is passed, whether the material identified as relevant and subject to disclosure attracts PII. The test is whether there is a real risk that disclosure would cause "real damage" or "serious harm" to the public interest – (certificate, paras 13 and 19). Thirdly, if applying the "real damage" test, the material attracts PII, the question arises as to whether the public interest in non-disclosure is outweighed by the public interest in disclosure for the purpose of doing justice in the proceedings …

11.58 In *Re C* Pauffley J explained how the three *ex parte Wiley* stages applied in that case, as more fully explained in Chapter 16.[57]

55 [2017] EWHC 692 (Fam), [2017] 2 FLR 1342; this case and its context is explained more fully in Chapter 16 Part 4.

56 [1994] UKHL 8, [1995] AC 274.

57 See 11.47.

5 COMMUNICATION: POLICE, LOCAL AUTHORITY AND THE COURTS IN CHILDREN PROCEEDINGS

The 2013 protocol

Police and local authorities in care proceedings

11.59 *Lancashire County Council v A, B and Z (A Child: Fact Finding Hearing: Police Disclosure)*[58] deals with the extent to which family courts can (if at all) seek production of material from the police. The *Lancashire County Council* case followed *Re L (A Child).*[59] Neither case makes any explicit reference to SCA 1981 section 34(2) which is explained in outline in Part 2 of this chapter. This will be explained further later in this Part.

11.60 *Lancashire County Council* and *Re L* can be read as guidance alongside the *Protocol and Good Practice Model: Disclosure of information in cases of alleged child abuse and linked criminal and care directions hearings* (October 2013:[60] 'the *2013 Protocol*'); but subject to what is said later at section (2) of this part. This protocol is intended to apply in care proceedings where both police and local authority have evidence which applies in care and prosecution proceedings.

11.61 The *2013 Protocol* encourages co-operation between police and local authorities over similar facts and information behind allegations in relation to children under 17, it does not – it cannot – alter the common law. There are all sorts of reasons why cooperation as envisaged by the *2013 Protocol* should be encouraged. As already considered,[61] the court has inherent powers to order non-parties to provide information about children;[62] but at present the law does not appear to permit disclosure orders save where statute allows.[63]

Police evidence and care proceedings

11.62 Where care and criminal proceedings are in contemplation, are under way or are concluded the procedures for communication of information are regulated against the backdrop of the contempt restrictions of AJA 1960 section 12(1)(a) (see below). The rules and guidance which deal specifically with release of information as between courts, police and the local authority are:

- Family Procedure Rules 2010 r 12.73.
- FPR 2010 *Practice Direction 12G – Communication of Information.*
- *2013 Protocol.*

58 [2018] EWHC 1819 (Fam), Gwyneth Knowles J.

59 Also called *A Local Authority* or *Southwark LBC v US)* [2017] EWHC 3707 (Fam) [2017] EWHC 3707 (Fam), Francis J.

60 Available at: www.cps.gov.uk/publications/docs/third_party_protocol_2013.pdf.

61 See 11.25.

62 *Re HM (Vulnerable Adult: Abduction)* [2010] EWHC 870 (Fam), [2010] 2 FLR 1057, Munby LJ sitting as a High Court judge.

63 CPR 1998 r 31.17, and now FPR 2010 r 21.2.

11.63 The *2013 Protocol* has been in force from 1 January 2014. Its object is to set up an exchange of information and to ensure full co-operation between the authorities involved in child protection and in bringing child abuse ('sexual and non-sexual') cases to the family and criminal courts. It sets up procedures for information and notification of proceedings from police and CPS; and for the passing on of information from the family justice system to the police (summarised in *Part 3: Aims and objectives*). The *2013 Protocol* uses the term 'family justice system' to mean care proceedings in the family courts.

11.64 The *2013 Protocol* is divided into three Parts:

(a) Part A: *Police information for care proceedings* – disclosure by the police of information into the care proceedings; confirmation by the police of the issue of criminal proceedings; and provision for court orders for disclosure by the police.

(b) Part B: *Information for criminal proceedings from care proceedings* – disclosure from care proceedings into the criminal justice system; disclosure of information by the local authority to the police; and provision for formal application by the police to the Family Court for release of information and the court's judgment.

(c) Part C: *Linked directions hearings* – 'linked criminal and care directions hearings' are to be considered by the allocated case management judge in the Family Court; and the local authority lawyers, in such cases, must liaise with the CPS as to what its then current position is in care proceedings (para 16.6). Part 17 sets out what must be considered at any linked directions hearing.

11.65 The emphasis in the *2013 Protocol* is on co-operation; but with all parties being aware that there may be times when full disclosure and co-operation is not possible on grounds of confidentiality. For example, specific provision is made in section 14 of the protocol for what happens if a local authority does not want information disclosed by the prosecution to the defence in the criminal proceedings (ie, to a parent, or parents, or other alleged perpetrator, in care proceedings). In the rare event that this is necessary, it is for CPS to make a public interest immunity application in the criminal proceedings (para 14.2; Criminal Procedure Rules 2013 r 22.3). The fact that 'documents in relation to Family Court proceedings' (ie, children proceedings) must not be included in files to be seen by the police is stressed at paragraph 10.4.

Co-operation: disclosure by the local authority and the court to the police

11.66 Sections 10 to 12 (in Part B) deals with 'disclosure' by the local authority to the police, and with applications by the police to the Family Court for material relating to family proceedings (including the text of any judgment). Section 11 deals mostly with procedural issues for police obtaining material, and in particular stresses the need for the police to give notice of any application to all parties where possible (para 11.7). Paragraph 11.8 asserts – without citation of authority – that the court may order release of material to the police or CPS 'without application having been made'.

11.67 Certain judgments will be published in any event.[64] Paragraph 12.2 states that the local authority must notify the police if there is a judgment not yet transcribed which it considers to be relevant to current criminal proceedings; and it must ask the Family Court to speed up transcription (para 12.3). Disclosure by the local authority to the police (summarised in Section 10, especially paras 10.3 to 10.6) and communication of other information must be seen in the light of the 'communication or information' provisions in FPR 2010 r 12.73 and *PD27G*.

The protocol: co-operation and the investigation of crime

11.68 In *Re X and Y (Disclosure of Judgment to Police)*[65] Baker J draws particular attention to the importance of the then relatively recently published *2013 Protocol*:[66]

> [46] ... The importance of [co-operation between police and local authorities] – recognised by the courts at the time of the *Re EC* decision – is now perceived as being crucial in maximising the protection given to children. This recognition underpins the recently published [2013 Protocol].
>
> [48] Linked to this ... is the fifth factor identified by Swinton Thomas LJ[67] – the public interest in the administration of justice, and the argument that barriers should not be erected between one branch of the judicature and another because this may be inimical to the overall interests of justice. Again, the importance of this principle has been widely accepted, and it is again reflected in the terms of the 2013 Protocol.

11.69 Baker J went on to support the 'public interest in prosecution of serious crime and the gravity of this offence' by reference to factors (6) and (7) and by drawing attention to the fact that it is not the job of a judge, but of the police, to investigate crime:

> [49] As has been acknowledged by many judges on previous occasions – for example, Baron J in *Re M (Care: Disclosure to Police)* [2008] 2 FLR 390 at para [18] – it is the police who have a duty to investigate crime and it is the CPS which has a duty to decide whether to bring criminal charges. It is not for the family court to decide whether prosecutions should be brought or pursued. Disclosure of the judgment will enable the police and CPS to decide whether or not to pursue the criminal investigation. In carrying out the balancing exercise as to disclosure of the judgments, this court recognises the importance of not impeding those bodies from carrying out their statutory duties.

---

64 See *Publication of Judgments Practice Guidance issued on 16 January 2014*. Available at: www.judiciary.gov.uk/wp-content/uploads/2014/01/transparency-in-the-family-courts-jan-2014-1.pdf.

65 [2014] EWHC 278 (Fam), [2015] 1 FLR 1218.

66 *2013 Protocol and Good Practice Model: Disclosure of information in cases of alleged child abuse and linked criminal and care directions hearings October 2013.*

67 See 7.22.

Police 'disclosure' under the 2013 Protocol

11.70 In *Re L (A Child)*[68] Francis J was dealing with CA 1989 Part 4 proceedings in respect of five children whose sister, L, died as a result of strangulation; but, said the judge, he must also decide whether or not she was 'sexually assaulted at some time shortly before her death and, again, whether such assault, if it occurred, was perpetrated by a member of her family'. The Home Office pathologist, who was instructed, considered that the death was a sexually motivated homicide. Emergency protection orders were made, followed by interim supervision orders with children living with the mother. The father and two older children were in the pool of possible perpetrators.

11.71 Francis J records that early in the proceedings '[8] I made a number of disclosure orders against the Metropolitan police'; though no authority in law for any power to order disclosure (ie production) is given by the judge. He goes on, later:

> [44] It is right, at this stage, that I refer briefly to the whole issue of police disclosure, a subject to which I return at the end of this Judgment. In short, however, I regard the disclosure of relevant material by the police in this case to have been woefully inadequate. It was only as a result of repeated orders made by me that several hundred pages of relevant material were produced during the course of this hearing. Some of what was part of the last minute disclosure has shaped the findings that I have made. It is important that lessons are learned from the way that the police have approached the issue of disclosure in this case and I set out some suggestions at the end of this Judgment.

11.72 It is said by Francis J that '[106] Compliance with [the *2013 Protocol*] is of course mandatory'. But, with respect to the judge, is it indeed mandatory? This will be considered in section (2) of this Part. First the parallel *Lancashire County Council* case must be considered.

Police production and the law

Lancashire County Council *and police production*

11.73 FPR 2010 r 21.2(1) is quite clear. Just as is required by CPR 1998 r 31.17(1) so too in r 21.2: 'disclosure' may only be ordered by the court where statute provides. In family proceedings it is generally agreed that this applies only to Bankers Book Evidence Act 1879 (not applicable here) and Senior Courts Act 1981 sections 33 and 34. In *Lancashire County Council* [69] proceedings were under way, so only section 34 could apply. The same applies to *Re L*. In neither case, it seems, was section 34(2) referred to.

---

68 Also called *A Local Authority* or *Southwark LBC v US)* [2017] EWHC 3707 (Fam), Francis J.

69 *Lancashire County Council v A, B and Z (A Child: Fact Finding Hearing: Police Disclosure)* [2018] EWHC 1819 (Fam) Gwyneth Knowles J; and see 11.59.

11.74 In *Lancashire County Council* the judge refers to FPR 2010 r 21.2 but only as follows:

> [8] [FPR 2010 Pt entitled] 'Miscellaneous Rules About Disclosure and Inspection of Documents makes provision for the disclosure and inspection of documents against persons who are not parties to the proceedings. Within family proceedings, disclosure is taken to mean the production of copies of documents though this is, strictly speaking, a means of providing for the inspection of documents. Rule 21.1(1) of the FPR states that: "A party discloses a document by stating that the document exists or has existed." The next logical step in the process is the inspection of a document by a party when that document has been disclosed by another person [Rule 21.1(2)]. Thereafter, Rule 21.2 makes provision for orders for disclosure against persons who are not parties to the proceedings. The relevant provisions are as follows (*sic*):
>
> ...
>
> (3) The court may make an order under this rule only where disclosure is necessary in order to dispose fairly of the proceedings or to save costs.
>
> (4) An order under this rule must –
>
> (a) specify the documents or the classes of documents which the respondent must disclose; and
>
> (b) require the respondent, when making disclosure to specify any of those documents –
>
> (i) which are no longer in the respondent's control; or
>
> (ii) in respect of which the respondent claims a right or duty to withhold inspection.

11.75 As can be seen, the omission marks show where Gwyneth Knowles J has deliberately left out the first two paragraphs of the rule.[70] Paragraph 21.2(1) specifically limits non-party disclosure – as opposed to, for example, production of documents by witness summons[71] – to circumstances where statute permits such disclosure. It is difficult to see how compliance with the statute would have produced a greatly different end result; but at least it would have ensured compliance with the statutorily required steps referred to about (and kept photocopying of irrelevant documents to a minimum).

Senior Courts Act 1981 section 34(2)

11.76 As mentioned in Part 2, section 34(2) is not only what the law imposes on the High Court when it makes this order.[72] Section 34(2) also prescribes a

70 Set out in full at 11.9.

71 FPR 2010 r 24.2(1)(b).

72 Probably the order can be made by the Family Court also: the Matrimonial and Family Proceedings Act 1984 s 31E(1)(a).

procedure which non-parties and the parties wanting to rely on their evidence must comply with, by statute. This seems to have been short-circuited by Francis and Knowles JJ. Statute directs that a list be prepared by the non-party. There is no evidence that the police provided a list of relevant documents in either of these cases (s 34(2)(a)). There is no information regarding exactly to whom (under s 34(2)(b)) the documents should have been produced; nor precisely to what the disclosed/produced documents related.

11.77 At the end of *Lancashire County Council* Gwyneth Knowles J cited with approval the judgment of Francis J in the earlier *Re L* (Southwark) case, and set out guidance issued by him, including:

> [48] … '(i) The local authority will make a protocol request to the police at least 14 days prior to the issue of s.31 proceedings. In cases where the issue of s.31 proceedings is immediately preceded by an application for an emergency protection order or the s.31 proceedings are listed upon short notice, the protocol request shall be made upon issue of the s.31 proceedings.
>
> (ii) Not later than seven days prior to the case management hearing, the local authority will issue an application for disclosure against the relevant police authority. The local authority will invite the court to list the application for disclosure on the same day as the case management hearing. The local authority will serve a copy of the application upon the police at least seven days prior to the case management hearing. The senior investigating police officer in the case should be invited to attend the case management hearing and be legally represented.
>
> (iii) In the event that the police wish to withhold any disclosure from the parties, any application should be made by them not less than two days prior to the case management hearing. The application should set out clearly the reasons why disclosure is being opposed and why a redacted version cannot be provided.
>
> (iv) Upon receipt of a protocol request or an application for disclosure, the police will provide a list or schedule of all the evidence and material they have within their possession that is relevant to the central issues in the Family Court case. This list shall address the following:
>
> (a) A short description of the evidence/material;
>
> (b) Whether the police agree to disclose that particular piece of evidence or material to the parties; and
>
> (c) In the event the police oppose disclosure of a particular piece of evidence or material clear reasons must be provided.

11.78 With the greatest respect to both judges, this list seems to take little account of the law in section 34(2). Section 34(2)(a) says what must be in the list (referred to at (iv) above). Section 34(2)(a) and FPR 2010 r 21.2(1) make it clear that is for the judge to make any order for disclosure, not a protocol or gloss on a protocol; and that order should, if possible, be made in the High Court. That is, as soon as any application is made under section 34(2), the court has control of the non-party disclosure process.

11.79 In *Re H (Children)* [2018] EWFC 61 Sir James Munby as a High Court judge provides a coda to this subject. Re H is not a judgment. It creates no new law; but it is a helpful commentary. Sir James accepted the local authority's invitation to look at the delay in care proceedings caused by production of documents by non-parties,[73] notably by the police, as follows:

(1) What can the family court do to avoid delay caused by concurrent care criminal proceedings?

(2) What can the family court do when delay is caused other government departments or agencies?

11.80 The courts cannot ever tell non-parties, especially public bodies, what they must do (what Sir James called the *A v Liverpool* principle: ie, per Lord Scarman in *A v Liverpool City Council* [1982] AC 363): 'The High Court cannot exercise its powers, however wide they may be, so as to intervene on the merits in an area of concern entrusted by Parliament to another public authority.' So, he said:

> [22] … A family court cannot dictate to another court or agency how [they are to exercise their] powers. [In the absence of] statutory provision to the contrary, the ambit of family court judicial decision-making is constrained by the extent of the resources made available by other public bodies. So, the family court cannot *direct* that resources be made available or that services be provided; it can merely seek to *persuade*. How far can *persuasion* go? The answer is that the family court can seek to *persuade* but must not apply *pressure*: *Holmes-Moorhouse v Richmond upon Thames London Borough Council* [2009] UKHL 7, [2009] 1 WLR 413 (per Lady Hale)' (judge's italics).

The court has powers as to issue a witness summons[74] under the jurisdiction conferred by Matrimonial and Family Proceedings Act 1984 section 31G

11.81 So what is a local authority to do? Section 31G does not create a jurisdiction which was not there before. It merely re-enacts County Courts Act 1981 section 55 which deals with witness summonses in the county court. Issue of a witness summons is defined by common law and is regulated by FPR 2010 r 24.2 (derived from CPR 1998 r 34.2). But, it must be emphasised, this can only happen where a party to the case requires a non-party – such as the police – to produce documents or by following the steps prescribed by FPR 2010 r 21.2. Section 31G cannot give a judge a free-standing power to call for evidence. The disappointing approach of the police to producing evidence into court proceedings and of which

73 Considered recently in David Burrows 'Who Must Disclose What & When?'(2018) *New Law Jourrnal* 9.
74 Sir James Munby at [31].

Sir James complains (understandably) (eg, under *2013 Protocol and Good Practice Model Disclosure of information in … linked criminal and care [proceedings]*) can probably only be corrected on formal application by a party to proceedings for a witness summons to produce documents (FPR 2010 r 24.2); not by the initiative of the judge.

12

RELEASE OR PUBLICATION OF COURT MATERIAL TO NON-PARTIES: THE LAW

1 INTRODUCTION

Supply of court documents and other forms of use by non-parties

12.1 This chapter and Chapter 13 look at circumstances in which documents and other information may be released to non-parties (or third parties), or otherwise 'used'[1] where the material has been filed at court: first in civil proceedings and then (Chapter 13) in family proceedings. Release may be to the press and other media, friends or supporters of a party to proceedings; and this may ultimately, and in various ways, involve publication or attempted publication.

12.2 This chapter deals with the law in relation to release at common law and in the inherent jurisdiction of the court. Chapter 13 deals with (1) the specific circumstances contemplated by the Civil Procedure Rules (CPR) 1998 r 31.22 – the 'implied undertaking' – as it applies to the Family Courts; and (2) with the extent to which the court can take it upon itself to release documents to non-parties in family proceedings.

12.3 In the absence of any provision in Family Procedure Rules 2010 (FPR 2010) and in the light of provisions in CPR 1998 and at common law (such as the 'implied undertaking' and the inherent jurisdiction of the courts[2] to order release of information), it will be assumed here that CPR 1998 and cases which explain

1 CPR 1998 r 31.22 (use of disclosed documents); the text of r 31.22 is at 12.46.

2 As explained in *Cape Intermediate Holdings Ltd v Dring (Asbestos Victims Support Group)* [2018] EWCA Civ 1795 see Chapter 13.

it represents the law in this area[3] for family as for civil proceedings. For example, CPR 1998 r 31.22(1) is intended to replace the former 'implied undertaking' not to 'use' disclosed documents and save in the circumstances described in r 31.22(1) not to permit their release to non-parties. Family proceedings, as hitherto – certainly until the introduction of CPR 1998 – has always been treated as 'civil proceedings'. The 'implied undertaking' has always therefore been treated as applicable to family proceedings.[4]

Divergence of family and civil proceedings; but the same common law

12.4 The common law, and the extent to which civil and family proceedings diverge from one another, is still in a state of development, as explained in, for example, discussion of hearings documents after *Cape Intermediate Holdings Ltd v Dring (Asbestos Victims Support Group)*[5] (*Cape Intermediate v Dring*). Certainly, it is by no means clear what documents or other information may be released to non-parties (such as media representatives or academics) who are permitted to attend a Family Court hearing by FPR 2010 r 27.11(2).[6]

Documents and Family Courts

12.5 The range and categories of documents which can be released from civil proceedings generally will be considered later, especially in Part 3. The types of Family Court hearing which will dictate the forms of document to be released, so far as this and the next chapter are concerned, are set out here. Each category of family hearing has different rules as will be explained in Chapter 13:

(1) Open court hearings (eg, divorce, committal proceedings, domestic abuse cases under the Family Law Act 1996 Part 4). Open justice principles apply to these hearings and the same rules are likely to apply as explained in *Cape Intermediate v Dring*.

(2) Hearings in private where media representatives and other can attend (FPR 2010 r 27.11(2)(f)–(g)): as long as anonymity is preserved, the *Cape Intermediate v Dring* rules could apply.

(3) Other hearings in private (see eg, *Clibbery v Allan* (above)).

---

3 See the Employment Tribunals (Constitution and Rules of Procedure) Regulations 2013 (SI 2013/1237), r 31 of which provides for disclosure by court order, Christopher Clarke LJ said in *IG Index Ltd v Cloete* [2014] EWCA Civ 1128: '[28] There is, however, no express provision in [the 2013 tribunal rules] restricting the use of disclosed documents. I would, however, regard it as implicit that the same restriction on disclosure by the recipient should apply as arises under CPR 31.22. The common law would necessarily imply some form of undertaking and the appropriate implication is that the person to whom disclosure is made pursuant to these Regulations should be under the same restriction as if he had given disclosure in the county court.' In principle there is no reason why the same cannot be said of rules for family proceedings.

4 See eg, *Clibbery v Allan* [2002] EWCA Civ 45, [200] Fam 261, [2002] 2 WLR 1511, [2002] 1 FLR 565.

5 [2018] EWCA Civ 1795; see Chapter 13.

6 See discussion in Chapter 13.

12.6 This chapter proceeds as follows:

- Part 2 looks generally at the subject of release of court documents to non-parties.
- Part 3 defines the common law and other sources for supply of court documents (CPR 1998 r 5.4C) for non-parties; and deals with the first category of documents considered here, namely court documents.
- Part 4 considers the case of *Cape Intermediate v Dring*[7] and documents as defined for release by the Court of Appeal in that case, in particular it considers documents which the court may be able in its inherent jurisdiction (especially in civil proceedings) to permit be released to a non-party[8] (eg, to anyone who attends a hearing, so that they may be able the better to understand the proceedings).
- Part 5 introduces the collateral use of court documents (the 'implied undertaking': CPR 1998 r 31.22), alongside consideration of the subject in family proceedings in Chapter 13 Part 6.

2 RELEASE OF COURT DOCUMENTS

Hearing documents in open court proceedings

12.7 For civil proceedings – indeed for all open court proceedings and, subject to privacy restrictions for hearing in private,[9] all civil proceedings – the law has been clarified and defined by the Court of Appeal in *Cape Intermediate v Dring*. The case opens up a fresh set of questions for non-parties in family proceedings which are taken up in the next chapter. The focus in this chapter will be on how relevant documents are dealt with in civil proceedings; and then to carry that forward for family proceedings.

12.8 Where Family Court proceedings are heard in open court it will be assumed here that the same common law approach and rules for release of hearings documents will apply to those proceedings, notwithstanding that FPR 2010 r 29.12 appears to say that documents may not be released from those proceedings (ie, open court hearings) to non-parties.

Open court principle and use of documents

12.9 In *R (Guardian News and Media Ltd) v City of Westminster Magistrates' Court*[10] (*Guardian News v Westminster*) Toulson LJ defined examples of the documents in question in this Part of Chapter 12:

7 *Cape Intermediate Holdings Ltd v Dring (Asbestos Victims Support Group)* [2018] EWCA Civ 1795.

8 The documents at issue in *Cape Intermediate Holdings Ltd v Dring (Asbestos Victims Support Group)* [2018] (above); considered further in Part 4.

9 CPR 1998 r 39.2(3).

10 [2012] EWCA Civ 420, [2013] QB 618.

> [6] In this case the question has arisen whether a District Judge, who made two extradition orders on the application of the US Government, had power to allow the Guardian Newspaper to inspect and take copies of affidavits or witness statements, written arguments and correspondence, which were supplied to the judge for the purposes of the extradition hearings. They were not read out in open court but they were referred to during the course of the hearings …

12.10 The principle of what hearing documents could be released to the press was considered by the Court of Appeal in *Guardian News v Westminster*. A magistrates' court district judge made two extradition orders on the application of the US Government; but did she have power to allow the *Guardian* to inspect and take copies of affidavits or witness statements, written arguments and correspondence, which were supplied to the judge for the purposes of the extradition hearings? They were not read out in open court, but they had been read by the judge and were referred to during the course of the hearings. The judge refused the *Guardian*'s application. The Administrative Court (Sullivan LJ and Silber J) agreed with her. The *Guardian* appealed against the refusal of its applications with leave of the court.

12.11 Toulson LJ started his judgment by placing the issue before the Court of Appeal firmly in the common law tradition of open justice:

> [1] Open justice. The words express a principle at the heart of our system of justice and vital to the rule of law. The rule of law is a fine concept but fine words butter no parsnips. How is the rule of law itself to be policed? It is an age old question. Quis custodiet ipsos custodes—who will guard the guards themselves? In a democracy, where power depends on the consent of the people governed, the answer must lie in the transparency of the legal process. Open justice lets in the light and allows the public to scrutinise the workings of the law, for better or for worse. Jeremy Bentham said in a well-known passage quoted by Lord Shaw in *Scott v Scott* [1913] AC 417, 477: 'Publicity is the very soul of justice. It is the keenest spur to exertion and the surest of all guards against improbity. It keeps the judge himself while trying under trial.'
>
> [2] This is a constitutional principle which has been recognised by the common law since the fall of the Stuart dynasty, as Lord Shaw explained. It is not only the individual judge who is open to scrutiny but the process of justice …

12.12 And if Sir Mark Potter's view of the 'watchdog' role for the media to be let into f in accordance with *Re Child X (Residence and Contact: Rights of Media Attendance: FPR Rule 10.28(4))* [11] is to mean anything, this version of Bentham's 'soul of justice' must surely be kept mind when release of documents is applied to those for whom FPR 2010 r 27.11(2) is intended (ie mostly the media).

11 [2009] EWHC 1728 (Fam), [2009] 2 FLR 1467, Sir Mark Potter P.

12.13 Toulson LJ continued in relation to open justice, especially in the context of release of court documents (and in passages cited by the Court of Appeal in *Cape Intermediate v Dring* by Hamblen LJ):

> [69] The open justice principle is a constitutional principle to be found not in a written text but in the common law. It is for the courts to determine its requirements, subject to any statutory provision. It follows that the courts have an inherent jurisdiction to determine how the principle should be applied.
>
> [70] Broadly speaking, the requirements of open justice apply to all tribunals exercising the judicial power of the state …

12.14 As Toulson LJ explained it was a matter for the courts to decide 'what open justice requires' and to determine what it required in terms of disclosure or release of documents:

> [71] The decisions of the courts in *Scott v Scott* [1913] AC 417, *GIO Personal Investments Services Ltd v Liverpool and London Steamship Protection and Indemnity Association Ltd (FAI General Insurance Co Ltd intervening)* [1999] 1 WLR 984 and *R v Howell* [2003] EWCA Crim 486 are illustrations of the jurisdiction of the courts to determine what open justice requires. For this purpose it is irrelevant how broadly or narrowly the last two cases should be interpreted. The significant point is that the decisions of the court in those cases, about disclosure of skeleton arguments to non-parties, were an exercise of the courts' power to determine whether such disclosure was required by the open justice principle.

Developments in the common law on release of hearing documents

12.15 In *GIO Personal Investment Services Limited v Liverpool and London Steamship P & I Association Limited*[12] (a case decided as CPR 1998 was coming into operation) the Court of Appeal distinguished between release of written submissions to the court, and parties' statements. In *Guardian News v Westminster* Toulson LJ explained this as follows:

> [35] In *GIO Personal Investment Services Limited v Liverpool* … a non-party applied to inspect written submissions and documents forming part of the evidence, including witness statements which had been referred to in open court but not read out. The application was refused at first instance. The Court of Appeal allowed an appeal in respect of the written submissions but not the evidence. As to the evidence, Potter LJ (with whose judgment the other members of the court agreed) said that historically there had been no right, and that there was currently no provision, which enabled a member of the public to see, examine

12 [1999] 1 WLR 984, CA in which the lead judgment was given by Potter LJ who, as Sir Mark Potter P, was to be a principle architect of the transparency reforms in family proceedings considered in the next chapter.

or copy a document on the basis that it had been referred to in court or read by the judge. He added that he did not consider that any recent development in court procedures justified the court in contemplating such an exercise under its inherent jurisdiction. On the other hand, he considered the arguments for such an exercise in respect of the written submissions of counsel to be a good deal stronger.

Civil Procedure Rules 1998: 'documents … from court records'

12.16 Neither of CPR 1998 r 5.4C (documents from court records) nor r 31.22[13] (use of disclosed documents) are provided for in FPR 2010 for family proceedings; though both rules in CPR 1998 have a well-developed case law. A question – mostly for Chapter 13 – will be to what extent these cases represent the common law and to what extent that common law applies to family proceedings.

12.17 CPR 1998 Part 5 deals in general with 'documents … from court records'. CPR 1998 r 5.4C provides for supply of 'documents … from court records'. The meaning of this term has been explained by *Cape Intermediate v Dring*. 'Documents from court records' can be obtained by a non-party; but what are these documents? And can the court order, on application, that individuals be prevented from receiving documents (r 5.4C(4) and (6)[14])? This subject is dealt with in Chapter 13 so far as it relates to family proceedings. Here, the civil proceedings position is considered.

12.18 CPR 1998 r 5.4C provides (as relevant here):

Supply of documents to a non-party from court records

(1) The general rule is that a person who is not a party to proceedings may obtain from the court records a copy of –

(a) a statement of case, but not any documents filed with or attached to the statement of case, or intended by the party whose statement it is to be served with it;

(b) a judgment or order given or made in public (whether made at a hearing or without a hearing), subject to paragraph (1B).

(1A) Where a non-party seeks to obtain a copy of a statement of case filed before 2nd October 2006 –

(a) this rule does not apply; and

(b) the rules of court relating to access by a non-party to statements of case in force immediately before 2nd October 2006 apply as if they had not been revoked.

13 The text of r 31.22 is at 12.46.

14 Consideration of the restrictions on release is at Part 3.

12.19 CPR 1998 r 31.22,[15] which is part of CPR 1998 Part 31 'Disclosure and Inspection of Documents', deals with – amongst other things – the 'use' outside court proceedings of documents disclosed in proceedings. It is only such documents, unless the court orders otherwise,[16] which may be published (ie the extent of overriding the 'implied undertaking').

Restrictions on release

12.20 Alongside the right of a non-party to obtain documents from court records[17] is the right of a party to proceedings or a person mentioned in a statement of case (a court pleading) to prevent release of a court record document (CPR 1998 r 5.4C(4)):

(4) The court may, on the application of a party or of any person identified in a statement of case –

- (a) order that a non-party may not obtain a copy of a statement of case under paragraph (1);
- (b) restrict the persons or classes of persons who may obtain a copy of a statement of case;
- (c) order that persons or classes of persons may only obtain a copy of a statement of case if it is edited in accordance with the directions of the court; or
- (d) make such other order as it thinks fit …

(6) Where the court makes an order under paragraph (4), a non-party who wishes to obtain a copy of the statement of case, or to obtain an unedited copy of the statement of case, may apply on notice to the party or person identified in the statement of case who requested the order, for permission.

15 Set out in full at 12.46.
16 CPR 1998 r 31.22(2).
17 CPR 1998 r 5.4C(1).

12.21 In addition to the above provisions, CPR 1998 r 5.4B and *Participation Direction 5A – Court documents* make formal provision for certain documents, as set out in paragraph 4.2A of the practice direction.[18] Rule 5.4B says:

> **Supply of documents to a party from court records**
>
> (1) A party to proceedings may, unless the court orders otherwise, obtain from the records of the court a copy of any document listed in paragraph 4.2A of Practice Direction 5A.
>
> (2) A party to proceedings may, if the court gives permission, obtain from the records of the court a copy of any other document filed by a party or communication between the court and a party or another person.

Documents in civil proceedings

12.22 What may be published or otherwise released from family proceedings will be defined and considered in Chapter 13. The remainder of this chapter deals with documents and other material in CPR 1998 rr 5.4C and 31.22, some by the common law (as will be explained):

(1) *Court documents* – Court documents for which a non-party is entitled to apply as a matter of formality (CPR 1998 r 5.4C).

(2) *Hearing documents* – Documents such as those pre-read by the judge or otherwise read at a hearing, for which a non-party may apply per *Guardian v Westminster*.[19]

---

18 4.2A A party to proceedings may, unless the court orders otherwise, obtain from the records of the court a copy of –
- (a) a certificate of suitability of a litigation friend;
- (b) a notice of funding;
- (c) a claim form or other statement of case together with any documents filed with or attached to or intended by the claimant to be served with such claim form;
- (d) an acknowledgment of service together with any documents filed with or attached to or intended by the party acknowledging service to be served with such acknowledgement of service;
- (e) a certificate of service, other than a certificate of service of an application notice or order in relation to a type of application mentioned in sub-paragraph (h)(i) or (ii);
- (f) a notice of non-service;
- (g) a directions questionnaire;
- (h) an application notice, other than in relation to –
  - (i) an application by a solicitor for an order declaring that he has ceased to be the solicitor acting for a party; or
  - (ii) an application for an order that the identity of a party or witness should not be disclosed;
- (i) any written evidence filed in relation to an application, other than a type of application mentioned in sub-paragraph (h)(i) or (ii);
- (j) a judgment or order given or made in public (whether made at a hearing or without a hearing);
- (k) a statement of costs;
- (l) a list of documents;
- (m) a notice of payment into court;
- (n) a notice of discontinuance;
- (o) a notice of change; or
- (p) an appellant's or respondent's notice of appeal.

19 See *R (ota Guardian News and Media Ltd) v City of Westminster Magistrates' Court (Article 19 Intervening)* [2012] EWCA Civ 420, [2013] QB 618.

(3) *Disclosed documents* – Documents whose production has been compelled by disclosure rules (CPR 1998 r 31.22(1)) and who release or other use the law restricts.

(4) *Other documents and information* which a party is entitled to publish or supply to others about proceedings where a court has sat in private.[20]

3 RELEASE OF HEARING DOCUMENTS

Documents for a non-party or court observer

12.23 The question as to what documents an observer of any court proceedings may have access, must be answered by reference to the common law in open court proceedings; and then by the common law as seen from the point of view of proceedings in private to which an observer has access (eg, under FPR 2010 r 27.11(2)).

12.24 In *Guardian News v Westminster*[21] the Court of Appeal considered release to a *Guardian* journalist of 'affidavits or witness statements, written arguments and correspondence, which were supplied to the judge for the purposes of [a court hearing]' (ie, extradition proceedings before a magistrates' court district judge).[22] As already mentioned,[23] Toulson LJ firmly based his judgment on the open justice principle. This applied where documents are placed before the court and are referred to in the course of a hearing:

> [85] … where documents have been placed before a judge and referred to in the course of proceedings, in my judgment the default position should be that access should be permitted on the open justice principle; and where access is sought for a proper journalistic purpose, the case for allowing it will be particularly strong.

The common law and family proceedings

12.25 The rules may be 'unchanged' (as *PD27B* says); but the common law, as it relates to civil proceedings, has developed since 2009. If application were made in family proceedings for release of information to a press representative or academic, a family judge will need to decide between, on the one hand, the line proposed by *Guardian News v Westminster* adapted to family proceedings and, on

20 See eg, *Clibbery v Allan* [2002] EWCA Civ 45, [2002] 1 FLR 565; *Clayton v Clayton* [2006] EWCA Civ 878, [2006] 1 FLR 11; Re *J (A Child)* [2013] EWHC 2694 (Fam) sub nom *Re J (Reporting Restriction: Internet: Video)* [2014] 1 FLR 523, Sir James Munby P.

21 [2012] EWCA Civ 420, [2013] QB 618, [2012] 3 WLR 1343.

22 Ibid at [6].

23 See 12.11.

the other hand, the approach of *PD27B* para 2.3 and Mostyn J. 'New ground' for civil proceedings was broken in *Guardian News v Westminster*:[24]

> [87] In this case the *Guardian* has put forward good reasons[25] for having access to the documents which it seeks. There has been no suggestion that this would give rise to any risk of harm to any other party, nor would it place any great burden on the court. Accordingly, its application should be allowed.

12.26 It is submitted that if – for similar, and other comparable, reasons – an observer were to apply alongside that observer's proposed attendance at court, then on principles equivalent to *Guardian News v Westminster* (save for its references to the open justice principle) a court would release documents to a journalist, academic, legal blogger or other responsible person permitted to attend court in family proceedings. Paragraph 2.3 of the *Practice Direction* implies that permission of the court can be applied for. It does not provide the same clarity with which such an application will be dealt with as does *Guardian v Westminster*.

'Evidence and argument must be publicly known'[26]

12.27 In *Harman v Secretary of State for the Home Department* [27] Lord Scarman[28] explained the importance, as he saw it, that people attending court were able to understand what went on in court and what was being said:

> [There is] another important public interest involved in justice done openly, namely, that the evidence and argument should be publicly known, so that society may judge for itself the quality of justice administered in its name, and whether the law requires modification. When public policy in the administration of justice is considered, public knowledge of the evidence and arguments of the parties is certainly as important as expedition: and, if the price of expedition is to be the silent reading by the judge before or at trial of relevant documents, it is arguable that expedition will not always be consistent with justice being seen to be done.

12.28 In *Smithkline Beecham Biologicals SA v Connaught Laboratories Inc*,[29] Lord Bingham CJ developed Lord Scarman's concerns in relation to hearing documents.

---

24 *R (Guardian News and Media Ltd) v City of Westminster Magistrates' Court (Article 19 intervening)* [2012] EWCA Civ 420, [2013] QB 618 at [90]: '... I recognise that this decision breaks new ground in the application of the principle of open justice, although not, as I believe, in relation to the nature of the principle itself.'

25 Toulson LJ had summarised the *Guardian's* reasons thus: '[13] the Guardian submitted that it was wrong for it to be denied the documentation sought. In particular, (a) it had a serious journalistic purpose in seeking production of the documents, because the case raised issues of public interest; (b) allowing it to see the documents would not frustrate or render impracticable the administration of justice; and (c) allowing it to see the documents would not interfere with any rights of the parties to the case or of third parties.'

26 See Lord Scarman in citation from *Harman v Home Department*.

27 [1983] 1 AC 280 at 316.

28 Quoted by Toulson LJ in *Guardian v Westminster* at [33].

29 [1999] EWCA Civ 1781, [1999] 4 All ER 498.

The case concerned a patent where documents had been disclosed by the defendants pursuant to a court order. The question was whether each of these documents had been 'read to or by the Court, or referred to, in open Court' (in the language of the then applicable Rules of the Supreme Court 1965 Order 24 r 14A, and as reproduced in CPR 1998 r 31.22(1)(a)). After the judge had pre-read all that he had been given, the respondent abandoned their case and the patent in issue was revoked. The appeal turned on confidentiality in the disclosed documents (or their 'use' in terms of CPR 1998 r 31.22). The Court of Appeal held that they had been referred to in open court[30] and that therefore 'we do not order that they should not be disclosed'.

12.29 In answering the question as to the confidentiality of the documents, Lord Bingham CJ (giving the judgment of the court[31]) discussed the matters raised by Lord Scarman in *Harman* and which are of direct concern here:

> Since the date when Lord Scarman expressed doubt in *Home Office v Harman* as to whether expedition would always be consistent with open justice, the practices of counsel preparing skeleton arguments, chronologies and reading guides, and judges pre-reading documents (including witness statements) out of court, have become much more common. These methods of saving time in court are now not merely permitted, but are positively required, by practice directions. The result is that a case may be heard in such a way that even an intelligent and well-informed member of the public, present throughout every hearing in open court, would be unable to obtain a full understanding of the documentary evidence and the arguments on which the case was to be decided.

Documents in SmithKline Beecham

12.30 Lord Bingham centred his review on 'skeleton arguments, chronologies and reading guides, and judges pre-reading' – essential to the saving of court time; balanced against the need for justice to be open:

> ... There may be some degree of unreality in the proposition that the material documents in the case have (in practice as well as in theory) passed into the public domain. That is a matter which gives rise to concern ...
>
> Some of those problems were explored in the judgment of Potter LJ in *GIO Personal Investment Services Ltd v Liverpool and London Steamship Protection and Indemnity Association Ltd (FAI General Insurance Co Ltd Intervening)* [1999] 1 WLR 984.[32] As the court's practice develops it will be

30 '... these were documents which had been referred to in open court. They were materials which the judge had read, on which SmithKline relied in seeking revocation of the patent and on which the judge must be taken to have relied, among other materials, when ruling that the patent should be revoked'.

31 Lord Bingham CJ and Otton and Robert Walker LJJ (passages cited here are also cited by Toulson LJ in *Guardian v Westminster* (at [34]) and by Bean J in *NAB v Serco* (at [26]).

32 Considered and explained at 12.15.

> necessary to give appropriate weight to both efficiency and openness of justice, with Lord Scarman's warning in mind. *Public access to documents referred to in open court (but not in fact read aloud and comprehensibly in open court) may be necessary, with suitable safeguards, to avoid too wide a gap between what has in theory, and what has in practice, passed into the public domain* (emphasis added).

12.31 In *Norfolk County Council v Webster and Others,*[33] Munby J took up the same point as Lord Scarman and Lord Bingham CJ, when he justified his decision to permit the press to see a party's position statement:

> [42] Today in the Family Division, as in the other divisions of the High Court and in the Court of Appeal, we have a system under which many matters that would in the days of purely oral advocacy have been spoken in court by counsel are now set out in written documents, prepared by counsel, which are pre-read by the judge before the hearing and which are therefore not read out in court during the hearing ... This system is intended to further the proper administration of justice. It does so in various ways including, in particular, by shortening hearings (and thereby increasing the throughput of cases through the court system) ...

12.32 In *Norfolk v Webster,* Munby J explained his decision on grounds of the importance to the press and therefore the public to understand the proceedings:

> [41] For if the media, and indeed the public generally, are not permitted to see the position statement [of counsel for the County Council], the ability of the media, and through the media the ability of the public, to understand what took place during the hearing would be severely compromised. This outcome would defeat the very purpose of permitting the media to be present.

4 DOCUMENTS AFTER CAPE INTERMEDIATE v DRING

Cape Intermediate v Dring: the case

12.33 The respondent to the appeal in *Cape Intermediate v Dring*[34] was a group, the Asbestos Victims Support Group (Mr Dring was their representative) who provided help and support to asbestos victims, and who acted also as a pressure group to raise awareness of the dangers of asbestos.

12.34 *Cape Intermediate* (CIH) had been involved in litigation taken by mesothelioma victims. The litigation settled before the end of a six-week trial.

33 [2006] EWHC 2898 (Fam), [2007] 2 FLR 415, Munby J.

34 *Cape Intermediate Holdings Ltd v Dring (Asbestos Victims Support Group)* [2018] EWCA Civ 1795.

A very substantial volume of documentation was involved. Following settlement, ASVG applied under Civil Procedure Rules 1998 (CPR 1998) r 5.4C for release to them of what amounted to a substantial proportion of the trial bundles. The Master granted the substantial part of their application. *CIH* appealed. The appeal was transferred direct to the full Court of Appeal (CPR 1998 r 52.23) because of the issues involved, instead of being dealt with by a single judge.

12.35 The main case relied upon by Hamblen LJ in the Court of Appeal is *GIO Personal Investment Services Ltd v Liverpool and London Steamship Protection* [1999] 1 WLR 984 (also cited in *Guardian News v Westminster*). He reviewed *GIO Personal* extensively at [61]–[68] and drew four main conclusions from it:

- That 'the court has an inherent jurisdiction to allow non-parties to obtain copies of skeleton arguments/written submissions used in lieu of oral submissions … open justice requires that the public have the same opportunity to understand the issues in a case as they would have had if the openings had been given orally' (at [69]).
- The court's inherent jurisdiction does not permit non-parties to have access to trial documents generally, even if they have been referred to in witness statements, in skeleton arguments, or in court, or have been read by the judge (see [70]).
- There is no inherent jurisdiction to allow non-party access to trial documents merely because they are referred to in eg, a skeleton argument or a witness statement (GIO Personal; [88]).
- GIO Personal 'emphasises the importance of the principle of open justice and recognised that the forthcoming CPR might provide for a wider right of access of non-parties to documents'; though, said Hamblen LJ 'the scheme and provisions of the most relevant provisions of the rules are materially similar under the CPR and the RSC' ([71]).

12.36 Once a document has been 'read or used in court' then any 'confidence in the document' goes (Buxton LJ in *Lilly Icos v Pfizer Ltd*[35]). And so, concluded Hamblin LJ, once a document has been read or treated as read by the judge, any confidentiality in it goes:

> [84] The trilogy of cases, *SmithKline Beecham, Barings [Barings v Coopers & Lybrand* [2000] 1 WLR 2353, CA, also earlier cited by the judge] and *Lilly Icos*, support a broad approach to what documents are to be treated as read by the court for the purpose of CPR 31.22(1)(a) and involve an assumption that the judge will have read documents to which he has been specifically referred. As is noted in *Lilly Icos* at [8], this only applies to documents "to which the judge has been specifically alerted, whether by reference in a skeleton argument or by mention in the 'reading guide' with which judges are now provided".

35 [2002] EWCA Civ 2, [2002] 1 WLR 2253 at [9]; CPR 1998 r 31.22(1)(a).

Release of documents: inherent jurisdiction

12.37 Hamblin LJ concluded this passage of the judgment by summarising the range of documents which might be covered by the inherent jurisdiction. These documents may be those which are released by the court to a person attending a family trial in private under FPR 2010 r 27.11(2) and subject to the constraints in civil proceedings of Administration of Justice Act 1960 section 12(1)(a). The following can be released to non-parties for inspection:

(1) *Skeleton arguments* and 'other advocates documents provided' to assist the court ([92]).

(2) *Witness statements*: under CPR 1998 r 32.13 non-parties are entitled to inspect witness statements. (There is no equivalent rule in FPR 2010.)

(3) *Experts reports*: the same applies as for expert's reports ([96]); but –

(4) *Documents read or treated as read in court* – CPR 1998 r 31.22 ([101]).

(5) *Other documents to meet the open justice principle* ([110]).

12.38 By contrast, *GIO Personal* is authority for the proposition that the court has no inherent jurisdiction to authorise inspection of exhibits ([97]); and this applies to non-inspection where they are referred to ([100]). Hamblen LJ saw no reason to try to diverge from the law set out in *GIO Personal.*

12.39 Of the list above, the last two require further comment. Documents treated as read in modern litigation will be numerous ([105]–[106]); but these must be clearly defined and must not leave non-parties in 'a markedly better position than they would have been when' everything was read out or otherwise orally dealt with in court ([107]). Thus, said Hamblen LJ:

> [108] Based on current civil court practices, I would accordingly confine the jurisdiction to documents which are read out in open court; documents which the judge is invited to read in open court; documents which the judge is specifically invited to read outside court, and documents which it is clear or stated that the judge has read. These are all documents which are likely to have been read out in open court had the trial been conducted orally.

Further documents

12.40 Finally, there may still be further documents which may need to be read to comply with the open justice principle. Thus, said Hamblen LJ, referring back to *Guardian News v Westminster*, the court has an inherent jurisdiction to decide how the open justice principle applies' ([111]). For himself, Hamblen LJ defined the open justice principle and in the context of hearing documents:

> [103] The principle of open justice requires seeking to place non-parties in an equivalent position to that which they would have been in had the trial been conducted orally, as trials used to be. It is in relation to the

reading of documents that the tension between efficient and open justice is most acute. It is increasingly common for judges to be invited to read documents for themselves. That may arise during the course of the hearing itself, or it may involve pre-reading, overnight reading or post-hearing reading.

12.41 The final question is to ask whether these clearly stated, mostly common law, principles can be said to apply to family proceedings where someone wants documents released, because they are planning to attend court or because they want to see material following a hearing. That question will be considered in the next chapter.

5 COLLATERAL USE OF DISCLOSED DOCUMENTS

The 'implied undertaking'

12.42 The requirement that a party must disclose documents (formerly discovery) and other private information in any civil proceedings is regarded as a very real invasion of that party's privacy. The retention of confidentiality in documents is treated as essential to encourage frankness between parties. Lord Denning MR explained this in *Riddick v Thames Board Mills*:[36]

> Compulsion is an invasion of a private right to keep one's documents to oneself. The public interest in privacy and confidence demands that this compulsion should not be pressed further than the course of justice requires ... In order to encourage openness and fairness, the public interest requires that documents disclosed on discovery are not to be made use of except for the purposes of the action in which they are disclosed.

12.43 The implied undertaking applied equally in family proceedings as in any other civil proceedings,[37] as will be explained in the next chapter. In *Harman v Secretary of State for the Home Department*,[38] Harriet Harman,[39] solicitor and legal officer of the National Council for Civil Liberties (NCCL), was acting for the plaintiff against the Home Office arising out of his treatment in prison. In the proceedings, the Home Office disclosed a large number of documents. They stated that they did not wish the documents to be used for other purposes by NCCL save in the action. Harman replied on the same day, saying she was aware of the rule that documents obtained on discovery should not be used for any purposes other than for the case in hand. The Home Office was later ordered to disclose six confidential documents that they had objected to producing on the ground of public interest immunity. Harman selected from the documents disclosed those required for use at the trial, and in due course they were read out by counsel at

36 [1977] 1 QB 881, CA at 896.

37 *Allan v Clibbery* [2002] EWCA Civ 45, [2002] Fam 261 sub nom *Clibbery v Allan* [2002] 1 FLR 565.

38 [1983] 1 AC 280, [1982] 2 WLR 338; and see *Harman* in the context of Lord Scarman's speech and the importance of release of hearing documents at 12.27.

39 Now a Labour MP and QC.

the hearing. A few days after the hearing, Harman allowed a journalist, whom she knew to be a feature writer and who had been present during part of the hearing, to have access to the documents that had been read out, including the confidential documents, for the purpose of writing a newspaper article. The article was critical of Home Office ministers and civil servants.

12.44 The Home Office applied for an order against Harman in contempt, alleging that she was in breach of the implied undertaking (implied by law and affirmed in her letter) not to use documents obtained on discovery (now disclosure) for purposes other than those of the action in which they were disclosed. Park J held that the solicitor was in contempt of court, but accepted that she had acted in good faith and imposed no penalty. The Court of Appeal dismissed an appeal by the solicitor. The House of Lords dismissed Harman's appeal (Lord Simon of Glaisdale and Lord Scarman dissenting). The majority held that a solicitor who in the course of discovery in litigation obtained possession of copies of documents belonging to his client's adversary gave an implied undertaking to the court not to use the copies, nor to allow them to be used, for any purpose other than the proper conduct of the action on behalf of her client. The fact that such documents were read out in open court at the hearing of the action, whether admitted in evidence or not, did not bring that implied undertaking to an end. Breach of the undertaking a civil contempt and Harman was guilty accordingly.

12.45 Lord Diplock explained the reason for the undertaking:[40]

> The use of discovery involves an inroad, in the interests of achieving justice, upon the right of the individual to keep his own documents to himself; it is an inroad that calls for safeguards against abuse, and these the English legal system provides, in its own distinctive fashion, through its rules about abuse of process and contempt of court.

12.46 CPR 1998 r 31.22 aims to make the position clearer and to assert that, unless the court orders otherwise, a document read out – or treated as read out – in open court may be 'used' by a party to the proceedings. As relevant here r 31.22 states:

> **31.22 Subsequent use of disclosed documents …**
>
> (1) A party to whom a document has been disclosed may use the document only for the purpose of the proceedings in which it is disclosed, except where –
>
> (a) the document has been read to or by the court, or referred to, at a hearing which has been held in public;
>
> (b) the court gives permission; or
>
> (c) the party who disclosed the document and the person to whom the document belongs agree.

40 [1983] 1 AC 280 at 300.

(2) The court may make an order restricting or prohibiting the use of a document which has been disclosed, even where the document has been read to or by the court, or referred to, at a hearing which has been held in public.

(3) An application for such an order may be made –

(a) by a party; or

(b) by any person to whom the document belongs.

Collateral use since Civil Procedure Rules 1998

12.47 The rationale for the implied undertaking, or 'collateral purpose rule', was explained by Rupert Jackson LJ in *Tchenguiz v Director of the Serious Fraud Office & Anor*[41] as follows:

> [55] Before the enactment of the Civil Procedure Rules 1998 it was an established rule that documents disclosed upon discovery could not be used for any collateral purpose without either the consent of the disclosing party or the leave of the court. See *Riddick v Thames Board Mills Ltd* [1977] QB 881; *Harman v Secretary of State for the Home Office* [1983] AC 280. I shall refer to this as 'the collateral purpose rule'.
>
> [56] The courts have stated the rationale of the collateral purpose rule on a number of occasions. First, a party receiving documents on discovery impliedly undertakes not to use them for a collateral purpose. Secondly, the obligation to give discovery is an invasion of the litigant's right to privacy and confidentiality. This is justified only because there is a public interest in ensuring that all relevant evidence is provided to the court in the current litigation. Therefore the use of those documents should be confined to that litigation. Thirdly the rule against using disclosed documents for a collateral purpose will promote compliance with the disclosure obligation.

12.48 The undertaking, refashioned since *Harman*, is now codified in CPR 1998 r 31.22(1) and (2), save where statute permits production of documents to third parties;[42] or where an applicant can show special circumstances why r 31.22(1) should be overridden and documents should be released. Eder J explained this in *Tchenguiz & Anor v Director of the Serious Fraud Office* (at first instance):[43]

> [18] ... However, given the compulsive nature of the disclosure process in legal proceedings and consistent with *Marlwood* and *Crest Homes*, I fully accept that the burden of proof lies on the applicant seeking permission and that the bar is high i.e. the applicant must show *cogent and persuasive reasons* why any particular document should be released

---

41 [2014] EWCA Civ 1409.

42 For example Crime (International Co-operation) Act 2003 s 9 as applied in *Crown Prosecution Service & Anor v Gohil* [2012] EWCA Civ 1550, [2013] 1 FLR 1095: see Chapter 13.

43 [2014] EWHC 1315.

amounting to *special circumstances* [(judicial emphasis added)]. In my view, it is important that these requirements are not in any way watered-down.

Collateral use: application to override prohibition on use

12.49 Whether the proceedings are heard in open court (and documents have not been read or referred to) or heard in private (whether or not read or referred to), permission will be required for a collateral use of documents or information. Similar principles apply where a judge considers release of documents to a third party on the judge's own initiative.[44]

12.50 In *Tchenguiz v Director of the Serious Fraud Office & Anor*,[45] the Court of Appeal heard an appeal against refusal of Eder J[46] to release for Guernsey proceedings documents disclosed in English proceedings. Rupert Jackson LJ explained that, upon his view of the authorities, in each case where application is made under r 31.22 (in this case under 31.22(1)(b): for permission to use documents) 'the decisions reached are highly fact sensitive. The court is weighing up conflicting public interests in a variety of different circumstances'.[47]

12.51 Rupert Jackson LJ reviewed a number of cases on applications to release documents; and in particular *Crown Prosecution Service & Anor v Gohil*.[48] In that case the CPS had obtained evidence from foreign states in a successful prosecution of G for fraud. In financial relief G's wife applied for an order that the CPS disclose that evidence. The Court of Appeal set aside the judge's order: the prohibition in Crime (International Co-operation) Act 2003, section 9(2) was absolute. The court had no discretion as whether to order disclosure in the absence of consent from the relevant overseas authority. If the UK were unable to give guarantees concerning collateral use of documents obtained from foreign authorities in criminal investigations, there would be a reduction in the level of international co-operation.

Collateral use in family proceedings

12.52 Collateral use of documents is not specifically dealt with in FPR 2010. The subject must therefore be approached by the common law (as outlined above). This is explained in the next chapter in Part 6.

---

44 *A v A; B v B* [2000] 1 FLR 701, Charles J: order of release of disclosed financial documents to the tax authorities.

45 [2014] EWCA Civ 1409.

46 *Tchenguiz & Ors v The Serious Fraud Office* [2014] EWHC 2597 (Comm).

47 Ibid at [65].

48 [2012] EWCA Civ 1550, [2013] 1 FLR 1095.

13

RELEASE OF COURT MATERIAL IN FAMILY PROCEEDINGS

1 INTRODUCTION

Release of documents to non-parties in family proceedings

13.1 Chapter 12 defined the law in civil proceedings in relation to release of documents to non-parties and their 'use' alongside or after court proceedings. This chapter applies that law, or the legal principles which apply, specifically to family proceedings. Much of the law which applies in family proceedings, though set down as procedural rules in CPR 1998 (eg, rr 5.4C and 31.22), can be defined from CPR 1998; though, as already explained, CPR 1998 does not strictly apply to family proceedings.[1] They can be taken to codify the common law which does apply to all family proceedings.

13.2 FPR 2010 r 27.10 says all family cases (except where stated otherwise) are heard 'in private'. That said, certain defined individuals (in addition to parties to the proceedings, their representatives and welfare officer) are permitted into court to hear the case.[2] A question which this chapter must answer is: to what extent does that mean that those who go into court are able to see any of the documents in the case, if only to help them understand what is going on during the hearing. The documents they can hope to see in a civil case has recently been fully considered by the Court of Appeal in *Cape Intermediate Holdings Ltd v Dring (Asbestos Victims Support Group)* [2018] EWCA Civ 1795 ('*Cape Intermediate v Dring*')[3] as explained in the previous chapter and below.

A right to see documents

13.3 A right to see documents goes further than this. In one of the main cases considered in this series the *Guardian* wanted to write up a case after the hearing; and successfully – on appeal to the Court of Appeal – managed to get to see the

1 CPR 1998 r 2.1(2); as explained in Chapter 1.
2 FPR 2010 r 27.11(2); and see this chapter, Part 3.
3 See Chapter 12, Part 4.

documents (*R (Guardian News and Media Ltd) v City of Westminster Magistrates' Court*[4]). The same would apply to anyone who for sound reason wanted access to hearings documents, perhaps more documents if the court so ordered in its inherent jurisdiction (as explained in *Cape Intermediate v Dring*).

13.4 As will be seen, all appeals to the Court of Appeal in family cases are in open court;[5] and parties must provide the media with copies of their skeleton arguments, anonymised in children cases.[6] The openness rules of the common law as codified in CPR 1998 apply to appeals, as does the provisions of such cases as *Cape Intermediate v Dring* in terms of release of documents (subject always to the provisions of Administration of Justice Act 1960 section 12(1)[7]).

13.5 This chapter proceeds as follows:

- Part 2 explains the restrictions on openness in family courts and the effect of sitting 'in private'; it looks at the statutory restrictions on publicity.
- Part 3 considers media representatives and other attendance at family courts where they sit in private; and defines and discusses FPR 2010 r 27.11(2) (which permits media and others into court); and how it affects different categories of those who may attend (eg, press and 'legal bloggers).
- Part 4 looks at where exclusion of the press may be permitted, especially in the light of *Spencer v Spencer.*
- Part 5 looks at the extent to which documents, especially hearing documents, is permitted in family proceedings, especially after *Cape Intermediate v Dring.*
- Part 6 looks at the 'implied undertaking' (see eg, *Clibbery v Allan*); and at collateral use and the application of CPR 1998 r 31.22 ('use' of court documents) to family proceedings.

2 RESTRICTIONS ON OPENNESS IN FAMILY COURT

Open justice and statutory restraints

13.6 For any civil court proceedings (including family proceedings) the common law and default position generally is that hearings be held in open court.[8] This is confirmed by CPR 1998 r 39.2(2) and in European Convention 1950 Article 6(1). Family proceedings, especially children hearings, are a particular exception to this. In *Re J (Reporting Restriction: Internet: Video),*[9] Sir James Munby P explained why he believed there was a pressing need for more openness – 'transparency' – in family proceedings (as explained in the next Part of this chapter). In *Re J*, Sir James was concerned to explain and to deal with the balance which may have to be struck

4 [2012] EWCA Civ 420, [2013] QB 618.
5 *Norman v Norman* [2017] EWCA Civ 49, [2017] 1 WLR 2523, [2018] 1 FLR 426.
6 CPR 1998 *PD52C* para 33.
7 See further at 13.9.
8 *Scott & Anor v Scott* [1913] UKHL 2, [1913] AC 417 explained further in Chapter 2.
9 [2013] EWHC 2694 (Fam), [2014] 1 FLR 523.

between the respect for privacy for children[10] (and see the European Convention 1950 Art 8) and the right of parents and the press (Art 10) to give publicity to family cases which concern them and their children.[11]

13.7 In doing this, Sir James summarised the legislative restrictions on publicity. He then went on to explain the importance to the family justice system itself, that it should receive publicity. He started by setting out the 'automatic constraints' on publicity, what these meant in practice and how they affect individual cases. Children Act 1989 (CA 1989) section 97 prohibits publication, but only until the conclusion of proceedings (*Clayton v Clayton*).[12] The Administration of Justice Act 1960 (AJA 1960) section 12 applies to all proceedings 'in private' and makes it a contempt of court to publish information in relation to children proceedings. These sections will now be set out, followed by Sir James's explanation of them.

Administration of Justice Act 1960 section 12(1)

13.8 The Administration of Justice Act 1960 section 12 is set out below in full. Typically family lawyers only refer to section 12(1)(a) (children proceedings); but section 12(1) read as a whole provides an insight into the breadth of the provision in relation to 'any court sitting in private' (and aligns the excepted types of proceedings with the views of the House of Lords over 100 years ago in *Scott & Anor v Scott*[13] and with CPR 1998 r 39.2[14]).

13.9 As amended, section 12 provides as follows:

> **12 Publication of information relating to proceedings in private**
>
> (1) The publication of information relating to proceedings before any court sitting in private shall not of itself be contempt of court except in the following cases, that is to say—
>
> (a) where the proceedings—
>
> (i) relate to the exercise of the inherent jurisdiction of the High Court with respect to minors;
>
> (ii) are brought under the Children Act 1989 or the Adoption and Children Act 2002; or
>
> (iii) otherwise relate wholly or mainly to the maintenance or upbringing of a minor;
>
> (b) where the proceedings are brought under the Mental Capacity Act 2005, or under any provision of the Mental Health Act 1983 ...;

10 See eg, *Scott v Scott* (above) and *Re K (Infants)* [1965] AC 201, also *Official Solicitor to Supreme Court v K* [1963] 3 WLR 408, (1963) FLR Rep 520.

11 The Article 8/Article 10 balance is considered more fully at 2.22.

12 [2006] EWCA Civ 878, [2006] 1 FLR 11.

13 [1913] UKHL 2, [1913] AC 417; discussed at 2.83.

14 Set out in full at 13.11.

(c) where the court sits in private for reasons of national security during that part of the proceedings about which the information in question is published;

(d) where the information relates to a secret process, discovery or invention which is in issue in the proceedings;

(e) where the court (having power to do so) expressly prohibits the publication of all information relating to the proceedings or of information of the description which is published.

(2) Without prejudice to the foregoing subsection, the publication of the text or a summary of the whole or part of an order made by a court sitting in private shall not of itself be contempt of court except where the court (having power to do so) expressly prohibits the publication.

(3) In this section references to a court include references to a judge and to a tribunal and to any person exercising the functions of a court, a judge or a tribunal; and references to a court sitting in private include references to a court sitting in camera or in chambers.

(4) Nothing in this section shall be construed as implying that any publication is punishable as contempt of court which would not be so punishable apart from this section (and in particular where the publication is not so punishable by reason of being authorised by rules of court).[15]

13.10 It is valuable to compare the restrictions in section 12(1) with the exceptions in European Convention 1950 Article 6(1) (see italicised passage below) and the open court rule exceptions in CPR 1998 r 39.2(3). Article 6(1) says:

> *Right to a fair trial*
>
> In the determination of his civil rights and obligations or of any criminal charge against him, everyone is entitled to a fair and public hearing within a reasonable time by an independent and impartial tribunal established by law. Judgment shall be pronounced publicly but *the press and public may be excluded from all or part of the trial in the interest of morals, public order or national security in a democratic society, where the interests of juveniles or the protection of the private life of the parties so require, or to the extent strictly necessary in the opinion of the court in special circumstances where publicity would prejudice the interests of justice.*

Civil proceedings and hearings 'in private'

13.11 CPR 1998 r 39.2(3) provides:

(3) A hearing, or any part of it, may be in private if –

(a) publicity would defeat the object of the hearing;

15 The meaning of s 12(4) was explained by the Court of Appeal in *Re F (a Minor) (Publication of Information)* [1977] Fam 58, [1976] 3 WLR 813.

(b) it involves matters relating to national security;

(c) it involves confidential information (including information relating to personal financial matters) and publicity would damage that confidentiality;

(d) a private hearing is necessary to protect the interests of any child or protected party;

(e) it is a hearing of an application made without notice and it would be unjust to any respondent for there to be a public hearing;

(f) it involves uncontentious matters arising in the administration of trusts or in the administration of a deceased person's estate; or

(g) the court considers this to be necessary, in the interests of justice.

13.12 Again, this list can be compared with that in AJA 1960 section 12(1) and the exceptions in European Convention 1950 Article 6(1) listed above.

Children Act 1989 section 97

13.13 As relevant CA 1989 section 97 provides:

> **97 Privacy for children involved in certain proceedings**
>
> (2) No person shall publish to the public at large or any section of the public any material which is intended, or likely, to identify –
>
> (a) any child as being involved in any proceedings before the High Court or the family court in which any power under this Act or the Adoption and Children Act 2002 may be exercised by the court with respect to that or any other child; or
>
> (b) an address or school as being that of a child involved in any such proceedings.
>
> (3) In any proceedings for an offence under this section it shall be a defence for the accused to prove that he did not know, and had no reason to suspect, that the published material was intended, or likely, to identify the child.

13.14 The ambit of section 97(2) is narrow. Its prohibition comes to an end at the conclusion of the proceedings as the Court of Appeal found in *Clayton v Clayton*;[16] but, said Wall LJ, in that case:

> [78] ... The fact that the provisions of s 97(2) of the 1989 Act cease to operate after the conclusion of the proceedings does not mean that parents are free at that point to draw their children into an ongoing public debate about their welfare or other wider issues. The court, after the conclusion of the proceedings, retains its welfare jurisdiction and will be able to intervene where a child's welfare is put at risk by

16 [2006] EWCA Civ 878, [2007] 1 FLR 11.

> inappropriate parental identification for publicity purposes. Quite where the line is to be drawn between s 1 of the 1989 Act and Arts 8 and 10 of the European Convention in this context remains to be seen, although I venture to think that in practice most parents will recognise it. But let those parents who do not, be in no doubt that the court's powers under the ss 1 and 8 of the 1989 Act remain, as do its powers to grant injunctions.

Children and Young Persons Act 1933

13.15 In addition to these two provisions for the control of publicity and privacy for family (mostly children proceedings) the Children and Young Persons Act 1933 section 39 prevents information about a child. Section 39(1) provides as follows:

> **39 Power to prohibit publication of certain matter ...**
>
> (1) In relation to any proceedings, other than criminal proceedings, in any court ... the court may direct that the following may not be included in a publication—
>
> (a) ... the name, address, or school ... of any child or young person concerned in the proceedings, either as being the person by or against or in respect of whom the proceedings are taken, or as being a witness therein;
>
> (aa) any particulars calculated to lead to the identification of a child or young person so concerned in the proceedings;
>
> (b) a picture that is or includes a picture of any child or young person so concerned in the proceedings ...;
>
> except in so far (if at all) as may be permitted by the direction of the court.

13.16 The Administration of Justice Act 1960 section 12(1) relates to 'proceedings in private', including children proceedings and (perhaps) certain other family proceedings. Its scope extends beyond the life of the proceedings; but, says Sir James, it narrows those proceedings to those in relation to children and only to 'proceedings before any court'; and it does not apply to 'anyone involved in the proceedings' (eg expert witnesses, social workers, the local authority etc; and see *Clayton* above). For example, injunctions for the anonymity of others involved in the proceedings – eg medical witnesses, social workers etc – will rarely be granted, 'unless there are compelling reasons'.[17]

Varying the 'automatic restraints'

13.17 The court may, by order, extend or reduce the automatic constraints publicity; but to do so it must conduct a balancing exercise within the

17 *Re J* at [24].

European Convention 1950 as described by Lord Steyn in the House of Lords in *Re S (Identification: Restrictions on Publication)*.[18] It is 'necessary to measure the nature of the impact ... on the child' of what is in prospect, said Lord Steyn. So, said Sir James, the interests of the child must be a primary consideration (*ZH (Tanzania) v Secretary of State for the Home Department*).[19] The balance must be drawn between respect for the child's private life (Art 8) and the right of the press and a parent or others who might want (as in *Re J*) to publicise information (Art 10).

13.18 In conducting that balancing exercise, the primacy of the best interests of the child must be considered. This was further explained by the Supreme Court in *H(H) v Deputy Prosecutor of the Italian Republic, Genoa (Official Solicitor intervening)*[20] where Lord Kerr said:

> [144] ... It is unquestioned that in each of these cases, the children's article 8 rights are engaged. As a matter of logical progression, therefore, one must first recognise the interference and then consider whether the interference is justified. This calls for a sequencing of, first, consideration of the importance to be attached to the children's rights (by obtaining a clear-sighted understanding of their nature), then an assessment of the degree of interference and finally addressing the question whether extradition justifies the interference ...
>
> [145] ... no factor must be given greater weight than the interests of the child.

13.19 *ZH* referred to proceedings for deportation of the parents of children. *H(H)* related to children in immigration proceedings. Neither were involved with publicity. However, the principles in relation to the interests of children are parallel.

Release of skeleton arguments in the Court of Appeal: a Practice Direction

13.20 Some Family Court appeals are to a circuit judge, some to a High Court judge sitting in the Family Court.[21] Many appeals from Family Court hearings are to the Court of Appeal.[22] Appeals in family cases in the Court of Appeal are heard in open court;[23] save that hearings of children cases are anonymised. For hearings in the Court of Appeal, law reporters and media representatives must be provided with copies of the parties skeleton arguments in accordance with CPR 1998 *Practice Direction – Appeals to the Court of Appeal* under the heading

18 [2004] UKHL 47, [2005] 1 AC 593, [2005] 1 FLR 591 at [17]; and see further at 2.22.
19 [2011] UKSC 4, [2011] 2 AC 166, [2011] 1 FLR 2170 at [33].
20 [2012] UKSC 25, [2013] 1 AC 338; though this case was not considered by Sir James.
21 FPR 2010 Pt 30; FPR 2010 *PD30A* para 2 sets out those appeals in the Family Court (para 2.1) and High Court, Family Division (para 2.2) which go to a High Court judge (ie, not to the Court of Appeal), such as appeals from a district judge ancillary relief decision or a circuit judge.
22 CPR 1998 Pt 52.
23 *Norman v Norman* [2017] EWCA Civ 49, [2017] 1 WLR 2523, [2018] 1 FLR 426.

'Documents to be provided to court reporters at the hearing of an appeal' paragraph 33, as relevant, provides:

(1) Where a party is legally represented at the hearing of an appeal, the legal representative must bring to the hearing two additional copies of the party's skeleton argument (including any supplementary skeleton argument) for provision to accredited law reporters and accredited media reporters in accordance with the following provisions of this paragraph.

(2) In appeals in family proceedings involving a child, the copies of the skeleton argument must be in anonymised form and must omit any detail that might, if reported, lead to the identification of the child.

13.21 There is no equivalent rule for family proceedings. The present arrangement is that appeals to the Family Court under FPR 2010 Part 30 are to be heard in chambers. It is not known whether the attention of Hamblen LJ was drawn to it: he does not mention in terms.

3 MEDIA AND OTHERS' ATTENDANCE AT PRIVATE HEARINGS

History of media and non-party attendance at family proceedings

13.22 The background to the attendance of media representatives at Family Court hearings is provided by the 2008 'Family Justice in View' (December 2008, Cm 7502[24]) which included in its review of Family Courts wider disclosure of information by parties. There were to be rules on those who may attend 'family proceedings involving children'; and to ensure that such proceedings would be 'readily accessible and easily understood'. The emphasis of the government response was on children proceedings (not all family proceedings). The conclusion of 'Family Justice in View' was:[25]

> ... that we must increase the volume of information available about the family courts and open up the courts; but a right of access to proceedings cannot mean an untrammelled right to report anything and in any manner regardless of its impact on the children involved. We propose to change the law to allow access to the court so that family justice can be seen.

13.23 This conclusion lead to introduction of the then FPR 1991 r 10.28, which is, in the same terms, what became FPR 2010 r 27.12(2). Rule 27.12(2) is backed by *Practice Direction 27B: Attendance of media representatives at hearings in [the family courts]* and *President's Guidance of 22 April 2009: Applications consequent upon the attendance of the media in family proceedings* [2009] 2 FLR 167. These directions and guidance were not been amended when the 2010 rules were introduced;

24 See www.gov.uk/government/uploads/system/uploads/attachment_data/file/238680/7502.pdf.
25 Ibid at p 31.

though there have been amendments (with effect from 1 October 2018) set out in FPR 2010 *PD36J*.[26]

Attendance of media representatives and other non-parties at Family Court hearings

13.24 The substantial majority of family hearings are intended by the rules to be in private is asserted by FPR 2010 r 27.10:

> **27.10 Hearings in private**
>
> (1) Proceedings to which these rules apply will be held in private, except –
>
> (a) where these rules or any other enactment provide otherwise;
>
> (b) subject to any enactment, where the court directs otherwise.
>
> (2) For the purposes of these rules, a reference to proceedings held 'in private' means proceedings at which the general public have no right to be present.

13.25 Thus divorce proceedings[27] and committal hearings (and ancillary relief hearings before Holman J,[28] but probably not other judges) will be in open court. Perhaps hearings under Family Law Act 1996 Parts 4 (domestic abuse) and 4A (forced marriage protection orders) should also be in open court. There is no pressing need for privacy. To that extent the *vires* of the Family Procedure Rules Committee to make r 27.10 in such wide terms may be in question.

13.26 Non-parties, for present purposes, include media representative and others who might be interested in the proceedings (eg, friends and family; academics, 'legal bloggers' etc). FPR 2010 r 27.11 (within the terms of r 27.10(1)(a)) provides exceptions to the exclusion rule in r 27.10:

> **27.11 Attendance at private hearings**
>
> (1) This rule applies when proceedings are held in private, except in relation to –
>
> (a) hearings conducted for the purpose of judicially assisted conciliation or negotiation;
>
> (b) proceedings to which the following provisions apply –
>
> (i) Part 13 (proceedings under section 54 of the Human Fertilisation and Embryology Act 2008);
>
> (ii) Part 14 (procedure for applications in adoption, placement and related proceedings); and

26 See 13.26 and 13.28.
27 FPR 2010 r 7.16.
28 *Fields v Fields* [2015] EWHC 1670 (Fam), [2016] 1 FLR 1186.

(iii) any proceedings identified in a practice direction as being excepted from this rule.

(2) When this rule applies, no person shall be present during any hearing other than –

(a) an officer of the court;

(b) a party to the proceedings;

(c) a litigation friend for any party, or legal representative instructed to act on that party's behalf;

(d) an officer of the service or Welsh family proceedings officer;

(e) a witness;

(f) duly accredited representatives of news gathering and reporting organisations;

(ff) duly authorised lawyers attending for journalistic, research or public legal educational purposes; and

(g) any other person whom the court permits to be present ...[29]

(6) This rule does not affect any power of the court to direct that witnesses shall be excluded until they are called for examination.

(7) In this rule 'duly accredited' refers to accreditation in accordance with any administrative scheme for the time being approved for the purposes of this rule by the Lord Chancellor.

13.27 The words in italics – r 27.11(2)(ff)[30] – have been added by a further practice direction, *Practice Direction 36J – Pilot Scheme: Transparency (attendance at hearings in private)*. This is intended to enable 'legal bloggers' to attend court as media representatives are able to do (subject to some convoluted requirements as to their documents and credentials which 'any other person' under (g) need not trouble with: though it is not clear why lawyers and academics who want to attend court cannot do so under the much simpler (ie, no documentary requirements) paragraph (g)).

'Legal bloggers'

13.28 *PD36J* has imposed a variety of requirements on anyone who wants to attend court under r 27.11(2)(ff). The purpose of the pilot scheme, which introduces (ff), is set out in its paragraph 2.1:

29 FPR 2010 r 27.11(3)–(5).

30 This may not be the place to question the power of the President of the Family Division to amend delegated legislation (a court rule) with sub-delegated legislation (a practice direction); but the point needs to be borne in mind (eg, if advice is being given to a child or parent who does not want an (ff) individual in court). This sub-rule seeks to amend a rule which is in accordance with the common law: Can the President alter the law by a practice direction? It is unlikely.

2.1 The purpose of the Pilot Scheme is to assess the use of new practices and procedures to allow for attendance at hearings in private by certain lawyers with a view to their being able to report on proceedings (as "legal bloggers") in addition to duly accredited representatives of news gathering and reporting organisations.

13.29 *PD36J* then goes on to define what is 'accredited' for purposes of the media (as in the original r 27.11) and what is a 'duly authorised lawyer' and a 'lawyer'. It amends r 27.11(7) to reframe it as follows:

(7) In this rule—

- (a) "duly accredited" refers to accreditation in accordance with any administrative scheme for the time being approved for the purposes of this rule by the Lord Chancellor;
- (b) "duly authorised lawyer" means—
  - (i) a person who is authorised by a practising certificate to conduct litigation or exercise a right of audience in the family court;
  - (ii) a lawyer working for the Law School, Faculty or Department of a Higher Education Institution designated as a recognised body pursuant to section 216 of the Education Reform Act 1988; or
  - (iii) a lawyer attending on behalf of a registered educational charity the name, objects and registered charity number of which have been provided to the President of the Family Division;
- (c) "lawyer" means a person who—
  - (i) holds a qualifying law degree as defined by the Bar Standards Board or Solicitors' Regulation Authority;
  - (ii) holds or has completed—
    - (aa) the Common Professional Examination (CPE);
    - (bb) an approved Graduate Diploma in Law (GDL) course or the Solicitors Qualifying Examination (SQE);
    - (cc) a postgraduate legal qualification; or
    - (dd) the CILEx Level 6 Diploma in Law and Practice or the CILEx Graduate Fast Track Diploma."

13.30 The practice direction then goes on to require identification for lawyers[31] who want to be regarded as 'authorised' (though no practising lawyer had been required to carry any such identification), namely at amendment paras 4A.1 to 4A.3 added to *PD27A* by *PD36J*. It is not clear why all this is required of a category (ff) applicant and not of one under (g); nor of any other practising lawyers who act for parties in family proceedings.[32] As already mentioned, a lawyer need not go through all that if that lawyer applies – as has been possible since 2009 – under (g).

'Duly accredited' press representative

13.31 A 'duly accredited'[33] press representative must obtain a card issued by the UK Press Card Authority to provide evidence of accreditation; though an unaccredited representative may be permitted to attend the hearing at the court's discretion.[34]

---

31 *Identification of lawyers as 'authorised'*

4A.1 Lawyers will be expected to carry with them identification sufficient to enable court staff, or if necessary the court itself, to verify that they are "authorised" lawyers within the meaning of the rule.

4A.2 The following forms of identification provide sufficient information, and production of such identification will be both necessary and sufficient to demonstrate that the lawyer is "authorised" within the meaning of rule 27.11(7)(b)(i), (ii) and (iii) respectively—

(a) a current practising certificate accompanied by picture identification of the lawyer and a signed written statement by the lawyer which complies with paragraph 4A.3;

(b) confirmation on headed notepaper from the relevant Higher Education Institution (or Law School, Faculty or Department of that Institution) of the lawyer's position and qualification, accompanied by picture identification of the lawyer and a signed written statement by the lawyer which complies with paragraph 4A.3;

(c) confirmation on headed notepaper from the relevant registered educational charity (specifying the registered charity number) of the lawyer's position and qualification, accompanied by picture identification of the lawyer and a signed written statement by the lawyer which complies with paragraph 4A.3.

4A.3 The signed written statement required by paragraph 4A.2 must—

(a) confirm that the lawyer's attendance is for journalistic, research or public legal educational purposes and that the lawyer has no personal interest in the proceedings and that he or she is not attending in the capacity of agent or instructed lawyer for any client; and

(b) confirm that the lawyer is aware of and will abide by any restrictions on publication, whether arising by operation of law (for example under section 97 of the Children Act 1989 and section 12 of the Administration of Justice Act 1960) or imposed by order of the court, which follow from the proceedings being in private.

32 Is this the thin end of a wedge for any practising lawyer who asserts that he or she is a solicitor or barrister when appearing as advocate?

33 FPR 2010 r 27.11(2)(f).

34 Ibid r 27.11(2)(g).

4 EXCLUSION OF THE MEDIA

Media representatives 'shall not attend the hearings ...'

13.32 FPR 2010 r 27.11(3)–(5)[35] deals with a set of provisions which enables the court on its own initiative, or the parties or witnesses or a child (if of age and understanding) to apply, to exclude the press where admitted under r 27.11(2)(f). None of the other non-parties can be required to be excluded under r 27.11(3). Rule 27.11(3)–(5) is in the following terms:

(3) At any stage of the proceedings the court may direct that persons within paragraph (2)(f) shall not attend the proceedings or any part of them, where satisfied that –

  (a) this is necessary –

    (i) in the interests of any child concerned in, or connected with, the proceedings;

    (ii) for the safety or protection of a party, a witness in the proceedings, or a person connected with such a party or witness; or

    (iii) for the orderly conduct of the proceedings; or

  (b) justice will otherwise be impeded or prejudiced.

(4) The court may exercise the power in paragraph (3) of its own initiative or pursuant to representations made by any of the persons listed in paragraph (5), and in either case having given to any person within paragraph (2)(f) who is in attendance an opportunity to make representations.

(5) At any stage of the proceedings, the following persons may make representations to the court regarding restricting the attendance of persons within paragraph (2)(f) in accordance with paragraph (3) –

  (a) a party to the proceedings;

  (b) any witness in the proceedings;

  (c) where appointed, any children's guardian;

  (d) where appointed, an officer of the service or Welsh family proceedings officer, on behalf of the child the subject of the proceedings;

  (e) the child, if of sufficient age and understanding.

Practice Direction PD27B: release of court documents

13.33 *PD27B* supports r 27.11 and deals with hearings in private. It deals mostly with exclusion of the press. Under a heading, 'Matters unchanged by [r 27.11]' court documents are dealt with in the following way in *PD27B*:

35 The remainder of r 27.11 is at 13.26.

> 2.3 The provisions of the rules permitting the attendance of media representatives and the disclosure to third parties of information relating to the proceedings do not entitle a media representative to receive or peruse court documents referred to in the course of evidence, submissions or judgment without the permission of the court ... (This is in contrast to the position in civil proceedings, where the court sits in public and where members of the public are entitled to seek copies of certain documents.)

13.34 It will be clear from its drafting (eg, references to 'High Court and County Courts') that this practice direction is relatively elderly, and that it has not been reviewed since eg, *Guardian News v Westminster*. It does not seem to take account of *Clibbery v Allan*.[36] It remains the case that the common law in relation to civil proceedings generally has developed since 2010 when that rule was probably last reviewed; and as will be explained it is clear that a party can release documents from Family Law Act 1996 Part 4 (occupation and non-molestation orders) can be released to the press or otherwise published where read in court.[37]

Exclusion of the media

13.35 The question of exclusion of the press under the predecessor of r 27.11(3) was considered on the day the new rule was introduced, by Charles J. In *D v D (Divorce: Media Presence)*,[38] Charles J stated:

> [14] It is said that the presence of a representative of the media might inhibit the husband from giving full and frank evidence. That submission also gives rise to a need to trawl a number of existing authorities in this field and others. To my mind, it is not a compelling submission, particularly when it is remembered that the more serious an issue that is raised in the context of a private hearing, the more likely it is that it would have to be reported by the court to the relevant public authority.

13.36 The subject of exclusion under r 27.11(3) was considered more fully by Munby J in *Spencer v Spencer*.[39] He was confronted by a joint application by the husband (H) and the wife (W) that the press be excluded. The fact that both parties agreed to exclusion meant the court should be even more vigilant, as Munby J explained.

13.37 In divorce proceedings W applied, long before the media representative extension (predecessor to r 27.11(2)), for financial relief. By the time the hearing

36 [2002] EWCA Civ 45, [200] Fam 261, [2002] 1 FLR 565.
37 See 13.32.
38 [2009] EWHC 946 (Fam), [2009] 2 FLR 324.
39 [2009] EWHC 1529 (Fam), [2009] 2 FLR 1416.

came on the rules had been changed.[40] The parties argued that in ancillary relief cases, unlike children cases, there was no jurisdiction to grant general injunctive relief against publication. Therefore, in a case in which there was an intense level of media interest without any real 'public interest' in the reporting of the proceedings (Earl Spencer was Princess Diana's brother), the court could protect the rights of the parties to respect for private and family life only by excluding the media altogether from the hearing. It was further argued that, given the allegations of conduct on both sides, there was a significant risk that a witness would not give full or frank evidence in the presence of media representatives.

13.38 On the parties' application under r 27.11(3), Munby J reflected on their rights under the European Convention 1950. First the parties were entitled to respect for their family rights (Art 8); but these must be balanced against the rights of the press (Art 10): a right, said Munby J, 'to receive information by sitting in court and ... to impart that information to the world at large'.[41]

13.39 However, he went on, there is a right for the community at large, protected by Article 6:

> [42] But there are also, as it seems to me, important rights protected by Art 6. There is – again there is much Strasbourg and domestic jurisprudence which there is no need for me to recite in detail – a well recognised public interest, an interest of the community as a whole, in promoting the administration of justice, in maintaining the authority of the judiciary and in maintaining the confidence of the public at large in the courts. And that public interest is protected by Art 6, quite apart from Art 10. But that interest typically pulls in two different directions. Viewed from the perspective of the media, and the market which the media are serving, that public interest is to be promoted and public confidence in the courts is to be maintained by justice being administered in public, or at least in a manner which enables its workings to be properly scrutinised, so that (and this is the modern European Convention version of the age-old Benthamite principle) the judges and other participants in the process remain visible and amenable to comment and criticism. This is the argument that Art 6 points in the direction of openness, specifically in this context in the direction of the media being permitted to remain in court.

13.40 Balanced against this Article 6 right, said Munby J, justice also demands privacy:

---

40 Of the change in the rules and how that should influence his disposal of the application before him, Munby J said: '[58] I am sympathetic to those involved in litigation which began before 27 April 2009 at their sense of grievance and injustice that the rules of the game have changed and the goal posts have been moved partway through their litigation. But the fact is that Parliament has seen fit to change the law and, without including any transitional provisions. And no one has suggested or could sensibly suggest that that itself involves any breach of the European Convention. So I have to take the law as it is, namely that the new arrangements apply to pending cases and, indeed, as I pointed out, to cases part-heard in which hearings happened to straddle the implementation date of 27 April 2009.'

41 Ibid at [41].

> [43] On the other hand, and the Art 6 jurisprudence equally recognises this right, there is the vital importance, as viewed from the perspective of the participants in the process, that if the administration of justice is to be promoted, and public confidence in the workings of the family court is to be maintained, then, so it is said, one needs to preserve the privacy of such proceedings, there being, for example, an important public interest in preserving faith with those who have launched upon the proceedings and given evidence in the family court in the belief that the proceedings and the evidence would remain confidential.

13.41 Munby J resolved the balance by holding that the press should not be excluded. Said the judge: '[45] ... despite their comparatively high media profile, the proceedings before me are typical of many ancillary relief cases. There is no great point of law or principle involved.' In the light of that (it was said), the parties settled their respective claims without need for further court involvement.

Parties agree to exclude: extra vigilance

13.42 As a postscript to this, a point made by judges from time to time: because the parties agree to exclusion of the press may be a reason for extra vigilance. If both agree, the press will not necessarily be excluded:

> [44] How then, in the circumstances of this particular case, is the balance to be struck? The fact that both parties join in making the application is not, of course, any reason why the application should succeed. If anything, quite the contrary – see the observation of Sir Christopher Staughton in *Ex parte P* (1998) *The Times*, 31 March, quoted with approval by Lord Woolf MR in *R v Legal Aid Board ex parte Kaim Todner* [1999] QB 966, [1998] 3 WLR 925 at 977 and 934 respectively: 'When both sides agreed that information should be kept from the public that was when the court had to be most vigilant.'

5 MEDIA AND OTHERS' ATTENDANCE: OPERATION OF THE RULE

Right to attend private hearings

13.43 An understanding of the subject matter of this chapter involves an explanation of how family proceedings have got to the point they have now arrived at. What are the rights of the media and non-parties generally? How do those rights affect their right to see documents?

13.44 The right of the media to attend a family hearing was explained by Baker J in *Re Al-Hilli (Children: Reporting Restrictions)*.[42] This, and the parallel right of other non-parties, must be looked at in the context of the case law subsequent to the

42 [2013] EWHC 2190 (Fam), [2014] 1 FLR 403.

original Family Proceedings Rules 1991 r 10.28(4) (predecessor to r 27.11(2)); and then, in the next Part, looked at in the context of what documents those attending might be entitled to see. In *Re Al-Hilli* Baker J said:

> [29] ... The media have a right to attend private family proceedings not falling within the exceptions in r 27.11(1) and can only be excluded if the court finds that one or more of the grounds in r 27.11(3) are established. It is for a person who wishes to exclude the media to satisfy the court of the necessity of the exclusion pursuant to one of the limited statutory criteria set out in FPR 2010, r 27.11(3); it is not for the media to justify their attendance (see Munby J in *Spencer v Spencer* at para [30], and Potter P in *Re Child X (Residence and Contact: Rights of Media Attendance: FPR Rule 10.28 (4))* at para [57]). In my view, the right of the media is properly characterised as an "assumption" and a "starting-point" by Munby J in *Re Child X (Residence and Contact: Rights of Media Attendance: FPR Rule 10.28(4)),* Potter P referred (at para [44]) to there being a "presumption" that the media representatives should attend hearings, and at para [65] to their "strong prima facie right" to attend. With respect to the former President, the language used by Munby J seems to me to be in line with the carefully-crafted words of r 27.11(3).

13.45 As it happens, both the cases referred to by Baker J in the quoted paragraph were transitional cases in that both applications were issued before the new rule was in place; but the issue of press attendance occurred after its introduction in Family Proceedings Rules 1991 with effect from 27 April 2009, though this did not alter their outcome. The judgments were delivered within days of one another: *Spencer v Spencer*[43] (an ancillary relief case) on 23 June 2009 and *Re Child X (Residence and Contact: Rights of Media Attendance: FPR Rule 10.28(4))*[44] (a child contact application) on 14 July 2009. In the first, Munby J said the press should be permitted to attend. In the second, Sir Mark Potter P said not. In the first, Munby J refused the application to exclude the press; and in the second Sir Mark allowed it, mostly on the ground of what he had heard of how press attendance and reporting affected the child concerned.[45]

'Watchdog role of the press'

13.46 Sir Mark Potter P was President of the Family Division when these reforms were introduced. In *Re Child X* he took the opportunity to explain what he understood the reforms to mean.

> [38] The net result of [what is now FPR 2010 r 27.11] is that, while the press are entitled to report on the nature of the dispute in the proceedings, and to identify the issues in the case and the identity of the participating witnesses (save those whose published identity would reveal the

43 [2009] EWHC 1529 (Fam), [2009] 2 FLR 1416, Munby J.
44 [2009] EWHC 1728 (Fam), [2009] 2 FLR 1467, Sir Mark Potter P.
45 Ibid at [59].

> identity of the child in the case), they are not entitled to set out the content of the evidence or the details of matters investigated by the court. Thus the position has been created that, whereas the media are now enabled to exercise a role of "watchdog" on the part of the public at large and to observe family justice at work for the purpose of informed comment upon its workings and the behaviour of its judges, they are unable to report in their newspapers or programmes the identity of the parties or the details of the evidence which are likely to catch the eye and engage the interest of the average reader or viewer.

13.47 He went on then to link this to children proceedings, to the European Convention 1950 balance (as between Articles 8 (respect for private life) and 10 (freedom of expression)) and especially to privacy questions in relation to what he called 'celebrities':

> [39] It is, of course, in the context of disputes over children between 'celebrities' in private law proceedings such as these that the media find the current statutory limitations most irksome. The line drawn is nonetheless one recognised as valid when balancing Art 8 and Art 10 considerations as between the privacy rights of individuals and the watchdog role of the press: see *Von Hannover v Germany (Application No 59320/00*) (2005) 40 EHRR 1, 16 BCHR 545, [2004] EMLR 379 at para 63: "A fundamental distinction needs to be made between reporting facts – even controversial ones – capable of contributing to a debate in a democratic society reacting to politicians in the exercise of their functions, for example, and reporting details of the private life of an individual who, moreover, as in this case, does not exercise official functions. While in the former case the press exercises its vital role of 'watchdog' in a democracy by contributing to 'imparting information and ideas on matters of public interest' it does not do so in the latter case."[46]

13.48 In *Appleton & Gallagher v News Group Newspapers Ltd & PA*,[47] Mostyn J explained the working of r 27.11 by reference to the passage – paragraph [38] – cited from *Re Child X*. Part 5 will deal with FPR 2010 r 29.12 and what it means in the context of court attendance and release of documents from family proceedings.

Limits on publication: Cooper-Hohn

13.49 In *Cooper-Hohn v Hohn*,[48] Roberts J dealt with the question of publicity in financial remedy proceedings. The judge found herself required to give a decision in a substantial money case where accredited members of the press had been present in court and in accordance with FPR 2010 r 27.11(2)(f). The question for

46 *Von Hannover*, he accepted, recognised 'the privacy rights of children, as an aspect of their welfare interests' (see [41]).

47 [2015] EWHC 2689 (Fam), [2016] 2 FLR 1.

48 [2014] EWHC 2314 (Fam), [2015] 1 FLR 19, Roberts J.

the judge was: '[2] … the extent to which [the media] should be able to report an account of the proceedings as they unfold on a daily basis and whether there is any restriction on their ability to do so.'

13.50 Application was made on behalf of the media for reporting restrictions to be lifted. Roberts J refused to impose full reporting restrictions (as Mr Hohn wanted) but restricted the press on terms as follows (para 98 of her judgment):

> The media shall be prohibited from publishing any such report that refers to or concerns any of the parties' financial information whether of a personal or business nature including, but not limited to, that contained in their voluntary disclosure, answers to questionnaire provided in solicitors' correspondence, in their witness statements, in their oral evidence or referred to in submissions made on their behalf, whether in writing or orally, save to the extent that any such information is already in the public domain.

13.51 Roberts J concluded – looking at her decision through the prism of the European Convention 1950 Articles 8 (respect for private life) and 10 (press freedom); and perhaps Article 6(1) (right to a fair trial; administration of justice) – that she should make the restriction order. She resolved the parties and the press's Convention rights as follows:

> [176] I find that the balance between the right of the media to freedom of expression and their ability to report to the public at large, and the right of the husband and wife to respect for their private and family life, in so far as it relates to the detail of their finances, weighed together with the overarching principle of open justice and the implied undertaking as to confidentiality, falls firmly in favour of privacy in relation to financial matters being maintained.

6 RELEASE OF DOCUMENTS TO NON-PARTIES

Release of material from family proceedings

13.52 There are no rules for inspection of documents in family proceedings – that is for release of documents – under FPR 2010 save FPR 2010 r 29.12 (set out below).[49] This raises the question of how the media can perform its 'watchdog' role, and how academics, legal bloggers and others with a legitimate interest in proceedings can make sense of a case which proceeds with many documents being read privately by the judge and the parties and their advocates. How can the concerns of judges such as Lord Scarman, Lord Bingham CJ and Toulson LJ be met in the absence of the media and other non-parties having access to the hearing documents?

49 And see discussion of *Appleton & Gallagher v News Group Newspapers Ltd & PA* [2015] EWHC 2689 (Fam), [2016] 2 FLR 1, Mostyn J at 13.48.

13.53 FPR 2010 r 29.12(1) provides as follows:

> **29.12 Access to and inspection of documents retained in court**
>
> (1) Except as provided by this rule or by any other rule or Practice Direction, no document or copy of a document filed or lodged in the court office shall be open to inspection by any person without the permission of the court, and no copy of any such document or copy shall be taken by, or issued to, any person without such permission ...

13.54 As can be seen from the words 'with permission of the court' it is anticipated that application can be made, including by a non-party, for inspection – and therefore of photocopying and reading – of any document filed in or lodged at court. Indeed, a fee for photocopying may be required, and is assumed as part of the question of a document on the court file being open to inspection. Hamblen LJ explained this in *Cape Intermediate v Dring*:

> [113] The court may order that copies be provided of documents which there is a right to inspect, but that will ordinarily be on the non-party undertaking to pay reasonable copying costs, consistently with CPR 31.15(c) ...

13.55 Of documents in family proceedings and in relation to FPR 2010 r 29.12 Mostyn J said, in passing:

> [13] This strict "watchdog" role is confirmed by the terms of the rules themselves. Rule 27.11 of the FPR 2010, which permits the admission of the press, confirms that the proceedings are held in private ... Further the press are not allowed any access to documents *whatsoever* – see FPR 2010, r 29.12. This is only consistent with a watchdog role, because without the documents the press can hardly be expected to be able to report the case intelligibly or even-handedly ... (italics added).

13.56 Mostyn J's assertion is open to a number of questions, such as:[50]

- His 'whatsoever' (italicised) is not born out by the rules, which say that the court can give permission for inspection of a document.
- The issue before the court was whether the press were to be allowed into court and what they could report.[51] The comment about documents was *obiter*.
- Mostyn J said was not considered by him in the light of *R (Guardian News and Media Ltd) v City of Westminster Magistrates' Court*.[52]

---

50 It is notable that Mostyn J makes no reference to *Spencer v Spencer* (above).

51 Mostyn J defined his judicial role thus: '[5] All I am being asked to decide today is whether the existing order, which restricts the reporting of the proceedings, should be lifted, or modified, at this point.'

52 [2012] EWCA Civ 420, [2013] QB 618; indeed it is unlikely any argument was heard on the point; but it would be necessary to see documents Mostyn J says cannot be seen to be clear on that point.

Release of information to the press and those covered by FPR 2010 r 27.11(2)

13.57 An answer to the question of the media understanding the issues before the court was provided by Munby J in *Norfolk County Council v Webster and Others*.[53] He was asked to allow the press to read the local authority position statement (ie, their proposals for three children at the start of care proceedings). A court order was required. If not, the press might be in contempt of court. 'It was essential' said the judge, 'for me to [release the statement] if the media, and through the media the general public, were to understand what had gone on' in the proceedings.[54]

13.58 In an earlier hearing involving the same family – *Re Webster; Norfolk County Council v Webster and Others*[55] – Munby J permitted access by the press on terms as to publication of the bundle only where documents had been read out or summarised or where the judge allowed further disclosure:

> [121] The other [matter to which I should refer] relates to the effect of my order permitting media access to the forthcoming hearing. The general public will not be able to attend the hearing. But since the media will be entitled to be present, the hearing will not, as it seems to me, be "in private" within the meaning of s 12 of the Administration of Justice Act 1960. Section 12 will therefore not apply in relation to that hearing. But this does not mean that s 12 ceases to apply altogether to the care proceedings. Save in relation to any particular hearing which has been opened to the media, s 12 will continue to apply ... Moreover, the effect of the order I am proposing to make is not to permit the dissemination of the entire contents of the court bundle prepared for a particular hearing merely because that hearing is not 'in private', nor to permit the publication of any or every part of a document merely because passing reference has been made to it during the course of the hearing. In principle, s 12 will continue to apply to everything in such a bundle save insofar as either: (a) particular parts of documents in the bundle have actually been read out or summarised during the course of the hearing (in which case, absent the imposition of further restrictions, the media will be able to report what has actually been said during the hearing); or (b) the judge authorises further disclosure.

13.59 As the law now stands, on application being made for inspection of hearings documents, the court must balance the arguments for and against release. Toulson LJ touched on this in *Guardian News v Westminster*; but was not tempted to try to define factors which might guide a judge in determining of an application:

> [85] ... I do not think that it is sensible or practical to look for a standard formula for determining how strong the grounds of opposition need to be in order to outweigh the merits of the application [for inspection of documents]. The court has to carry out a proportionality exercise

53 [2006] EWHC 2898 (Fam), [2007] 2 FLR 415 Munby J.

54 *Norfolk County Council v Webster and Others* [2006] EWHC 2898 (Fam), [2007] 2 FLR 415, Munby J at [43].

55 [2006] EWHC 2733 (Fam), [2007] 1 FLR 1146.

which will be fact-specific. Central to the court's evaluation will be the purpose of the open justice principle, the potential value of the material in advancing that purpose and, conversely, any risk of harm which access to the documents may cause to the legitimate interests of others.

Court documents: towards a classification

13.60 So, what can any of these court attenders expect to see and before the hearing? These being family proceedings, no one will be surprised to hear that the answer is unclear. *Cape Intermediate v Dring* has gone some way to explain the position in civil proceedings (which does not include family cases). One thing this note will seek to do is to explain how far the position in *Cape Intermediate v Dring* may affect family cases. Because civil proceedings are (mostly) in open court their rules are different.

13.61 The following is a classification of the categories of document concerned, which will be used in this article, and are more fully explained in *Cape Intermediate v Dring* as explained below:

(1) *Court documents* – Documents 'from the court records' for which a non-party is entitled to apply as a matter of formality (CPR 1998 r 5.4C; CPR 1998 *PD5A* paragraph 4.2A, and as explained in *Cape Intermediate v Dring*).

(2) *Hearing documents* – Court documents for which a non-party is entitled to apply: eg, to make sense of the proceedings or for a particular journalistic purpose (eg, skeleton arguments, parties statements, expert reports etc).

(3) *Disclosed documents* – Use, or other release, of documents whose production has been compelled by disclosure rules (CPR 1998 r 31.22(1)) and whose release or other use the law restricts or may prevent, in cases of breach (r 31.22(2)).

(4) *Trial documents* – The composite set of documents prepared for the judge and at a court hearing.

(5) *Other material* – Documents and information which a party is entitled to publish about proceedings where a case has been heard in private (see eg, *Clibbery v Allan* [2002] EWCA Civ 45, [200] Fam 261, [2002] 1 FLR 565).

13.62 There are three categories of Family Courts hearing. Each is likely to have different rules (though the law is not clear on this):

(1) Open court hearings (eg, divorce, committal proceedings, domestic abuse cases under Family Law Act 1996 Pt 4). Open justice principles apply to these hearings and the same rules are likely to apply as explained in *Cape Intermediate v Dring*.

(2) Hearings in private where media representatives and other can attend (r 27.11(2)(f)–(g)): so long as anonymity is preserved the *Cape Intermediate* rules could apply.

(3) Other hearings in private (see eg, *Clibbery v Allan* (above)).

13.63 To that list must be added those who may want to see documents after the hearing and to whom the principles considered here apply (eg, the journalist who appealed successfully to the Court of Appeal in *Guardian News v Westminster*).

Cape Intermediate v Dring: the case

13.64 The respondents to the appeal in *Cape Intermediate v Dring* were a group (Asbestos Victims Support Group: Mr Dring was their representative) who provided help and support to asbestos victims, and who acted also as a pressure group to raise awareness of the dangers of asbestos. Cape Intermediate had been involved in litigation taken by mesothelioma victims. The litigation settled before the end of a six-week trial. A very substantial volume of documentation was involved. Following settlement ASVG applied under CPR 1998 r 5.4C for release to them of what amounted to a substantial proportion of the trial bundles. The Master granted the substantial part of their application. Cape Intermediate appealed. The appeal was transferred direct to the full Court of Appeal (CPR 1998 r 52.23) because of the issues involved, instead of being dealt with by a single judge.

13.65 CPR 1998 apply to this case. These rules, and therefore the case, do not formally apply to family proceedings. However, so far as the case and CPR 1998 define the common law in relation to the release of documents, they may apply to family proceedings (subject to the provisions of AJA 1960 section 12(1)). What first may be said to be the common law after *Cape Intermediate v Dring*?

The common law position after *Cape Intermediate v Dring*

13.66 For Hamblin LJ the case of *GIO Personal Investment Services Ltd v Liverpool and London Steamship Protection*[56] (also cited in *Guardian News v Westminster*) is central to his reasoning. He reviewed the case extensively at [61]–[68]; and drew the following main conclusions from it:

- That 'the court has an inherent jurisdiction to allow non-parties to obtain copies of skeleton arguments/written submissions used in lieu of oral submissions ... open justice requires that the public have the same opportunity to understand the issues in a case as they would have had if the openings had been given orally'.[57]
- The court's inherent jurisdiction does not permit non-parties to have access to trial documents generally, even if they have been referred to in witness statements, in skeleton arguments, or in court, or have been read by the judge.[58]
- *GIO Personal* 'emphasises the importance of the principle of open justice and recognised that the forthcoming CPR might provide for a wider right of access of non-parties to documents'; though, said Hamblen LJ, 'the scheme

56 [1999] 1 WLR 984.
57 *Cape Intermediate v Dring* at [69].
58 Ibid at [70].

and provisions of the most relevant provisions of the rules are materially similar under the CPR and the RSC'.[59]

13.67 However, he said, *GIO Personal* is also authority for the view that there is no inherent jurisdiction in the court to allow non-party access to trial documents merely because they are referred to in, for example, a skeleton argument or witness statement.[60] As explained below the same applies to documents as exhibits to witness statements or to experts' reports.

13.68 Once a document has been 'read or used in court' then any 'confidence in the document' goes.[61] That is, the document ceases to be confidential. So, concluded Hamblen LJ:

> [84] The trilogy of cases, *SmithKline Beecham, Barings* [*Barings v Coopers & Lybrand* [2000] 1 WLR 2353, CA, also earlier cited by the judge] and *Lilly Icos,* support a broad approach to what documents are to be treated as read by the court for the purpose of CPR 31.22(1)(a) and involve an assumption that the judge will have read documents to which he has been specifically referred. As is noted in *Lilly Icos* at [8], this only applies to documents "to which the judge has been specifically alerted, whether by reference in a skeleton argument or by mention in the 'reading guide' with which judges are now provided".

Release of documents: inherent jurisdiction

13.69 Hamblen LJ summarised the range of documents which might be covered by an order from the court under its inherent jurisdiction (ie, with permission, in the terminology of FPR 2010 r 29.12(1)). These documents may be those which are released by the court to a person attending a family trial in private under r 27.11(2) and still within the ambit of r 29.12(1). Any such release must be subject to the constraints in civil proceedings of the Administration of Justice Act 1960 section 12(1).

13.70 On the basis of Hamblen LJ's list and explanation in *Cape Intermediate v Dring* at [91–113] the following can be released to non-parties for inspection:

(1) *Skeleton arguments* and 'other advocates documents provided' to assist the court.[62]

(2) *Witness statements*: under CPR 1998 r 32.13 non-parties are entitled to inspect witness statements. (There is no equivalent rule in FPR 2010.)

(3) *Experts' reports*: the same applies as for experts' reports.[63]

59 Ibid at [71].
60 *GIO; Cape Intermediate v Dring* at [88].
61 Buxton LJ in *Lilly Icos v Pfizer Ltd* [2002] EWCA Civ 2, [2002] 1 WLR 2253 at [9]; CPR 1998 r 31.22(1)(a).
62 *Cape Intermediate v Dring* at [92].
63 Ibid at [96].

(4) *Documents read or treated as read in court.*[64]

(5) *Other documents to be read and thus to meet the open justice principle.*[65]

By contrast, the *Exhibits to statements/reports* do not come into the same category as the above list. There is no inherent jurisdiction which guarantees their release to non-parties.

13.71 Of these, the last two require further comment. Documents treated as read in modern litigation will be numerous; but where these are ordered by the court in its inherent jurisdiction, these documents must be clearly defined and must not leave non-parties in 'a markedly better position than they would have been when' everything was read out or otherwise orally dealt with in court.[66] Thus said Hamblen LJ:

> [108] Based on current civil court practices, I would accordingly confine the jurisdiction to documents which are read out in open court; documents which the judge is invited to read in open court; documents which the judge is specifically invited to read outside court, and documents which it is clear or stated that the judge has read. These are all documents which are likely to have been read out in open court had the trial been conducted orally.

Further documents

13.72 Finally, there may still be further documents which may need to be read to comply with the open justice principle. Thus, said Hamblen LJ, referring back to *Guardian News v Westminster*, 'the court has an inherent jurisdiction to decide how the open justice principle applies' ([111]). For himself, Hamblen LJ defined the open justice principle and in the context of hearing documents:

> [103] The principle of open justice requires seeking to place non-parties in an equivalent position to that which they would have been in had the trial been conducted orally, as trials used to be. It is in relation to the reading of documents that the tension between efficient and open justice is most acute. It is increasingly common for judges to be invited to read documents for themselves. That may arise during the course of the hearing itself, or it may involve pre-reading, overnight reading or post-hearing reading.

13.73 If the criterion for exercise of its jurisdiction by the Family Courts is to enable those who attend court to understand the proceedings then, subject to non-parties' compliance with privacy restrictions (eg, AJA 1960 s 12(1)), the question must be: why should not the non-parties have access to documents to enable them to understand what is happening. Release of the *Cape Intermediate v Dring* list of types of document must, in most family cases, go a long way to

---

64 Ibid at [101]; CPR 1998 r 31.22(1)(a); and see 13.68.

65 Ibid at [110].

66 Ibid at [107].

telling a non-party what is going on; or telling a non-party looking into the case, who has also read any judgment (anonymised in family cases), what happened.

13.74 Such release would enable courts, in most cases, to pay full regard to what was said by Toulson LJ in *Guardian News v Westminster*:

> [83] The courts have recognised that the practice of receiving evidence without it being read in open court potentially has the side effect of making the proceedings less intelligible to the press and the public. This calls for counter measures. In *SmithKline Beecham Biologicals SA v Connaught Laboratories Inc* [1999] 4 All ER 498 Lord Bingham referred to the need to give appropriate weight both to efficiency and to openness of justice as the court's practice develops. He observed that public access to documents referred to in open court might be necessary. In my view the time has come for the courts to acknowledge that in some cases it is indeed necessary.

13.75 If the common law permits release to non-parties of documents for civil proceedings, the family courts will surely need to answer the question: why should not family courts do the same for non-parties who are permitted to attend private court hearings (under FPR 2010 r 27.11(2))? And perhaps the same applies, for those non-parties who, for good reason (per *Guardian News v Westminster*), want to see material listed by Hamblen LJ, but after a hearing (as with the journalist in the *Guardian* case, subject always to the contempt provisions of AJA 1960 section 12(1) and other statutory provisions referred to in Part 2).

7 COLLATERAL USE OF COURT DOCUMENTS IN FAMILY PROCEEDINGS

The 'implied undertaking'[67] in family proceedings

13.76 In the absence of a rule equivalent to r 31.22 in FPR 2010, family proceedings are governed by the jurisprudence from civil proceedings. The existence of CPR 1998 r 31.22 is noted by Dame Elizabeth Butler-Sloss P in *Clibbery v Allan*[68] but at that stage the Court of Appeal did not apply it directly to family proceedings. CPR 1998 r 31.22 will be treated here as having subsumed the 'implied undertaking'. It will be said here that in that form the provisions of CPR 1998 r 31.22 apply in family proceedings as they do in family proceedings.

67 The 'implied undertaking' and r 31.22 are considered in the context of civil proceedings in Chapter 12, Pt 6.

68 [2002] EWCA Civ 45, [2002] Fam 261 sub nom *Clibbery v Allan* [2002] 1 FLR 565 at [65].

13.77 CPR 1998 r 31.22, as relevant here, provides as follows:

31.22 Subsequent use of disclosed documents …

(1) A party to whom a document has been disclosed may use the document only for the purpose of the proceedings in which it is disclosed, except where –

(a) the document has been read to or by the court, or referred to, at a hearing which has been held in public;

(b) the court gives permission; or

(c) the party who disclosed the document and the person to whom the document belongs agree.

(2) The court may make an order restricting or prohibiting the use of a document which has been disclosed, even where the document has been read to or by the court, or referred to, at a hearing which has been held in public.

13.78 Munby J had been appointed a High Court judge for eight months (from 2 October 2000) when he delivered his judgment in *Clibbery v Allan*,[69] Munby J. The appeal against his decision was allowed:

[83] In the present appeal, the court has no information at all about the evidence which was adduced at the hearing in the county court, other than that reported in the newspapers. There is a blanket objection by the appellant [(ie A)] to publication, based on the general premise that the case was heard in chambers and consequently must remain secret. On the information available to this court and to Munby J it was an issue of jurisdiction … This appeal has to be decided on what the court knows. Applying the principles which I have set out above, I can see no ground upon which, on the present facts, there cannot be publication of the proceedings …

13.79 Dame Elizabeth Butler-Sloss P went on to say: '[83] … Although I consider, for the reasons set out above that he has expressed his general propositions too widely, I agree with the conclusions of Munby J on the facts of the appeal.' Seventeen years after Munby J set out his judgment in *Clibbery v Allan*, to what extent are some of his comments now more apt to privacy in family proceedings in 2018? But first, the case and the appeal and some of the older law on release of court documents.

Clibbery v Allan

13.80 *Clibbery v Allan*[70] concerned proceedings where a circuit judge had refused to make an occupation order injunction (under Family Law Act 1996 Part 4) on the

69 [2001] 2 FLR 819.

70 Though Mr Allan was the appellant, the case is generally known by family lawyers and in many law reports by its name before Munby J.

application of the applicant Miss Clibbery (C). After the hearing she passed some of the documents in the case to the *Daily Mail.* Mr Allan (A) sought an injunction to prevent publication of the contents of these documents. The injunction was granted on an interim basis but refused by Munby J on the return date hearing.[71] Much of the judgment in the Court of Appeal turned on the extent to which proceedings such as these (under Part 4 of the 1996 Act) were private, and to what extent confidentiality of documents applied as a matter of course to such private proceedings.

13.81 One of the difficulties with *Allan v Clibbery* is that, though the discussion of the case by the court was wide-ranging, the court's findings – the *ratio decidendi* – applied to a relatively narrow span of legal principle. The issue for disposal was: where proceedings were in private – as the court held were the proceedings of Ms Clibbery and Mr Allan[72] – could there be subsequent publication or other release of documents, the oral evidence or submissions of judgment?[73]

13.82 Dame Elizabeth Butler-Sloss P (with whom Thorpe and Keene LJJ agreed) held that publication by C was permitted. A's injunction was discharged.

Collateral release of material in family proceedings

13.83 In *S v S (Inland Revenue: Tax Evasion)*[74] in financial relief proceedings, Wilson J found that the husband had evaded payment of tax. The wife's brother sent a copy of the judgment to the Inland Revenue. The Inland Revenue applied to Wilson J keep the transcript and also sought leave to inspect affidavits and documents produced at the substantive hearing and to obtain a transcript of the oral evidence. The judge dismissed the application: the seriousness of the husband not paying tax was outweighed by the importance of the public interest that in financial relief proceedings the parties should be candid with the court.

13.84 Six months after *S v S*, in *R v R (Disclosure to Revenue)*,[75] Wilson J considered a similar point. In financial relief proceedings he had found that a husband had failed to declare all his income but that it was unlikely that the under-declaration would be discovered. The judge assessed the husband's income without making any provision for tax on the hidden income. The Inland Revenue received a copy of the judgment and made tax assessments based on the undeclared income: (a) The husband applied for an order that the Inland Revenue deliver to the court all copies of the judgment in its possession. (b) On the Inland Revenue being ordered to produce to the court all copies of correspondence between them and the wife or her accountant, the Inland Revenue applied to set aside the order for production.

13.85 The judge refused both applications: (a) the court had a duty to discover who was responsible for sending the transcript of the judgment to the Inland

71 *Clibbery v Allan* [2001] 2 FLR 819.
72 See Dame Elizabeth Butler-Sloss P at [50].
73 Summarised at [14].
74 [1997] 2 FLR 774, Wilson J.
75 [1998] 1 FLR 922, Wilson J.

Revenue, so the order for 'production' stood; and (b) the Inland Revenue had had possession of the judgment for many months and that the process of levying the tax in the light of it was well underway so the Inland Revenue should be allowed to keep the transcript.[76] The husband's application was dismissed.

Court order for release of information: not to release would 'cheapen the law'

13.86 In *A v A; B v B*[77] financial relief claims in two divorces were heard together, because the husbands' joint business interests meant a considerable overlap between the two cases. By the time of the hearing the husbands had admitted attempting to hide assets. Agreement was reached and consent orders were approved by the court. Charles J indicated was considering passing on the papers to various third parties, including the Inland Revenue and the DPP. The cases were adjourned to enable the parties to reply. Charles J ordered disclosure of certain documents to the Isle of Man court and to the Law Society (an order for the Revenue was unnecessary because the parties themselves had agreed to make the necessary disclosure to the authorities). The judgment was obiter but the judge considered it appropriate to pass on information where parties had evaded or failed to pay taxes.

13.87 In direct opposition to Wilson J's decision in *S v S*,[78] and of whether the court should decide a case knowing that there has been tax evasion and that liabilities to HMRC have not been taken fully into account, Charles J took the view:[79]

(12) In my judgment, in general terms the problem is that an argument that there is a public interest in a court, or other public body, seeking to promote or encourage disclosure on the basis that it will generally proceed on the basis that:

(a) illegal or unlawful conduct, will not be reported to the proper authorities, and

(b) the product of such conduct will be retained and divided between individuals

is built on flawed foundations and is unattractive.

---

76 Per Wilson J at 927–928: '[In *S v S*] at 777G–H I observed that it was greatly in the public interest that all tax due should be paid and that evaders of tax should be convicted and sentenced. On the other hand, I reminded myself of the public interest that in proceedings for ancillary relief the parties should make full and frank disclosure of their resources; and observed that, were it to be understood that candour would usually lead to exposure of under-declarations to the Revenue, the pressure wrongfully to dissemble within the proceedings might be irresistible to a significant number of litigants. I went on to suggest that between these two opposing public interests should the individual circumstances be weighed.

I am clearly of the view that in the present case the weighing exercise results in a conclusion that the Inland Revenue should keep the copy pages that it irregularly has; and indeed that my order should specifically regularise its possession of them. It follows that the husband's application is dismissed.'

77 [2000] 1 FLR 701, Charles J.

78 *S v S (Inland Revenue: Tax Evasion)* [1997] 2 FLR 774.

79 Ibid at 746.

13.88 Putting it more strongly than Wilson J, Charles J held that not to report 'illegal or unlawful conduct' to the appropriate authorities positively 'would cheapen the law':[80]

Collateral use where a party has lied

13.89 Charles J's 'reflections' were cited with approval by Bodey J in *Y v Z (Disclosure to Police and Financial Conduct Authority: Publicity)*[81]

> [23] Perhaps the most comprehensive reflections on the various competing considerations, although completely obiter, are those of Charles J in *A v A; B v B* [2000] 1 FLR 701. That case was specifically about disclosure to the Inland Revenue of tax evasion, as to which the public interest considerations are different from where the wrongdoing and 'loss' can be reasonably enough remedied within the family proceedings themselves. At 737E Charles J noted that: "... the court does not regularly send papers to the prosecuting authorities when a litigant admits that he has lied or is found to have lied to the court ... It seems to me that, with a view to promoting the public interest in a civil court having all relevant material before it, a general practice can be adopted pursuant to which the court does not report the matter to the prosecuting authorities, particularly if the person involved makes full and frank disclosure and apology. There will naturally be exceptions having regard to the nature and circumstances of the case." As Charles J pointed out however that pragmatic approach, which probably accords with the general experience of most who practise in this area, is much less readily applicable where the exposed criminality is 'external' to the case, such as tax evasion or defalcation of a third party's money. In such circumstances as those, he said at 739E, that he generally favoured disclosure to the appropriate authorities. There is thus a discernible and reasonably logical distinction between:
>
> (i) those non-disclosures and lies which by their nature can be reasonably well remedied within the family proceedings, which may include by restorative financial orders and/or costs orders, or even by committal or a fine for contempt of court (subject to procedural formalities and to proof to the criminal standard); and
>
> (ii) those which by their nature cannot be.
>
> In the latter situation, disclosure to outside agencies may generally be seen as more likely in practice than in the former, although no sanctions can ever be ruled out in either case.

80 Ibid.

81 [2014] EWHC 650 (Fam), [2014] 2 FLR 1311.

13.90 In *Y v Z*, Bodey J was dealing with variation of a CA 1989 Sch 1 claim; and there were parallel domestic violence proceedings. During the course of those proceedings it became clear that the father had lied on oath to the court about his financial position in the original Sch 1 proceedings. He was chief executive officer and chairman of a company funded by investors. The mother wanted to disclose to the criminal authorities and the Financial Conduct Authority (FCA) the fact that he had lied. The district judge made an order which prevented the mother from disclosing information or documents in the proceedings without permission. Bodey J refused to alter that order on appeal; though had he been dealing with the case at first instance it must be open to question whether he would have made refused to restrain the mother from publication and release of documents. His conclusion on the mother's appeal was follows:

> [32] … I am not here exercising a fresh discretion of my own, but reviewing the decision below; and I am not in the end persuaded that the district judge carried out the balancing exercise in a way which can be characterised as wrong. I consider this case came close to the line, particularly in respect of disclosure to the FCA; but that is not to say that it crossed it, as the district judge decided it did not. No one should however regard this case as a green light for failing to disclose relevant information and/or for lying to the family courts. There is and always has been a probability that anyone who does so will be the subject of sanctions of one sort or another, and of differing types and severity, including in appropriate circumstances disclosure to relevant outside agencies.

Referral of a family case to appropriate authorities

13.91 In *Re Jones (Alleged Contempt of Court)*,[82] Sir James Munby P[83] approved the approach of Charles J in his consideration of the law on reporting to appropriate government authorities. He held that in his view the plainly allowed the court to refer matters to an outside agency, such as the police, Crown Prosecution Service or HM Revenue and Customs (italicised passage below):

> [12] It is well known that, on occasions, judges refer the papers in a case which has been before them to some outside agency with a view to that agency considering whether or not to take any steps arising out of the matters referred by the judge. Sometimes the papers are referred to the police, the CPS or the DPP with a view to the possible commencement of criminal proceedings. Sometimes the referral is to some professional or other regulator. Sometimes the referral is to HMRC. Sometimes, as here, the referral is to the Law Officers. No doubt there are other instances. Although the basis upon which such referrals are made has not very often been explored in any depth – the judgment of Charles J in *A v A; B v B* [2000] 1 FLR 701 is an exception – *there can be no*

82 [2013] EWHC 2579 (Fam) sub nom *The Solicitor General v J M J (Contempt)* [2014] 1 FLR 852, Sir James Munby P; court's invitation to the Attorney-General to apply for committal of a mother in child abduction proceedings.

83 Who represented the husbands in *A v A; B v B*.

> *question about the right of the judges to act in this way*. Nor, in my judgment, can there be any objection to a judge, as here, referring the papers to the Law Officers with a view to them considering whether or not to bring proceedings for contempt; and, I should make clear, whether the contempt is criminal or, as in the present case, civil … (italics added).

14

RELEASE OF CONFIDENTIAL MATERIAL FROM FAMILY PROCEEDINGS

1 INTRODUCTION

Confidential documents

14.1 Chapter 11, in part, considered the extent to which family courts could compel non-parties to produce documents into family court proceedings (Family Procedure Rules 2010 (FPR 2010) rr 21.2 and 24.2). Chapters 12 and 13 considered to what extent family courts can go in permitting confidential material to go from family proceedings to non-parties who may have an interest in those proceedings. This chapter looks at the extent to which family courts can expect to receive documents from non-parties (such as the police) outside the statutory scheme envisaged by FPR 2010 r 21.2 or by means of a witness summons to produce documents.

14.2 Restrictions dictated by the common law and under the rules (mostly FPR 2010) are dealt with at various point in this this book. It is necessary here only to draw attention to the following:

- That the common law[1] and the law on contempt (see s 12(1)(a)) below makes private all court hearings in relation to children.
- That proceedings governed by Family Procedure Rules 2010 (FPR 2010) are said to be heard in private, save where otherwise provided.[2]
- That because a hearing is in private, it does not mean that certain documents from the case (where not disclosed under compulsion of court order) cannot be released to the media.[3]

---

1 *Scott & Anor v Scott* [1913] UKHL 2, [1913] AC 417.

2 FPR 2010 r 27.10.

3 *Clibbery v Allan* [2002] EWCA Civ 45, [200] Fam 261, [2002] 1 FLR 565.

- Application can be made to the court by a non-party to proceedings for release of a defined range of documents.[4]

14.3 This chapter proceeds as follows:

- Part 2 looks at the extent to which information available to parties to children proceedings may be communicated to non-parties and in the best interests of children: see especially FPR 2010 Part 12 Chapter 7 (communication of information).
- Part 3 deals with the specific question of orders for release of family proceedings documents to non-parties under FPR 2010 Part 12 Chapter 7.

2 COMMUNICATION OF INFORMATION: CHILDREN PROCEEDINGS

Family Procedure Rules 2010 Part 12, Chapter 7: children proceedings

14.4 FPR 2010 Part 12, which deals with most aspects of children proceedings, concludes with Chapter 7 (headed as the heading to this Part). Chapter 7 comprises FPR 2010 rr 12.72 to 12.75, of which only two are operative (one is an 'Interpretation' rule and another has been revoked). These rules are accompanied by *Practice Direction 12G – Communication of information (PD12G).*

14.5 FPR 2010 rr 12.73 and 12.75 deal respectively with:

- Documents which can be communicated to those involved in the proceedings (such as legal representatives, CAFCASS officers etc), and with release on individuals or others (such as the police) with permission of the court (r 12.73).
- Circumstances in which a party or their representative can pass on information for example for a mediation meeting or to pursue a complaint relating to the proceedings.

14.6 Although r 12.73 refers to the generic 'proceedings in private', it is clear from the context in which the rule appears – FPR 2010 Part 12: 'Children proceedings etc' – and from the prominent reference to children proceedings in *PD12G*, that the rule is intended only for children cases.

Information from children proceedings

14.7 Under the heading 'Communication of information: general' FPR 2010 r 12.73(1) creates a list of three categories of individual to whom 'information

4 FPR 2010 r 29.12; *Cape Intermediate Holdings Ltd v Dring (Asbestos Victims Support Group)* [2018] EWCA Civ 1795.

relating to proceedings in private' can be communicated in such a way as not to be a contempt of court. FPR 2010 r 12.73 says:

> **12.73 Communication of information: general**
>
> (1) For the purposes of the law relating to contempt of court, information relating to proceedings held in private (whether or not contained in a document filed with the court) may be communicated –
>
> (a) where the communication is to –
>
> (i) a party;
>
> (ii) the legal representative of a party;[5]
>
> (iii) a professional legal adviser;
>
> (iv) an officer of the service or a Welsh family proceedings officer;
>
> (v) the welfare officer;
>
> (vi) the Director of Legal Aid Casework ...;
>
> (vii) an expert whose instruction by a party has been authorised by the court for the purposes of the proceedings;
>
> (viii)a professional acting in furtherance of the protection of children;
>
> (ix) an independent reviewing officer appointed in respect of a child who is, or has been, subject to proceedings to which this rule applies;
>
> (b) where the court gives permission; or
>
> (c) subject to any direction of the court, in accordance with rule 12.75 and *Practice Direction 12G*.

14.8 *Practice Direction 12G* is entitled *Communication of Information* and provides three tables which set out which communications in children proceedings can be passed on to particular bodies or individuals. Paragraph 2.1 of *PD12G* is the first of these. It sets out a table which deals with 'any information relating to the proceedings'. This information can be passed on by specified individuals – for example, a party, a legal representative or others lawfully in possession of the information – for specified purposes, other than the proceedings. For example, information can be communicated to a person conducting 'an approved research project'. Any communication in accordance with the provisions of *PD12G* is, by paragraph 1.2, 'Subject to any direction of the court ...'

5 The terms 'legal representative' and a 'professional legal adviser' are, with other terms, defined by FPR 2010 r 2.3(1) (the rules' interpretation rule). 'Professional legal adviser' is distinguished from 'legal representative' because the former gives advice but is not instructed to represent. In *Re B (A Child: Disclosure of Evidence in Care Proceedings)* [2012] 1 FLR 142, Bodey J held that 'professional legal adviser' covered the respective parents' defence solicitors in possible criminal proceedings. No permission was therefore required for the respective defence solicitors to receive disclosure of the transcripts of evidence given in care proceedings.

Communication of information in children proceedings: application to restrict release

14.9 The operation of r 12.73 was considered by Baker J in *Re X and Y (Disclosure of Judgment to Police)*.[6] In that case the judge concluded that the child, Y, had sustained non-accidental injuries while in the care of the parents and that the parents had not told the truth about what happened. It was probable that one of the parents was responsible for the injuries and that the other was withholding information to protect the perpetrator. The judgment indicated that if a frank account were given, the children would be rehabilitated. It was published anonymised. It was not passed on to the police. Two days later, the father admitted he had inflicted the injuries and the parents separated. The finding in relation to the mother was reviewed. A supervision order was put in place for 12 months which provided for the children to be rehabilitated to the mother's care and the father was to have supervised contact.

14.10 The father applied for an order preventing the disclosure of any material connected to the proceedings to the police or Crown Prosecution Service (CPS). The police had closed their file on the matter when they were unable to conclude which parent had caused the injuries to Y. The police applied for any information which had come to light during the proceedings so that a decision as to prosecution could be taken. The father resisted the application and claimed that there had been a failure fully to explain the repercussions of his telling the truth in breach of his European Convention 1950 Article 6 rights.

14.11 Baker J ordered release of the judgments to the police and the CPS. It could not be said that the court's failure to give a warning of the ramifications amounted to a breach of the father's right to a fair trial in the proceedings. By urging both parties to tell the truth, the court was seeking to ensure a fair trial for all parties, in particular the parents and the children. The inducement held out was that, if the perpetrator of Y's injuries gave a frank account, the children could be rehabilitated within the family. The father did not resile from his confession and the outcome of the proceedings was manifestly fair to all parties.

Disclosure and PD12G

14.12 The local authority is one of the specified individuals in *PD12G* as a party to the proceedings, in paragraph 2.1. They did not need permission under r 12.73(1)(b) to release information to the police. The judgment was required by the police 'for the purpose of a criminal investigation' and thus – subject to any order – was eligible for communication within the terms of paragraph 2.1. The resultant position under the rules, as summarised by Baker J, is as follows:

> [16] Thus the scheme of the current rules is that communication of information relating to care proceedings falls into three categories:
>
> (1) communications under r 12.73(1)(a), which may be made as a matter of right;

6 [2014] EWHC 278 (Fam), [2015] 1 FLR 1218.

(2) communications under r 12.73(1)(c) and *PD 12G* paras 1 and 2, which may be made, but are subject to any direction by the court, including, in appropriate circumstances, a direction that they should not be made; and

(3) other communications, which under 12.73(1)(b) may only be made with the court's permission.

Plainly, whereas the onus in respect of proposed communications under r 12.73(1)(b) lies on the party seeking permission to communicate, the onus in respect of communications that would otherwise be permitted under r 12.73(1)(c) and Practice Direction 12G paras 1 and 2 lies on the party contending that such communication should not be permitted.

Re EC and disclosure of material from care proceedings

14.13 As to whether he should release his judgment to the police, Baker J relied on *Re EC (Disclosure of Material)*[7] (*Re EC*).[8] He treated that case as still the leading authority on release of information to the police. The factors in *Re EC* listed by Swinton Thomas LJ,[9] and as relevant in the present context, are:

(1) The welfare and interests of the child or children concerned in the care proceedings. If the child is likely to be adversely affected by the order in any serious way, this will be a very important factor.

(2) The welfare and interests of other children generally.

(3) The maintenance of confidentiality in children cases.

(4) The importance of encouraging frankness in children's cases …

(5) The public interest in the administration of justice. Barriers should not be erected between one branch of the judicature and another because this may be inimical to the overall interests of justice.

(6) The public interest in the prosecution of serious crime and the punishment of offenders …

(7) The gravity of the alleged offence and the relevance of the evidence to it. If the evidence has little or no bearing on the investigation or the trial, this will militate against a disclosure order.

(8) The desirability of co-operation between various agencies concerned with the welfare of children …

(9) …

(10) Any other material disclosure which has already taken place.

---

7 *Re C (A Minor) (Care Proceedings: Disclosure)* [1997] Fam 76, [1997] 2 WLR 322, sub nom *Re EC (Disclosure of Material)* [1996] 2 FLR 725, CA.

8 *Re EC*, predominantly a case on self-incrimination privilege, is considered more fully in Chapter 7.

9 Ibid at [85] and [733] respectively.

14.14 Any order for release of the judgment in *Re X and Y* was to be limited to 'criminal investigation', said Baker J. Any further onward release by the police (eg, for disclosure in a criminal trial) would only be with permission from the court, as the judge made clear.[10]

14.15 Finally, Baker J affirmed the view of Thorpe LJ in the Court of Appeal in *Re H (Care Proceedings: Disclosure)*[11] as to the importance of *Re EC* in the context of release of confidential information from care proceedings:

> [35] As indicated in *Re H* by Thorpe LJ, *Re EC* remains the leading authority when deciding whether to disclose confidential information arising in care proceedings. The analysis conducted by Swinton Thomas LJ was comprehensive and the 10 factors identified by him all remain relevant to such a decision.

Release of child protection information to the police by CAFCASS

14.16 The case of *S v SP and CAFCASS*[12] deals with the extent to which a Cafcass officer may provide child protection information when asked for it. SP, the Cafcass officer in question, was asked to provide information to the police about a mentally unstable parent in private law proceedings. Confronted by an application for committal by the father of Cafcass and their officer, Baker J emphasised the importance of a children's guardian (ie, the 'Cafcass officer') being able to pass on information to the police 'in furtherance of child protection'. This was entirely within the meaning of the terms 'child protection' in FPR 2010 r 12.73.[13]

14.17 In *S v SP* a father (S) had been permitted only indirect contact with his children. There were concerns as to his mental health. He was not permitted directly to communicate with the mother or the children. He made a complaint concerning SP, their Cafcass officer, as to her conduct of the case. She had received a call about S from a police officer and in the course of it gave to the police officer certain information about the proceedings. Acting in person, S applied for findings of contempt against SP and against Cafcass, for 'deliberately disclosing inappropriate information'.

14.18 The judge gave short shrift to S's argument that this passing on of information was 'publication' as anticipated by the Administration of Justice (AJA) 1960 section 12(1)[14] and that is could therefore contempt within the terms of section 12(1). He dwelled however on the meaning of FPR 2010 r 12.73(1)(a)(viii): that for any alleged contempt in relation to children proceedings, 'information… may be communicated [by] (viii) a professional acting in furtherance of the protection of children …'.[15]

10 Ibid at [21] and [25].
11 [2009] EWCA Civ 704, [2009] 2 FLR 1531.
12 [2016] EWHC 3673 (Fam) Baker J.
13 See *S v SP* at [37]. For the text of r 12.73(1) see 14.7.
14 For the text of s 12(1) see 2.78.
15 *S v SP* at [24].

14.19 In *S v SP*, as he had done in *Re X and Y*, Baker J stressed the importance of professionals working together to share information. If in doubt before passing on information, a professional should make application in the children proceedings.[16] In this case, the guardian was not acting unlawfully in passing on the information, said the judge; and neither SP nor CAFCASS were in contempt of court in any way. On the contrary, in passing on information to the police the guardian was acting entirely in accordance with what was intended by FPR 2010 r 12.73(1)(b).

Release of documents to third parties outside PG12G

14.20 In *Re X, Y and Z (Disclosure to the Security Service)*,[17] McDonald J dealt with an application by the Metropolitan Police (MPS) to release a judgment and mother's statement in unconcluded care proceedings to the Security Service (ie, MI5). The child was aged three and it was suspect that her mother wanted to take her to Islamic State. MPS had received the documents on their own earlier application. MI5 were not a party to that application. MPS wanted to release the documents, and to do so unconditionally, in case MI5 could assist them in their own enquiries (eg, to provide them with information about any criminal information, including radicalisation, about the mother).

14.21 The case turned on whether there should be, and if so what, conditions upon the onward release of the children proceedings documents by the police to MI5. MPS said release by them should be unconditional. On behalf of the child it was said release should be conditional. McDonald J agreed. He explained the background law (providing an excellent summary in the process) at paras [16] to [35]. He said that release of documents in the proceedings was not a 'binary issue': to disclose or not to disclose. He explained this:

> [26] ... The court may order disclosure but impose appropriate conditions on the disclosure of documents where such conditions are necessary to ensure fair balance between the rights engaged (*Re X (Children)* [2007] EWHC 1719, [2008] 1 FLR 589 [Munby J] at [38] and *Re X and Y (Disclosure of Judgment to Police)* [[2014] EWHC 278 (Fam), [2015] 1 FLR 1218, Baker J] at [21] and [38]).

14.22 McDonald J ordered release but subject to conditions which essentially maintained control of confidentiality in the documents with the court. And an essential aspect of the judge's decision-making turned on the right of the parties and child, or children, to confidentiality. Further the security services are not in the lists in *PD12G*. The must therefore make application – or, in this case, the police on their behalf. In making any order for release, the court will be concerned to preserve, as far as possible, the parties' rights and any confidentiality in documents.

---

16 Ibid at [38]; FPR 2010 r 12.73(1)(b).

17 [2016] EWHC 2400 (Fam), [2017] 2 FLR 583 sub nom *Commissioner of Police of the Metropolis v A Local Authority and others* [2016] 4 WLR 153.

Purposes connected with children proceedings

14.23 FPR 2010 r 12.75 contains a rule which enables a party to children proceedings, or their legal representative, to communicate information to anyone comprised in the list in r 12.75(1), and for the purposes there mentioned:

> **12.75 Communication of information for purposes connected with the proceedings**
>
> (1) A party or the legal representative of a party, on behalf of and upon the instructions of that party, may communicate information relating to the proceedings to any person where necessary to enable that party –
>
> (a) by confidential discussion, to obtain support, advice or assistance in the conduct of the proceedings;
>
> (b) to attend a mediation information and assessment meeting, or to engage in mediation or other forms of non-court dispute resolution;
>
> (c) to make and pursue a complaint against a person or body concerned in the proceedings; or
>
> (d) to make and pursue a complaint regarding the law, policy or procedure relating to a category of proceedings to which this Part applies.

14.24 FPR 2010 r 12.75(2) and (3) set limits on further communication of information:

(2) Where information is communicated to any person in accordance with paragraph (1)(a) of this rule, no further communication by that person is permitted.

(3) When information relating to the proceedings is communicated to any person in accordance with paragraphs (1)(b), (c) or (d) of this rule –

(a) the recipient may communicate that information to a further recipient, provided that –

(i) the party who initially communicated the information consents to that further communication; and

(ii) the further communication is made only for the purpose or purposes for which the party made the initial communication; and

(b) the information may be successively communicated to and by further recipients on as many occasions as may be necessary to fulfil the purpose for which the information was initially communicated, provided that on each such occasion the conditions in sub-paragraph (a) are met.

14.25 The editors of *Family Court Practice*[18] describe this rule as introducing 'sweeping changes to the disclosure of information without the prior sanction of the court'. They point to the 'safeguards' in the rules. First any communication

18 *Family Court Practice* (London: LexisNexis 2018) under commentary to FPR 2010, r 12.75.

must be 'necessary' which, said Munby J, in *Spencer v Spencer*,[19] when speaking of the word in the context of another form of publicity (exclusion of the press from family proceedings: FPR 2010 r 27.11(3)(a)). Munby J said:

> [31] … It is not for nothing, as it seems to me, that the rule uses the word 'necessary', that being a word familiar from the Strasbourg jurisprudence and, in my judgment, a word used here with the intention that it should be understood in the sense spelt out in the Strasbourg jurisprudence. Necessity, in the Strasbourg sense, has a meaning lying somewhere between 'essential' or 'indispensable', on the one hand, and 'useful', 'reasonable' or 'desirable' on the other hand …

14.26 FPR 2010 r 12.73(2) puts an absolute bar on any communication of information to the public as a whole; or to any section of the public. As *Family Court Practice* goes on: 'It may no longer be necessary to obtain prior judicial sanction for disclosures permitted by r 12.75.' The editors suggest that 'someone communicating information in circumstances that would otherwise involve a contempt of court because of the operation of Administration of Justice Act 1960 (AJA 1960) section 12(1) will be able to rely on Chapter 7 and *PD12G* as disapplying section 12(1), if AJA 1960 section 12(4) applies – that is, that is authorised by rules of court.

Administration of Justice Act 1960 section 12: permitted publication

14.27 As already mentioned, AJA 1960 section 12(1) (in a part of the Act headed 'Contempt of court, habeas corpus and certiorari') is a section which is written mostly in negative terms: it says what is not contempt (publication of information from proceedings in private), save in the case of, for instance, children proceedings – unless rules permit such publication. For present purposes it is necessary only to set out section 12(1)(a) and (4) (as amended):

> **12 Publication of information relating to proceedings in private**
>
> (1) The publication of information relating to proceedings before any court sitting in private shall not of itself be contempt of court except in the following cases, that is to say—
>
> (a) where the proceedings—
>
> (i) relate to the exercise of the inherent jurisdiction of the High Court with respect to minors;
>
> (ii) are brought under the Children Act 1989 or the Adoption and Children Act 2002; or
>
> (iii) otherwise relate wholly or mainly to the maintenance or upbringing of a minor; …

19 [2009] EWHC 1529 (Fam), [2009] 2 FLR 1416.

(4) Nothing in this section shall be construed as implying that any publication is punishable as contempt of court which would not be so punishable apart from this section (and in particular where the publication is not so punishable by reason of being authorised by rules of court).

14.28 FPR 2010 rr 12.73 and 12.75 authorised departure from section 12(1)(a) as carefully defined in Chapter 7. A party who keeps within the bounds of r 12.75(1) is within section 12(4); but anyone who communicates onwards (eg, a family member on to the media) risks committal proceedings.

3 MATERIAL FROM FAMILY PROCEEDINGS TO NON-PARTIES

Release of documents to non-parties

14.29 In *A Health Authority v X (Discovery: Medical Conduct)*[20] Munby J dealt with an application in earlier care proceedings where the health authority wanted to consider compliance by a GP practice whose doctors had been involved in earlier care proceedings. The health authority applied for disclosure of certain documents which had been produced in the care proceedings. Munby J ordered disclosure on strict conditions; and in passing commented on the extent to which disclosure of documents could be ordered in the Family Division. Counsel for the health authority had argued that, said the judge, a public body can apply for 'a mandatory order requiring the delivery up to it by anybody of documents required by it for the purpose of carrying out its public or regulatory functions'.[21]

14.30 Munby J rejected the idea that there was any such wide jurisdiction. It was not possible to obtain documents from an 'innocent third party' save in very restricted circumstances; and that if it could be said that the Family Division did have such power then that would 'set at nought' the *Norwich Pharmacal* rule:[22]

> [60] There is, in my judgment, no such principle and I cannot believe that Kennedy LJ had any such type of application in mind. In the first place it seems to me to set at nought the well-established rule, recognised in *Norwich Pharmacal Co and Others v Customs and Excise Commissioners* [1972] Ch 566 (ChD), [1974] AC 133 (HL), that neither at common law nor in equity does any independent action (that is, an action unlinked with any sustainable claim for substantive relief) lie against an innocent third party for the purpose of obtaining papers or information. The only permissible course is to issue a [witness summons]. After all, the whole point in the *Norwich Pharmacal* case was whether or not there was, as the House of Lords eventually held, reversing the Court of Appeal and restoring the

20 [2001] 2 FLR 673.

21 Ibid at [59].

22 Explained at 11.31.

judgment of Graham J, an exception to this rule where the third party against whom disclosure was sought had become, albeit innocently, involved in the tortious acts of another.

Re X and Y: communication of information to the police

14.31 A practical application of the procedures in the *2013 Protocol*[23] – at a time when it was coming into force[24] – and of FPR 2010 r 12.73 can be seen in operation in *Re X and Y (Disclosure of Judgment to Police)*.[25] Baker J was dealing with an application by the police who wanted to see a judgment in which he had recorded that the father of a child had admitted, after the making of a care order, that he had perpetrated the injuries on one of three children. In his first judgment, in relation to fact-finding, the judge had found that the injuries were probably caused by one of the parents. He urged both parents, despite that finding, that they should be to be more frank with the court about what had really happened. Two days later the father confessed that he had caused the injuries to the child. The parents separated.

> [5] … The matter was therefore restored before me and I directed a further fact-finding hearing to be listed urgently before me. The father duly filed a statement in which he described in detail the circumstances in which he had come to inflict the injuries. The mother filed a statement setting out her response to the father's confession. Two experts filed addendum reports in which they accepted that the injuries could have been sustained in the incidents described by the father.

14.32 The judge resumed the fact-finding hearing and, at the end of it, delivered a second judgment which was transcribed, but not released for publication nor communicated to the police. Baker J concluded that 'on a balance of probabilities, that the injuries had been inflicted by the father in the manner described in his statement'.[26] The mother was exonerated. The children remained in her care subject to a supervision order.

14.33 Meanwhile, the father applied for an order prohibiting the local authority or any other party from communicating any information to the police or CPS (as explained above). Section 12 of the *2013 Protocol* deals with release of the text of judgments to the police or CPS and asserts that there is a duty on the local authority to do this where they have the judgment.[27]

14.34 Alternatively, police can obtain a transcript from the court under *PG27A*.[28] Subject to r 12.73(1) and *PG27A*, were the local authority to have released the

---

23 *2013 Protocol and Good Practice Model Disclosure of Information in Cases of Alleged Child Abuse and Linked Criminal and Care Directions Hearings October 2013*.

24 The judgment under consideration here, the third in a series, was given on 12 February 2014.

25 [2014] EWHC 278 (Fam), [2015] 1 FLR 1218 (see also at 14.9).

26 Ibid at [6].

27 *2013 Protocol* para 12.1.

28 Ibid para 12.2; though it is not clear under what provision of *PG27A* the police are entitled to expect the court to release the judgment.

judgment to the police following any care proceedings they risked contempt proceedings in the light of AJA section 12(1)(a).[29] The rule and practice direction are intended to avoid this and to ensure that there can be more openness in relation to children proceedings.

29 See further at 2.78.

15

CLOSED MATERIAL PROCEDURES

1 INTRODUCTION

Exclusion from disclosure to a party to proceedings

15.1 Use of any closed material procedures will be very rare indeed in family or any other proceedings. Such a procedure is not provided for in Family Procedure Rules 2010 (FPR 2010). It is therefore approached here analogically with the procedures in civil proceedings in the High Court under Justice and Security Act 2013 (JSA 2013) and Civil Procedure Rules 1998 (CPR 1998) Part 82. This is the only source from which the rare procedure can, at present, be approached.

15.2 A closed material procedure (CMP) permits the High Court to restrict disclosure of certain documents – to be defined in this Chapter as 'sensitive material'. The procedure makes possible restricted disclosure to:

- one or more parties to the proceedings (excluded parties); and
- specially appointed advocates for the excluded parties.

15.3 The general rule is that only a statute can authorise CMP. In the majority of proceedings it cannot, for example, be done in the inherent jurisdiction of the court. Children proceedings have been treated as an exception to this general rule.[1] If a CMP is to be authorised in children proceedings, it can only be by the Family Division of the High Court.[2]

15.4 A CMP was defined by Lord Neuberger in *Bank Mellat v Her Majesty's Treasury (No 1)*[3] as:

> [1] ... A closed material procedure involves the production of material which is so confidential and sensitive that it requires the court not only to sit in private, but to sit in a closed hearing (ie a hearing at which the court considers the material and hears submissions about it without one of the parties to the appeal seeing the material or being present), and

1 See Chapter 15, Part 2(4).

2 *Re X, Y and Z (Disclosure to the Security Service)* [2016] EWHC 2400 (Fam), [2017] 2 FLR 583 sub nom *Commissioner of Police of the Metropolis v A Local Authority and others* [2016] 4 WLR 153, McDonald J.

3 [2013] UKSC 38, [2014] AC 700.

to contemplate giving a partly closed judgment (ie a judgment part of which will not be seen by one of the parties).

15.5 The starting point in any case must always be to protect a party's right to an open trial and with all material which will be considered by the court available on the same terms to all parties. However, CMPs have been used to protect national security[4] and in proceedings before the Information Commissioner where sensitive information is required to be protected.[5] In tightly controlled circumstances such procedures may be justified in children proceedings.[6]

15.6 This chapter proceeds as follows:

- Part 2 explains the severe restrictions on CMPs and that (save perhaps in children proceedings) such procedures in civil proceedings can only be permitted as authorised by statute.
- Part 3 deals with how a closed material declaration may be obtained under the Justice and Security Act 2013 section 6, so that any similar procedure which is attempted in children proceedings can be understood analogically with proceedings under CPR 1998 Part 82. The role of special advocates is explained.
- Part 4 differentiates production of material only to parties advocates (which has in any event been disapproved of by Court of Appeal and Supreme Court); and considered it in the light of the *Re HI* case.[7]
- Part 5 looks at the role of the special advocate: (1) in proceedings under JSA 2013; and (2) in children proceedings (especially in the light of *Re T*[8]).

Closed material procedures and public interest immunity

15.7 The distinction between public interest immunity (see Chapter 15) and a CMP must be made clear immediately. With a CMP the judge, certain particular parties and any special advocates for the excluded parties will see the sensitive material; though the excluded parties will not (by definition). By contrast, in the case of public interest immunity only the party who has the documents has access to the information they contain. This is denied to other parties and eve to the judge.

15.8 In the case of a CMP at least the judge a restricted category of the parties see the sensitive material. With public interest immunity the court must decide the case with sight only of part of the relevant evidence. In *Local Authority X v HI and*

4 See eg, *Bank Mellat v Her Majesty's Treasury (No 2)* [2013] UKSC 39, [2014] 1 AC 700.

5 *Browning v The Information Commissioner & Anor* [2014] EWCA Civ 1050, [2014] 1 WLR 3848.

6 As explained in *Al Rawi & Ors v The Security Service & Ors* [2011] UKSC 34 [2012] AC 531, [2011] 3 WLR 388 and considered at 15.9 and 15.15.

7 *Local Authority X v HI and Others* [2016] EWHC 1123 (Fam), [2017] 1 FLR 1362, Roberts J.

8 *Re T (Wardship: Impact of Police Intelligence)* [2009] EWHC 2440 (Fam), [2010] 1 FLR 1048, McFarlane J.

Others,[9] the court permitted release of documents only to the parties' advocates, as explained in Part 4 of this chapter. With respect to the judges involved, it is unlikely that any such practice is lawful.[10]

2 RULE AGAINST CLOSED MATERIAL PROCEDURES

Restricted scope for closed material procedures

Closed material procedures in civil proceedings

15.9 In *Al Rawi & Ors v The Security Service & Ors*[11] the Supreme Court explained that the common law, on its own, could not generally be used to set up a CMP. Such a procedure can only be provided for by specific statutory provision (the *Bank Mellat* case proceeded under Counter-Terrorism Act 2008). European Convention 1950 and the right to a fair trial does not on its own prevent CMPs, provided strict conditions as to the procedure are met.

15.10 In *Bank Mellat (No 1)* Lord Neuberger summarised the conditions for a CMP to be ordered, as follows:

> [5] … Those conditions, in very summary terms, would normally include the court being satisfied that (i) for weighty reasons, such as national security, the material has to be kept secret from the excluded party as well as the public, (ii) a hearing to determine the issues between the parties could not fairly go ahead without the material being shown to the judge, (iii) a summary, which is both sufficiently informative and as full as the circumstances permit, of all the closed material has been made available to the excluded party, and (iv) an independent advocate, who has seen all the material, is able to challenge the need for the procedure, and, if there is a closed hearing, is present throughout to test the accuracy and relevance of the material and to make submissions about it.

15.11 In *Re A (Sexual Abuse: Disclosure)*[12] (a vulnerable young adult witness confronted by an argument that her confidentiality should be breached so she could give evidence against a father in children proceedings) Lady Hale dealt with a suggestion that closed material procedures could be used in a case where a vulnerable witness wanted to restrict a father's access to her evidence. Her reply was as follows:

> [34] … It has been suggested that the court might adopt some form of closed material procedure, in which full disclosure was made to a

9 [2016] EWHC 1123 (Fam), [2017] 1 FLR 1362, Roberts J.

10 *Somerville and others v Scottish Ministers (HM Advocate General for Scotland Intervening)* [2007] UKHL 44, [2007] 1 WLR 2734.

11 [2011] UKSC 34 [2012] AC 531.

12 [2012] UKSC 60, [2013] 1 FLR 948.

> special advocate appointed to protect the parents' interests, but not to the father himself. It faces two formidable difficulties. The first is that this Court has held that there is no power to adopt such a procedure in ordinary civil proceedings: *Al Rawi v Security Service (JUSTICE intervening)* [2011] UKSC 34, [2012] 1 AC 531 … It is arguable that a greater latitude may be allowed in children cases where the child's welfare is the court's paramount concern. But the arguments against making such an inroad into the normal principles of a fair trial remain very powerful …

15.12 Further, she went on to say, there are difficulties inherent in the fairness of the procedures; and, by definition, in relation to a person's ability of to mount a defence which is based on all the material available to the court and to some other parties. So, said Lady Hale:

> [34] … The essential requirement of any fair procedure is that the person who stands to lose his rights has an opportunity effectively to challenge the essence of the case against him. There may be cases in which this can be done by offering him a "gist" of the allegations and appointing a special advocate to scrutinise the whole of the material deployed against him…. Even if it were theoretically possible to devise some form of closed material procedures, therefore, it would not meet the minimum requirements of a fair hearing in this case.

Closed material procedures: children proceedings and Al Rawi

15.13 So where does that leave the possibility of use of a CMP in children proceedings? *Al Rawi & Ors v The Security Service & Ors* [13] provides the starting point. The case arose as a preliminary issue on disclosure in a damages claim. The claimants said that the security services had been complicit in their detention and ill-treatment of them by foreign authorities, including at Guantanamo Bay. The pleaded causes of action included false imprisonment, trespass to the person, conspiracy to injure, torture and breach of the Human Rights Act 1998.

15.14 The Security Service, the defendants, said that the disclosure question could not be dealt with on ordinary public interest immunity grounds. They said there was so much material: this might take three years just to decide in respect of which material public interest immunity should be claimed. The judge said a CMP was permitted. The Court of Appeal disagreed; and the Supreme Court disallowed the Security Service's appeal from that decision (with Lord Clarke dissenting). In that case, and as a general rule in civil proceedings, it was held that CMPs could not be permitted save where statutory provision provided for it in a specific class of case.

13 [2011] UKSC 34 [2012] AC 531, [2011] 3 WLR 388.

Open justice principles as against private children proceedings

Objections to closed material procedures

15.15 Lord Dyson, who gave the main judgment for the majority in *Al Rawi*, summarised the open trial principles. First, he said, trials must always be in public (subject to certain 'limited exceptions'):

> [10] There are certain features of a common law trial which are fundamental to our system of justice (both criminal and civil). First, subject to certain established and limited exceptions, trials should be conducted and judgments given in public. The importance of the open justice principle has been emphasised many times: see, for example, *R v Sussex Justices, Ex p McCarthy* [1924] 1 KB 256, at p 259, per Lord Hewart CJ, *Attorney General v Leveller Magazine Ltd* [1979] AC 440, at pp 449H–450B, per Lord Diplock, and recently *R (Mohamed) v Secretary of State for Foreign and Commonwealth Affairs (No 2) (Guardian News and Media Ltd intervening)* [2011] QB 218, paras 38–39, per Lord Judge CJ.

15.16 Certain basic principles of natural justice must be observed by the courts:

> [12] ... A party has a right to know the case against him and the evidence on which it is based. [and] he is entitled to have the opportunity to respond to any such evidence and to any submissions made by the other side. The other side may not advance contentions or adduce evidence of which he is kept in ignorance ...
>
> [13] ... The parties should be given an opportunity to call their own witnesses and to cross-examine the opposing witnesses. As was said by the High Court of Australia in *Lee v The Queen* (1998) 195 CLR 594, at para 32: "Confrontation and the opportunity for cross-examination is of central significance to the common law adversarial system of trial."

15.17 As already mentioned, a CMP must be distinguished from public interest immunity. In the case of the former the judge, certain parties and perhaps special advocates for the excluded parties will see the sensitive material. The excluded parties themselves will not. By contrast, in the case of public interest immunity only the party who has the documents has access to the information they contain. The court therefore decides the case with only a part of the relevant evidence.

Proceedings in private

15.18 It is not in question that proceedings in relation to children are one of the exceptions to the open justice principle. Hearings will almost invariably be in private even though an anonymised version of the judgment may be published. However, CMPs go much further than privacy. Accordingly, in *Al Rawi* Lord Dyson continued:

> [27] It is one thing to say that the open justice principle may be abrogated if justice cannot otherwise be achieved. As Lord Bingham said

> in *R v Davis* [2008] UKHL 36, [2008] 1 AC 1128 at [28], the rights of a litigating party are the same whether a trial is conducted in camera or in open court and whether or not the course of the proceedings may be reported in the media. It is quite a different matter to say that the court may sanction a departure from the natural justice principle (including the right to be present at and participate in the whole or part of a trial). *Scott v Scott* is no authority for such a proposition.

15.19 Lord Dyson concluded his judgment by referring to the exceptions to the normal rule which prohibits CMPs. He agreed with Lord Clarke's minority judgment to the following extent; and especially to the extent that it recognised that CMPs might in effect operate in wardship, and in other case which concern the interests of children (see italicised passage below):

> [63] ... there are certain classes of case where a departure from the normal rule may be justified for special reasons in the interests of justice. Thus as Baroness Hale of Richmond said in *Secretary of State for the Home Department v MB* [2007] UKHL 46, [2008] 1 AC 440 at para 58: "If ... the whole object of the proceedings is to protect and promote the best interests of a child, there may be exceptional circumstances in which disclosure of some of the evidence would be so detrimental to the child's welfare as to defeat the object of the exercise." Wardship proceedings are an obvious example of such a case: see *In re K (Infants)* [1965] AC 201, per Lord Devlin at p 241A. Cases involving children raise different considerations from those which arise in ordinary civil litigation. *That is because the interests of children are paramount. It follows that where the interests of the child are served, so too are the interests of justice* (emphasis added).

15.20 Where the interests of a child are served, so too are the interests of justice, said Lord Dyson. This is the main rationale for accepting CMPs in children proceedings.

Closed material: Justice and Security Act 2013

Justice and Security Act 2013: national security alongside interests of children

15.21 The Justice and Security Act 2013 (JSA 2013) may provide a framework for CMP in children proceedings. However, any question related to closed material must be considered always with European Convention 1950 Article 6 (right to a fair trial) fully in mind. For example, Article 6 includes the following:

> (1) ... the press and public may be excluded from all or part of the trial in the interest of morals, public order or national security in a democratic society, where the interests of juveniles or the protection of the private life of the parties so require, or to the extent strictly necessary in the opinion of the court in special circumstances where publicity would prejudice the interests of justice.

15.22 JSA 2013 deals with national security. Public order and national security and 'the interests of juveniles [(ie the welfare of children)] or the protection of the private life of the parties' are bracketed in Article 6(1) as justifying exclusion of public and press. In a similar way in CPR 1998 r 39.2(3) 'national security'[14] is included with 'the interests of any child or protected party'[15] as amongst those proceedings where the court is able to consider ordering that a hearing should be in private. There seems to be no reason in underlying principle why similar criteria, at least in terms of evidence and procedure, should not be applied, in the very limited circumstances where it may be demanded, in children proceedings as in proceedings which concern national security under JSA 2013 and CPR 1998 Part 82.

Closed material and wardship

Children proceedings and the inherent jurisdiction

15.23 In *Re K (Infants)*,[16] the House of Lords considered whether, in wardship proceedings, they were entitled to deny to a mother access to a medical report which had been prepared specifically for the Official Solicitor. They held that a judge was entitled, as a matter of discretion, to deny access to information to a party, in the interests of a child. Lord Devlin started from 'the ordinary principles of a judicial inquiry' (as had Upjohn LJ in the Court of Appeal):

> They include [said Lord Devlin] the rules that all justice shall be done openly and that it shall be done only after a fair hearing; and also the rule that is in point here, namely, that judgment shall be given only upon evidence that is made known to all parties. Some of these principles are so fundamental that they must be observed by everyone who is acting judicially, whether he is sitting in a court of law or not; and these are called the principles of natural justice. The rule in point here is undoubtedly one of those.

15.24 Lord Devlin explained the difference between the judge who sits – as in most cases – as 'arbiter between two parties'; and where a judge has a duty in respect of the interests (as of a child) of an individual who is 'outside the conflict':[17]

> This is the essence of the matter. Where the judge sits as an arbiter between two parties, he need consider only what they put before him. If one or other omits something material and suffers from the omission, he must blame himself and not the judge. Where the judge sits purely as an arbiter and relies on the parties for his information, the parties have a correlative right that he should act only on information which they have had the opportunity of testing. Where the judge is not sitting purely, or even primarily, as an arbiter but is charged with the paramount duty of protecting the interests of one

14 CPR 1998 r 39.2(3)(b).
15 Ibid r 39.2(3)(d).
16 [1965] AC 201.
17 Ibid at [240]–[241].

outside the conflict, a rule that is designed for just arbitrament cannot in all circumstances prevail.

15.25 Where the interests of a child require it, the position remains as it was in 1965: that the court can restrict disclosure to a party to protect the interest of a third party, the child. A form of CMP can operate where such principles apply; but how far?

Closed material and the High Court

15.26 In the rare event that a CMP order (akin to a closed material declaration in JSA 2013 proceeding) is to be made in family proceedings it is like that the application must be made in proceedings transferred to the Family Division of the High Court?[18] In *Re X, Y and Z (Disclosure to the Security Service)*[19] McDonald J considered, amongst the issues before him, the aptness of, and procedure for, CMPs in family proceedings.

15.27 The case concerned continuing proceedings under CA 1989 Part 4 (care proceedings) concerning a three-year-old child. The local authority obtained an order which enabled them to disclose to the police and the Crown Prosecution Service the mother's statement lodged immediately prior to a hearing to be held in private. The police further applied for permission to disclose the mother's statement and the judgment to the Security Service. The application was not actively opposed in principle but all the parties to the care proceedings contended that any permission should involve the imposition of conditions regulating any onward disclosure by the Security Service.

15.28 In dealing with the question of onward disclosure the judge pointed out that the Security Service was not specified in FPR 2010 r 12.73(1)(a) as a 'person' to whom disclosure of information confidential to family proceedings could be made as of right and therefore the burden lay on the police to demonstrate to the court that the disclosure sought should be permitted.[20] The police therefore needed to seek permission to disclose to the Security Service a copy of the mother's statement and a copy of the judgment. It was not necessary to impose conditions regarding the handling of documents by the Security Service internally, it was appropriate to impose a condition that the Security Service apply for the court's permission if it intended to disclose beyond itself. Were that to occur, it might become necessary for the Service to seek a CMP to pass on information outside itself.

15.29 As to the possible need for a procedure for closed material should the Security Service wish to refer the documents from the proceedings on to others, McDonald explained the position as follows:

---

18 A procedure for a CMP application in family proceedings is proposed in *Family Court Practice* at Procedural Guide F7.

19 [2016] EWHC 2400 (Fam), [2017] 2 FLR 583 sub nom *Commissioner of Police of the Metropolis v A Local Authority and others* [2016] 4 WLR 153, McDonald J.

20 Ibid at [19]–[20].

> [89] My decision raises the possibility of the Security Service needing to make an application to this court for permission to disclose the material outside the Service. Whilst such applications are ordinarily straightforward, as set out above, given the nature of the Security Service and its manner of operation, an application in this context presents specific potential difficulties. In particular, the practice of neither confirming nor denying an interest or involvement means that it is unlikely that the Security Service will wish to give notice of such an application in circumstances where, in some situations, simply confirming or denying that an agency is interested in information or seeks information will result in risk that that agency will disclose its interest in, or alert suspects. In addition, the nature of the disclosure sought means that it is likely the Security Service will thereafter wish to adopt a closed procedure. Given the impact of these contentions on the Art 6 rights of the parties, they will need to be the subject of rigorous examination by the court …

Closed material: a procedure

15.30 That said MacDonald J went on to explain how he envisaged that any CMP application could proceed. He set out the analogy with JSA 2013 and CPR 1998 Part 82:

> [92] As to the applicable principles for determining whether a closed procedure should be adopted (if requested), the Justice and Security Act 2013 s 6(11) provides for the making of a declaration in any proceedings (other than proceedings in a criminal cause or matter) before the High Court that the proceedings are proceedings in which a closed material application may be made to the court. No such provision is made however, in respect of proceedings in the Family Court. Further, the rules of court which govern the determination of an application for such a declaration, and any subsequent closed material application are those set out in the CPR Part 82. By CPR r 2.1(2), CPR Part 82 does not apply to family proceedings and CPR Part 82 is not otherwise incorporated into the FPR 2010.

15.31 He explained that there was a history of what amounts to closed material procedures in the family courts. The likelihood is that by paragraphs [92] to [94] of his judgment he was intending to say that MCP orders in family proceedings should be made in the High Court. A procedure derived from JSA 2013 and CPR 1998 Part 82 is proposed by *Family Court Practice* at Procedural Guide F7.[21]

15.32 In his review of the procedural position McDonald J made particular reference to the following:

- *Re T (Wardship: Impact of Police Intelligence)* [2010] 1 FLR 1048 at [31] to [34] and [112];[22]

21 It will be noted that MacDonald J and this author are both contributors to *Family Court Practice*.

22 *Re T* is considered in full in Part 6 of this chapter.

- *BCC v FZ, AZ, HZ and TVP* [2013] 1 FLR 974 at [13] to [48]);
- *A Chief Constable v YK and Others,*[23] in which, whilst the court declined the use of special advocates, Sir Nicholas Wall P observed that 'there will be undoubtedly be circumstances in family proceedings in which they are appropriate'.

15.33 He concluded by mentioning the President's Guidance entitled *Radicalisation Cases in the Family Courts* dated 8 October 2015 and the President's Guidance entitled *The Role of the Attorney General in Appointing Advocates to the Court of Special Advocates in Family Cases* dated 26 March 2016, both of which contemplate the use of closed hearings and special advocates in family proceedings.

Case management of closed material cases in family proceedings

15.34 McDonald J concluded his judgment with suggestions for case management of a case involving an application for closed material by the Security Service:[24]

(1) Is the application properly made (as it was here, and as may often be the case) without notice in the first instance? The application should contain brief reasons for seeking to pursue the application initially without notice to the parties by reference to the principles.[25]

(2) Whether the application is appropriate to be dealt with by means of the use of a closed procedure utilising special advocates having regard to the guidance set out in the cases referred to in 15.32 (above).

(3) Any further directions for the hearing having regard to the court's decision in respect of the foregoing matters, again having regard the guidance in the authorities set out at (2).

3 CLOSED MATERIAL PROCEDURES IN CIVIL PROCEEDINGS

Prevention of access to disclosed documents

15.35 CMPs arise mostly in cases where damage to national security is alleged; and to this end CPR 1998 has been amended to include Part 82 (entitled 'Closed Material Procedure', in operation from June 2013) which is in support of JSA 2013. However, CMPs may arise in other proceedings where state or other private interests are threatened and where a party has access to highly sensitive information which needs to be produced in court; but from which one or more parties, says the applicant, must be excluded.

23 *A Chief Constable v YK and Others* [2010] EWHC 2438 (Fam) [2011] 1 FLR 1493, Sir Nicholas Wall P at [112].

24 Ibid at [95].

25 *Re S (Ex Parte Orders)* [2001] 1 FLR 308, *KY v DD* [2012] 2 FLR 200, and *Re C (A Child)* [2013] EWCA Civ 1412.

15.36 Such exclusion may arise in children proceedings where a child's welfare or the safety of a party to proceedings[26] is at risk if confidential material is produced. It may arise where forced marriage or female genital mutilation is in issue, and material from the police of security services is wanted to be produced but not be seen by one or both of the parents.

15.37 To deal with restriction on production of documents which such a procedure demands, CPR 1998 r 82.2 (in the context of JSA 2013) requires that for purposes of JSA 2013, the overriding objective in CPR 1998 r 1.1 'be read and given effect to in a way which is compatible'[27] with CPR 1998 r 82.2(2). Rule 82.2(2) provides as follows:

(2) The court must ensure that information is not disclosed in a way which would be damaging to the interests of national security.

Closed material procedures in civil proceedings: closed material declaration

15.38 A short introduction to the framework of CMPs under JSA 2013 will be provided here, only to show how the process works under the 2013 Act and to the extent that that operation is analogous to family proceedings. An application for a closed material declaration, where application is made by the government (whether or not a party to the proceedings) or one of the parties are such that a closed material application can be made:[28] that is to say, an application within the terms of CPR 1998 Part 82 and JSA 2013 section 6(2).

6 Declaration permitting closed material applications in proceedings

(1) The court seised of relevant civil proceedings may make a declaration that the proceedings are proceedings in which a closed material application may be made to the court.

(2) The court may make such a declaration—

(a) on the application of—

(i) the Secretary of State (whether or not the Secretary of State is a party to the proceedings), or

(ii) any party to the proceedings, or

(b) of its own motion.

15.39 If both the conditions in section 6(3) and (4) then are met in relation to material which should otherwise be disclosed in proceedings,[29] JSA 2013 section

26 See eg, *Re T (Wardship: Impact of Police Intelligence)* [2009] EWHC 2440 (Fam), [2010] 1 FLR 1048, McFarlane J (police believed there was a credible threat to the life of the mother of the wards); considered below at 15.67.

27 CPR 1998 r 82.2(1).

28 JSA 2013 s 6(2).

29 Ibid s 6(6).

6(2) permits the court to make a closed material declaration.[30] The conditions which are required to be met are set out in JSA 2013 section 6(4) and (5). JSA 2013 section 6(3)–(5) states (as amended) as follows:

(3) The court may make such a declaration if it considers that the following two conditions are met.

(4) The first condition is that—

(a) a party to the proceedings would be required to disclose sensitive material in the course of the proceedings to another person (whether or not another party to the proceedings), …

(5) The second condition is that it is in the interests of the fair and effective administration of justice in the proceedings to make a declaration.

15.40 Application for a closed material declaration can only be made in 'relevant civil proceedings' which means 'any proceedings (other than proceedings in a criminal cause or matter)' in the High Court, Court of Appeal or Supreme Court.[31] A consequence of a closed material declaration is that the court will give notice of the declaration to the Attorney-General who then has power to appoint a special advocate.[32] But to what extent are the procedures under JSA 2013 and CPR 1998 Part 82 in any way helpful in the context of children proceedings?

Conditions for allowing a closed material procedure

15.41 Any order which completely restricts access of a party to documents seen by the court and by other parties will need to comply with these conditions. Each case will depend on its own facts, and will be assessed by an exacting proportionality and rationality test as explained by Lord Sumption in *Bank Mellat v Her Majesty's Treasury (No 2)*:[33]

> [20] The requirements of rationality and proportionality, as applied to decisions engaging the human rights of applicants, inevitably overlap. [That is] the question depends on an exacting analysis of the factual case advanced in defence of the measure, in order to determine (i) whether its objective is sufficiently important to justify the limitation of a fundamental right; (ii) whether it is rationally connected to the objective; (iii) whether a less intrusive measure could have been used; and (iv) whether, having regard to these matters and to the severity of the consequences, a fair balance has been struck between the rights of the individual and the interests of the community. These four requirements are logically separate, but in practice they inevitably overlap because the same facts are likely to be relevant to more than one of them.

30 Ibid s 6(3)–(5).
31 Ibid s 6(11).
32 JSA 2013 s 9(1); CPR 1998 r 82.9(1).
33 [2013] UKSC 39, [2014] 1 AC 700.

15.42 That is to say, in outline: does the CMP means justify the non-disclosure end, having regard to the incursion on open justice principles which will result if a closed material declaration is made?

4 DISCLOSURE TO LEGAL REPRESENTATIVES ONLY

Disclosure only to a legal representative

15.43 Is it sufficient to allow for release of documents to a legal representative? This is still being permitted in family courts. So far as it is happening, it is probably unlawful.[34]

15.44 The question was considered in *Browning v The Information Commissioner & Anor,*[35] where the Court of Appeal heard an appeal from the Upper Tribunal (Administrative Appeals Chamber)[36] by a journalist Jonathan Browning.[37] The appeal was against a refusal of the Information Commissioner to permit disclosure of information to Mr Browning because, said the Commissioner, it was not in the public interest that it should be disclosed. The question on appeal was whether the court (ie, Upper Tribunal, in the particular case) could see material that neither the appellant nor his representative could see.

15.45 Neither the statute under which the tribunals are set up nor their rules[38] provide expressly for a CMP. And, as Maurice Kay LJ acknowledged, the case was concerned with 'part of the substantive hearing' before the tribunal:

> [32] ... the present case is not concerned with public interest immunity. Nor is it concerned with an interlocutory determination of what may or may not form part of a trial. The closed session with which we are concerned was part of the substantive hearing.

15.46 In *Browning,* Mr Browning accepted that he should himself be excluded from sight of the material. The decision related to whether the material could be seen only by his legal representative, subject to the representative giving an undertaking not to disclose confidential material to his or her client.[39] Though the case did not directly concern closed material procedures it did relate to a particular means, sometimes used by courts, of limiting disclosure, or of preventing a party, personally, from seeing material.

---

34 *Somerville and others v Scottish Ministers (HM Advocate General for Scotland Intervening)* [2007] UKHL 44, [2007] 1 WLR 2734, considered further at 15.48.

35 [2014] EWCA Civ 1050, [2014] 1 WLR 3848.

36 The unsuccessful appeal to the Court of Appeal was from the Upper Tribunal (UKUT 236 AC) consisting of Charles J, then President of the Chamber, Mitting J and Upper Tribunal Judge Andrew Bartlett QC.

37 Maurice Kay LJ described Mr Browning is a 'respected journalist'.

38 Tribunals, Courts and Enforcement Act 2007 and Tribunal Procedure (First-tier Tribunal)(General Regulatory Chamber) Rules 2009.

39 As had been the case, said the Court of Appeal (at §[8]), *British Union for the Abolition of Vivisection v ICO and anor* EA 2010/0064.

15.47 Maurice Kay LJ gave judgment based on the question of whether Mr Browning's legal representative should be excluded from seeing the undisclosed documents, which the court would see. He found[40] that the rules under the Tribunals, Courts and Enforcement Act 2007 did permit the procedure used in this case to exclude the appellant and his legal representative. But, he said, courts were generally averse to allowing lawyers to have access to documents which they could not disclose to their client. It was not appropriate for a legal representative only to see documents from which his or her client was excluded. He continued:

> [32] Our Courts have shown an aversion to permitting counsel to see or hear evidence which he is not at liberty to disclose to his client. In the context of criminal litigation, this is illustrated by *R v Davis* [1993] 1 WLR 613, 616 to 617, per Lord Taylor CJ; *R v Preston* [1994] 2 AC 130 at 152–153, per Lord Mustill; and *R v G* [2004] 1 WLR 2932, at paragraph 13, per Rose LJ.

15.48 However, said Maurice Kay LJ, this approach of courts being unwilling to let advocates see documents which their clients may not see, can arise also in civil litigation. The point was dealt with by Lord Rodger in *Somerville v Scottish Ministers*:[41] [42]

> [152] In terms of an agreement contained in a "protocol", under conditions of the strictest confidentiality, senior counsel for the petitioners was allowed to inspect the complete versions of the documents for which the respondents were claiming public interest immunity. Although devised with the best of intentions, this procedure was, in my view, wrong in principle. As a result, it not only gave rise to very real practical difficulties but led the court to adopt a mistaken approach to the inspection of the documents by the [judge].
>
> [153] If the respondents claim that, in the public interest, the redacted parts of the documents should not be revealed was valid, then, in normal course, it was valid against counsel … who should therefore not have seen the full version. As it was, counsel … was left in a very difficult situation where, as a result of reading the documents, he had information that he was not able to reveal to, or discuss with, his clients or instructing solicitors. He even felt inhibited from revealing it to the [judge].

15.49 Lord Rodger concluded:[43] 'In agreement with all of your Lordships, I am satisfied that no such procedure should be followed in future.' Advocates should not see documents in circumstances where their clients are not permitted access to those documents.

---

40 Ibid at [28].

41 *Somerville v Scottish Ministers (Scotland)* [2007] UKHL 44, [2007] 1 WLR 2734.

42 And see Lord Mance at [203].

43 *Somerville v Scottish Ministers (Scotland)* at [153].

Restricted material and HI

15.50 In *Local Authority X v HI and Others*[44] the court – Russell J and Holman J, respectively – set up what amounted to a closed material procedure to try a preliminary issue. The issue was: should evidence – which might or might not be relevant to an issue in care proceedings concerning HI – be disclosed to all parties, including the child's parents, by the local authority. HI (known as 'I' in the judgment) did not want the material seen by his father and step-mother. They were confidential as between him and the local authority worker to whom they had been released.

15.51 HI, a 15-year-old – nearly 16 – was involved in care proceedings. He had said things to professionals which he wanted them to be prevented from disclosing to his father and step-mother, with whom he had previously been living. They were parties to the care proceedings. They pressed for disclosure. So far as the evidence was relevant to an issue before the court they would normally be entitled to it. The question was: could they be prevented from seeing it?

15.52 On release of the case to her by Holman J, Russell J considered an application by his guardian on behalf of HI for withholding of the evidence (FPR 2010 r 21.3: the thrust of the case is blunted, since Russell J thought the evidence to be of only tangential relevance; and its disclosure could have been refused on that ground alone); and from the local authority as to whether they should pass on the information in any event. HI wanted what he had said to remain confidential.

Withholding disclosure as a preliminary issue

15.53 The preliminary issue was set up in the following way (Holman J was to be the judge who tried the ultimate care application):

> [10] When the matter came before Holman J on 18 April 2016, none of the three respondents had been given notice of the guardian's application. In those circumstances, and following the guidance given in *Re M (Disclosure)* [1998] 2 FLR 1028 and *Official Solicitor to the Supreme Court v K and Another* [1965] AC 201, (1963) FLR Rep 520,[45] the matter was adjourned to today on the basis that the respondents would be served with notice of the application. In accordance with the practice recommended in those authorities, his Lordship directed that the papers were to be released to counsel instructed to attend today but on the basis that those legal representatives should not disclose the papers or the information contained in them to their respective clients. Pending adjudication of the issue, the local authority were ordered not to disclose the information to any of the respondents.

44 [2016] EWHC 1123 (Fam), [2017] 1 FLR 1362, Russell J.

45 *Re K (Infants)* [1965] AC 201, also *Official Solicitor to Supreme Court v K* [1963] 3 WLR 408, (1963) FLR Rep 520.

15.54 The 'guidance given by *Re M*[46] etc' (referred to in the above passage), with respect to Russell J, has been overtaken by FPR 2010 r 21.3, and by such cases as *Browning* and the jurisprudence in relation to closed procedures[47] (which she was in effect operating). *Re M* turned on whether the judge should have heard from the party to whom material was not to be disclosed (in this case the parents). That the judge should have heard from that party before making the order is clear from, for example, Pill LJ (who sat with Thorpe LJ):[48]

> It is essential that any party to whom it is proposed information is not to be revealed should have the opportunity of making representations to the court. In *Re C (Disclosure)* [1996] 1 FLR 797 Johnson J stated at 801F that: '... the procedure in each case will be determined by the court in the light of the particular circumstances and demands of the particular case.'

15.55 A procedure for dealing with FPR 2010 r 21.3 applications in proceedings is set out in Chapter 11.

Information and the advocates only

15.56 It can be seen that the judge and all parties' lawyers, but not the lay adult parties, had read H's information; but on terms that the lawyers could not discuss the content of the information with their clients. It was, in a sense, a de facto closed material procedure with the parties' lawyers doubling up as special advocates.

15.57 The position of the parties was that HI (represented by his guardian throughout), supported by his mother, opposed inspection by his parents. Inspection (ie, so they had copies) was pressed for by the father and stepmother. The local authority sought the judge's 'guidance' as to whether the information should be passed on. It is a feature of the case that it seems to have been dealt with without reference to rules or common law as to the court's powers to restrict disclosure; or to permit advocates only – and to the exclusion of their clients – to see documents under consideration by the judge. For example, if the jurisprudence on release to parties' advocates only referred to above[49] was submitted to the judge it is not referred to in her judgment; nor, it seems, was she referred to FPR 2010 r 21.3 and the case law considered in Chapter 11 Part 3.

15.58 The judge took account of the fact that H was *Gillick*-competent. His views 'deserve the court's respect' ([60]); but he was but one party in relation to the disclosure issue. The rights of his parents, affected by her decision, must be taken into account.

46 *Re M (Disclosure)* [1998] 2 FLR 1028.

47 See Part 2 of this chapter.

48 *Re M (Disclosure)* at [1033].

49 See eg, *Somerville and others v Scottish Ministers (HM Advocate General for Scotland intervening)* [2007] UKHL 44, [2007] 1 WLR 2734; *Browning v The Information Commissioner & Anor* [2014] EWCA Civ 1050, [2014] 1 WLR 3848.

Non-disclosure and Article 6 rights

15.59 As to the parents' Article 6 rights (ie, to see the documents): Russell J had the jurisprudence discussed by Lord Bingham and Lady Hale in *MB* [50] and by Munby J in *Re B* in mind when she said:

> [58] ... The [parents'] rights to a fair trial are, of course, absolute but, as Hale LJ acknowledged in *Re X*,[51] in deciding how to conduct a fair trial, it is perfectly reasonable to take account of the facts and circumstances of the particular case with which the court is dealing. The concept of a fair trial is inviolable but the *content* (including the evidence) which is placed before the court is flexible and depends upon context and the issues with which the court is dealing. Whilst I accept that any departure from the usual requirements in relation to the disclosure of evidence in an adversarial trial must be for a legitimate aim and proportionate to that aim, the Court of Appeal has held that protecting the welfare of vulnerable young persons is a specific and undoubtedly a legitimate aim.

15.60 Thus, the procedure for the fair trial will normally depend on the facts of the particular case; and the procedure adopted must be proportionate to its aims. The right to a fair trial was absolute, but denying the father and step-mother access to the information here – even so far as it was relevant – would not deprive them of a fair trial. The harm which would be caused to HI would, said Russell J, be 'wholly disproportionate to any legitimate forensic purposes served'.[52]

5 SPECIAL ADVOCATES

Special advocates and the Justice and Security Act 2013

Special advocates to the court

15.61 The Justice and Security Act (JSA) 2013 section 9 enables the Attorney-General to appoint a qualified lawyer 'to represent the interests of a party in

50 *Secretary of State for the Home Department v MB* [2007] UKHL 46 [2008] 1 AC 440, [2007] 3 WLR 681, considered above at 15.79.

51 *Re X (Adoption: Confidential Procedure)* [2002] EWCA Civ 828, [2002] 2 FLR 476: a case where prospective adopters, who were known to the natural parents, nevertheless wanted their adoption to be anonymous. Of the fair trial aspect, Hale LJ said: '[13] Unlike the right to respect for family and private life in Art 8, the right to a fair trial in Art 6 is absolute and unqualified. But the content of a fair trial in any particular case is more flexible and depends upon the context: as Lord Bingham of Cornhill said in *Brown v Stott (Procurator Fiscal, Dunfermline) and Another* [2001] 2 WLR 817, at 824: "What a fair trial requires cannot, however, be the subject of a single unvarying rule or collection of rules. It is proper to take account of the facts and circumstances of particular cases, as the European Court has consistently done." Departures from the usual requirements of an adversarial trial must, of course, be for a legitimate aim and proportionate to that aim. Protecting the welfare of these very vulnerable children is undoubtedly a legitimate aim.'

52 Ibid at [59].

any [closed material declaration application] from which the party (and any legal representative of the party) is excluded'.[53] The person 'appointed as a special advocate is not responsible to the party to the proceedings whose interests the person is appointed to represent'.[54]

15.62 CPR 1998 Part 82 Section II provides a procedure for appointment of a special advocate in civil proceedings.[55] FPR 2010, not surprisingly, provides no such procedure. A procedure analogous to that in CPR 1998 Part 82 may work for children proceedings. Where application for a closed material declaration is made on behalf of a government department or a party to proceedings the Attorney-General will be notified.[56] The Attorney-General can then give consideration under JSA 2013 section 9(1) to arrangements for representation of the specially represented party.

15.63 The functions of the special advocate of are to 'represent the interests of the specially represented party',[57] and are defined by CPR 1998 r 82.10 as follows:

> **82.10 Functions of a special advocate**
>
> The functions of a special advocate are to represent the interests of a specially represented party by—
>
> (a) making submissions to the court at any hearing or part of a hearing from which the specially represented party and the specially represented party's legal representatives are excluded;
>
> (b) adducing evidence and cross-examining witnesses at any such hearing or part of a hearing;
>
> (c) making applications to the court or seeking directions from the court where necessary; and
>
> (d) making written submissions to the court.

---

53 JSA 2013 s 9(1).

54 Ibid s 9(4); and cf the duties of the advocate to the court appointed in civil proceedings: *Memorandum of 19 December 2001*, para 4: the 'advocate to the court represents no one'.

55 The *Attorney-General's Memorandum of 19 December 2001*is silent on the subject of appointment of special advocates. The President's guidance of 25 March 2015 explains that appointment is by a separate procedure: '*Special Advocates* – These are not the subject of [25 March 2015 guidance], or any, Memorandum. Usually a Special Advocate is required because a public body that is party to the litigation, often a local authority or the police, resists disclosure of sensitive documents. The Attorney General has asked that at the point of requesting him to instruct a Special Advocate the court should specifically consider and make provision (after, of course, hearing submissions from the parties) as to which party should pay the costs of the Special Advocate. The essential point is that this is not a service which the Attorney General will normally cover ...'

56 CPR 1998 r 82.9(1).

57 But note the assertion in JSA 2013 s 9(4) that the 'special advocate is not responsible to the party to the proceedings whose interests the person is appointed to represent'.

Sensitive material

15.64 CPR 1998 r 82.11 defines how a special advocate can communicate about the proceedings, and depends on the date on which a 'relevant person'[58] serves the material – 'the sensitive material'[59] – in respect of which a declaration is claimed. Before service of the material, the special advocate is permitted to communicate with the represented party. CPR 1998 r 82.11(1) and (2) provide as follows:

> **82.11 Special advocate: communicating about proceedings**
>
> (1) The special advocate may communicate with the specially represented party or the specially represented party's legal representative at any time before a relevant person serves sensitive material on the special advocate.
>
> (2) After the relevant person serves sensitive material on the special advocate, the special advocate must not communicate with any person about any matter connected with the proceedings, except [as provided in r 82.11] …

15.65 The remainder of CPR 1998 r 82.11 deals with:

- with whom the special advocate may communicate, without direction of the court (r 82.11(3): eg the court, the relevant person or (where different) the government representative);
- the fact that the special advocate may seek directions from the court to communicate with the specially represented party or his/her representative (r 82.11(4)); and in that case the court must notify the Secretary of State and the relevant person; and
- the fact that the specially represented party may communicate with the advocate after service, but only 'in writing through the specially represented party's legal representative'; and the special advocate can only reply as directed by the court (r 82.11(6)).

'Scepticism and stringency'

15.66 The role of the special advocate in JSA 2013 is defined in CPR 1998 r 82.10 (set out in the Appendix to this chapter). The House of Lords has urged[60] *scepticism on the part of special advocates and of the judges who are asked to make a closed material declaration:*

> [66] The [applicant] must give as full as possible an explanation of why she considers that the grounds [for a declaration] are made out. The

---

58 JSA 2013 s 6(8) defines a 'relevant person' – eg the police in *Re T (Wardship: Impact of Police Intelligence)* [2009] EWHC 2440 (Fam), [2010] 1 FLR 1048 – as the person who held the material in respect of which a declaration under s 6 was to be sought.

59 'Sensitive material' under JSA 2013 s 6(11) is material the disclosure of which – under JSA 2013 – would be damaging to the interests of national security.

60 *Secretary of State for the Home Department v MB* [2007] UKHL 46, [2008] 1 AC 440 per Lady Hale.

> fuller the explanation given, the fuller the instructions that the special advocates will be able to take from the client before they see the closed material. Both judge and special advocates will have to probe the claim that the closed material should remain closed with great care and considerable scepticism ... Both judge and special advocates will have stringently to test the material which remains closed. All must be alive to the possibility that material could be redacted or gisted in such a way as to enable the special advocates to seek the client's instructions upon it ... The nature of the case may be such that the client does not need to know all the details of the evidence in order to make an effective challenge.

Special advocate and children proceedings

Special advocate and Re T

15.67 In *Re T (Wardship: Impact of Police Intelligence)*[61] McFarlane J explained his view of the role of the special advocate in wardship proceedings; and on the basis of the case law then available (the judgment is dated 7 October 2009).[62] He drew, in particular, on *Secretary of State for the Home Department v MB*[63] and the speech of Lady Hale. He referred to the speech of Lord Hoffman (in which there are echoes, perhaps, of Lord Devlin in *Re K (Infants)*[64] and of the question of limiting access to disclosed material): that there may be interests other than those of the parties only, to consider in a CMP decision:

> [54] ... From the point of view of the individual seeking to challenge the order [the special advocate procedure] is of course imperfect. But the Strasbourg Court has recognised that the right to be informed of the case against one, though important, may have to be qualified in the interests of others and the public interest ...

15.68 In *Re T (Wardship: Impact of Police Intelligence)*[65] a child, aged five at the time of the hearing, had been made a ward of court when he was taken to India by the father (F), but without the mother's (M) consent. F returned with the child to England two years later. Neither he nor his solicitors[66] disclosed the child's whereabouts to the court. The child was ultimately recovered by the police. F applied for contact from prison. His parents also applied for contact.

15.69 On the day that a directions hearing was to take place, the police informed the family judge that there was credible intelligence that F had taken

61 [2009] EWHC 2440 (Fam), [2010] 1 FLR 1048, McFarlane J.

62 Ibid at [19]–[28].

63 [2007] UKHL 46, [2008] 1 AC 440 (to what extent can the Special Immigration Appeals Commission restrict access to materials before them).

64 [1965] AC 201 at [240]–[241].

65 [2009] EWHC 2440 (Fam), [2010] 1 FLR 1048, McFarlane J.

66 There was no general duty, absent a court order, requiring solicitors to disclose information as to the whereabouts of a ward, in breach of the duty of confidentiality owed to a client: paras [102]–[105].

out a contract to have M murdered when she came to the hearing. The police had therefore decided to take M and the child into police protection. This protection would be withdrawn if interim contact was ordered. The police initially requested that none of this information be disclosed to F, his family or any of the family's representatives. The court was required to investigate these allegations, whilst at the same time affording due protection to their material, which the police asserted must, in the public interest, remain confidential and undisclosed to the parties and, crucially, undisclosed to their representatives.

15.70 Special advocates were appointed for F and his family – possibly for the first time in family proceedings, said the judge – to see the police material, and with that information then to represent the interests of F and his parents at the closed hearings. They filtered the evidence, whose disclosure was resisted by the police. Following a proper evaluation by the court, the police eventually agreed to disclose the great bulk of its material at the non-closed fact-finding hearing; though certain information concerning the original intelligence as to the contract remained closed and known only to the judge and the special advocates throughout the process.

Special advocate and wardship

15.71 In wardship the family court had always had a duty to investigate all of the relevant circumstances that might touch upon the ward's future welfare, the wardship court could, unlike a criminal court, receive anonymous, hearsay evidence. For the Family Division the question was the weight which could be given to such material. McFarlane J explained this as follows:

> [89] [The court's] investigation must include receiving evidence, even if it is anonymous, hearsay evidence from an unknown individual, as part of the process. Thus, for the wardship court, it is not a case that a certain category of evidence cannot be acceptable or must be excluded, rather, it is a question of what weight is to be attached to that evidence when the court comes to evaluate it. During the exercise of determining the weight to be given to material ..., the principles underpinning the House of Lords decision in *R v Davis*[67] will be of substantial relevance and may well be determinative, but the issue will be weight rather than admissibility.

---

67 In *R v Davis* [2008] UKHL 36, [2008] 1 AC 1128, [2008] 3 WLR 125, the House of Lords held that in a criminal trial the use of anonymous evidence was not acceptable and did not satisfy the requirements of European Convention 1950 Art 6. In wardship the judge held (para [89]) there was a 'distinction between the criminal jurisdiction and the wardship jurisdiction'. Unlike the criminal jurisdiction, where the sole issue before the court is determining the guilt or otherwise of the defendant on a particular charge, the wardship court has a duty to investigate all of the relevant circumstances that may touch upon the ward's future welfare. That investigation must include receiving evidence, even if it is anonymous, hearsay evidence from an unknown individual, as part of the process'. For the wardship court 'it is a question of what weight is to be attached to that evidence when the court comes to evaluate it'.

Appointment of special advocate: procedure in Re T

15.72 In *Re T* the procedure[68] favoured by McFarlane J was in wardship. Procedurally there need be no difference between wardship and other children proceedings: either as a FPR 2010 Part 18 application in existing proceedings transferred to the High Court; or as a FPR 2010 Part 19 originating application in the Family Division. As explained by MacDonald J in *Re X, Y and Z (Disclosure to the Security Service),*[69] any application must be before a High Court judge.

15.73 The pre-requisites for any application were summarised by McFarlane J in *Re T*:[70]

(1) The two special advocates retained were 'fully briefed' by the lawyers acting for F and for his parents (the two excluded parties).

(2) The special advocates met their respective lay clients in conference. Thereafter the special advocates had little or no direct contact with the paternal family or their legal representatives.

(3) The parties' representatives remained able at all times to communicate with and pass information to the special advocates.[71]

(4) The special advocates could not communicate with the open parties save with their legal representatives in writing and with the permission of the court.

15.74 The next stage of the process, said the judge, was geared to the special advocates' challenge to the police assertion of public interest immunity:

> [32] ... involved the police disclosing what was thought to be the entirety of their files to the special advocates. There followed a detailed discussion between the special advocates and the police as to which parts of the material could be disclosed to the 'open' parties, the role of the special advocates at this stage being to challenge the assertion of PII made by the MPS.

15.75 It then became possible, as a result of the 'process of the special advocates and the [police] consideration of the detailed material' that the majority of undisclosed material could be disclosed to the 'open parties', and public interest immunity was accepted as being applicable to certain restricted categories of document (eg, to protect arrangements for the mother and to avoid identification of informants).[72] The resulting material in full, redacted or 'gisted' (summarised) could then be disclosed to the open parties; and, said the judge

> [34] ... It is also right to record that this degree of disclosure had been achieved through discussion between the [police] legal team and the

68 A procedure for a CMP is proposed in *Family Court Practice* at Procedural Guide F7.

69 [2016] EWHC 2400 (Fam), [2017] 2 FLR 583 sub nom *Commissioner of Police of the Metropolis v A Local Authority and others* [2016] 4 WLR 153, McDonald J.

70 See especially paras [34]–[37].

71 Cf CPR 1998 r 82.11.

72 *Re T* at [33].

special advocates, and did not at any stage of that process require a ruling from the court on any disclosure issue.

Statutory provision

15.76 As already mentioned, in *Al Rawi & Ors v The Security Service & Ors*[73] it was held by the Supreme Court that, in the absence of statutory authority, it was not open to the courts to set up CMP, including in civil proceedings. In *Secretary of State for the Home Department v MB*,[74] Lady Hale explained why, in her opinion, children proceedings might be different from other civil proceedings in terms of the court being able to order that not all material be disclosed to all parties:

> [57] The object of all legal proceedings is to do justice according to law: but this is easily said and not so easily done. Doing justice means not only arriving at a just result but arriving at it in a just manner. The overriding objective of the Civil Procedure Rules is to enable the court to deal with cases justly: CPR r. 1.1(1). Of the fundamental importance of the right to a fair trial there can be no doubt. But there is equally no doubt that the essential ingredients of a fair trial can vary according to the subject matter and nature of the proceedings.

15.77 Thus, though the requirements of fairness in given case vary according to the issues for hearing, the basic requirements remain: to know the case against that party, and to have an opportunity of meeting it – so long as the principle serves the justice of the case. As Lord Devlin in the House of Lords stressed in *Re K (Infants)*:[75] a procedural rule must be the servant of justice, not its master:

> ... a principle of judicial inquiry, whether fundamental or not, is only a means to an end. If it can be shown in any particular class of case that the observance of a principle of this sort does not serve the ends of justice, it must be dismissed: otherwise it would become the master instead of the servant of justice.

Best interests of children: special circumstances

15.78 If the requirement is to promote the best interests of a child, there might be exceptional circumstances where disclosure might harm the child. In *MB* Lady Hale continued:

> [58] The basic requirement is to know the case against one and to have an opportunity of meeting it. But in *In re K (Infants)* [1963] Ch 381, 405, Upjohn LJ identified more detailed principles of a judicial inquiry: "the right to see all the information put before the judge, to comment on it, to challenge it and if needs be to combat it, and to try to establish by

73 [2011] UKSC 34 [2012] AC 531.
74 [2007] UKHL 46, [2008] 1 AC 440.
75 [1965] AC 201 at 238.

> contrary evidence that it is wrong." However, as Lord Devlin pointed out in the same case in the House of Lords, at [1965] AC 201, 238 [per passage cited above]. If, as in that case, the whole object of the proceedings is to protect and promote the best interests of a child, there may be exceptional circumstances in which disclosure of some of the evidence would be so detrimental to the child's welfare as to defeat the object of the exercise: the modern principles are explained in *In re D (Minors)(Adoption Reports: Confidentiality)* [1996] AC 593, [1995] 2 FLR 687.

15.79 As Lady Hale says: modern principles for limits on disclosure are set out in *Re D (Minors) (Adoption Reports: Confidentiality)*,[76] by Lord Mustill in the House of Lords. *Re D* was an adoption case in which the question of whether a mother should see a section of a report in the proceedings relating to the children's wishes and feelings was in question. The judge held as a matter of his discretion that she should not. The House of Lords said the wider principles of openness, even within the privacy of adoption proceedings, should have been taken into account by the judge. They sent the case back for him to reconsider. Lord Mustill (who gave the only reasoned opinion) commented:

> For my part I have no hesitation in saying that a strong presumption in favour of disclosing to a party any material relating to him or her is the point at which the judge should start. It is true, as frequently emphasised, that the requirements of natural justice are not invariable, and that circumstances must alter cases. Nevertheless the opportunity to know about and respond to adverse materials is at the heart of a fair hearing. Adoption is an unusual process, but it calls for fairness as much as any other, and indeed with special intensity, for the reasons already given.

15.80 It remains the case that in the interests of a child special procedures may be set up to prevent a party to children proceedings – it may be a parent, but it could be another family member who is a party to the case – having full access to material seen by the court and by other parties.[77] 'Very powerful' arguments will be needed to justify the extreme step of a CMP.[78]

76 [1996] AC 593, sub nom *Re D (Adoption Reports: Confidentiality)* [1995] 2 FLR 687, HL.

77 See eg, *D (Minors)(Adoption Reports: Confidentiality)* [1996] AC 593, [1995] 2 FLR 687; *Secretary of State for the Home Department v MB* [2007] UKHL 46, [2008] 1 AC 440; *Re T (Wardship: Impact of Police Intelligence)* [2009] EWHC 2440 (Fam), [2010] 1 FLR 1048, McFarlane J.

78 *Re A (Sexual Abuse: Disclosure)* [2012] UKSC 60, [2013] 1 FLR 948 per Lady Hale at [34].

16

PUBLIC INTEREST IMMUNITY

1 INTRODUCTION

Public interest immunity and 'privilege'

16.1 In *Duncan v Cammell Laird,*[1] Lord Simon pointed out that what was then known as 'Crown privilege', now public interest immunity (PII), was not properly a branch of the law of privilege at all. It was a 'rule that the interests of the state must not be put in jeopardy by production of documents'. It is not therefore, properly part of the subject of privilege. It is included here for completeness' sake; so that, it can be called upon, if need be, to protect the confidentiality of public body documents; and to contrast its role from that of a closed material procedure (CMP).[2]

16.2 Public interest immunity is a rule which can be called into play by the court (if need be) 'even though no objection [to disclosure] is taken at all' by the party entitled to seek the immunity.[3] Lord Simon explained the distinction between privilege and PII: the former is for the protection of the individual litigant. It can be waived by him or her. However, a rule that the interests of the state require protection if documents were disclosed was a matter of public law and related to the administration of justice. It was unconnected with the private law interests of parties to court proceedings which define privilege.

Claims to immunity in civil proceedings

16.3 CPR 1998 r 31.19 and FPR 2010 r 21.3 (which is derived from r 31.19) both deal with an application to withhold the disclosure of documents which the applicant claims are covered by PII. This procedure is the same as for documents covered by privilege and confidentiality and are considered fully in Chapter 11; save that in the case of PII it is for the body seeking the immunity to apply to the court to withhold disclosure (rather than, as with privilege) for the party seeking production of documents to apply.

1 [1942] AC 624.
2 See Chapter 15.
3 [1942] AC 624 at 641.

16.4 This chapter proceeds as follows:

- Part 2 defines the modern law (staring from *ex parte Wiley*) and traces the extent to which it applies in family proceedings, starting from the premise that full disclosure is the general rule to which PII is a significant exception.
- Part 3 deals with PII: public and private interests.
- Part 4 considers immunity – such as it is – for informers who provide information to public bodies.
- Part 5 looks at evidence required of non-parties (eg, the police of Home Office) and how application may be made by those non-parties for immunity.

Public interest immunity and closed material procedures contrasted

16.5 The subject of a CMP (which can follow from a PII claim) is dealt with separately in Chapter 15. It is emphasised here, as in Chapter 15, that if PII is ordered only the party with the material covered by PII sees it; whereas in a CMP it is only the excluded party (and just possibly his or her special advocate) who does not see material. At least with a CMP the judge and other parties to the case see the sensitive material.

2 PUBLIC INTEREST IMMUNITY

Public interests: confidentiality balanced against justice

16.6 The foundation of the modern law on public interest immunity was laid by *R v Chief Constable of the West Midlands, ex p Wiley*[4] ('*ex p Wiley*'). The main speech in *exp Wiley* was given by Lord Woolf; but in a short introductory speech Lord Templeman summarised the law on PII and disclosure (then 'discovery'). He stressed the concern of the courts to balance the public interest in preserving confidentiality of material as against that of 'securing justice'.

16.7 Disclosure – that is to say openness – must be the starting point in all cases. Specific documents may be immune from disclosure, but each document will generally be expected to be assessed for importance as against disclosure or of harm to the public interest, if disclosed. Lord Templeman explained this:[5]

> If public interest immunity is approached by every litigant on the basis that a relevant and material document must be disclosed unless the disclosure will cause substantial harm to the public interest, the distinction between a class claim and a contents claim loses much of its significance. As a general rule the harm to the public interest of the disclosure of the whole or part of a document dealing with defence or national security or diplomatic secrets will

4 [1994] UKHL 8, [1995] AC 274.
5 At [1995] AC 274, 281.

be self-evident and will preclude disclosure. On the other hand it is difficult to see how the disclosure of documents generated by the activities of the Police Complaints Authority can cause any harm.

Open justice and a fair trial

16.8 Common law development in the past ten years in the area of disclosure and PII has been influenced considerably by the development of CMPs. In *Bank Mellat v Her Majesty's Treasury (No 1)*,[6] under the heading 'Open justice and natural justice', the common law principle of documents being available in open court to all parties to a case was explained by Lord Neuberger:

> [2] The idea of a court hearing evidence or argument in private is contrary to the principle of open justice, which is fundamental to the dispensation of justice in a modern, democratic society.

16.9 But, said Lord Neuberger, there were 'rare cases' where the court has powers to override open justice – including, as he emphasised, in children cases (see italicised passage below). He continued in *Bank Mellat (No 1)*:

> [2] … However, it has long been accepted that, in rare cases, a court has inherent power to receive evidence and argument in a hearing from which the public and the press are excluded, and that it can even give a judgment which is only available to the parties. Such a course may only be taken (i) if it is strictly necessary to have a private hearing in order to achieve justice between the parties, and, (ii) if the degree of privacy is kept to an absolute minimum … *Examples of such cases include litigation where children are involved*, where threatened breaches of privacy are being alleged, and where commercially valuable secret information is in issue (emphasis added).

Ex p Wiley a starting point: rejection of class immunity

16.10 *Exp Wiley* rejected authoritatively the concept of class – or blanket – immunity for a batch of documents on application by a public body. (Class immunity is to be contrasted with contents immunity, which concerns an immunity claim based on the specific content or subject matter of particular individual documents.) The House of Lords said – as subsequent case law has confirmed – that it will be rare since *ex p Wiley* that PII will apply automatically and merely because a document falls into a class (eg, a social work file or medical records). PII would only be ordered by the court according to the content of each individual document within that class.

16.11 In *Durham County Council v Dunn*[7] Munby LJ confirmed this approach. In a short judgment supplementary to the main judgment he concluded his survey of

---

6 [2013] UKSC 38.
7 [2012] EWCA Civ 1654.

recent case law on PII by commenting, with approval, on Charles J's assessment of the role and function of *ex p Wiley*, as follows:

> [44] … I share Charles J's scepticism as expressed in *Re R (Care: Disclosure: Nature of Proceedings)* [2002] 1 FLR 755. I agree with his observation that: "any case on public interest immunity that precedes *R v Chief Constable of West Midlands Police ex parte Wiley; R v Chief Constable of Nottinghamshire Police ex parte Sunderland* [1995] 1 AC 275 or post-dates it but does not include a careful consideration of that case and the developments in the law and practice relating to public interest immunity that followed should be regarded with caution and carefully reconsidered. For example, in my judgment, that applies to the decision of the Court of Appeal in *Re M (A Minor: Disclosure of Material)* [1990] 2 FLR 36."

Disclosure: identities protected

16.12 In *Durham County Council v Dunn*,[8] the Court of Appeal considered a civil claim arising from the alleged abuse of a person at a young people's centre. The case provides a summary of the application of the rules on disclosure (CPR 1998 Part 31 (ie, FPR 2010 Part 21 in family proceedings)) as distinct from when it might be appropriate to seek information under the Data Protection Act 1998 (DPA 1998), which was how the lawyers for Mr Dunn (D) had approached disclosure in his claim. The case explained why it is almost invariably more appropriate to proceed under CPR 1998 Part 31 (especially once proceedings are issued). (Judgment was handed down in *Durham CC v Dunn* only a day or two before the judgment in the Supreme Court in *Re A (A Child)* (below).)

16.13 D, a former resident of Aycliffe Young People's Centre in County Durham, alleged that he had been abused while he was there. He wanted a disclosure order against the Council seeking information as to the names and other details of those people who may have abused him. His solicitors initially sought information under the DPA 1998. When the information proffered proved inadequate, they applied before the district judge again under the DPA 1998. Redacted disclosure was ordered by the district judge; but he gave both parties permission to appeal. The circuit judge allowed D's appeal and ordered all references to redaction to be removed from the order. The council appealed to the Court of Appeal.

16.14 Maurice Kay LJ looked both at disclosure under CPR 1998 Pt 31 and at the issue of information under the DPA 1998. No application had been made by the council for PII in respect of the documents sought by D.[9] However, Maurice Kay LJ touched on the subject and reviewed disclosure and how it should be approached in the context of the European Convention 1950. He looked for a balance between Article 8 privacy for the staff of the centre (whose names and addresses D was seeking) and a fair trial (Art 6) based on all relevant evidence available to the defendants:

---

8 Ibid.

9 Per CPR 1998 r 31.19.

> [21] … The true position is that CPR 1998 Part 31, read as a whole, enables and requires the court to excuse disclosure or inspection on public interest grounds. In a case such as the present one, it may be misleading to describe the issue as one of [PII] … The requisite balancing exercise is between, on the one hand, a party's right to a fair trial at common law and pursuant to Article 6 of the … (ECHR) and, on the other hand, the rights of his opponent or a non-party to privacy or confidentiality which may most conveniently be protected through the lens of Article 8. It is a distraction to start with the DPA 1998, as the Act itself acknowledges …

16.15 The Court dismissed the appeal (so the claimant got his disclosure); but to protect the identities of non-parties (ie, the names and details sought by the claimant) it protected their privacy by including in the order 'a provision that the identities of non-parties be not disclosed beyond the parties and their legal advisers and that the information to be disclosed be used solely for the purpose of those proceedings until further order …' (para [25]).

'Automatic immunity from production of' local authority records

16.16 Munby LJ explained in *Dunn* that there had been a significant break with previous court procedural management of disclosure in children proceedings occurred in 1990 with *Re M (A Minor) (Disclosure of Material)*.[10] In that case, the Court of Appeal recognised that PII might, in appropriate cases, attach to social work records, but proceeded on the basis that 'the practice of giving automatic immunity from production of such records "needs to be reconsidered"'.[11] If a party sought production of a social work file, whether it should be made available must be reviewed and determined by the court in each case.

16.17 In *R v Hampshire County Council ex parte K and Another*,[12] the Divisional Court considered disclosure of local authority records in the context of care proceedings. There were allegations of sexual abuse against a parent; but the court (Watkins LJ and Waite J) stressed the importance of the interests of the child concerned:

> [37] [The court] emphasised (page 336) the interest of the child "as part and parcel of its general welfare, not only in having its own voice sympathetically heard and its own needs sensitively considered but also in ensuring that its parents are given every proper opportunity of having the evidence fairly tested and preparing themselves in advance to meet the grave charges against them". They went on: "Local authorities therefore have a high duty in law, not only on grounds of general fairness but also in the direct interest of a child whose welfare they serve, to be open in the disclosure of all relevant material affecting that child in their possession or power (excluding documents

10 [1990] 2 FLR 36, CA.

11 Ibid at [43].

12 [1990] 1 FLR 330.

protected on established grounds of public immunity) which may be of assistance to the natural parent or parents in rebutting charges against one or both of them of in any way ill-treating the child."

16.18 Disclosure, said Munby LJ, is not 'simply a binary question: yes or no'. There might be cases where disclosure might be ordered, but subject – as in *Durham v Dunn* – to safeguards, such as:

> [50] ... limiting the use that may be made of the documents and, in particular, safeguards designed to ensure that the release into the public domain of intensely personal information about third parties is strictly limited and permitted only if it has first been anonymised. Disclosure of third-party personal data is permissible only if there are what the Strasbourg court in *Z v Finland* (1998) 25 EHRR 373, paragraph 103, referred to as "effective and adequate safeguards against abuse". An example of an order imposing such safeguards can be found in *A Health Authority v X (Discovery: Medical Conduct)* [2001] 2 FLR 673, 699 (appeal dismissed *A Health Authority v X* [2001] EWCA Civ 2014).

'Key stages' in a public interest immunity application

16.19 In Part 5 the application of the Home Secretary (SSHD) to set aside – or to consider setting aside – an a non-party order in care proceedings based on radicalisation will be considered in *Re C (A Child) (Care Proceedings: Disclosure)*.[13] Here it is relevant to note Pauffley J's approach to the factors relevant to any application – had one been made – by SSHD for a certificate that PII applied to the information they were being ordered to produce into the care proceedings.

16.20 In *Re C*, the Home Department was a non-party to the case. It will be assumed here that the stages in any application by the Department, as contemplated by Pauffley J, would be the same as an application under FPR 2010 r 21.3(1) by a party (generally a public body) to family proceedings.

16.21 The first step, she says, is to assess relevance and materiality of the evidence:

> [14] ... Is for legal advisers to consider whether the material sought or held is relevant and material to the proceedings. In a case of this kind, it would only be disclosable if it is necessary to dispose fairly of the proceedings. To judge relevance and materiality, it is necessary to consider the issues in play in the proceedings, ie the orders and factual findings sought as well as the evidence already before the court.

16.22 The next step[14] requires 'officials' – Home Department staff, or others in the public body concerned – to carry out 'a more detailed assessment of the sensitivity of the information'. For them, the 'critical question is whether there is a real risk that disclosure would cause substantial harm to an important public

13 [2016] EWHC 3171 (Fam), [2017] 1 FLR 1665, Pauffley J.

14 Ibid at [15].

interest'. If no harm to the public interest was likely, material should be disclosed: that is, tendered for inspection. However, if 'the assessment was that disclosure would harm the public interest then material' may attract PII and a claim must be considered.

16.23 The final step involves the decision as to whether to make a PII claim. In particular is the public interest in immunity outweighed, in the mind of the decision-maker, by the need to do justice in the case?

> [16] … This is a decision taken by the SSHD assisted by advice from those involved at stages 1 and 2. The decision maker will have to consider the importance of the information to the issues the court has to decide, and form a view as to whether the public interest in non-disclosure is outweighed by the public interest in disclosure, in order to do justice within the proceedings: "If a document is relevant and material then it must be disclosed … unless a breach of confidentiality will cause harm to the public interest which outweighs the harm to the interests of justice caused by non-disclosure".[15]

3 PUBLIC AND PRIVATE INTERESTS

'Suppression of evidence'

16.24 *Wade & Forsyth* entitle their treatment of PII as 'Suppression of evidence in the public interest'.[16] This may sound a little harsh: 'suppression' sounds a little harsh. However, as a matter of fact, suppression on grounds of public interest is what the court is being asked to order. In each case 'the court has a power and the duty to weigh the public interest of justice to litigants against [any] public interest asserted by the government'.[17] In that passage, the authors were commenting on *Conway v Rimmer*[18] where the House of Lords disapproved of blanket immunity for types of documents. They pointed out that, if need be, the court must look at the documents themselves (without the claimant having seen them) to decide whether immunity should be ordered.[19]

Private law – public interest

16.25 The rule can apply, exceptionally, in private law proceedings. For example, *D v National Society for the Prevention of Cruelty to Children*[20] concerned

15 Per Lord Templeman in *R v Chief Constable of the West Midlands, ex p Wiley* [1994] UKHL 8, [1995] AC 274, [1994] 3 WLR 433, at 281F.

16 HWR Wade and CF Forsyth *Administrative Law* 11th edn (Oxford: Oxford University Press, 2014) at 711.

17 Ibid at 714.

18 [1968] AC 910.

19 The House later looked at the documents (reports on a police probationer who was suing his former employers) and held that disclosure would not be against the public interest.

20 [1978] AC 171.

an applicant private body, albeit with a public law (then child care proceedings) role. In that case, the House of Lords considered whether the identity of an NSPCC informant should be protected in proceedings by a mother, Mrs D, who had been the subject of a complaint to the NSPCC. Mrs D sued the NSPCC for damages claiming that their enquiry was negligent; and in the course of that civil claim she sought discovery (ie, disclosure) of their documents which were likely to disclose the identity of the informant. The House of Lords unanimously allowed the NSPCC appeal. They permitted a form of PII which applied in private law proceedings. They could see an analogy, for example, between protection to a NSPCC informant and the protection permitted to police informers.

16.26 Lord Diplock explained his view of the immunity which should be extended to informers in children proceedings:[21]

> I would extend to those who give information about neglect or ill-treatment of children to a local authority or the N.S.P.C.C. a similar immunity from disclosure of their identity in legal proceedings to that which the law accords to police informers. The public interests served by preserving the anonymity of both classes of informants are analogous; they are of no less weight in the case of the former than in that of the latter class, and in my judgment are of greater weight than in the case of informers of the Gaming Board to whom immunity from disclosure of their identity has recently been extended by this House.[22]

16.27 Thus, Lord Diplock made clear his own view: that the interest of protecting child informers was greater than, for examples, Gaming Board informants.

Disclosure and harm to a child

16.28 In the context of adoption proceedings PII was considered by the House of Lords in *Re D (Adoption reports: confidentiality)*.[23] Lord Mustill summarised the principles on which suppression of evidence could be ordered and where harm to a child might arise:[24]

---

21 Ibid at 219.

22 Reference to *R v Lewis Justices exp Secretary of State for the Home Department* [1973] AC 388. In that case applications made to the Gaming Board by R for certificates in relation to five bingo clubs which were refused. R commenced proceedings for criminal libel for a letter written by the assistant chief constable in reply to a request for certain information about him. The Home Secretary applied for an order of certiorari to set aside two witness summonses directed to the chief constable and the secretary of the board to give evidence and produce certain documents (including the letter requesting the information). The board made a similar application in relation to the summons directed to their secretary. On the Home Secretary's application, the Divisional Court ordered that the two witness summonses should be set aside; it made no order on the board's application. On appeal to the House of Lords, they held that the public interest required that the letters should not be produced, since, if the information given to the board was liable to be disclosed, it might be withheld and they would thereby be hampered in the discharge of the duty imposed on them by statute to identify and exclude persons of dubious character and reputation from obtaining a licence to conduct a gaming establishment; this depended on the public interest, and an order setting aside the witness summonses should accordingly be made.

23 [1996] AC 593, [1995] 2 FLR 687.

24 [1995] 2 FLR 687 at 699–700.

(1) It is a fundamental principle of fairness that a party is entitled to the disclosure of all materials which may be taken into account by the court when reaching a decision adverse to that party …

(2) … the court should first consider whether disclosure of the material would involve a real possibility of significant harm to the child.

(3) If it would, the court should next consider whether the overall interests of the child would benefit from non-disclosure, weighing on the one hand the interest of the child in having the material properly tested, and on the other both the magnitude of the risk that harm will occur and the gravity of the harm if it does occur.

(4) If the court is satisfied that the interests of the child point towards non-disclosure, the next and final step is for the court to weigh that consideration, and its strength in the circumstances of the case, against the interest of the parent or other party in having an opportunity to see and respond to the material. In the latter regard the court should take into account the importance of the material to the issues in the case.

(5) Non-disclosure should be the exception not the rule. The court should be rigorous in its examination of the risk and gravity of the feared harm to the child and should order non-disclosure only when the case for doing so is compelling.

16.29 As can be seen, the stress is on fairness and therefore in favour of disclosure. Non-disclosure is very much the exception. The withholding of evidence is justified only on the court finding the real possibility of significant harm to the child. 'Non-disclosure should be the exception not the rule. The court … should order non-disclosure only when the case for doing so is compelling' (per para (5) of the summary of *Re D* (above)). However, this may be overridden where the public interest demands that a PII application be allowed; and in children cases there is the added concern for a child's welfare.[25]

Public interest immunity in the light of the Human Rights Act 1998

16.30 Following the coming into operation of the Human Rights Act 1988 (HRA 1998) in *Re B (Disclosure to other parties)*,[26] Munby J set out three propositions in relation to disclosure and PII in family proceedings (especially in children proceedings) in the light of the European Convention 1950:

(1) Entitlement to a fair trial under the European Convention 1950 Article 6(1) is absolute; but this does not mean that any party, as a matter of right, is entitled to see all the documents in the case.

(2) It is not only the interests of children involved in the litigation which may justify the denial of access to documents. The interests of anyone else who is involved, whether as victim, party or witness and who can demonstrate that

25 As emphasised by Lord Diplock in *D v NSPCC* (see 16.39).

26 [2001] 2 FLR 1017.

their European Convention 1950 Article 8 rights are sufficiently engaged, may apply for documents to be withheld from a party to the proceedings.[27]

(3) A limited qualification of the right to see the documents may be acceptable if directed towards a clear and proper objective; that is non-disclosure must be limited to what the situation imperatively demands and is justified only when the case is compelling or strictly necessary. The court must be careful to balance the feared harm and any difficulty caused to the litigant counterbalanced by procedures designed to ensure a fair trial.

Public interest immunity and special advocate

16.31 In *Chief Constable & Anor v YK & Ors*,[28] Sir Nicholas Wall P considered PII in the context of two forced marriage protection order applications. He considered the PII question at the beginning of his judgment:

> [10] The legal conundrum potentially thrown up by the instant case (and certainly likely to arise at some point in the future) is one which, potentially, goes to the root of family justice, namely how is it possible to achieve a fair hearing (i.e. comply with ECHR Article 6) if parts of the evidence which it is necessary for parties to know in order to enable them to meet allegations made against them cannot safely be revealed to them on the ground that disclosure of the information or its source is likely to identify the informant (and thus place him or her at risk)?

16.32 The issues which the court confronts in the special advocate jurisdiction were considered by the House of Lords in *Secretary of State for the Home Department v MB and AF*.[29] The means of achieving justice, said Lady Hale, can sometimes be as important as achieving a just result. Lady Hale explained the issues as follows:

> [57] The object of all legal proceedings is to do justice according to law: but this is easily said and not so easily done. Doing justice means not only arriving at a just result but arriving at it in a just manner: … the essential ingredients of a fair trial can vary according to the subject matter and nature of the proceedings.
>
> [58] The basic requirement is to know the case against one and to have an opportunity of meeting it. But in *In re K (Infants)* [1963] Ch 381, 405, Upjohn LJ identified more detailed principles of a judicial inquiry: "the right to see all the information put before the judge, to comment on it, to challenge it and if needs be to combat it, and to try to establish by contrary evidence that it is wrong." However, as Lord Devlin pointed out in the same case in the House of Lords, at [1965] AC 201, 238: "… a principle of judicial inquiry, whether fundamental or not, is only a means to an end. If it can be shown in any particular class of case

---

27 And see *Local Authority X v HI and Others* [2016] EWHC 1123 (Fam), [2017] 1 FLR 1362, Roberts J where disclosure to a 15-year-old's father and step-mother was denied on his application, though not as a PII issue.

28 [2010] EWHC 2438 (Fam).

29 [2007] UKHL 46, [2008] 1 AC 40; and see Chapter 15.

that the observance of a principle of this sort does not serve the ends of justice, it must be dismissed: otherwise it would become the master instead of the servant of justice".

Disclosure ordered

16.33 *A Local Authority v A Mother & Ors,*[30] Hedley J raised in children proceedings issues which related mostly to private law matters between the mother and her husband and their family. Suppression of evidence was sought by the local authority as much as anything in the private interests of the mother and Hedley J decided the case on that basis.

16.34 In that case the local authority started care proceedings. Various parental shortcomings were alleged concerning a child, whose family originated from Pakistan and were practising Muslims. The child's parents were first cousins, there were difficulties in their relationship, but the father was hoping that the parents would be able to present as a couple in the proceedings. When the mother returned from a holiday to Turkey (spent with the child and with her aunt and sister) she told the social worker that she had had sexual relations with three different men while away and that, on one occasion, the child had been in the room. The mother's sister subsequently confirmed much of the mother's account. The mother made comments suggesting gender and sexual ambivalence. The foster carer had noted some inappropriate touching of her by the mother.

16.35 All three women were adamant that the male members of the family should not be told about any of this, as they feared that the mother's safety and both her life and theirs would be in danger for having 'dishonoured' the family. The information formed part of the social work records and the social worker's statement, as, in part, evidence relevant to the mother's capacity to parent.

16.36 The local authority applied for a direction that the information should not be disclosed. The father consented on a temporary basis to disclosure of the information to his legal team without disclosure to him. [31]

16.37 Hedley J's disposal of the local authority's application for PII was to adopt as his starting point the speech of Lord Mustill in *Re D (Minors) (Adoption Reports: Confidentiality).*[32] Disclosure should be the norm. He could not find a real risk to the mother, and refused to order immunity from disclosure in the following terms:

> [14] I am satisfied that this risk apart, this information is discloseable. It is relevant to the assessment of the mother's capacity to parent A and to provide stability and consistency; it is, therefore, relevant to the father's case of presentation as a couple in circumstances where

30 [2009] EWHC 1574 (Fam), [2010] 1 FLR 545.

31 See Chapter 15 and *Somerville and others v Scottish Ministers (HM Advocate General for Scotland intervening)* [2007] UKHL 44, [2007] 1 WLR 2734 on the law's distaste for disclosure of material only to lawyers.

32 *Re D (Minors) (Adoption Reports: Confidentiality)* [1996] AC 593, [1995] 2 FLR 687, [1996] 1 FCR 205.

> the local authority would be bound to assess him as a sole carer if he so requested. I emphasise that I have not been asked to nor have I inquired into the truth of the relevant allegation though no one has yet sought to deny it, indeed the reverse is the case. I acknowledge that it may have consequences directly for the mother and other female family members and quite possibly indirectly for A but they are not of the nature or degree that would justify non-disclosure …

4 IMMUNITY FOR INFORMANTS

Public interest in informers informing

16.38 A variety of public bodies rely upon informers to provide information. That private individuals provide information in this way is regarded as in the public interest: for example for the prevention of crime and of the abuse of children. It is assumed that in many such cases informants will only provide information if they can do so anonymously. They rely on the public body to whom information is supplied (eg, the police) to assure them of anonymity; and in the interests of maintaining a flow of information the law supports this anonymity by making informer evidence generally immune from disclosure in the proceedings in which it arose, or in any subsequent civil proceedings arising from it. In criminal proceedings, a balance may still have to be drawn between immunity for the informer and fairness of any trial of the accused concerned.

16.39 So is the same the position for informers in children cases? Confidentiality and what may be treated as an informer's evidence has recently been considered by the Supreme Court in *Re A (Sexual Abuse: Disclosure)*[33] (reheard in the Court of Appeal as Re *J (A Child: Disclosure)*[34]). Despite what was said in *Re A,* the welfare of a child, protected by the information of an informer (like X in the *Re A* case), may yet permit an immunity from disclosure of confidential information which is wider than the relatively narrow approach adopted in *Re A*. Another decision of the House of Lords touched on only in *Re A* – namely *D v National Society for the Prevention of Cruelty to Children*[35] (*D v NSPCC*) – remains unaffected by the later decision.

Police informants: civil proceedings

16.40 In *D v NSPCC,* Lord Diplock reflected on the similarity between a public interest immunity application to seek immunity for a police informer and that for an informer in respect of a child's welfare. On this point he said:

> The public interest which the NSPCC relies upon as obliging it to withhold from the plaintiff and from the court itself material that could disclose the

33 [2012] UKSC 60, [2013] 1 FLR 948.

34 [2012] EWCA Civ 1204.

35 [1978] AC 171, (1977) FLR Rep 181.

identity of the society's informant is analogous to the public interest that is protected by the well-established rule of law that the identity of police informers may not be disclosed in a civil action, whether by the process of discovery or by oral evidence at the trial: *Marks v Beyfus* (1890) 25 QBD 494.

16.41 The principle to which he refers (derived from *Marks v Beyfus*) remained as much part of the law then as it does now. For example, in *Powell & Anor v Chief Constable of North Wales Constabulary*,[36] a chief constable asserted that hearsay evidence from a policeman concerning an informer's evidence was immune from disclosure in the public interest and that the judge had no discretion to admit it.

16.42 The Court of Appeal (Scheiman, Roch and Beldam LJJ) held that, on the contrary, in such circumstances a judge was required to balance the interests of someone seeking damages, with those of the public interest in maintaining the anonymity of informers. Once it was accepted that the balance fell on the side of a public interest in concealing the identity of the informer, the court had no discretion in the matter. Beldam LJ explained the position as follows:

> In ... *R v Lewis Justices exp Home Secretary* [1973] AC 388 and *D -v- NSPCC* [1978 AC 171], the immunity from disclosure of the identity of an informant was upheld notwithstanding recognition of the public interest that information should not be withheld which is relevant to issues a judicial tribunal has to decide. If it came to be thought that there was a general and wider discretion to admit evidence of the kind sought to be admitted in this case, it would greatly sap the confidence in anonymity which is so important a factor in encouraging the provision of information. I therefore agree ... that the judge has no residual discretion once he has determined that evidence concerning the informant should not be disclosed.

Immunity for informers in children proceedings

16.43 In *Re A (A Child) (Sexual Abuse: Disclosure)*,[37] the Supreme Court was called upon to balance the interests of justice against, or alongside, the welfare of a child. The welfare of the child was linked entirely with justice ('the interests of that little girl ... in having an allegation properly investigated and tested'[38]) rather than in the abstract: the public interest in ensuring that those with information about abuse of children come forward (as was the case in *D v NSPCC*).

16.44 The issue before the Court was whether disclosure of the identity of a father's accuser (X) and the substance of her allegations against him should be given to the parties; and whether X should be required to give evidence in those proceedings. A (the child in the proceedings) was aged 10 and her parents, G and J, had separated in 2002. J lived in Australia. He applied for contact and a final order, made in 2009, provided staying contact for him with A. X made serious allegations

36 Case No: CCRTI 1999/0904/B1) CA 1999 WL 1142622.

37 *Re A (Sexual Abuse: Disclosure)* [2012] UKSC 60, [2013] 1 FLR 948, [2013] 1 FCR 69 sub nom *Re A (Family Proceedings: Disclosure of Information)* [2013] 2 AC 66.

38 Ibid at [1].

to social workers of sexual abuse by J, which were said to have taken place when she was a child. She made the allegations in confidence (as she thought) and did not wish to take them any further. Social Services considered the allegations to be credible and contacted G. She was told that allegations of sexual abuse had been made against J by an unnamed person, and that she should take steps to protect A. G applied to vary the contact order based on this information. J and A's guardian applied for disclosure of X's identity, the substance of the allegations and of her medical records.

16.45 The local authority claimed public interest immunity in proceedings taken by the mother to reduce J's contact with her daughter. X suffered from significant mental and physical health problems which, at times, had been life threatening. Her psychiatric report said that forcing her to give evidence in the proceedings would have a seriously detrimental effect on her.

16.46 The Supreme Court rejected X's appeal against disclosure of her evidence: the information from X must be disclosed to all parties. The parties' right to a fair trial (European Convention 1950 Art 6(1)) overrode the right of X to her privacy (Art 8) and to any suggested inhuman or degrading treatment (Art 3).

> [24] To what extent, if at all, are these principles affected by the Human Rights Act 1998? In *A Local Authority v A* [2010] 2 FLR 1757, the Court of Appeal accepted that the principles of non-disclosure might now have to be extended to other people whose Convention rights might be violated by disclosure.
>
> [25] It is common ground that several Convention rights are, or may be, in play in this case. There are the article 6 rights of all three parties to the proceedings, A, M and F, to have a fair trial in the determination of their civil rights. The right to a fair trial is absolute but the question of what is fair may depend upon the circumstances of the case. There are the article 8 rights of A, M and F to respect for their private and family lives. There is also the article 8 right of X to respect for her private life. Article 8 rights are qualified and can be interfered with if it is necessary in a democratic society in order to protect the rights of others.

16.47 All that said, as the Court explained, it might be possible for X actually to give her evidence in family proceedings in a way that her distress was not unduly heightened.[39] Ultimately, the Court of Appeal decided that X was unable to give evidence and that any case against the father must fail.

Public interest immunity and *Re A*

16.48 The local authority had claimed immunity 'because of the public interest in maintaining the confidentiality of information given to the authorities responsible for protecting children from abuse'. The court explained the part which public interest immunity played in the case as follows:

39 *Re A (Sexual Abuse: Disclosure)* at [36].

> [15] ... That this is a class of information to which public interest immunity attaches has been established since the decision of the House of Lords in *D v National Society for the Prevention of Cruelty to Children* [1978] AC 171. That case accorded to people who informed the authorities of allegations of child abuse the same protection as informants to the police and the gaming authorities. It is not the fact that the information is communicated in confidence which attracts the immunity, but the public interest in encouraging members of the public to come forward to help the authorities to protect children. That this may also protect an untruthful or malicious informant is the necessary price to be paid. Although *D v National Society for the Prevention of Cruelty to Children* was concerned with a neighbour who claimed to have witnessed the alleged abuse, rather than a victim, I can see no reason why the same rationale should not also apply to the victims of alleged abuse.

16.49 Thus, Lady Hale associated the reasoning in *D v NSPCC* with the position of X. However, she went on, matters did not end there. Without PII all documents must be disclosed, for confidentiality alone does not confer privilege nor guarantee privacy. The Supreme Court echoed the words of the Court of Appeal in *Powell & Anor v Chief Constable of North Wales Constabulary* but reached an opposite conclusion:

> [16] ... Public interest immunity is not absolute. The public interest in maintaining confidentiality must be balanced against the public interest in a fair trial, according to principles which have developed since the landmark case of *Conway v Rimmer* [1968] AC 910 required the court to strike that balance.

5 PUBLIC INTEREST IMMUNITY: ORDERS FOR AND AGAINST NON-PARTIES

PII and the evidence of non-parties

16.50 In *Re C (A Child) (Care Proceedings: Disclosure)*[40] and *Re C (A Child) (Application for Public Interest Immunity)*,[41] Pauffley J developed a procedure whereby a non-party who was subject to a 'disclosure order' against another non-party (in this case it was the Home Department: no statutory source for the order is indicated) sought to set it aside. The non-party was Counter Terrorism Command Special Operations Branch (SO15) (ie the Secretary of State for the Home Department (SSHD)). The proceedings concerned possible child radicalisation issues. Under the *President's Guidance of 8 October 2015 on Radicalisation Cases in the Family Courts*,[42] it had been transferred to the High Court. The SSHD objected to disclosure on what were treated as PII grounds.

40 [2016] EWHC 3171 (Fam), [2017] 1 FLR 1665, Pauffley J.

41 [2017] EWHC 692 (Fam), [2017] 2 FLR 1342, Pauffley J.

42 See www.judiciary.uk/wp-content/uploads/2015/10/pfd-guidance-radicalisation-cases.pdf; and see *Family Court Practice* Part V.

16.51 Pauffley J made a without notice disclosure order against the SSHD, making clear that the court needed 'all information' about the parents which the Department was at liberty to disclose. The SSHD had declined to make disclosure and would, if necessary, consider making an application for a closed material procedure under the Justice and Security Act 2013. Pauffley J's order gave a detailed preamble of the requirements, should such an application be made. The SSHD applied for a discharge of the disclosure order arguing that the authority's approach did not accord with the *Guidance* in making an inappropriately wide request, that it did not comply with FPR 2010, r 21.2(3) as to necessity and that seeking the underlying assessment of the decision to refuse to issue a replacement passport was erroneous.

16.52 Pauffley J dismissed the application. The order, she said, had been legitimately made on the basis of necessity and had to be maintained. The order as a whole was transparently clear and amply substantiated the requirement for disclosure. Considerations of counter terrorism policy or operations did not eclipse the paramount consideration of the welfare of the child.

16.53 The correct course of action for the SSHD, said the judge, was for the Secretary of State to have signed a PII certificate if she considered it were necessary. The present application appeared to be an attempt to short-circuit or head-off what would otherwise be a necessary process of administrative decision making leading in all probability to such a claim. Until there was a PII certificate containing the views of the Secretary of State as to the harm to the public interest that would be caused by disclosure and the weight to be given to competing public interests, there was no appropriate mechanism for action. Pauffley J explained this as follows:

> [46] Until there is a PII Certificate containing the SSHD's judgment as to the harm to the public interest that would be caused by disclosure and the weight to be given to competing public interests, there is no appropriate mechanism for action. So soon as the claim for PII is made, consideration will be given to whether or not it should be upheld.

Application for public interest immunity by a non-party; *ex parte Wiley*

16.54 In the next case in the same series, namely *Re C (A Child) (Application for Public Interest Immunity)*,[43] Pauffley J considered the SSHD's application for PII in respect of their material. A closed hearing took place to enable the SSHD to make submissions in relation to sensitive material; in particular its assertion that the disclosure of the material would create a real risk of damage to national security. Following that closed hearing, the SSHD issued a PII certificate and applied for PII. The report is the judgment in respect of the hearing of that application.

43 [2017] EWHC 692 (Fam), [2017] 2 FLR 1342.

16.55 Pauffley J reminded herself of the three steps required by *R v Chief Constable of the West Midlands, ex p Wiley*:[44]

> [29] There are three required steps when the SSHD considers whether to make a claim for PII. First, whether the material is relevant and passes the threshold test for disclosure in the applicable proceedings – (certificate, para 11). Secondly, if the threshold test is passed, whether the material identified as relevant and subject to disclosure attracts PII. The test is whether there is a real risk that disclosure would cause "real damage" or "serious harm" to the public interest – (certificate, paras 13 and 19). Thirdly, if applying the "real damage" test, the material attracts PII, the question arises as to whether the public interest in non-disclosure is outweighed by the public interest in disclosure for the purpose of doing justice in the proceedings …

16.56 Applying principles set out in *R v Chief Constable of the West Midlands, ex p Wiley*,[45] Pauffley J held that it was clear that the material was relevant. It therefore passed the first test for disclosure. There were clear reasons for agreeing with the SSHD's evaluation as to the risk of real damage to national security if the material was disclosed, and based upon the materials the judge had seen in the closed hearing. The remaining two steps applied; and a PII certificate was ordered accordingly.

44 [1994] UKHL 8, [1995] AC 274.

45 Ibid.

INDEX

[*all references are to paragraph number*]